Leadership
Priorities and Practice

ASHFORD
UNIVERSITY
FOUNDED 1918

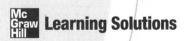

Boston   Burr Ridge, IL   Dubuque, IA   New York   San Francisco   St. Louis
Bangkok   Bogotá   Caracas   Lisbon   London   Madrid
Mexico City   Milan   New Delhi   Seoul   Singapore   Sydney   Taipei   Toronto

Leadership: Priorities and Practice
Ashford University

This book is a McGraw-Hill Learning Solutions textbook and contains select material from the following sources:
Management Communication: Principles and Practice, Third Edition by Michael E. Hattersley and Linda McJannet. Copyright © 2008 by The McGraw-Hill Companies, Inc.
Behavior in Organizations: An Experiential Approach, Eighth Edition by A.B. Shani and James B. Lau. Copyright © 2005, 2000, 1996, 1992, 1988, 1984, 1978, 1975 by The McGraw-Hill Companies, Inc.
Business Ethics: A Global & Managerial Perspective, by David J. Fritzsche. Copyright © 2005, 1997 by The McGraw-Hill Companies, Inc.
Leading Corporate Citizens: Visions, Values, Value Added, Second Edition by Sandra Waddock. Copyright © 2006, 2002 by The McGraw-Hill Companies, Inc.
Beyond Feelings: A Guide to Critical Thinking, Seventh Edition by Vincent Ryan Ruggiero. Copyright © 2004 by The McGraw-Hill Companies, Inc.
Perspectives in Business Ethics, Third Edition by Laura P. Hartman. Copyright © 2005, 2002, 1998 by The McGraw-Hill Companies, Inc.
Classroom Assessment: Concepts and Applications, Fifth Edition by Peter W. Airasian. Copyright © 2005, 2001, 1997, 1994, 1991 by The McGraw-Hill Companies, Inc.
All are reprinted with permission of the publisher. Many custom published texts are modified versions or adaptations of our best-selling textbooks. Some adaptations are printed in black and white to keep prices at a minimum, while others are in color.

2 3 4 5 6 7 8 9 0 PAH PAH 0 9 8

ISBN 13: 978-0-697-77523-8
ISBN-10: 0-697-77523-2

Custom Publishing Specialist: Judith Wetherington
Production Editor: Carrie Braun
Printer/Binder: P.A. Hutchison Company

Contents

Leading Corporate Citizenship: Vision, Values, Value Added

I want to challenge you to join me in taking our relationship to a still higher level. I propose that you [corporate leaders] . . . and we, the United Nations, initiate a global compact of shared values and principles, which will give a human face to the global market.

Globalization is a fact of life. But I believe we have underestimated its fragility. The problem is this. The spread of markets outpaces the ability of societies and their political systems to adjust to them, let alone to guide the course they take. History teaches us that such an imbalance between the economic, social and political realms can never be sustained for very long. . . .

We have to choose between a global market driven only by calculations of short-term profit, and one which has a human face. Between a world which condemns a quarter of the human race to starvation and squalor, and one which offers everyone at least a chance of prosperity, in a healthy environment. Between a selfish free-for-all in which we ignore the fate of the losers, and a culture in which the strong and successful accept their responsibilities, showing global vision and leadership.

Kofi Annan, Secretary-General of the United Nations[1]

Corporations: Citizens of the (Natural and Human) World

Kofi Annan's words highlight an important and often forgotten reality: Business is integrally connected to both the social context in which it operates and the natural environment on which we all depend. With the statement above, Annan launched what has become the United Nations' Global Compact and signaled an important shift in the long-term relationships that businesses can expect to have with their many constituencies—their stakeholders as well as how they treat the natural environment.[2] As businesses have grown larger and more powerful, their attendant responsibilities to be good corporate citizens wherever they operate have also grown. Indeed, some argue that the rise of the very term *corporate citizenship* since the late 1990s came about in part because some companies in the process of globalization began to assume responsibilities formerly assigned solely to governments.[3]

Corporate citizenship is an integral part of the whole corporation as it exists in whole communities and whole societies, with whole people operating within. In this sense of wholes within other wholes, corporations are what Ken Wilber terms *holons*, that is, both wholes in and of themselves and parts of something larger. As holons, they are embedded in and affect the web of relationships that constitutes societies, just as biological systems are also interrelated webs.[4] In administering some of the responsibilities of citizenship, companies are increasingly finding themselves held accountable for their impacts on society and social rights (e.g., not polluting or otherwise contributing to deteriorating environmental conditions), on individual or civil rights (e.g., freedom from abusive working conditions), and on political rights (e.g., being held accountable when participating in countries whose governments do not uphold basic political and individual rights).[5]

The embeddedness of corporations in societies—that is, their existence as socially constructed holons in economic, political, and societal contexts—means that careful attention needs to be given to how they behave. Being or becoming a leading corporate citizen implies that companies must understand their relationships to both primary and secondary stakeholders in society, must learn to treat those stakeholders as well as the natural environment respectfully, and must understand the global context in which businesses operate. Sustainability depends on these systemic understandings, whether it is the ecological sustainability so in question today by many environmentalists, the sustainability of the societies and communities where businesses operate, or the longevity of the business itself.

If we conceive companies in terms of their relationships to stakeholders and the natural environment, then we come to the following definition of leading corporate citizenship:

> Leading corporate citizens are companies that live up to clear constructive visions and core values consistent with those of the broader societies within which they operate, respect the natural environment, and treat well the entire range of stakeholders who risk capital in, have an interest in, or are linked to the firm through primary and secondary impacts. They operationalize their corporate citizenship in all of their strategies and business practices by developing respectful, mutually beneficial relationships with stakeholders and by working to maximize sustainability of the natural environment. They recognize that they are responsible for their impacts and are willing to be held accountable for them.

Corporate citizenship by this definition involves far more than meeting the discretionary responsibilities associated with philanthropy, volunteerism, community relations, and otherwise doing "social good," which some people think is sufficient[6] and which constitutes corporate *social* responsibility.[7] This broad understanding of citizenship means paying attention to how fundamental responsibilities—some of which are those traditionally assumed by governments, such as labor and human rights, environmental sustainability, and anticorruption measures—are being met in all of the company's strategies and operating practices, as well as to the outcomes and implications of corporate activities. For many companies, it means developing a "lived" set of policies, practices, and programs that help the company achieve its vision and values. The decision to be a *leading* corporate citizen is, of course, probably still voluntary on the part of companies; however, companies do bear responsibility for the ways in which they treat their stakeholders and nature—and can be judged on their impacts—whether they proactively or interactively assume the role of "good corporate citizen."

Given the preceding definition of *leading corporate citizens*, let's start with a proposition: The core purposes of the corporation include but go far beyond generating shareholder wealth. Indeed, wealth and profits are simply important by-products of the firm's efforts to create a product or service for customers that adds enough value that customers are willing to pay more than they would otherwise pay. Value-added goods and services are produced through the good offices of employees, managers, suppliers, and allies, using a wide range of forms of capital. Management thinker Charles Handy puts the issue straightforwardly:

> To turn shareholders' needs into a purpose is to be guilty of a logical confusion, to mistake a necessary condition for a sufficient one. We need to eat to live, food is a necessary condition of life. But if we lived mainly to eat, making food a sufficient or sole purpose of life, we would become gross. The purpose of a business, in other words, is not to make a profit, full stop. It is to make a profit so that the business can do something more or better. That "something" becomes the real justification for the business.[8]

Investments in businesses go way beyond those made by shareholders. Capital does, of course, include the important financial resources supplied by the owners or shareholders. Equally important, capital also encompasses the intellectual and human capital provided by employees, the trust and loyalty of customers that products or services will meet expectations and add value (for which they will pay), and various forms of social capital. Further, capital includes the infrastructure and social relations supplied by the communities and other levels of government in locations where the company has facilities. It includes interdependent relationships developed among its business partners, suppliers, and distributors, and it exists in the social contract written or unwritten by a range of local, state, and national governments, which have provided the social—and legal—contract and necessary physical infrastructure on which the firm's existence is premised.

All of these capitals are supplied to the firm by stakeholders. A stakeholder, generally, is any individual or group who is affected by or can affect an organization.[9] Companies exist in relationship to and because of their stakeholders. Simply stated, despite the prevailing idea that the purpose of the firm is to maximize shareholder wealth (and although it is absolutely essential that companies do produce wealth to survive), because of their numerous impacts, corporations are considerably more than profit-maximizing efficiency machines. Corporations are inherently and inextricably embedded in a web of relationships with stakeholders that create the very context in which they do business and that enable the enterprise to succeed. Without its core stakeholders, the corporation cannot survive, nor can it begin to make a profit, never mind maximize profits. Indeed, in many ways, the corporation is nothing more and nothing less than its primary relationships.

Therefore, we begin with this premise: Profits are essential to corporate success, and indeed corporate survival. Profits are critical to sustaining democratic capitalism, but they are in fact a by-product of the many relationships on which a corporation—or any other organization—depends for its legitimacy, power, resources, and various kinds of capital investments. This perspective, which differs from the traditional economics perspective on the firm (which says that the one and only purpose of the firm is to maximize profits or shareholder wealth), is called the *stakeholder capitalism concept of the firm*.

In this stakeholder view, stakeholder relationships and the operating practices (policies, processes, and procedures) that support those relationships are the basis of leading corporate citizenship.[10] Much is being written about global corporate citizenship these days. The neoclassical economics model, which dominates much business thinking, suggests that the corporation should maximize wealth for one set of stakeholders: the owners or shareholders. Conformance to existing law and meeting ethical responsibilities come next, especially in the view of economist Milton Friedman, who espouses the neoclassical economics perspective. In his classic article against the concept of social responsibility, entitled "The Social Responsibility of Business Is to Increase Its Profits," Friedman states:

But the doctrine of "social responsibility" taken seriously would extend the scope of the political mechanism to every human activity. It does not differ in philosophy from the most explicitly collectivist doctrine. It differs only in professing to believe that collectivist ends can be attained without collectivist means. That is why in my book *Capitalism and Freedom*, I have called it a "fundamentally subversive doctrine" in a free society, and have said that in such a society, there is one and only one social responsibility of business—to use its resources and engage in activities designed to increase its profits so long as it stays within the rules of the game, which is to say, engages in open and free competition without deception or fraud.[11]

The basis for Friedman's assertion, echoed by other economists as well, that shareholders are the only important stakeholder is that owners have taken a risk with their investments in the firm and are therefore owed a profit. But this view is too constricted to be useful in a world in which it is increasingly recognized that other stakeholders are equally important to the survival and success of the firm and that they too make significant investments in the welfare of the firm.

Recent thinking about corporate citizenship has significantly broadened the scope of its definition to recognize that citizenship inherently involves the rights and duties of membership. Chris Marsden and Jörg Andriof of the University of Warwick, United Kingdom, summarize this perspective:

> As Peter Drucker . . . says, however, citizenship is more than just a legal term, it is a political term. "As a political term citizenship means active commitment. It means responsibility. It means making a difference in one's community, one's society, one's country." Drucker might have added, in today's global economy, "one's world." Good corporate citizenship, therefore, is about understanding and managing an organisation's influences on and relationships with the rest of society in a way that minimises the negative and maximises the positive.[12]

Stakes and Stakeholders

Let's start this journey into leading corporate citizenship by considering the definition of a *stake* and therefore a *stakeholder* in more detail. The word *stake* can have one of three different general meanings, each representing a different type of relationship between the stakeholder and the entity in which a stake exists (see Table 1.1). A stake is a claim of some sort, for example, a claim of ownership based on a set of expectations related to principles of ethics, such as legal or moral rights, justice or fairness, the greatest good for the greatest number, or the principle of care.

TABLE 1.1   **The Types of Stakes**

Stake As:	Stake Is Based On:
• Claim	• Legal or moral right • Consideration of justice/fairness • Utility (greatest good for the greatest number) • Care

• Risk
  1. Owner
  2. Community
  3. Employee
  4. Customer
  5. Supplier
	• Investment of capital, including:
	  1. Financial capital
	  2. Social/infrastructure capital
	  3. Knowledge/intellectual/human capital
	  4. Franchise (trust) capital
	  5. Technological, infrastructure capital

• Bonds (tether, tie)	• Identification (process)

Each type of stake creates a relationship that, when constructive and positive, is:
1. Mutual
2. Interactive
3. Consistent over time
4. Interdependent

Second, a stake can signify that a stakeholder has made an investment, thereby putting some sort of capital at risk.[13] In this usage, a stake is an interest or a share in some enterprise or activity, a prize (as in a horse race or other gamble) or perhaps a grubstake (for which the provider expects a return for the risk taken). Typically, the type of risk under consideration relates specifically to the type of capital invested. Thus, for example, owners invest financial capital in the firm, while communities may invest social capital—or relationships built on trust and association—in the firm's local presence or create infrastructure to support the firm's activities. Employees invest their human capital, their knowledge, and their intellectual energies—all forms of capital—in the firm. Customers invest their trust as part of the firm's franchise and hence their willingness to continue to purchase the goods and services produced by the firm. Suppliers may invest in specific technology, equipment, or infrastructure so that they can enhance their relationship to the firm over time and make the bonds tighter

The third meaning of *stake* is a bond, such as a tie or tether, something that creates links between two entities, including tangible links that bind the entities together (e.g., contracts or long-term relationships for purchasing supplies) as well as intangible relational links. Intangible bonds can come about because a stakeholder identifies in some way with the organization and therefore feels an association with the organization that potentially creates one of the other types of stakes, a claim or a risk.[14]

Stakeholder Relationships

Notice that each of the types of stakes identified in Table 1.1 creates a *relationship* between the stakeholder and the organization in which there is a stake.[15] For example, owners are clearly stakeholders. By making an investment, the stakeholder owner creates a relationship with the organization. Similarly, the stakeholder who puts something at risk for possible benefit through an enterprise creates a relationship with that enterprise, as communities do when they invest in local infrastructure that supports a firm's activities. Bonds of identity also create ongoing relationships. The important point, then, is that whichever meaning we use for *stake*, being a stakeholder creates an ongoing and interactive relationship between the stakeholder and the enterprise or activity.[16]

Stakeholder relationships also create a boundary around managerial responsibilities so that corporations are responsible not for all of the problems of society but only for those that they create or those that affect them. Thus, when we think about corporate responsibility, we can think in terms of the public responsibility of managers, which is limited to the areas of primary and secondary involvement of their enterprises. The principle of public responsibility, which was developed by scholars Lee Preston and James Post, comes about in part because companies are granted permission or charters (literally, incorporation papers) by the states in which they are established and in part as a result of the impacts that companies have on their various stakeholders and the natural environment, and for which society wishes to hold them accountable.[17]

The scope of managers' public responsibilities is quite wide given the resources that companies, particularly multinational companies, command and the resulting power they hold. According to Preston and Post, management's responsibilities are limited by the organization's primary and secondary involvements (see Figure 1.1). Primary involvement arenas are related to the main business mission and purpose of the firm as attempts to live out its vision in society. Thus, as Preston and Post state, "Primary involvement relationships, tested and mediated through the market mechanism, are essential to the existence of the organization over time."[18]

Primary involvement arenas are those that affect primary stakeholders, that is, those stakeholders without whom the company cannot stay in business.[19] For most companies, primary stakeholders include owners, customers, employees, suppliers, and allies. Although some people believe that the environment is a stakeholder, because it supplies the raw materials necessary to the company's existence,[20] we will take the perspective that the environment is not a stakeholder but rather an essential underpinning to all human civilization, an underpinning that needs to be healthy for human civilization to survive.[21]

Managerial public responsibilities do not end with primary involvement arenas; they extend also to arenas of secondary involvement, which include those arenas and relation-

FIGURE 1.1   **Primary and Secondary Stakeholders of the Corporation**

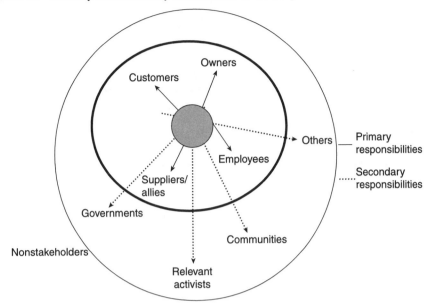

ships that affect or are affected by the firm's activities. Secondary stakeholders are those who affect or are affected by the company's activities indirectly or as a by-product. Secondary stakeholders may not be in direct transactions with the corporation or necessary to its survival. Because they can impact the firm or are affected by the firm's activities, it is important that secondary stakeholders' needs and interests be taken into consideration in much the way that the needs and interests of primary stakeholders are.[22] Thus, the governments that create the rules of the game by which companies operate, as well as the communities that supply the local infrastructure on which companies depend, can be considered secondary stakeholders.

Stakeholders interact with—or in the case of primary stakeholders actually constitute— organizations; that is, they are in relationship to an organization or company. For example, activists may attempt to influence corporate environmental policy but may not be in a position to put the company out of business; thus, they are secondary stakeholders. Similarly, towns and cities located downstream from a company may feel the impact of its polluting a river that flows through and thus are secondary stakeholders. Firms ignore these impacts at their peril, because secondary stakeholders can be demanding or dangerous when their needs are urgent, when, for a variety of reasons, they have power or, if they are inactive, when they are awakened into action.[23]

Companies are typically started and financed by owners, who in the current thinking of many business leaders are considered to be the dominant (and sometimes only important) stakeholder. Other stakeholders are critical to the success of companies as corporate citizens because they too have placed various forms of their capital at risk, are invested in, or tied in relationship to companies. For example, *employees* as stakeholders develop, produce, and deliver the company's products and services. A company's existence is also contingent on the goodwill and continued purchases of *customers*. Companies also depend on the earth for raw materials (ultimately) and *suppliers and allies or partners*, who produce the raw materials necessary for the company to generate its own goods and services. Relationships with these stakeholder groups constitute any leading corporate citizen's *primary stakeholder relationships*.

There are also *critical secondary stakeholder relationships* without which most companies could not survive. For example, companies rely on *governments*—local, state/provincial, national, and increasingly international—to create rules of society that make trading, economic, and political relationships feasible over time. Corporate citizens rely on their local *communities* for an educated workforce and for the infrastructure that makes production of goods and services possible (e.g., roads, local services, and zoning

In 1999, swine production contributed $1 billion to the North Carolina economy, surpassing tobacco. Swine production has experienced explosive growth under the stimulus of franchises offered by large meat-processing corporations, like Murphy Family Farms, which give growers a set price for the output of their mass-production operations. Many of the estimated 10 million porkers who populate North Carolina's eastern lowland counties spend their lives confined to pens in huge high-tech facilities that deliver food to the front and dispose of waste at the rear via conveyor belts. Since a hog produces four times as much waste as a human being, one corporate hog farm can generate a waste stream equivalent to that of a city of 250,000 people. A Web site titled Hog Watch posted by the Environmental Defense Fund notes that North Carolina's hogs "produce a mind-boggling amount of waste: 19 million tons of feces and urine a year, or over 50,000 tons every single day. That's more waste in one year than the entire human population of Charlotte, North Carolina, produces in 58 years! To make matters worse, almost all of North Carolina's hogs are concentrated in the eastern coastal plain, an economically important and ecologically sensitive network of wetlands, rivers, and coastline." The traditional method for dealing with this prodigious outflow has been to dig a waste lagoon, followed by spraying the liquefied waste on nearby fields as an organic fertilizer.

By the mid-1990s, the growth of these swine factories in North Carolina was generating a political backlash against the externalities imposed on neighboring communities by corporate hog farm practices. Beyond the obvious "public bad" of a downwind stench and the incremental impact of acid rain from evaporating ammonia, the waste lagoon and field spray system create a nitrogen-rich effluent carried by rain into nearby streams. Excessive nitrogen in the streams feeds the bloom of algae, turning the streams emerald green. When this algae collects in wetlands near the ocean, it dies and sinks to the bottom. Bacteria, feeding on the dead algae, rob the water of oxygen, causing periodic fish kills near fishing and tourist areas. The failure of one industry to recognize and internalize its externality costs imposes an economic burden on other industries, while also negatively impacting society and the ecological system.

In the summer of 1995, public concern about the negative environmental impacts of corporate pig farming reached new heights in the soggy, smelly aftermath of Hurricane Floyd. Torrential rains in June swelled the state's more than 3,600 waste lagoons to near overflowing, weakening their retaining walls and threatening a deluge of liquid waste on downstream fisheries and communities. Many hog farmers illegally drained excess lagoon waste into streams and swamps to prevent a breach in their dikes. In the end, Hurricane Floyd washed out 50 waste lagoons and drowned more than 30,000 hogs. Defenders of corporate hog farm practices sought to divert public blame and

political retribution by claiming that this environmental calamity was an act of God. A critic in the state legislature countered that this was a sign from God that conventional methods for dealing with the industry's societal mess were inadequate and had to change.

State politicians, previously concerned with promoting economic development and highly sensitive to the political clout and campaign contributions of "Boss Hog," responded to public pressure for increased regulatory controls and oversight. In 1997, the general assembly imposed a temporary moratorium on new hog farms and stepped up regulatory oversight of swine operations. In 1999, Governor Jim Hunt decreed that existing waste lagoons must be phased out over 10 years. The following year, the Democratic state attorney general Mike Easley, in charge of the regulatory crackdown, ran for governor on a platform calling for more balance between the push for economic growth and the pull for corporate accountability and environmental sustainability.

The search is on for a new, more sustainable swine waste processing technology, at an estimated cost to taxpayers and hog farmers of at least $400 million. One of the most promising approaches is a bacterium that reduces the waste to amino acids that can be reconstituted as animal feed. In the end, the solution to this problem will be political rather than scientific. Some have called on the government to promote a "systems solution" by creating a market for the processed swine waste, whether as compost, animal feed, or crab bait. This would give farmers some added income to cover the higher cost of managing manure. Many hog farmers have borrowed heavily to finance expansion at a time when overproduction has driven the price of pork bellies below the break-even point for many producers. A more sustainable industry may also be a smaller industry, with limits to growth to accompany limits on waste.

DISCUSSION QUESTIONS

1. Take the perspective of different actors in this situation (e.g., farmers, local communities downriver and downwind of the hog farms, politicians, customers). How would being in these different situations shift your perspective on the viability and importance of keeping local pig farms operating?

2. What would be the best solution to this situation from each stakeholder's perspective? How can an overall solution be reached?

Sources: Jerry Calton, University of Hawaii, Hilo. This case is based on the *Raleigh News-Observer* investigative series entitled "Boss Hog," which won the 1996 Pulitzer Prize for public service journalism. For an in-depth look at this messy issue, go to www.nando.net/sproject/hogs. See also Environmental Defense Fund Web site titled Hog Watch, www.environmentaldefense.org/system/templates/page/subissue.cfm?subissue=10 (accessed March 16, 2004).

regulations). And there are other critical secondary stakeholders depending on the particular circumstances of the company and the nature of its business (see Case 1.1).

Corporate Responsibility and Citizenship

By defining *corporate citizenship* through the lens of a company's strategies and operating practices, we are taking a practice-based stakeholder view of the corporation, which significantly broadens understanding of the stakeholders to whom a firm is accountable. This view moves the conversation directly toward the quality and nature of the relationships that companies develop with stakeholders and assessment of the impacts of corporate activities on those stakeholders, as well as on the natural environment, whose interests are frequently represented by environmental activists though it is not itself a stakeholder.[24] Such a perspective moves our thinking away from a largely descriptive and even instrumental (or usefulness) perspective on stakeholder relationships. We move, in this book, toward a more normative model, that is, a model of how, in the best of worlds, stakeholder relationships *ought* to be, as the opening quotation by Kofi Annan, secretary-general of the United Nations, suggests.[25]

In support of this perspective, the Business Roundtable (BRT), a major association for business leaders, issued a document titled "Statement on Corporate Responsibility" as long ago as 1980, even before the term *stakeholder* itself became popularized.[26] In this statement, the BRT argued that "it is clear that a large percentage of the public now measures corporations by a yardstick beyond strictly economic objectives."[27] In the words of the BRT, which are even truer now that business impacts frequently have a global scope:

> [The corporation's] economic responsibility is by no means incompatible with other corporate responsibilities in society. In contemporary society all corporate responsibilities are so interrelated that they should not and cannot be separated.
>
> The issue is one of defining, and achieving, responsible corporate management which fully integrates into the entire corporate planning, management, and decision-making process consideration of the impacts of all operating and policy decisions on each of the corporation's constituents. Responsibility to all these constituents *in toto* constitutes responsibility to society, making the corporation both an economically and socially viable entity. Business and society have a symbiotic relationship: The long-term viability of the corporation depends upon its responsibility to the society of which it is a part. And the well-being of society depends upon profitable and responsible business enterprises.[28]

In other words, responsible leaders and managers cannot operate blindly with respect to the impacts that their actions have on any and all of their stakeholders or the natural environment, especially if they hope to do well over the long term. Gaining the respect and commitment of employees, customers, suppliers, communities, and relevant government officials, as well as owners, is essential to productivity and performance. Because corporations are part of and interdependent with the communities and societies in which they operate, they need to actively engage with their stakeholders. Maintaining positive stakeholder relationships involves establishing constructive and positive relationships with them, and being constantly aware of both the status and health of each stakeholder group. These relationships, then, are the essence of corporate global and local citizenship.

Stakeholder Relationship Management

Respect for others is at the heart of good stakeholder relations. While it is frequently true that companies have a great deal of power because they command significant resources, they need to recognize the importance of maintaining good relationships with their stakeholders to experience outstanding long-term performance. Recent research, for example, shows that when companies score highly in *Fortune* magazine's reputational ratings, they are also consistently high performers with respect to their primary stakeholders.[29] Further, companies that are more responsible also appear to perform better financially, thus creating a virtuous circle.[30]

Companies' stakeholder relationships can evolve in one of three ways: reactively, proactively, or interactively.[31] Good stakeholder relationships can be sustained only if the company takes an interactive stance.

Reactive Stance

When companies or their managers take a reactive stance, they may not be paying attention very much to what is going on outside the company's boundaries. They may deny their responsibility for establishing and maintaining positive policies toward stakeholders, engage in legal battles to avoid responsibility, or do the bare minimum to meet the letter but not the spirit of the law.[32] Reaction puts the company and its managers on the defensive rather than in a more positive mode. Because managers have failed to anticipate problems from stakeholders, they may find themselves wondering how things evolved in such a negative fashion.

Proactive Stance

Better, but probably still insufficient to establish truly positive stakeholder relationships is the stance that companies sometimes take when they work to proactively anticipate issues arising from external stakeholders. They may do this by establishing one of any number of what are called boundary-spanning functions to cope with their external relations.

Boundary-spanning functions are those that cross organizational boundaries, either internally or externally, and attempt to develop and maintain relationships with one or more stakeholder groups. For example, modern multinational corporations typically will have at least some of the following functions: public affairs, community relations, public relations, media relations, investor relations, employee relations, government relations, lobbyists, union relations, environmental officers, issues management, and (in one recent instance) a vice president for corporate responsibility.

Interactive Stance

Even a proactive stance falls short of the ideal unless the company's boundary-spanning functions are managed interactively and with respect for the claims, risks, and bonds that stakeholders have. Because stakeholders exist in relationship to the firm, they are embedded in a network that makes them interdependent for their mutual success in activities where their interests overlap. Thus, arguably the best stance for showing ongoing respect for the firm's stakeholders is a mutual and interactive one that is consistent over time and that acknowledges both the mutuality of the relationship and the interdependence of the two entities.

Such constructive and positive relationships between organizations and their stakeholders are built on a framework of interaction, mutual respect, and dialogue, as opposed to management or dominance. That is, progressive companies no longer attempt to manage or dominate their stakeholders. Rather, they have recognized the importance of engaging with them in a relationship based on respect and dialogue or talking *with* each other rather than talking at each other, which is more one-sided. Building this relationship is not a one-time thing but rather an evolving long-term process that requires commitment, energy, a willingness to admit mistakes, and a capacity for both parties to change when necessary.

Understanding the Spheres of Influence: The Ecological Underpinning

Even at present population levels, nearly a billion people go to bed hungry each night. Yet the soils on which we depend for food are being depleted faster than nature can regenerate them, and one by one the world's once most productive fisheries are collapsing from overuse. Water shortages have become pervasive, not simply from temporary droughts but also from depleted water tables and rivers taxed beyond their ability to regenerate. We hear of communities devastated by the exhaustion of their forests and fisheries and of people much like ourselves discovering that they and their children are being poisoned by chemical and radioactive contamination in the food they eat, the water they drink, and the earth on which they live and play.

As we wait for a technological miracle to resolve these apparent limits on continued economic expansion, some 88 million people are added to the world's population every year. Each new member of the human family aspires to a secure and prosperous share the planet's dwindling bounty . . . Bear in mind that population projections are produced by demographers based only on assumptions about fertility rates. They take no account of what the planet can sustain. Given the environmental and social stresses created by current population levels, it is likely that if we do not voluntarily limit our numbers, famine, disease, and social breakdown will do it for us well before another doubling occurs.[33]

Modern business activities occur in an intensely competitive, even hypercompetitive, and relatively newly globalized environment.[34] Change is considered to be a constant, and there is ever-increasing pressure for enhanced productivity and performance. For many businesses, growth and efficiency come by way of dog-eat-dog competition in which the winner takes all in terms of market share and supposedly maximized profits for shareholders.

Without diminishing the importance of competition—and competitiveness—for corporate success, we can add another perspective. Consider that companies operate in a sphere or sector of activities we can call the economic sphere. This sphere has all of the imperatives of growth, efficiency, productivity, and competition inherent in the current capitalistic paradigm, which, with the fall of communism and the rapid evolution of e-commerce, now is operating at some level in most free societies in the world. We know, however, that the economic sector cannot operate independent of society. The economic system is a creature of society.

There is more to society than economics. Living well—that is, living the good life, by almost anyone's definition—has important elements of long-term sustainability with regard to community and ecological health, and also requires some form of governance, or government, to function well. Each of these spheres (which will sometimes be called sectors) intersects and overlaps to some extent with all the others; hence, they must be viewed together as a system, inextricably and unavoidably interwoven. The success of any one of these sectors requires that there be an appropriate balance of power and interests among all of them as well with the ecological surround on which they depend. To complete this picture and provide for an integrated view of what is frequently called the global village (i.e., the world of communities in which we all live and to which we are all connected), we must deeply understand the critical role of the ecological or natural environment. The ecological environment or sphere forms the essential foundation on which all else rests. Without the diversity inherent in the natural environment, without its sustaining resources (which provide raw materials for production), and without appropriate balance in human activities to protect those natural resources, industry and human society quite literally cannot sustain themselves. In that sense we are dependent on this foundation of ecology and the web of life that it supports for our very existence.[35] Leading corporate citizenship needs to be understood as a system characterized by ecological interdependence and mutuality among entities operating in the different spheres (see Figure 1.2). The following are definitions for each of the spheres that form a core structure for understanding leading corporate citizenship:

1. The *economic* sphere encompasses the businesses, profit-generating enterprises, and associated supplier/distributor relationships that produce the goods and services on which human civilization depends.

2. The *political* or *public policy* sphere encompasses government bodies at the local, state, regional, national, and global (international) levels that create the rules by which societies operate and establish what is meant (within and among societies) by the public interest.

3. The *civil society* or civilizing sphere encompasses all other organized forms of activity, such as nongovernmental organizations (NGOs), nonprofit enterprises, schools, religious organizations, political organizations, families, and civic and societal enterprises. This sphere generates the civilizing relationships and sense of community that characterize human society.

4. The *natural or ecological environment* underpins and supports all else, providing sources of raw materials for sustaining human civilization and healthy societies. A healthy ecology is essential to the long-term health of all of human civilization.

Understanding how these spheres intersect and influence each other necessitates a brief journey into system thinking, followed by a more in-depth look at the ecological sphere that underpins what we call society.

Systems Thinking: The Need to Integrate the Environment

Western philosophy and Western science underpin the capitalistic economic system in which we live today throughout much of the developed world. Western science, including

FIGURE 1.2 Spheres of Influence: Economic, Political, Social, Ecological

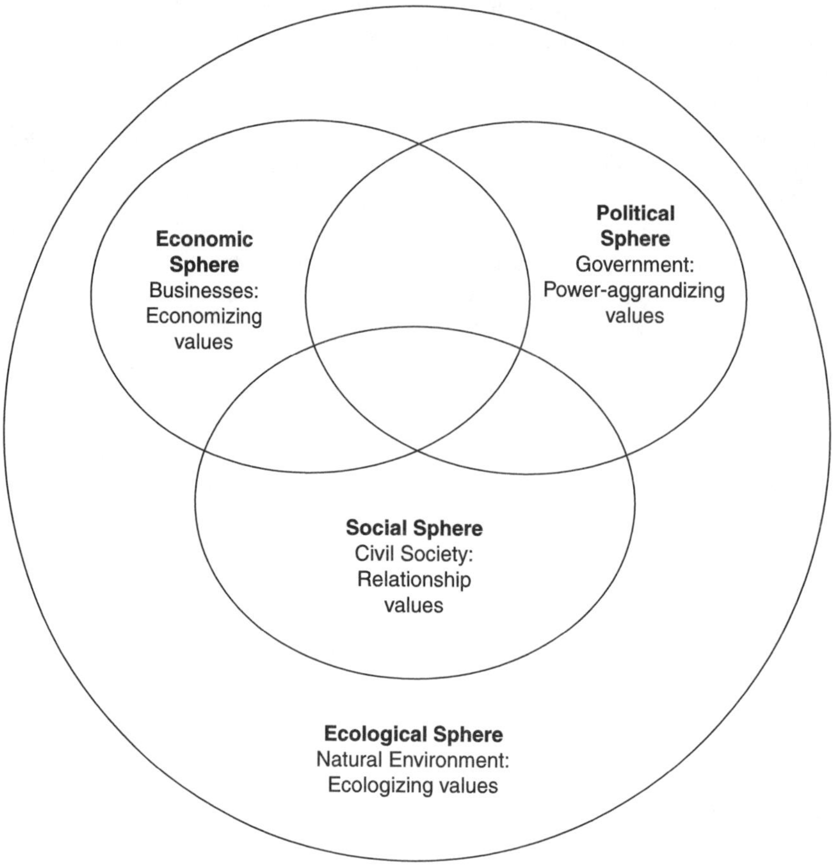

the social science of economics, tends to approach its subjects by taking them apart and reducing them to their smallest elements. Once the smallest elements or fragments have been understood, the Western approach hopes to reintegrate the subject and thereby figure out how it works as an integrated whole. This approach derives from thinkers like Descartes, is premised on Newtonian physics, and is empiricist in its orientation in that it seeks observable evidence in coming to its conclusions.

But this approach, which essentially reduces things to their fundamental parts or atomistic elements, also separates the material elements (body) from nonmaterial aspects of the world like consciousness, emotions, aesthetic appreciation, and spirituality. In simple terms, Western thinking has largely separated and broken into fragmented parts the mind and body, with little mention at all of heart, spirit, community, or meaning, none of which are directly observable. It has, in some respects, done much the same thing to the environment, making some people forget (or ignore) our very human interdependency with nature. Additionally, technological advances have sometimes made progress seem inevitable, as if a solution to whatever problems arise is always just around the corner. The Western approach has a major drawback in that it tends to lessen people's ability to think about the system as a whole, which also reduces their ability to think about systemic and ecological impacts of business actions.

The fragmented or atomistic approach has come under severe criticism in recent years, for reasons that management thinker Peter Senge highlights (see Note 1.1). Many people now believe that a more integrated approach, in part ecologically based and in part based on an integration of mind and body (or material and nonmaterial), better speaks to the long-term needs of human beings and the communities and organizations to which they belong. Such an approach will be particularly critical in the technologically complex and ecologically resource-constrained future, in which an understanding of the impacts of one part of the system on the other will be increasingly necessary.

A cloud masses, the sky darkens, leaves twist upward, and we know that it will rain. We also know that after the storm, the runoff will feed into groundwater miles away, and the sky will grow clear by tomorrow. All these events are distant in time and space, and yet they are all connected within the same pattern. Each has an influence on the rest, an influence that is usually hidden from view. You can only understand the system of a rainstorm by contemplating the whole, not any individual part of the pattern.

Business and other human endeavors are also systems. They, too, are bound by invisible fabrics of interrelated actions, which often take years to fully play out their effects on each other. Since we are part of that lacework ourselves, it's doubly hard to see the whole pattern of change. Instead, we tend to focus on isolated parts of the system, and wonder why our deepest problems never seem to get solved.

Source: Peter Senge, *The Fifth Discipline: The Art and Practice of the Learning Organization* (New York: Double day, 1991), pp. 6–7.

This systemic approach to leading corporate citizenship has been fueled by the development of chaos and complexity theories, which are shedding greater light on the behavior of complex systems, a set to which human systems clearly belong. It has been further advanced by quantum physics, astrophysics, and biology's new understandings of the nature of matter and the interconnectedness among all living things, as well as between living and nonliving matter.[36]

Such developments have highlighted the need for a more integrated approach to understanding the impact of human beings, and the economic organizations they create, on the world and in particular on the natural environment. One seminal work emphasizing a systems approach to management is Peter Senge's influential book *The Fifth Discipline*. Systems thinking emphasizes wholes or, more accurately, holons—whole/parts—and the interrelationships and interdependencies among them.[37] As noted earlier in this chapter, a holon is anything that is itself whole and also a part of something else. Thus, for example, a neutron is an entity, a whole, and it is also a part of an atom. A hand is an entity in itself and also a part of an arm, which is part of a body, and so on. In social systems, an individual (whole) is part of a family (whole) that is part of a community, and so on. In organizations, individuals are part of departments, which are units of divisions, which are parts of the corporate entity, which are part of their industry whole, which in turn are part of society. Holons are integrally linked to the other holons of which they are a part. When something shifts in one holon, the other holons are affected as well because all holons in a given system are interdependent.

We can think of holons as being nested within each other. Each holon is nested within the next level of holon, assuring their interconnectedness and interdependence. What this means in system terms is that anything that affects one part of the system also affects (at some level and in some way) the whole system. Thinking about systems in this way changes our perspective on the corporation: No longer can we consider that a company operates independently of its impacts on stakeholders, society, or nature. Because the companies are part of the larger holon of the communities, societies, and the global village in which they are nested, these systems must, by this way of thinking, impact each other reciprocally.

For example, a company might think of itself as separate from a nonprofit organization to which it has given money in the past or a supplier in its supply chain. When the company withdraws funding—cuts the nonprofit off or decides to use another supplier—the company's leaders may believe that they have ended their impact and responsibility. But the withdrawal of funding creates shifts in the financial stability of the nonprofit or the supplier and has multiple ramifications both within these enterprises and the clients they serve. And while the company may believe that it is immune from these impacts, there may be subtle shifts in employee morale or important customer relationships that ultimately affect the business. All actions within holons have impacts.

The general approach in the Western world to support a given position has been to look for empirical evidence, that is, objective data. Rather than looking at subjectively (or in collective settings, intersubjectively) experienced realities, the typical Western approach is to focus on the material evidence that can be gathered to support the case. But thinkers like Senge (and ecologists like Gladwin, physicists like Capra, and theorists like Wheatley, among many others)[38] propose that it is important to incorporate not only the objective data

FIGURE 1.3 Wilber's Framework for Understanding Holons

Left-hand Side	Right-hand Side

	Interior	**Exterior**
Individual	Subjective Intentional Realm of "I" experienced	Objective Behavioral Realm of "It" observed
Collective	Intersubjective Cultural Realm of "We" experienced	Interobjective Social Realm of "It(s)" observed

but also the nonmaterial, that is, the elements of consciousness and conscience, of emotion and feelings, of meaning and meaningfulness, of spirit and indeed of spirituality, if the work of enterprise is to be approached holistically.

Philosopher Ken Wilber has worked to construct an integrative developmental framework for understanding the world's systems.[39] He notes that the Western tradition has focused almost exclusively on objective, empirically observable elements of individual and collective systems. Wilber generates a two-by-two matrix (see Figure 1.3) in which he places individual and collective exterior elements (i.e., what is objective) on what he terms the right-hand side. On the left-hand side, he places the individual and collective interior aspects of the world. Complete understanding of any system therefore encompasses (1) interior, or nonobservable, elements that we must ask about, such as thoughts, feelings, meanings, aesthetic appreciation, and (2) exterior, or observable, elements. Additionally, both interior elements and external elements also contain individual and collective aspects. Wilber names three categories of holons—*I, we*, and *it* (by collapsing both individual and collective exterior elements into the single category of observable behaviors—it/its).

As you move through this book, try to keep in mind that really understanding anything, including business decisions, requires dealing with all four ways of viewing the world (interior/individual, interior/collective, exterior/individual, and exterior/collective). We are all familiar with traditional data-gathering efforts that focus on the importance of objective information, whether individual or group. For example, traditional financial measurement both for individuals (i.e., pay) and companies (i.e., profits) is a normal measure. At the same time, subjective individual aspects—that is, how individuals experience their organizations or what the group experiences—are also meaningful in creating visionary organizations.

By taking an integrative and holistic systems perspective, we can reshape how we see our impact on the world and the world's on us. In the words of Peter Senge:

> Systems thinking is a discipline for seeing the "structures" that underlie complex situations and for discerning high from low leverage change. That is, by seeing wholes we learn how to foster health . . . [Systems thinking and the related disciplines of personal mastery, mental models, shared vision, and team learning] are concerned with a shift of mind from seeing parts to seeing wholes, from seeing people as helpless reactors to seeing them as active participants in shaping their reality, from reacting to the present to creating the future.[40]

Starbucks (see Case 1.2) is one company that understands the importance of taking a systemic approach to its business and its many stakeholder—as well as one that

Starbucks' Moving Targets Sustainability, Fair Trade, and Supplier Relations

Can a huge company with enormous retail clout, a company that dominates its industry, gain credibility with consumers and critics alike by promoting more ecologically sensitive shade-grown coffee for the environment, supply chain management, and fair trade pricing for its suppliers? That is exactly what coffee giant Starbucks is trying to do, but not without criticism. By 2004, Starbucks had more than 7,500 retail locations in North America, Latin America, Europe, the Middle East and the Pacific Rim. It sells its coffee in a wide range of restaurants, businesses, airlines, hotels, and universities, as well as through mail-order and online catalogs. Ubiquitous as it has become, Starbucks seems well on its way to achieving its goal of establishing itself as the most recognized and respected brand in the world. So how does a company that has achieved such market dominance by selling coffee (and related) products move toward ecological sustainability and fair treatment of its suppliers and their workers in its growing operations?

In 1992 Starbucks established its first environmental mission statement (see Exhibit 1). After being roundly and publicly criticized for its labor and sourcing practices, the company had, by 1995, developed its Framework for a Code of Conduct, becoming the first coffee company to acknowledge its responsibility for working conditions, wages, and rights of coffee workers on the farms of its suppliers. By 1998 Starbucks had formed an ongoing partnership with Conservation International (CI) intended to support shade cultivation, which protects biodiversity, encourages use of environmentally sustainable agricultural practices, and helps the farmers earn more money. This partnership, which was renewed and upgraded in the summer of 2000, permits CI to work in five coffee-growing projects in Latin America, Asia, and Africa. Through a program called Conservation Coffee, Starbucks enables CI to help small farmers grow coffee in the buffer zone of the reserve under the shade of the forest canopy. Growing coffee in the shade helps protect the reserve's forests, streams, and wildlife, while providing substantial income benefits for the farmers.

In 2001 the company, still facing criticism about its percentage of purchased shade-grown coffee and increasing attacks on wages and working conditions on suppliers' farms, established a Preferred Supplier Program to "encourage continuous improvement in sustainable coffee production." This program established a point system in which suppliers could become preferred suppliers not only by meeting certain quality standards (a given for the quality-conscious company) but also by focusing on environmental impacts (e.g., soil management, water reduction, and various waste management and conservation

approaches); social conditions of workers (e.g., wages and benefits, health and safety, and living conditions); and economic issues, especially economic transparency. By late 2003 the company's experience with this program had evolved into its Supplier Code of Conduct, which required suppliers to live up to Starbucks' own standards (see Exhibit 2).

Since that time, the company has moved progressively forward in its efforts to establish a leadership position on environmental sustainability issues within the coffee industry. Using The Natural Step's sustainability framework (discussed in the next section of this chapter), Starbucks identified three primary areas of environmental impact on which to assess its ecological footprint: sourcing; transportation; and store design and operations, including energy, water, recycling, and waste reduction. In 2002, Starbucks president and chief executive officer Orin Smith accepted a Humanitarian Medal of Merit for Starbucks' leadership on sustainability from the Coffee Quality Institute.

Still, critics were not satisfied with Starbucks' performance on human rights, labor, and ecological issues. The activist group Global Exchange, which has an ongoing campaign to pressure Starbucks to procure and promote more fair trade coffee, pointed out in 2004 that prices for coffee were at an all-time low (around 50 cents a pound) and that while some 235 million pounds of coffee were recorded by the Fair Trade Coffee Register in 2003, only some 32 million pounds were sold. The group further charged that Starbucks still does not offer brewed fair trade coffee in its stores, nor does it promote that coffee as the "coffee of the day." The activist group advocated that consumers exert pressure on Starbucks by requesting brewed fair trade coffee in retail shops and otherwise making their preferences known.

For Starbucks, the quest for credibility with its customers, activists, and investors presents a series of ever-new challenges around its supply chain management, environmental, and purchasing policies. These challenges over time have pushed the company in the direction of recognition of new and expanding responsibilities in line with society's changing expectations for large and powerful companies.

Sources: Bart Slob and Joris Oldenziel, "Coffee and Codes: Overview of Codes of Conduct and Ethical Trade Initiatives in the Coffee Sector," www.somo.nl/somo_ned/publicaties/Coffee%20&%20Codes,%20SOMO,%202003%20-%20Enhanced.pdf (accessed February 24, 2004); Elliot J. Schrage, "Promoting International Worker Rights through Private Voluntary Initiatives: Public Relations or Public Policy," Report to the U.S. Department of State (Iowa City: University of Iowa Center for Human Rights, 2004); and www.starbucks.com/aboutus/pressdesc.asp?id=380 (accessed February 24, 2004).

EXHIBIT 1 **Starbucks' Environmental Mission Statement**

Source: www.starbucks.com/aboutus/envapproach.asp (accessed February 24, 2004).

Starbucks is committed to a role of environmental leadership in all facets of our business. We will fulfill this mission by a commitment to:

- Understanding of environmental issues and sharing information with our partners (employees).
- Developing innovative and flexible solutions to bring about change.
- Striving to buy, sell and use environmentally friendly products.
- Recognizing that fiscal responsibility is essential to our environmental future.
- Instilling environmental responsibility values.
- Measuring and monitoring our progress for each project.
- Encouraging all partners to share in our mission.

EXHIBIT 2 **Starbucks' Supplier Code of Conduct**

Source: www.starbucks.com/aboutus/supplier_code.asp (accessed February 24, 2004).

Starbucks strives to be a great, enduring company by employing business standards and practices that produce social, environmental and economic benefits for the communities where we do business. We believe that conducting business responsibly benefits society as well as our various stakeholders, including employees, customers, suppliers, investors, and community members.

As a global company, Starbucks does business with suppliers from many countries of diverse cultural, social, and economic circumstances. We strive to work with suppliers that are committed to our universal principles of operating their business in a responsible and ethical manner, respecting the rights of individuals, and helping to protect the environment.

Our suppliers are required to sign an agreement pledging compliance with Starbucks' Supplier Code of Conduct and specific standards, which include the following:

- Demonstrating commitment to the welfare, economic improvement and sustainability of the people and places that produce our products and services
- Adherence to local laws and international standards regarding human rights, workplace safety, and worker compensation and treatment
- Meeting or exceeding national laws and international standards for environmental protection, and minimizing negative environmental impacts of suppliers' operations
- Commitment to measuring, monitoring, reporting and verification of compliance to this code
- Pursuing continuous improvement of these social and environmental principles

recognizes the growing imperative of sustainability, which will be discussed in the next section of this chapter.

Natural Ecology: The Biological Basis of Citizenship

Why do companies like Starbucks move toward sustainable ecological practices in addition to recognizing the importance of stakeholders throughout their supply chains? Let us begin to understand the overall system in which businesses operate at the foundation: the natural environment. With the earth's population at more than 6 billion and projected to double within the next century (if trends don't change), there is an increasing imperative to understand the impact of human beings on the ecology that sustains them. One organization that has taken a creative and systemic approach to understanding ecological sustainability and business's role in it is the Swedish nonprofit organization The Natural Step (TNS).

Founded in 1989 by Dr. Karl-Henrik Robert, TNS works to develop a consensus about the ecological environment, the role of humans in that environment, and the ways in which humans are threatening not only other forms of life on earth but also themselves by engaging in activities that result in deteriorating natural conditions.[41] Robert, joined by a Swedish physicist, John Holmberg, defined a set of important system conditions based on the laws of thermodynamics and natural cycles that form TNS's framework for environmental sustainability.

Sustainability, as the biologist Humberto Maturana notes, is critical not just to the environment but also to human beings, and particularly to the natural environment's capacity to sustain human civilization. The environment, Maturana points out, will go on in one form or another, no matter what humans do to it. The real question is, Can human society survive major ecological changes?[42] TNS's framework is aimed at helping both individuals and organizations understand ecology systemically so that the use (and abuse) of natural resources can be reduced and newer sustainable approaches to production developed. In addition, TNS hopes to help focus the development of new, less resource-intensive technologies and to provide a common language and set of guiding principles for sustainable enterprise. TNS has relatively recently been introduced into the United States, Canada, the United Kingdom, Japan, and Australia; however, TNS is a household word in Sweden.

The Natural Step's Four System Conditions for Sustainability

The Natural Step system conditions, also called principles of sustainability, define the basic conditions that need to be met in a sustainable society. By looking at the three ways we are damaging nature, and then adding the word "not," The Natural Step has defined the three basic principles for an ecologically sustainable society. However, because we are talking about sustainability for people and for the planet, a basic social principle is also needed—that human needs are met worldwide. From this assessment, we articulate four basic principles for a sustainable society:

In a sustainable society, nature is not subject to systematically increasing:

1. concentrations of substances extracted from the earth's crust;
2. concentrations of substances produced by society;
3. degradation by physical means; and, in that society,
4. human needs are met worldwide.

Source: www.naturalstep.org/about/ faq.php#system_conditions (accessed March 1, 2004).

Thinking Systemically about Ecology: The Natural Step Framework[43]

TNS highlights some of the problematic aspects of human economic development on the ecology. Because of the impact of the 6 billion people currently alive on earth, multiple ecological systems—including croplands, wetlands, the ozone layer, rain forests, fisheries, and groundwater—are facing serious trouble. Visible garbage is filling up landfills, while various pollutants accumulate less visibly in the atmosphere. The ozone hole is increasing, with negative consequences for human life. Rain forests continue to be depleted with almost unimaginable impact on world ecology, for not only do rain forests provide fresh water but they also cleanse the atmosphere. Some ecologists believe that a sustainable number of people on earth would be between 1 and 2 billion, well below current population levels.

According to environmentalist Paul Hawken, "We are far better at making waste than at making products. For every 100 pounds of product we manufacture in the United States, we create at least 3,200 pounds of waste. In a decade, we transform 500 trillion pounds of molecules into nonproductive solids, liquids, and gases."[44] Clearly, if we believe that the earth's resources are limited and that demands on the system cannot be sustained at this rate of "progress," then a new approach to productivity is necessary. TNS's framework provides a set of system conditions that, according to the scientists who originally created the system in Sweden (and others where it is being replicated throughout the world), will be needed to prevent the world from hitting a wall of unsupportable demands on the natural environment. Note 1.2 lists the system conditions for sustainability as developed by TNS, which works with companies such as Home Depot, Bank of America, and McDonald's on implementing these conditions.

The TNS system is aimed at sustainable development. Sustainable development can be defined as "a process of achieving human development . . . in an inclusive, connected, equitable, prudent, and secure manner," according to ecological scholar Thomas Gladwin and his colleagues.[45] Gladwin has defined five elements that represent a set of constraints on human development, similar to those for the material world that TNS produced (see Table 1.2).

Inclusiveness connotes an expansive view of the space, time, and component parts of the observed ecology, embracing both ecological and human conditions in the present and the future. *Connectivity* means understanding the inherent interconnectedness and interdependence of elements of the world and problems in the world. *Equity* means a fair distribution of resources and property rights within and between generations. Putting connectivity and equity together suggests greater comprehension of the unavoidable links between, for example, creating better ecological health and efforts to reduce poverty or the gap between rich and poor.

Prudence means taking care of the resources of the world, as suggested by the TNS constraints. In practice, being prudent means keeping ecosystems and socioeconomic systems

TABLE 1.2 **Constraints on Sustainable Human Development**

Source: Thomas N. Gladwin, James J. Kennelly, and Tara-Shelomith Krause, "Shifting Paradigms for Sustainable Development: Implications for Management Theory and Research," *Academy of Management Review* 20, no. 4 (October 1995), pp. 847–907.

Inclusiveness	Expansive view of space, time, and elements of ecology (present and future)
Connectivity	Understanding inherent interconnectedness and interdependence of world's elements and problems
Equity	Fair distribution of resources and property rights (within and between generations)
Prudence	Taking care of world's resources so they are healthy and resilient
Security	Sustainability of health, high quality human life for present and future generations

healthy and resilient; avoiding irreversible losses of ecological or other resources; and, again as the TNS constraints indicate, keeping human activities within the earth's regenerative capacity. Finally, *security* focuses on the sustainability of human life, that is, ensuring "a safe, healthy, high quality of life for current and future generations."[46]

Later in this book, we will consider some of the ecological problems that have arisen as a result of human and economic development, technological advances, and the process of industrialization as part of the systemic thinking process. For now, what is important is to recognize that systemic thinking fundamentally means thinking in new ways about the relationships that exist among human beings, the enterprises they create, and the rest of the natural world.

Indeed, thinking about ecological sustainability may mean complementing traditional (Western) ways of viewing human beings' relationship to the natural world with more holistic perspectives. It may even mean shifting our perspective away from an anthropomorphic (human-centered) or technocentric (technologically oriented) worldview beyond even an ecocentric (ecological) worldview.[47] It may mean a wholly integrative approach to economic development focused on sustainability.

A fully integrative perspective would synthesize the three critical spheres of civilization (economic, political, and societal) with the ecological, and would also integrate the subjective and intersubjective elements of emotions, intuition, aesthetics, and culture, among others, into our perspective. The result would be better understanding of the values that underpin each sphere of activity and an integration of them into an ecologically sustainable and holistic worldview.

The Need for Balance

Just as nature requires a balance among elements to sustain any healthy ecological environment, we must think about corporate global citizenship as part of the social ecology. Balance among the interests of all three important sectors of human civilization is of paramount concern. In sustaining this balance among sectors and with the natural world, we must also marry competition and competitiveness with cooperation and collaboration, in the process that biologists call symbiosis. Competition *and* collaboration, with sustainability, are necessary and important to societal—and business—health and success. The physicist Fritjof Capra perhaps puts it best:

> The recognition of symbiosis as a major evolutionary force has profound philosophical implications. All larger organisms [and organizations], including ourselves, are living testimonies to the fact that destructive practices do not work in the long run. In the end the aggressors always destroy themselves, making way for others who know how to cooperate and get along. Life is much less a competitive struggle for survival than a triumph of cooperation and creativity. Indeed, since the creation of the first nucleated cells, evolution has proceeded through ever more intricate arrangements of cooperation and coevolution.[48]

Mastering systems thinking is a critical element of creating continually improving and learning enterprises.[49] An integrative systems approach is essential if we are to conceive of operating businesses, as well as governments and civil society enterprise, in sustainable ways, giving due consideration to the seventh generation out, as our Native American ancestors would have noted.

Leading Challenges: A New Paradigm for Corporate Citizenship

Fundamentally, leading corporate citizenship cannot evolve into constructive stakeholder relationships without the active participation of effective, aware, and progressive leaders. Aware leaders have thought deeply about their own values and vision, and as a result are prepared for the complex world they must face. Being prepared won't necessarily lessen the complexity or the difficulty of the decisions they must make, but awareness does help leaders make the right decisions when challenges are high, as they inevitably are in the complex social and political environment. Particularly in an era in which activists and other stakeholders can mobilize nearly instantaneously and globally, awareness of and response to the demands of leading a corporate citizen is a must. In effect, this mobilization is what happened in 1999 when activists prevented the World Trade Organization from meeting in Seattle, in 2001 when terrorists struck the World Trade Center and the Pentagon, and since that time in the increasing antiglobalization sentiments expressed by activists around the world.

In light of challenges like these, the goal of this book is to help those managers leading corporate citizens to understand the real world of complex dilemmas leaders face and the multiple perspectives embedded in every decision. The book also seeks to build awareness of the impacts and implications of those decisions on the people—the stakeholders— whom they affect. The book is organized as follows:

- Part 1, *A Context for Leading Corporate Citizens*: This chapter explores the context in which businesses operate today. In this chapter, we explored the spheres of human civilization as they are built on a healthy ecological environment. We will continue to explore the interrelationship of the corporation (as it exists within the economic sphere) and the organizations and enterprises that exist in the political and civil or societal spheres.

- Part 2, *Leading Corporate Citizens with Vision, Values, and Value Added*: Mere understanding of the need for balance among the spheres is insufficient to guide organizations successfully. Both individuals and organizations need clear and constructive visions embedded with constructive end values to get the kinds of added value that sustain a business. Successful leaders develop personal and organizational vision and awareness, growing intellectually, emotionally, and morally so that they can cope with the complexity and challenges of the global business arena. Higher levels of individual and organizational awareness and development, ongoing learning, and empowerment are also necessary for organizations to succeed in the complexity of the modern world. We will explore the realities and links among vision, values, and value added.

- Part 3, *Leading Corporate Citizens and Their Stakeholders*: Provide significant evidence that developing positive operating practices with respect to multiple stakeholders is likely to be the key to organizational success in the future. We will explore relationships with stakeholders directly by assessing the links companies create with their many stakeholders so that they can get to value added. Then we will explore how an emphasis on multiple bottom lines rather than a single bottom line can be productive. In taking this approach, we will learn that the "soft stuff" is really the "hard stuff," but that it can be and is being measured.

We will explicitly look at the ways in which corporate responsibility and citizenship can be managed internally. We will explore the ways in which operating with integrity adds value—and values—to business enterprises through living up to articulated visions as well as established codes promoting respect and human dignity. We will assess the ecology of leading corporate citizenship, exploring both the natural environmental and sustainability implications of corporate activities, and moving toward an understanding of what a broader awareness of the impact of economic activities on the environment means for long-term economic development. The intersection of the knowledge economy, the blurring of boundaries with increased technological connectivity, and the need for respecting human dignity will serve as a foundation for this exploration.

- Part 4, *Leading Corporate Citizens into the Future*: The exploration of vision, values, and value added as ways of managing corporate responsibility provides a framework for businesses to operate with integrity amid complexity and change, that is, living up to codes of conduct and emerging global standards and operating with value added rather than in a value-neutral stance. Finally, we will focus on developing an integrated vision of what a new paradigm corporation would look like if it were fully implemented. How and where would individuals fit in? What does this new paradigm organization look, feel, and act like? How can we manage effectively and efficiently, doing the right thing and doing things right, for the future?

Endnotes

1. Kofi Annan, "Business and the U.N.: A Global Compact of Shared Values and Principles," World Economic Forum, Davos, Switzerland, January 31, 1999. Reprinted in *Vital Speeches of the Day* 65, no. 9 (February 15, 1999) pp. 260–61. For further information on the Global Compact, see www.unglobalcompact.org.

2. The classic references are R. Edward Freeman, *Strategic Management: A Stakeholder Approach* (New York: Basic Books, 1984), and William M. Evan and R. Edward Freeman, "A Stakeholder Theory of the Modern Corporation: Kantian Capitalism," in *Ethical Theory and Business*, ed. T. Beauchamp and N. Bowie (Englewood Cliffs, NJ: Prentice Hall, 1998). Max Clarkson identifies stakeholders as primary and secondary, depending on the level of risk they have taken with respect to the organization. See Max B. E. Clarkson, "A Stakeholder Framework for Analyzing and Evaluating Corporate Social Performance," *Academy of Management Review* 20, no. 1 (1995), pp. 92–117.

3. Dirk Matten and Andrew Crane, "Corporate Citizenship: Towards an Extended Theoretical Conceptualization," *Academy of Management Review* 29 (2004).

4. See the works of Ken Wilber, for example, *A Brief History of Everything* (Boston: Shambala, 1996); *Eye of the Spirit: An Integral Vision for a World Gone Slightly Mad* (Boston: Shambala, 1998); and *The Marriage of Sense and Soul: Integrating Science and Reason* (New York: Random House, 1998). For a discussion of the web that constitutes life and the ways in which all matter is interrelated see Fritjof Capra, *The Web of Life* (New York: Anchor Doubleday, 1995).

5. Matten and Crane, "Corporate Citizenship."

6. Michael Porter's views on corporate (social) responsibility are characteristic of this perspective. See Michael Porter and Mark R. Kramer, "The Competitive Advantage of Philanthropy," *Harvard Business Review* 80, no. 12 (December 2002), pp. 56–69.

7. Sandra Waddock, "Companies, Academics, and the Progress of Corporate Citizenship," *Business and Society Review* 109 (March 2004), pp. 5–42.

8. Charles Handy, "What's a Business For?" *Harvard Business Review* (December 2002). Reprinted by permission of *Harvard Business Review*. Copyright 2002 by the Harvard Business School Publishing Corporation; all rights reserved.

9. Freeman, *Strategic Management*.

10. See, for example, James E. Post, Lee E. Preston, and Sybil Sachs, "Managing the Extended Enterprise: The New Stakeholder View," *California Management Review* 45, no. 1 (2002), pp. 6–29; and James E. Post, Lee E. Preston, and Sybil Sachs, *Redefining the Corporation* (New York: Oxford University Press, 2002).

11. Milton Friedman, "The Social Responsibility of a Business Is to Increase Its Profits," *New York Times Magazine*, September 13, 1970. Copyright © 1970. The New York Times Company. Reprinted with permission.

12. Chris Marsden and Jörg Andriof, "Towards an Understanding of Corporate Citizenship and How to Influence It," *Citizenship Studies* 2, no. 2 (1988), pp. 329–52.

13. See Clarkson, "A Stakeholder Framework," for an extended discussion of stakes. See also Ronald K. Mitchell, Bradley R. Agle, and Donna J. Wood, "Toward a Theory of Stakeholder Identification and Salience: Defining the Principle of Who and What Really Counts," *Academy of Management Review* 22, no. 4 (October 1997), pp. 853–86.

14. For a perspective on this, See Tammy MacLean, "Creating Stakeholder Relationships: A Model of Organizational Social Identification—How the Southern Baptist Convention Became Stakeholders of Walt Disney," paper presented at the annual meeting of the Academy of Management, San Diego, CA, 1998.

15. Thanks are owed to Max B. E. Clarkson for providing a basis for thinking about corporate social performance in terms of stakeholder relationships. See Clarkson, "A Stakeholder Framework."

16. See, for example, Freeman, *Strategic Management*, and Evan and Freeman, "A Stakeholder Theory of the Modern Corporation." See also Clarkson, "A Stakeholder Framework,"

and, more recently, Mitchell, Agle, and Wood, "Toward a Theory of Stakeholder Identification and Salience."

17. The concepts of primary and secondary involvement come from Lee E. Preston and James E. Post, *Private Management and Public Policy: The Principle of Public Responsibility* (Englewood Cliffs, NJ: Prentice Hall, 1975).

18. Ibid., p. 95.

19. This definition is from Clarkson, "A Stakeholder Framework," p. 106. However, the distinction goes back to Freeman, *Strategic Management*.

20. For example, Mark Starik, "Should Trees Have Managerial Standing? Toward Stakeholder Status for Non-Human Nature," *Journal of Business Ethics* 14 (1995), pp. 204–17.

21. See, for example, Robert A. Phillips and Joel Reichart, "The Environment as a Stakeholder? A Fairness Based Approach," *Journal of Business Ethics* 23 (January 2000), pp. 183–97.

22. Clarkson, "A Stakeholder Framework," p. 107.

23. Mitchell, Agle, and Wood, "Toward a Theory of Stakeholder Identification and Salience." Mitchell, Agle, and Wood's model has been somewhat modified by Steven L. Wartick and Donna J. Wood, *International Business and Society* (Malden, MA: Blackwell Press, 1998), in the fashion incorporated into this discussion.

24. See Duane Windsor, "Stakeholder Responsibilities: Lessons for Managers," in *Unfolding Stakeholder Thinking: Theory, Responsibility and Engagement*, ed. Jörg Andriof, Sandra Waddock, Bryan Husted, and Sandra Sutherland Rahman (Sheffield: Greenleaf, 2002), pp. 137–54.

25. For background on descriptive, instrumental, and normative branches of stakeholder theory, see Thomas Donaldson and Lee E. Preston, "The Stakeholder Theory of the Corporation: Concepts, Evidence, and Implications," *Academy of Management Review* 20 (January 1995), pp. 1, 65–91.

26. See Business Roundtable, "Statement on Corporate Responsibility," in *Business and Society: Economic, Moral, and Political Foundations*, ed. Thomas G. Marx (Englewood Cliffs, NJ: Prentice Hall, 1985), p. 152. The term *stakeholder* entered the popular parlance in 1984 with the issuance of Freeman, *Strategic Management*.

27. Business Round table, "Statement on Corporate Responsibility," p. 152.

28. Ibid., p. 157.

29. Note that this link is the basis of the instrumental argument for positive stakeholder relationships, as discussed by Donaldson and Preston, "The Stakeholder Theory of the Corporation."

30. See for example, Joshua D. Margolis and James P. Walsh, *People and Profits? The Search for a Link between a Company's Social and Financial Performance* (Mahwah, NJ: Erlbaum, 2001); Joshua D. Margolis and James P. Walsh, "Misery Loves Companies: Rethinking Social Initiatives by Business," *Administrative Science Quarterly* 48 (2003), pp. 268–305; S. A. Waddock and S. B. Graves, "Quality of Management and Quality of Stakeholder Relations: Are They Synonymous?" *Business and Society* 36, no. 3 (September 1979), pp. 250–79; and S. A. Waddock and S. B. Graves, "The Corporate Social Performance–Financial Performance Link," *Strategic Management Journal* 18, no. 4 (1997), pp. 303–19.

31. For a discussion of this framework, see Preston and Post, *Private Management and Public Policy*.

32. See also Clarkson, "A Stakeholder Framework," p. 109. Clarkson's "postures" are different from the stances outlined here.

33. David C. Korten, *When Corporations Rule the World* (San Francisco: Berrett-Koehler, 1995), p. 21.

34. See Richard D'Aveni, *Hyper-Competition: Managing the Dynamics of Strategic Maneuvering* (New York: Free Press, 1994).

35. For a marvelous and accessible description of the interconnectedness of living and material entities, see Capra, *The Web of Life*.

36. For some insight into these topics, you can start with James Gleick, *Chaos: Making a New Science* (New York: Viking, 1987); Stuart Kauffman, *At Home in the Universe: The Search for the Laws of Self-Organization and Complexity* (New York: Oxford University Press, 1995); Capra, *The Web of Life*; Humberto R. Maturana and Francisco J. Varela, *The Tree of Knowledge: The Biological Roots of Human Understanding*, rev. ed. (Boston: Shambala, 1998); and of course Peter Senge, *The Fifth Discipline: The Art and Practice of the Learning Organization* (New York: Doubleday, 1991).

37. The term *holon* is from Arthur Koestler and is extensively developed in Ken Wilber's work. Relevant works by Wilber include *Sex, Ecology, Spirituality: The Spirit of Evolution* (Boston: Shambala, 1995), *Eye of the Spirit*, and *A Brief History of Everything*.

38. Thomas N. Gladwin, James J. Kennelly, and Tara-Shelomith Krause, "Shifting Paradigms for Sustainable Development: Implications for Management Theory and Research," *Academy of Management Review* 20, no. 4 (October 1995), pp. 874–907; Fritjof Capra, *The Turning Point: Science, Society, and the Rising Culture* (New York: Bantam Books, 1983); and Margaret J. Wheatley, *Leadership and the New Science: Learning about Organization from an Orderly New Universe* (San Francisco: Berrett-Koehler, 1992).

39. See Wilber, *Sex, Ecology, Spirituality; Eye of the Spirit;* and *A Brief History of Everything*.

40. Senge, *The Fifth Discipline*, p. 69.

41. Information on The Natural Step can be found at www.naturalstep.org.

42. This paragraph is based on a talk by Humberto Maturana at the 1998 annual meeting of the Society for Organizational Learning (SoL). A version of this talk by Humberto Maturana Romesin and Pille Bunnell, entitled "Biosphere, Homosphere, and Robosphere: What Has That to Do with Business?" is available at www.solonline.org/res/wp/maturana/index.html (accessed June 29, 2004).

43. This section is based on The Natural Step Web site, www.naturalstep.org (accessed February 25, 2004).

44. Quoted in ibid.

45. Gladwin, Kennelly, and Krause, "Shifting Paradigms for Sustainable Development."

46. U.S. President's Council on Sustainable Development, quoted in Gladwin, Kennelly, and Krause "Shifting Paradigms for Sustainable Development." Much of the discussion in these paragraphs is based on this article.

47. These terms are developed in Gladwin, Kennelly, and Krause, "Shifting Paradigms for Sustainable Development."

48. Capra, *The Web of Life*, p. 243.

49. Senge, *The Fifth Discipline*.

What Is Evidence?

To state an opinion is to tell others what we think about something; to present evidence is to *show* others that what we think makes sense. Being shown is much more interesting and impressive than being told—we've all known this since grade school. Why, then, does so much writing and speaking consist of piling one opinion on another, with little or no evidence offered in support of any of them? One reason is that the human mind is a veritable opinion factory, so most people have an abundance of opinions to share. Another reason is that people tend to remember their opinions and forget the process by which they got them, much as students remember their final grade in a course long after they have forgotten the tests and homework grades that it comprises.

A third, and in some ways more significant, reason is that sometimes there is little or no evidence to remember—in other words, the opinion is based on nothing substantial. For example, in early 1999 many people held the opinion that William Jefferson Clinton's lying under oath did not "rise to the level of an impeachable offense." When asked to explain why they thought that, some people repeated the assertion in identical or similar words: "He shouldn't be removed from office for what he did," "It's between him and Hillary." Or they offered related opinions: "It's a right-wing conspiracy," "Independent counsel Kenneth Starr is on a witch-hunt." Though it is impossible to be *certain* why they thought as they did, the fact that they expressed the opinion in the very same words incessantly repeated by a half dozen White House advisors and innumerable other Clinton supporters suggests that they simply borrowed the opinion without evaluating it.*

We can all identify with those people. More often than most of us would care to admit, when called on to support our opinions, we manage to produce only the flimsiest of evidence. We may soothe ourselves with the notion that a thick folder of evidence lies misfiled in our minds, but the very real possibility remains that flimsy evidence was all we ever had. Critical thinkers are tempted to commit the same self-deception that plagues others, but they have learned the value of resisting that temptation. More important, they have developed the habit of checking the quality and quantity of the evidence before forming an opinion. Also, before *expressing* an opinion, they review their evidence. The extra time this takes is more than compensated by the confidence that comes from knowing what they are talking about.

---

*The fact that many people embraced this opinion without much evidence does not mean that no evidence could be marshalled for the view. Other supporters of President Clinton responded more substantively.

Kinds of Evidence

To evaluate your own and other people's opinions, you will need to understand the various kinds of evidence. This entails knowing the value and limitations of each kind, as well as the appropriate questions to ask. The most important kinds of evidence are *personal experience, unpublished report, published report, eyewitness testimony, celebrity testimony, expert opinion, experiment, statistics, survey, formal observation, and* research review.

It is important to note that the arrangement here is not in ascending or descending order of reliability but rather in rough order of familiarity—*personal experience* being very familiar to most people and *research review* much less familiar

Personal Experience

Personal experience is the one kind of evidence we don't have to go to the library or the Internet to get. We carry it with us in our minds. For this reason, it tends to exert a greater influence than other kinds of evidence. The individuals we've met, the situations we've been in, the things that have happened to us seem more authentic and meaningful than what we have merely heard or read. We are confident about our personal experience. Unfortunately, this confidence can cause us to attach greater significance and universality to particular events than they deserve. If we ride in a New York City taxicab on one occasion, we may think we are acquainted with New York City taxicab drivers. If we have a Korean friend, we may feel that we know Koreans in general or even Asians in general. However, it takes more than one or a few examples to support a generalization; for sweeping generalizations, even a dozen may not be enough.

To evaluate personal experience—your own or other people's—ask: Are the events typical or unique? Are they sufficient in number and kind to support the conclusion? Remember that the vividness and dramatic quality of an anecdote cannot compensate for its limitedness.

Unpublished Report

Unpublished reports are stories we hear from other people, often referred to as gossip or hearsay. The biggest problem with such reports is that it is difficult to confirm them. In many cases, we don't know whether the stories are secondhand or third-, fourth-, or *fiftieth*-hand. And stories have a way of changing as they are passed from person to person. The people who repeat them may not be dishonest; they may, in fact, try to be accurate but then inadvertently leave out some words, add others, or change the details or order of events.

To evaluate an unpublished report, ask: Where did the story originate? How can I confirm that the version I heard is accurate?

Published Report

This kind of evidence is found in a wide variety of published or broadcast works, from scholarly books, professional journals, and encyclopedia articles, to magazine or newspaper articles, news broadcasts, and radio or television commentaries. In scholarly works the sources of the material are usually carefully documented in footnotes and bibliographic citations. In nonscholarly works, the documentation may be informal, fragmentary, or in some cases, nonexistent. Even when the source is not cited, we can assess the author's and publisher's reliability. Facts and opinions are often mingled in contemporary publications, particularly nonscholarly ones, so careful reading may be necessary to reveal which statements constitute evidence and which should *themselves* be supported with evidence.

To evaluate a published report, ask: Does the report cite the sources of all important items of information? (If so, you may wish to check them.) Does the author have a reputation for careful reporting? Does the publisher or broadcaster have a reputation for reliability? Which statements in the published report constitute evidence, and which should themselves be supported with evidence? (Another way to ask this question is, Which statements might a thoughtful person challenge? Does the author answer the challenges satisfactorily?)

Eyewitness Testimony

Because eyewitness testimony is commonly considered to be the most reliable kind of evidence, you may be surprised to find that it is sometimes badly flawed for any one of several reasons. The external conditions may not have been optimal—for example, the incident may have occurred late on a foggy night and the eyewitness may have been some distance away. The eyewitness may have been tired or under the influence of alcohol or drugs; his or her observation may also have been distorted by preconceptions or expectations. Finally, the person's memory of what occurred may have been confused by subsequent events. Such confusion can be a special problem when considerable time has elapsed between the event and the testimony.

To evaluate eyewitness testimony, ask: What circumstances surrounding the event, including the eyewitness's state of mind, could have distorted his or her perception? (If any such distortion was likely, try to determine whether it actually occurred.) What circumstances since the event—for example, the publication of other accounts of the event—could have affected the eyewitness's recollection?

Celebrity Testimony

Increasingly, celebrities are seen endorsing products and services in commercials and "infomercials." In addition, when they appear as guests on radio and television talk shows, they are encouraged to state their personal views about whatever happens to be in the news at the time. On any given day you may hear singers, actors, and athletes discussing religion, criminal justice, education, economics, international relations, campaign finance reform, and psychology, among other topics. For example, a TV host once asked an actor, "How big a factor in human life do you believe is chance in the universe?"

Your respect for celebrities as entertainers may lead you to assume that they know what they are talking about in interviews. This assumption is often mistaken. They may be very well informed. Or they may have been caught unawares by the host's question and, not wanting to seem ignorant, uttered whatever happened to come to mind. Some may be so impressed with their own importance that they imagine whatever they say is profound for no other reason than that they say it! In the case of testimonials for products or services, the celebrities may have been paid to read words about products that they know little or nothing about.

To evaluate celebrity testimony, ask: In the case of advertisements or "infomercials," is the celebrity a paid spokesperson? (This is often indicated in small print at the end of the ad.) In the case of talk show comments, does the celebrity offer any support for his or her views—for example, citing research conducted by more qualified people? Also, does the host ask for such support? If the discussion consists of little more than a series of assertions expressing the celebrity's unsupported opinion, you would do well to discount it no matter now much you may admire the person.

Expert Opinion

As you might expect, expert opinion is generally more reliable than most of the varieties of evidence we have considered so far. The advantage it enjoys over personal experience is that it can usually address the crucial question of what is typical and what is not. Nevertheless, not even expert opinion is consistently reliable. The most significant reason for unreliability is that knowledge in virtually every field is rapidly expanding. A century ago it was possible to gain expertise in more than one discipline. Today's scholars typically have expertise in *a single narrow aspect of one discipline* and may have difficulty keeping abreast of significant developments in that one. Unfortunately, some people can't resist the temptation to think of themselves as experts in everything. A well-known astronomer, for example, used to write articles in popular magazines and offer his opinions on ethics, anthropology, and theology.

To evaluate expert opinion, ask: Does the person have, in addition to credentials in the broad field in question, *specific* expertise in the particular issue under discussion? This is not always easy to ascertain by those outside the field, but one good indication is that the person does not just state his or her opinion but also supports it with references to current research. Also ask whether the expert was paid. The acceptance of money does not necessarily taint expert opinion, but it may raise questions about the person's objectivity. Finally, ask whether other authorities agree or disagree with the expert's view.

Experiment

There are two broad types of experiments. The *laboratory* experiment enables researchers to vary the conditions and thereby identify causes and effects more precisely. One disadvantage of the laboratory experiment, however, is its artificiality. The *field* experiment has the advantage of occurring in a natural setting, but the presence of the researchers can influence the subjects and distort the findings.

To evaluate experimental evidence, ask: For a laboratory experiment, has it been replicated by other researchers? For a field experiment, have other researchers independently confirmed the findings? If replication or confirmation has been unsuccessfully attempted, it is best to postpone your acceptance of the experimental findings.

Statistics

In the broad sense, the term *statistics* applies to any information that can be quantified; for example, the changes in average temperature over a period of time to determine whether the phenomenon of global warming is occurring. The term *statistics* may also be used more narrowly to mean quantifiable information about a group that is obtained by contacting, or otherwise accounting for, every individual in the group. The U.S. Census is one example of statistics in this sense. Others are the voting records of U.S. senators, the percentage of automobile fatalities involving drunk driving, the fluctuations in immigration patterns over the past century, the percentage of unwed mothers who come from one-parent homes, and the comparative education and income levels of various racial-ethnic groups.

When evaluating statistical information, ask: What is the source of the statistics? Is the source reliable? How old are the data? Have any important factors changed since the data were collected?

Survey

Surveys are among the most common tools used by professionals, particularly in the social sciences. Since the data obtained from surveys are quantifiable, surveys are often included under the broad heading of "statistics." However, we are considering them separately to highlight one distinguishing characteristic: Surveys typically obtain data by contacting, not every individual in the group (known as a *population*), but a representative *sample* of the group. Surveys are conducted by telephone contact, mail, or personal interview. The sampling may be *random, systematic* (for example, every tenth or hundredth person in a telephone directory), or *stratified* (the exact proportion of the component members of the group; for example, 51 percent women and 49 percent men).

When evaluating a survey, ask: Was the sample truly representative? That is, did all members of the total population surveyed have an equal chance of being selected? Were the questions clear and unambiguous? Were they objectively phrased rather than slanted? In the case of a mailed survey, did a significant number fail to respond? If so, how might non-respondents differ from respondents? Also, do other surveys corroborate the survey's findings?

Formal Observation

There are two kinds of formal observational studies. In *detached* observation the observer does not interact with the individuals being studied. A child psychologist, for example, might visit a school playground and watch how the children behave. In *participant* observation the researcher is involved in the activity being studied. An anthropologist who lived with a nomadic tribe for a period of months, sharing meals with them and taking part in their communal activities, would be a participant observer.

When evaluating formal observation, ask: Is it likely that the presence of the observer distorted the behavior being observed? Was the observation of sufficient duration to permit the conclusions that were drawn? Do the conclusions overgeneralize? (For example, the observations made of a single nomadic group might be generalized to all nomadic groups, ignoring the fact that other nomadic groups may differ in important ways.)

Research Review

This kind of study is undertaken when a considerable body of research has already been done on a subject. The reviewer examines all the scholarly studies that have been done and then summarizes and compares their findings. Often dozens or even hundreds of studies are examined. A thorough review of research reveals areas of agreement and disagreement and provides a valuable overview of the current state of knowledge on the subject.

When evaluating a research review, ask: Do the reviewer's conclusions seem reasonable given the research covered in the review? Has the reviewer omitted any relevant research? (As a lay person, you may find the latter question impossible to answer yourself. You could, however, ask it of another expert in the field who is familiar with both the actual research and the review.)

One additional question is applicable to all kinds of evidence: Is this evidence *relevant* to the issue under consideration? If it is not relevant, it deserves no consideration, no matter how excellent it may be in other respects. Here is an actual example of an issue that has been badly confused by the use of irrelevant evidence. Many college administrators have rejected instructors' requests for a reduction in class size for courses such as writing, speaking, and critical thinking. The administrators cited scholarly studies demonstrating that teaching effectiveness is unrelated to class size—in other words, that teachers can be as effective with fifty students in the classroom as they are with fifteen. Yet the scholarly studies in question examined only courses that impart information, not those that develop skills. For the latter, the very courses in question, the evidence had no relevance.

Evaluating Evidence

We all like to think of ourselves as totally objective, equally open to either side of every issue. But that is rarely the case. Even if we have not yet taken a firm position on an issue at the outset of our evaluation, we will usually be "tilted" in one direction or the other by our overall philosophy of life, our political or social views, our opinions on related issues, or our attitude toward the people associated with the various views. This tilting, also known as *bias,* may be so slight that it has little or no effect on our judgment. On the other hand, it may be significant enough to short-circuit critical thinking. The more we tilt on an issue, the greater our thinking deficit is likely to be.

How can you tell when bias is hindering your evaluation of evidence? Look for one or more of these signs:

- You approach your evaluation *wanting* one side to be proven right.
- You begin your investigation assuming that familiar views will prove correct.
- You look for evidence that supports the side of the issue you favor and ignore evidence that opposes it.
- You rate sources by how favorable they are to your thinking rather than by their reliability and the quality of their research.
- You are nitpickingly critical of evidence for views you oppose and uncritical of evidence for views you favor.
- When you encounter evidence that opposes your bias, you begin arguing against it, often before you have completed examining it.

Although you may not be able to eliminate your biases, you can nevertheless identify and *control* them, and that is all that is necessary. The purpose of evaluating evidence is to discover the truth, regardless of whether it is pleasant or unpleasant, and the only way to do so is to evaluate *fairly.* Such an evaluation will sometimes require you to conclude that the view you leaned toward (or actually held) is mistaken. Never hesitate to do so. Changing your mind is not dishonorable, but maintaining a false view in order to save face is not only foolish but also intellectually dishonest.

What Constitutes "Sufficient" Evidence?

It is seldom easy to decide when your evidence, or that of the person whose opinion you are evaluating, is sufficient. In making your determination you will have to consider both the quantity and the quality of the evidence. No simple formula exists, but these general guidelines will help you decide particular cases:

1. *Evidence is sufficient when it permits a judgment to be made with certainty.* Wishing, assuming, or pretending that a judgment is correct does not constitute certainty. Certainty exists when there is no good reason for doubt, no basis for dispute. The standard for conviction in a criminal trial, for example, is "guilt beyond a reasonable doubt." Certainty is a very difficult standard to meet, especially in controversial issues, so generally you will be forced to settle for a more modest standard.

2. *If certainty is unattainable, evidence is sufficient if one view of the issue has been shown to have the force of probability.* This means that the view in question is demonstrably more reasonable than any competing view. In civil court cases this standard is expressed as "a preponderance of the evidence." *Demonstrating* reasonableness is, of course, very different from merely *asserting* it, and all possible views must be identified and evaluated before any one view can be established as most reasonable.

3. *In all other cases, the evidence must be considered insufficient.* In other words, if the evidence does not show one view to be more reasonable than competing views, the only prudent course of action is to withhold judgment until sufficient evidence is available. Such restraint can be difficult, especially when you favor a particular view, but restraint is an important characteristic of the critical thinker.

Applications

1. Many years ago an expert on thinking made this observation: "Probably the main characteristic of the trained thinker is that he does not jump to conclusions on insufficient evidence as the untrained man is inclined to do."[1] (Note: At that time, *he* and *man* were commonly used to denote both men and women.) Think of several recent occasions when you formed opinions with little or no evidence. In each case state the opinion and explain what kind of evidence would be necessary to support it adequately.

2. Some years ago, a well-known television actress was on a talk show, discussing a number of topics, including an episode of her show in which two lesbians kissed on camera. The actress volunteered this opinion: "This is a time in our society when homophobia is really huge and crimes against gays are at an all-time high." If the talk show host had been a critical thinker, what questions would he have asked at that point? What kind of evidence would be helpful in testing the reasonableness of her opinion?

3. Respond to each of the following questions with an opinion. Review those opinions and the evidence you offered in support of them. In each case classify the evidence as *personal experience, unpublished report, published report, eyewitness testimony, celebrity testimony, expert opinion, experiment, statistics, survey, formal observation,* or *research review.* Decide whether your evidence was sufficient. If you find it was not, explain what kind of evidence would be necessary to support the opinion adequately.

   a. In divorce cases what guidelines should the courts use in deciding which parent gets custody of the children?

   b. Until what age should children be spanked (if indeed they should be spanked at all)?

---

[1] W. I. B. Beveridge, *The Art of Scientific Investigation* (New York: W. W. Norton, 1951), p. 54.

c. Should the minimum drinking age be sixteen in all states?

d. In what situation, if any, should the United States make the first strike with nuclear weapons?

e. Do evil spirits exist? If so, can they influence people's actions?

f. Does the end ever justify the means?

g. Does attending class regularly increase one's chances for academic success?

h. Were teachers more respected fifty years ago than they are today?

i. Does binge drinking on weekends constitute alcoholism?

j. Is antisocial behavior increasing, or are the media just doing a better job of reporting it?

4. Expressed an opinion about each of the statements listed below. Reexamine each of your responses, following the directions in application 3, above.

a. Health care workers should be required to be tested for HIV/AIDS.

b. Beauty contests and talent competitions for children should be banned.

c. Extremist groups like the Ku Klux Klan should be allowed to hold rallies on public property or be issued permits to hold parades in city streets.

d. Freshman composition should be a required course for all students.

e. Athletes should be tested for anabolic steroid use.

f. Creationism should be taught in high school biology classes.

g. Polygamy should be legalized.

h. The voting age should be lowered to sixteen.

i. The prison system should give greater emphasis to the punishment of inmates than to their rehabilitation.

j. Doctors and clinics should be required to notify parents of minors when they prescribe birth control devices for the minors.

k. A man's self-esteem is severely injured if his wife makes more money than he makes.

l. Women like being dependent on men.

A Difference of Opinion

The following passage summarizes an important difference of opinion. After reading the statement, use the library and/or the Internet and find what knowledgeable people have said about the issue. Be sure to cover the entire range of views. Then assess the strengths and weaknesses of each. If you conclude that one view is entirely correct and the others are mistaken, explain how you reached that conclusion. If, *as is more likely,* you find that one view is more insightful than the others but that they all make some valid points, construct a view of your own that *combines* the insights from all sides and explain why that view is the most reasonable of all. Present your response in a composition or an oral report, as your instructor specifies.

Improving children's role models. Some years ago Charles Barkley, at the time a National Basketball Association All-Star, commented to reporters that he didn't want to be considered a role model for young people and he didn't think other athletes should be considered as such either. In any case, it is well established that many young people follow the example of athletes, as well as that of rock musicians and movie/television stars, even though that example is not always worthy of imitation. Two questions remain controversial: What kinds of people are the best role models for young people? And how can young people be persuaded to accept these role models?

PART TWO

CHAPTER THREE

Giving and Receiving Feedback

Giving and receiving feedback are essential managerial skills. A manager's tasks include directing, coaching, and evaluating the work of subordinates. Informally, managers review and respond to the performance of those who work both over and under them every day, clarifying expectations, praising success, and correcting misunderstandings. Most companies require formal appraisals once or twice a year to evaluate performance and encourage growth. Since a manager's own results depend heavily on those whom she or he supervises or reports to, effective feedback benefits the giver as much as the receiver.

In addition, as the previous discussion has suggested, listening to your audiences before, during, and after a business communication will often determine whether your message achieves your goal. This means receiving constant feedback: the data you need to build your case, the preconceptions of key audiences, how your proposals are coming across, what reasonable alternatives are possible, why important constituencies are likely to oppose you, whether superiors are merely nodding their agreement or actually implementing your proposals. Thus, seeking and wisely interpreting feedback are essential to your personal success as a manager and communicator.

Two major factors inhibit both downward and upward feedback in many business communication situations.

First, nobody likes to get bad news. Any manager wants to hear that she or he has done a good job. It's very easy to send verbal or nonverbal signals that you don't want to be criticized. As a result, subordinates, colleagues, or superiors may be reluctant to share crucial information that may help you redefine your goal, revise your communication strategy, or use your energy in a more productive direction.

Second, hierarchical organizations have a tendency to become less and less receptive to both downward and upward feedback. Several factors inhibit feedback in organizations.

Human beings prefer to command rather than confer. Immediate subordinates easily adapt to this style. Consequently, habits or systems develop that prevent managers from getting the information they need or understanding the concerns of those who are working for them. Often, this can result in drastic losses in morale and productivity.

Managers like to hoard information because it gives them a sense of power. Sometimes extra information will give them a leg up over a colleague or additional authority over a subordinate. Most of the time, however, successful managers share information widely because they benefit if others know what they need to know to do their jobs. Numerous studies have demonstrated that information hoarding by middle managers is one of the greatest drags on productivity in large organizations.

Everyone is prone to tell the boss what she wants to hear.

Listening takes time. Busy managers with the best intentions in the world often flub opportunities to get invaluable feedback from subordinates. Managers may send unintentional messages that they're too busy to be bothered, not respond to subtle hints, or simply fail to schedule regular feedback opportunities. Surveys of most organizations regularly demonstrate that, by and large, managers feel their superiors really don't care much about their opinions. Top managers are often surprised to hear this.

Successful organizations maintain and improve internal channels designed to drive accurate information both downward and upward.

General Considerations

Both *giving* and *receiving* feedback are among the high arts of management, and demand very special skills. Several key factors determine the effectiveness of most managerial feedback, whether it's informal day-to-day coaching, formal performance evaluation, or talking to your boss. As you provide feedback to superiors, peers, and subordinates, keep the following four factors in mind:

Timing

Delayed feedback rarely works. Over time, the specifics may have faded from memory, or, more likely, have been transformed in the mind to shore up individual egos. The recipient may wonder why you've waited so long; has the incident rankled all these months? Occasions also exist where feedback can come too soon. If a presentation has clearly not gone well, the communicator may need time to salve his wounds before he can hear suggestions for improvement. The most timely feedback is a regular flow while a project is underway. This can prevent feedback from becoming an extraordinary—and often painful—experience for both parties.

Objectivity

Total objectivity is impossible, and even often undesirable, as we discussed in Chap. 4, Point of View. Still, effective feedback provides concrete support for judgments that inevitably have a subjective element. Were projects completed on time? Were agreed-upon goals met? Did a communication have the desired effect? When and where did the recipient display the particular strength or weakness under discussion? Without such specifics, your feedback won't be credible or interpretable. Saying "Here are the objective results of your actions" or "Here's how your actions have affected me" will sound less accusatory than "You're failing." Saying "You're doing a great job" will be less effective than "Here are the types of accomplishments I want you to keep delivering."

Empowerment

Feedback must focus on things the recipient has the power to change, whether the recipient is a boss who can approve a project or an employee who's been slacking off. Most people can't change basic personality traits such as timidity or hotheadedness, but they can learn to modify their behavior to accomplish goals or perform more effectively. They're most likely to do so if you've given them the tools to do the job. Have you provided the boss with the information to make your case? Have you given a subordinate the resources to meet specified goals?

Trust

While people occasionally learn valuable lessons from someone with whom they don't get along, feedback is always more readily accepted if it comes from a trusted source. A foundation for trust cannot be established in a single exchange; it develops by experience, over the life of a working relationship. But skillful managers use each feedback opportunity to contribute to the fund of trust and mutual respect. The best single tool for building trust is legitimate *praise*. Managers and employees alike too rarely receive congratulations for a job well done. If you've recognized their accomplishments, people are more likely to heed you when you point out their deficiencies. An equally powerful tool, over the long term, is *honesty*.

Giving Feedback to Peers and Subordinates

The following guidelines can improve your informal, day-to-day experiences as a giver of feedback as well as your formal evaluation of subordinates.

Evaluate Strengths and Weaknesses in Light of Agreed-upon Goals and Objectives

This basic principle undergirds the "management by objectives" school of performance evaluation, but it applies in a commonsense way to all effective feedback. Workers' performances cannot be usefully evaluated unless the specific tasks and overall objectives they were charged with are reasonably clear. Arriving at mutually agreed-upon, or at least mutually understood, goals and criteria for performance is itself an important part of providing effective feedback.

Commend Where Possible

A totally negative critique not only disheartens the recipient but also is easy to ignore. He will likely shrug it off on the grounds that successful communication with such a harsh superior is impossible. Remember that praise and affirmation are more powerful motivators for most people than is criticism. Don't neglect these important management communication tools.

Be Specific

General comments such as "Great job" or "Poor presentation" won't be of much use. Instead, refer to specific instances, and describe the particular virtues you noticed or the specific problems you encountered: "The change you proposed will save us a great deal of paperwork" or "Your recent presentation needed more preparation and better graphics."

Strive for a Matter-of-Fact Tone

When you are providing feedback across or down, it's easy to sound obsequious, coy, apologetic, or condescending. Use superlatives sparingly, and avoid, except in extreme instances, questioning the recipient's competence or motives. As much as possible, keep yourself out of the picture. Statements such as "As one who appreciates good writing," or "I hate to be a nitpicker, but . . . " will make you sound like a prima donna.

Avoid Overkill

Most subordinates appreciate a frank and thoughtful response to their work, but there's a limit to how much anyone can absorb at one time. Focus on the most significant issues. A clear point of view on your part will ensure that you put minor points in their proper place.

Practice What You Preach

It's hard to complain about another's interpersonal skills if your own are somewhat lacking. It's unwise to point out missed deadlines if you are known to procrastinate. A badly written critique or an incoherent oral response to a subordinate's written or oral report won't command much authority.

Soliciting Feedback

When do you need feedback, and how can you get it? You need feedback in the *planning stages* to determine the attitudes of your audiences and the feasibility of achieving your goal. This means gathering factual information to support your case and sounding out those you need to persuade. Determine their bias (positive, neutral, or hostile); their familiarity with your topic; and their likely questions, concerns, and objections. How you solicit this feedback will depend on the size and variety of your audiences. If you're trying to persuade one person, you may feel out her views ahead of time in informal conversations and by asking others what types of arguments and approaches she has found convincing in the past. If you're addressing a small group, you may test your ideas against representative members whom you trust. With large audiences, such as all the employees of a corporation or the general public, you may need to conduct focus groups or to commission a professional survey.

Often, eliciting feedback during the planning stages gives you a double advantage; not only does it provide you with information you need to develop your communication plan, but also it can begin to build advocacy ahead of time with influential members of your future audience. Irrespective of audience size, you need feedback on each communication before you deliver it. This may mean asking a colleague to edit a memo or practicing a speech in front of your partner.

You need feedback during the *execution stages* so you can adjust your message according to the reaction you're getting. Build in as many response opportunities as possible. You'll keep your finger on the pulse of the audiences; by engaging in a dialog with you, they will become invested in the process and may develop a commitment to help you achieve your goal. Opportunities for feedback during the execution stages include inviting written responses, seeking out informal one-on-one reactions to formal communications, inviting questions from the audience, conferring in small groups, and polling large audiences.

You need feedback during the *follow-up stages* to ensure that your plan is being executed. Many a manager has promulgated a great plan, to universal applause, and then seen nothing happen. Before you send a message, determine how you will measure its success. Then put mechanisms in place to provide you with a regular series of updates on whether you're making progress toward your goal. These can include data (Are sales going up?), fixed deadlines (Have all the branch offices reported back by the specified date?), specific results (Did the union sign the contract?), or attitude surveys (Have my audience's views changed in the direction I wish since my communication?).

Receiving Feedback

Hearing is even harder than telling, because few pieces of feedback you receive will be entirely positive, especially during performance evaluations. Here are some guidelines:

Listen First

As a recipient of feedback, you must cultivate the habit of listening to your sources. Anyone who has devoted time and thought to reviewing your work has earned the right to be heard. You can't benefit from responses that you haven't understood.

Strive to Understand Your Respondent's Goals

Whether you're listening to bosses or subordinates, you won't fully understand them unless you temporarily set aside your own goals and focus on what they want to accomplish. While ideal feedback is explicit, keep in mind that secondary or subtle purposes may be in play. Ascertain what your source wants out of this interaction. A boss who is mildly suggesting a change in your project or approach may actually be issuing an order. A subordinate's memo reviewing a recent meeting may be intended to set certain decisions in stone.

Don't Get Defensive

Most of us must make a conscious effort to receive criticism constructively. Our impulse is not to listen, but to devise a self-protective reply. We interrupt our respondent to explain the constraints on us; we try to direct attention back to our goal or interest. Such responses will provoke the reaction "She just doesn't want to hear me," and they will rarely serve you well. At the same time, listening should *not* be passive; ask questions that clarify your respondent's remarks. You'll communicate courtesy and appreciation by following your source's train of thought rather than directing it. Save your main reactions until you've elicited your respondent's point of view.

Evaluating Feedback

Evaluating feedback means evaluating your sources. Are they reliable? Do they have your best interests at heart, or are they pursuing their own agenda? Are they likely to be flattering you? Does their response demonstrate an adequate knowledge of your subject?

People giving you feedback on a specific performance-period, communication, or proposal may respond in three ways:

1. They can report their experiences as workmates, readers, or listeners.
2. They can identify strengths and weaknesses.
3. They can suggest improvements in your analysis or plan of action.

In receiving such feedback, first, look for *misunderstanding:* Have your words, proposals, or actions been misinterpreted? If so, you probably need to modify your communication strategy. Second, look for *valid arguments against your position:* Has your respondent discovered real flaws? If so, perhaps you need to go back to the drawing board. Third, look for unanticipated *grounds of opposition;* these can help you reshape your message or performance. Perhaps your behavior or proposal will hurt your respondent in a way you hadn't considered. Fourth, value those *suggestions on how you can perform or communicate better.*

Two quotes aptly summarize the challenges of giving and receiving useful feedback. Rosabeth Moss Kanter and Derick Brinkerhoff write, "No amount of human relations techniques can change the fact that evaluations represent the exercise of power and authority by superiors over subordinates."[1] Admiral Hyman Rickover, the developer of the nuclear submarine, once said, "Always use the chain of command to issue orders, but if you use the chain of command for information, you're dead."[2] Kanter and Brinkerhoff are saying that no one enjoys the boss's criticism. Rickover is warning: "Don't believe yes-men." Managers must exert constant sensitivity to the human situations of those to whom they are giving feedback and of those who are giving feedback to them.

Consideration of feedback also leads to a more general observation implicit in the previous chapters. Effective business communication is not something you "add on" at the end of a decision-making process. No business strategy will succeed unless communication considerations are factored in from the beginning of your planning. At each step along the way—examining yourself as a source, analyzing your audiences, defining your goal, considering the context, shaping your message, choosing your media, achieving appropriate style and tone—you need to reexamine your project in light of the feedback you've received. At any point, you may find that, to succeed, you have to revise your original approach.

The following case explores the uses and abuses of feedback, including performance evaluation in business situations.

---

[1] See "Appraising the Performance Appraisal," *Sloan Management Review,* Vol. 21, 1980, pp. 10–11.
[2] *Newsweek*, Oct. 10, 1994.

In early spring, 2005, the Executive Committee of Bailey & Wick, a first-tier New York accounting firm of 150 accountants and 200 staff, approved the hiring of HK Communications to explore the issue of giving and receiving feedback at B&W. In particular, HK Communications was asked to report to B&W management on whether associates were receiving enough useful feedback on their work from partners. A year before, at B&W's fall retreat, an Associate Retention Committee had noted "the lack of formal and informal mentoring, training, or feedback—either positive or negative." B&W had also ranked low in a nationwide poll on associates' job satisfaction and career advancement prospects.

Two questions most concerned the Executive Committee: (1) Was the firm losing prominent candidates for promotion because insufficient attention was being paid to associates' development? (2) Was productivity being hampered because partners were not helping associates improve performance? The Professional Development Committee—two partners, four associates, and a director—felt the feedback issue merited serious review. HK's job: to assess the situation and propose options to the decision makers.

HK'S METHODOLOGY

The consultants planned to interview a representative cross-section of B&W's executives on the issue of partner-associate feedback. But before speaking to anyone, they needed to define clear goals for the project. After two meetings with the Professional Development Committee, HK decided to focus on five key questions:

1. *Was there a problem?* Apprentices are always grumbling about their jobs, and there is bound to be a good deal of grousing in a service organization where the competitive edge is sharpened by the implied message: UP OR OUT. Generally, associates who survived the three-year review could stay on until year seven, when they either left or attained partnership. Suppose there were weak links in professional nurturing; were they really damaging the performance of associates, particularly those willing and able to succeed at B&W?

2. *If the problem was real, how, specifically, was it hurting the firm?* Was B&W actually losing associates it wanted to retain? If partners were not providing effective feedback and if associates were therefore not performing at capacity, were partners doing work that associates should be performing and thereby wasting billable hours on routine tasks—and thus risking burnout? Did a lapse in professional development suggest a lapse in total quality management?

3. *Was this a perception problem, a question of no feedback, or of not enough feedback?* Juniors always want more attention and affirmation from seniors. Given the times and apparent uncertainties, was the perceived need for more and better feedback satisfiable? How did partners see their side of the feedback equation?

4. *What reasonable range of actions could improve partner-associate feedback?* Would a renewed effort at consciousness-raising be enough? In the relatively informal world of B&W, could feedback mechanisms be institutionalized?

5. *Were the benefits of any given solution worth the costs?* Perhaps many associates would welcome improved coaching and critiquing; yet would the results justify the investment of partners' time and B&W's resources? How good were the B&W partners and associates at giving and receiving feedback? How much

training would be required to realize any sustainable change? To what extent, in a horizontal organization like B&W, was resistance to confrontation a cultural norm?

Beyond these questions, HK also planned to approach the interviews with a flexible definition of "feedback" itself. The word had a wide spectrum of meanings at B&W—from the offhandedly responsive to the directly judgmental—and the consultants didn't want to inhibit free exchange in the interviews by narrowing the use of jargon. "Feedback" also included the single most important appraisal associates received: their performance evaluation, conducted twice a year for the first two years and annually thereafter. In years one and two, the review assessed basic competence within the associates' departments. The third-year review was especially important, because it was conducted by all the partners, many of whom by that time had worked with a given associate. Historically, such reviews had involved both a discussion and a written evaluation. More recently, the written feedback had been discontinued; instead, two partners visited the associate and summarized the review. The consultants' brief charged them with examining the effectiveness of feedback outside the review process, but they wondered if such a distinction could actually be made. Perhaps if the reviews were functioning better, there would be less demand for day-to-day feedback.

Feedback really included any reactions partners gave associates. Most often, this meant editing of associates' draft audit reports or other documents. But it also included every partner-associate interaction: praise or criticism of a task, comments on a client interaction, warmth or coolness at a social occasion, responsiveness to associates' questions, greetings in the elevators or hallways, even name-recognition. Which of these mattered, and which, if any, could be influenced by the firm?

INTERVIEW RESULTS

Simple ground rules applied to the interviews: any questions could be asked; confidentiality would be maintained in reporting results. Fourteen interviews were conducted, seven with associates (three female, four male) and seven with partners (two female, five male). After collating the interview results, HK Communications decided that two composite views essentially represented the Alpha and Omega of the feedback issue:

Alpha (mid-level associate):

I never know what's wanted of me or how I'm doing. Frankly, I need more affirmation, if only for self-respect. I spend too much time here worrying about people's expectations of me—worrying if they think I'm just slacking off, worrying whether no news is good news. There's too much stress. I work for everybody and nobody. What one partner likes, another hates. When I manage to get a response from a partner on my work, I can't tell if it's a casual suggestion or a coded but devastating critique of my performance in general. Of course I know that my reports are going to be refined by my seniors; but how do I know if it's a good draft or hopelessly inept? My evaluations are particularly hard to read. They're incredibly general, like: "We think you're doing fine. Just do better. We think you could improve your client presentations." How? I have peers who come out of their reviews serenely confident that they're going to make partner. Some of these have been eased out. But most associates report hearing the same things I did. I think I'm pulling my weight but I want to know, specifically, how I can do better. Most of us know we're not going to make partner, and for many of us, that's not even the goal. We want to learn, contribute, and be respected while we're here. If we didn't have to spend so much time second-guessing and reading partners' minds, we'd be more productive. If partners spent a little time giving us feedback, we'd be better at what we do, and save the firm money. I'm not looking for a formal report card—I'd dread that. I'd like some direct, honest assessment of my work on a major project.

Omega (senior partner):

Let's face it: accountants aren't good at direct teaching of subordinates. We're not educating associates, we're looking them over. Training is a secondary consideration, especially the first two years, when we need to get a lot of grunt work out of them. They're in boot camp, and they know it. It's the exceptional associate who's productive before year three. But you can tell quickly whether someone has it or not. The one who reaches out, finds training and mentoring, is the one who gets the plum assignments. The partners are looking for that as they decide who has to go, who's partner material, and who can be productive for a few years before she or he moves on. It's often said that the way to become a partner at B&W is to start somewhere else. We're probably not good at nurturing, but the truth is, it's easy to find someone out there to fill a gap. Juniors always want to change the rules, to box seniors in and guarantee their own security. But a busy partner has little time for wet-nursing and schoolmarming. It's easier to rewrite a bad report than use it as a training vehicle. If there's to be more direct feedback, it should go to associates who are going to be around here for a while.

Most of HK's interviews fell between these two extremes, and helped to round out the picture. Some samples:

Associate:

If I'm concerned with a problem about my work, I ask. I've always gotten a straight answer. But many associates are very unsure of themselves, and a good many of them are suckered by the p.r.—that B&W is committed to training—and they become disillusioned very quickly. They want assurance that they're doing well when often they're not. I started going for feedback because I got badly burned in my first evaluation. I'd had no indication that I was doing poorly; then I got slammed in my review. Maybe that was a good sign— they thought I could improve. Half of us came here for the experience, the other half to make partner. Maybe one or two of my class of twenty actually will. This isn't kindergarten, and partners shouldn't have to do remedial education. But let's take a competent associate who may not be partner material in the current climate. An hour of focused feedback a month would make that person so much more productive—maybe, even, happy in his work—and save the partner a lot of time currently spent running around with a pooper scooper.

Senior partner:

When I came here years ago, I worked with two of the younger partners. One took pride in teaching, in marking up the product and getting me to see the relevance of detail and the importance of craftsmanship. The other took no interest at all; she essentially ignored me. With her, I had to get better on my own. This is a big organization. You have to develop a thick skin; it's a meritocracy. While we value collegiality, we don't necessarily foster it; winnowing out is part of the process. Actually, among peers, we have a lot of feedback, but there's a structural problem. When an associate clearly isn't going to make it, it's harder for a partner to

take interest. We need a senior associate group to do training of juniors. And the junior partners could do more. I accept the associates' claim that "if you give me useful feedback I'll do a better job and save the firm money." But I accept it abstractly. I welcome juniors who visit my office to ask for advice, but I know it's intimidating. That's part of the job.

Mid-level associate:

We suffer a lot from attrition. Lots of the best associates seem to be leaving. One senior associate I knew was particularly willing to provide feedback to younger associates. She saved the firm a lot of time and money. But this commitment to training didn't show up in her performance review. She received mediocre evaluations and ended up leaving the firm. Our main competitor has an associate committee that's in-the-know about partners' personal styles and walks you through the feedback. Maybe partners here should sit down with associates after each major transaction and tell them what worked and what didn't—not a long meeting, just a brief review while the memory is still fresh.

Partner:

Today's clients want senior people and fewer people. It's difficult to foist new associates on impatient clients. Why waste trained talent? Recently, we've created a Professional Development Staff— but their real title should be: "How to Help Decent Associates Who Won't Make Partner." The ones who will make partner are too good and too busy. We've hired a lot of people we shouldn't have, people we know aren't going to make it here. We're also losing people we need to keep because the pipeline has gotten too narrow. We haven't admitted to ourselves that we've gotten "partnered up" and sometimes mislead the associates about their chances. The truth is, associates have become disposable, and the smart ones know that. So we don't project excitement and communicate our enthusiasm downward. We're not building loyalty because we can't satisfy the expectation that would generate.

Senior associate:

Most corporations today recognize that they get a big payback from training employees. People who feel some sense of ownership clearly do a better job. But there's clearly a caste system here: associates don't feel they're on the same team as the partners. There are code words: everyone not partner is "staff"; we don't "work with someone," we "give them an assignment." It's not "our client," it's "my client." It's not in the firm's interest to signal someone they're not going to make it until the last possible moment: carrot and stick, like anywhere else. Otherwise, what performance would you get out of them?

Junior partner:

Consciousness-raising isn't enough; it seems to me we have to institutionalize feedback. One idea currently floating around is to have associates give anonymous feedback to the partners. But do we really need more forms to fill out? Any institutionalized feedback would have to be tailored from department to department, and who has the time for that? Maybe there should be a new class of billable time—training hours. It's never going to work until you build it into the system. Still, why should partners do training unless they get some credit for it? A lot of the top people here are brilliant eccentrics who can't be told what to do. When I needed feedback, I didn't wait. I asked for it, and I got it. But for many people, this place is too courtly and too chilly.

IMPLEMENTATION

HK decided there were two ways B&W could go. One was to continue current practice. Although it generated anxiety among the associates and probably caused some good prospects to leave while they were ahead, it worked. On the other hand, B&W could reorganize its feedback processes to develop permanent talent, using more carrot, less stick. Steps the firm might implement to improve feedback included:

1. Encouraging partners to be more responsive to associates' requests for feedback;
2. Teaching associates how to solicit feedback, perhaps in initial orientation sessions;
3. Adding a third category of "training hours" to billable and pro-bono hours;
4. Rewarding senior associates who provided feedback by crediting them in their evaluations;
5. Institutionalizing feedback by requiring seniors to provide it to juniors after each major project;
6. Requiring each department to propose, then implement, a feedback program appropriate to its size and needs; and
7. Encouraging partners to see themselves less as independent craftsmen, more as team leaders. Any significant change in feedback practices would require the sustained and active support of top management.

This case was prepared by Michael Hattersley, © 2006.

Study Questions

1. What are the most important ways people communicate with one another in a complex, high-pressured organization?
2. What are the trade-offs among responsibility, legitimate self-interest, and training at Bailey & Wick?
3. What are the differences between how juniors can talk to seniors and how seniors can talk to juniors?
4. What institutional changes in communication practice could benefit this organization? How might they be communicated?

Performance Assessments

Chapter Objectives

After reading this chapter, you will be able to:

- Define checklist, rating scale, rubric, performance criteria, and other basic terms
- Contrast performance processes and performance products
- Contrast performance assessment with other assessment types
- Write well-stated performance criteria for a given process or performance
- Apply different scoring approaches for performance assessments
- Construct a scoring rubric
- Discuss portfolios and their use in assessment
- Identify strategies to improve the validity and reliability of classroom performance assessments

■■■ Thinking About Teaching

In what ways can teachers use the results of assessments to improve pupil learning?

This chapter describes **performance assessment,** which is any form of assessment in which pupils carry out an activity or produce a product in order to demonstrate learning. This chapter tells how to develop such assessments and discusses their pros and cons, including questions of validity and reliability.

The following examples describe common classroom assessment practices. How could the validity of these practices be improved?

> Ms. Landers taught her ninth grade science class a unit on microscopes. She taught her pupils how to set up, focus, and use a microscope. Each pupil used a microscope to identify and draw pictures of three or four objects on glass slides. At the end of the unit, she assessed the pupils' achievement by giving a paper-and-pencil test that asked them to label parts of a diagrammed microscope and answer multiple-choice questions about the history of the microscope.

In Mr. Cleaver's third grade class, oral reading skills are strongly emphasized, and he devotes a great deal of energy to helping pupils use proper phrasing, vocal expression, and clear pronunciation when they read aloud. All of the tests that Mr. Cleaver uses to grade his pupils' reading achievement are paper-and-pencil tests that assess pupils' paragraph comprehension and word recognition.

These examples illustrate an important limitation of many paper-and-pencil tests: they allow teachers to assess some, but not all, important school learning outcomes. In each of the two classrooms, the teacher relied solely on tests that measured *knowledge of performance* (remember factual knowledge), but not ability to actually *perform the skill* (apply procedural knowledge).

The General Role of Performance Assessments

There are many classroom situations for which valid assessment requires that teachers gather formal information about pupils' performances or products. Teachers collect pupil products such as written stories, paintings, lab reports, and science fair projects, as well as performances such as giving a speech, holding a pencil, typing, and cooperating in groups. Generally, products produce tangible outcomes—things you can hold in your hand—while performances are things you observe or listen to. Table 4.1 contrasts the selection and supply items with typical examples of performance and product assessments.

Performance assessments may also be called alternative or authentic assessments. They permit pupils to show what they can do in real situations (Wiggins, 1992). The difference between describing how a skill should be performed and actually knowing how to perform it is an important distinction in classroom assessment. Teachers recognize this distinction, as the following comments illustrate.

I want my pupils to learn to do math for its own intrinsic value, but also because math is so essential for everyday life. Making change, balancing checkbooks, doing a budget, and many other practical, real-world activities require that pupils know how to use their math knowledge.

The kids need to learn to get along in groups, be respectful of others' property, and wait their turns. I don't want kids to be able to recite classroom rules, I want them to practice them. These behaviors are just as important for kids to learn in school as reading, writing, and math.

Just because they can write a list of steps they would follow to ensure laboratory safety does not mean that in a given situation they could actually demonstrate that knowledge.

Performance assessments allow pupils to demonstrate what they know and can do in a real situation. Performance assessments are also called alternative and authentic assessments.

TABLE 4.1   Examples of Four Assessment Approaches

Selection	Supply	Product	Performance
Multiple choice	Completion	Essay, story, or poem	Musical, dance, or dramatic performance
True-false	Label a diagram	Research report	Science lab demonstration
Matching	Short answer	Writing portfolio	Typing test
	Concept map	Diary or journal	Athletic competition
		Science fair project	Debate
		Art exhibit or portfolio	Oral presentation
			Cooperation in groups

Source: *If Minds Matter: A Forward to the Future,* vol. 2, edited by Arthur L. Costa, James Bellanca, and Robin Fogarty. © 1992 IRI/Skylight Publishing Inc. Reprinted by permission of Skylight Professional Development. www./skylightedu.com

Some types of paper-and-pencil test items can be used to provide information about the thinking processes that underlie pupils' performance. For example, a math problem in which pupils have to show their work provides insight into the mental processes used to solve the problem. An essay question can show pupils' organizational skills, thought processes, and application of capitalization and punctuation rules. These two forms of paper-and-pencil test items can assess what pupils can do as opposed to the majority of paper-and-pencil test questions that reveal what pupils know. With most selection and supply questions, the teacher observes the *result* of the pupil's intellectual process, but not the thinking process that produced the result. If the pupil gets a multiple-choice, true-false, matching, or completion item correct, the teacher *assumes* that the pupil must have followed the correct process, but there is little direct evidence to support this assumption, since the only evidence of the pupil's thought process is a circled letter or a single written word. On the other hand, essays and other extended response items provide a product that shows how pupils think about and construct their responses. They permit the teacher to see the logic of arguments, the manner in which the response is organized, and the basis of conclusions drawn by the pupil (Bartz et al. 1994). Thus, paper-and-pencil assessments like stories, reports, or "show-your-work" problems are important forms of performance assessments. Table 4.2 shows some of the differences between objective test items, essay tests, oral questions, and performance assessments.

Teachers observe their pupils' performance in order to learn about them and also to obtain information about the moment-to-moment success of their instruction. Such observations are primarily informal and spontaneous. In this chapter, we are concerned with assessing more formal, structured performances and products, those that the teacher plans in advance, helps each pupil to perform, and formally assesses. These assessments can take place during normal classroom instruction (e.g., oral reading activities, setting up laboratory equipment) or in some special situation set up to elicit a performance (e.g., giving a speech in an auditorium). In either case, the activity is formally structured—the teacher arranges the conditions in which the performance or product is demonstrated and judged. Such assessments permit each pupil to show his or her mastery of the same process or task, something that is impossible with informal observation of spontaneous classroom performance and events.

TABLE 4.2 **Comparison of Various Types of Assessments**

Source: Adapted from R. J. Stiggins, "Design and Development of Performance Assessments," *Educational Measurement: Issues and Practice,* 1987, 6(3), p. 35. Copyright 1987 by the National Council on Measurement in Education Adapted by permission of the publisher.

	Objective Test	**Essay Test**	**Oral Question**	**Performance Assessment**
Purpose	Sample knowledge with maximum efficiency and reliability	Assess thinking skills and/or mastery of how a body of knowledge is structured	Assess knowledge during instruction	Assess ability to translate knowledge and understanding into action
Pupil's Response	Read, evaluate, select	Organize, compose	Oral answer	Plan, construct, and deliver an original response
Major Advantage	Efficiency—can administer many items per unit of testing time	Can measure complex cognitive outcomes	Joins assessment and instruction	Provides rich evidence of performance skills
Influence on Learning	Overemphasis on recall encourages memorization; can encourage thinking skills if properly constructed	Encourages thinking and development of writing skills	Stimulates participation in instruction, provides teacher immediate feedback on effectiveness of teaching	Emphasizes use of available skill and knowledge in relevant problem contexts

Performance Assessment in Schools

The amount of attention that has recently been focused on performance assessment in states, schools, and classrooms might lead one to believe that performance assessment is new and untried, and that it can solve all the problems of classroom assessment. Neither of these beliefs is true (Madaus and O'Dwyer, 1999). Performance assessment has been used extensively in classrooms for as long as there have been classrooms. Table 4.3 provides examples of five common, long-standing areas of performance assessment in schools.

Performance assessments reflect the recent emphasis on real-world problem solving.

Many factors account for the growing popularity of performance assessment (Ryan and Miyasaka, 1995; Quality Counts, 1999). First, performance assessment is being proposed or mandated as part of formal statewide assessment programs. Second, increased classroom emphasis on problem solving, higher-level thinking, and real-world reasoning skills has created a reliance on performance and product assessments to demonstrate pupil learning. Third, performance assessments can provide some pupils who do poorly on selection-type tests an opportunity to show their achievement in alternative ways.

Performance-Oriented Subjects

All schools expect pupils to demonstrate communication skills, so reading, writing, and speaking are perhaps the most common areas of classroom performance assessment. Likewise, simple psychomotor skills such as being able to sit in a chair or hold a pencil, as well as more sophisticated skills such as setting up laboratory equipment or using tools to build a birdhouse, are a fundamental part of school life. Closely related are the athletic performances taught in physical education classes.

Assessing students' understanding of concepts through hands-on demonstrations is becoming more common.

There also is a growing emphasis on using performance assessment to determine pupils' understanding of the concepts they are taught and measure their ability to apply procedural knowledge. The argument is that if pupils really grasp a concept or process, they can explain and use it to solve real-life problems. For example, after teaching pupils about money and making change, the teacher may assess learning by having pupils count out the money needed to purchase objects from the classroom "store" or act as storekeeper and make change for other pupils' purchases. Or, rather than giving a multiple-choice test on the chemical reactions that help identify unknown substances, the teacher could give each pupil an unknown substance and have them go through the process of identifying it. These kinds of hands-on demonstrations of concept mastery are growing in popularity.

Teachers also constantly assess pupils' feelings, values, attitudes, and emotions. When a teacher checks the "satisfactory" rating under the category "works hard" or "obeys school rules" on a pupil's report card, the teacher bases this judgment on observations of the pupil's performance. Teachers rely upon observations of pupil performance to collect evidence about important behaviors such as getting along with peers, working independently, following rules, and self-control.

TABLE 4.3   Five Common Domains of Performance Assessment

Communication Skills	Psychomotor Skills	Athletic Activities	Concept Acquisition	Affective Skills
Writing essays	Holding a pencil	Shooting free throws	Constructing open and closed circuits	Sharing toys
Giving a speech	Setting up lab equipment	Catching a ball	Selecting proper tools for shop tasks	Working in cooperative groups
Pronouncing a foreign language	Using scissors	Hopping	Identifying unknown chemical substances	Obeying school rules
Following spoken directions	Dissecting a frog	Swimming the crawl	Generalizing from experimental data	Maintaining self-control

Most teachers recognize the importance of balancing supply and selection assessments with performance and product assessments, as the following comments indicate.

> It's not reasonable to grade reading without including the pupil's oral reading skills or their comprehension of what they read. I always spend some time when it's grading time listening to and rating my pupils' oral reading and comprehension quality.

> My kids know that a large part of their grade depends on how well they follow safety procedures and take proper care of the tools they use. They know I'm always on the lookout for times when they don't do these things and that it will count against them if I see them.

> I wouldn't want anyone to assess my teaching competence solely on the basis of my students' paper-and-pencil test scores. I would want to be seen interacting with the kids, teaching them, and attending to their needs. Why should I confine my assessments of my pupils solely to paper-and-pencil methods?

Early Childhood and Special Needs Pupils

While performance assessment cuts across subject areas and grade levels, it is heavily used in early childhood and special education settings. Because preschool, kindergarten, and primary school pupils are limited in their communication skills and are still in the process of being socialized into the school culture, much assessment information is obtained by observing their performances and products. Assessment at this age focuses on gross and fine motor development, verbal and auditory acuity, and visual development, as well as social behaviors. Key Assessment Tools 4.1 illustrates some of the important early childhood behaviors and skills that teachers assess by performance-based means. These examples provide a sense of how heavily the early childhood curriculum is weighted toward performance outcomes.

Many special needs pupils—especially those who exhibit multiple and severe disabilities in their cognitive, affective, and psychomotor development—are provided instruction focused on self-help skills such as getting dressed, brushing teeth, making a sandwich, and operating a vacuum cleaner. Pupils are taught to carry out these performances through many, many repetitions. Observation of pupils as they perform these activities is the main assessment technique special education teachers use to identify performance mastery or areas needing further work.

To summarize, performance assessment gathers evidence about pupils by observing and rating their performance or products. Although appropriate at all grade levels, it is especially useful in subjects that place heavy emphasis on performances or products of some kind, such as art, music, public speaking, shop, foreign language, and physical edu-

---

Key Assessment Tools 4.1
EARLY CHILDHOOD BEHAVIOR AREAS

Gross motor development: Roll over, sit erect without toppling over, walk a straight line, throw a ball, jump on one or two feet, skip.

Fine motor development: Cut with scissors, trace an object, color inside the lines, draw geometric forms (e.g., circles, squares, triangles), penmanship, left-to-right progression in reading and writing, eye-hand coordination.

Verbal and auditory acuity: Identify sounds, listen to certain sounds and ignore others (e.g., tune out distractions), discriminate between sounds and words that sound alike (e.g., "fix" vs. "fish"), remember numbers in sequence, follow directions, remember the correct order of events, pronounce words and letters.

Visual development: Find a letter, number, or object similar to one shown by the teacher; copy a shape; identify shapes and embedded figures; reproduce a design given by the teacher; differentiate objects by size, color, and shape.

Social acclimation: Listen to the teacher, follow a time schedule, share, wait one's turn, respect the property of others.

cation. It is also very useful with early childhood and special needs pupils whose lack of basic communication, psychomotor, and social skills forces the teacher to rely upon pupil performances to assess instructional success.

Developing Performance Assessments

A diving competition is an instructive example of a skill that is assessed by a performance assessment. Submitting a written essay describing how to perform various dives or answering a multiple-choice test about diving rules are hardly appropriate ways to demonstrate one's diving *performance*. Rather, a valid assessment of diving performance requires seeing the diver actually perform. And, to make the assessment reliable, the diver must perform a series of dives, not just one.

Diving judges rate dives using a scale that has 21 possible numerical scores that can be awarded (e.g., 0.0, 0.5, 1.0 . . . 5.5, 6.0, 6.5, . . . 9.0, 9.5, 10.0). They observe a very complicated performance made up of many body movements that together take about 2 seconds to complete. The judges do not have the benefit of slow motion or instant replay to review the performance and they cannot discuss the dive with one another. If their attention strays for even a second, they miss a large portion of the performance. Yet, when the scores are flashed on the scoreboard the judges inevitably are in very close agreement. Rarely do all judges give a dive the exact same score, but rarely is there more than a 1-point difference between any two judges' scores. This is amazing agreement among observers for such a short, complicated performance.

With this example in mind, let's consider the four essential features of all formal performance assessments, whether it be a diving competition, an oral speech, a book report, a typing exercise, a science fair project, or something else. This overview will then be followed by a more extensive discussion of each feature. Briefly, every performance assessment should:

1. Have a clear purpose that identifies the decision to be made from the performance assessment.
2. Identify observable aspects of the pupil's performance or product that can be judged.
3. Provide an appropriate setting for eliciting and judging the performance or product.
4. Provide a judgment or score to describe performance.

Define the Purpose of Assessment

In a diving competition, the purpose of the assessment is to rank each diver's performance in order to identify the best divers. Each dive receives a score and the highest total score wins the competition. Suppose, however, that dives were being performed during practice, prior to a competition. The diver's coach would observe the practice dives, but the coach's main concern would be not with the overall dive, but with examining the many specific features of each dive that the judges will score during a competition. Consequently, the coach would "score" the practice dive formatively, identifying the diver's strengths and weaknesses for all aspects of each dive. The specific areas in which the diver was weak would likely be emphasized in practice.

Performance assessments are particularly suited to such diagnosis because they can provide information about how a pupil performs each of the specific criteria that make up a more general performance or product. This criterion-by-criterion assessment makes it easy to identify the strong and weak points of a pupil's performance. When the performance criteria are stated in terms of observable pupil behaviors or product characteristics, as they should be, remediation is made easy. Each suggestion for improvement can be described in specific terms—for example, "report to group project area on time," "wait your turn to speak," "do your share of the group work."

Teachers use performance assessment for many purposes: grading pupils, constructing portfolios of pupil work, diagnosing pupil learning, helping pupils recognize the important steps in a performance or product, providing concrete examples of pupil work for parent conferences. Whatever the purpose of performance assessment, it should be specified

Performances and products are normally broken down into specific, observable criteria, each of which can be judged independently.

Performance assessments are particularly suited to diagnosis because they provide information about how pupils perform each specific criterion in a general performance.

at the beginning of the assessment process so that proper performance criteria and scoring procedures can be established.

Teachers need to think ahead about whether a performance assessment's purposes will be formative or summative because their judgment task is very different depending on which is the case. When the goal of assessment is formative, the focus is on giving feedback to pupils about their strengths and weaknesses. When the goal is summative, the focus is on rating the ultimate level of achievement.

Identify Performance Criteria

Performance criteria are the specific behaviors a pupil should display in properly carrying out a performance or create a product. They are at the heart of successful performance assessment, yet they are the area in which most problems occur.

When teachers first think about assessing performance, they tend to think in terms of general performances such as oral reading, giving a speech, following safety rules in the laboratory, penmanship, writing a book report, organizing ideas, fingering a keyboard, or getting along with peers. In reality, such performances cannot be assessed until they are broken down into the more specific aspects or characteristics that comprise them. These more narrow aspects and characteristics are the performance criteria that teachers will observe and judge.

Studies show that many classroom teachers lack skill in assessing and are unprepared to assess their pupils, especially on performance assessments (Fager, Plake, and Impara, 1997). Relatively few teachers are required to pass a course in classroom assessment in their teacher preparation. Only about 20 states require that preservice teachers take an assessment course (Stiggins, 1999). Teachers tend to be better at providing interesting tasks and performances for their pupils than they are at identifying the criteria that describe what makes a good task or performance. Often, the first question a teacher asks is "What will we do?" A more appropriate question to ask first, especially with performance assessments, is "What do I want my pupils to learn?" (Arter, 1999.)

Key Assessment Tools 4.2 shows three sets of criteria for assessing pupils' performance when (1) working in groups, (2) playing the piano, and (3) writing a book report. Criteria such as these focus teachers' instruction and assessments in the same way that diving criteria enable judges to evaluate diving performance. Notice how the performance

---

Key Assessment Tools 4.2

EXAMPLES OF PEFRFORMANCE CRITERIA

Working in Groups	**Playing the Piano**	**Writing a Book Report**
Reports to group project area on time	Sits upright with feet on floor (or pedal, when necessary)	States the author and title
Starts work on own	Arches fingers on keys	Identifies the type of book (fiction, adventure, historical, etc.)
Shares information	Plays without pauses or interruptions	Describes what the book was about in four or more sentences
Contributes ideas	Maintains even tempo	
Listens to others	Plays correct notes	States an opinion of the book
Waits turn to speak	Holds all note values for indicated duration	Gives three reasons to support the opinion
Follows instructions		
Courteous to other group members	Follows score dynamics (forte, crescendo, decrescendo)	Uses correct spelling, punctuation, and capitalization
Helps to solve group problems	Melody can be heard above other harmonization	
Considers viewpoints of others		
Carries out share of group-determined activities	Phrases according to score (staccato and legato)	
Completes assigned tasks on time	Follows score pedal markings	

criteria clearly identify the important aspects of the performance or product being assessed. Well-stated performance criteria are at the heart of successful efforts to instruct and assess performances and products.

To define performance criteria, a teacher must first decide if a process or a product will be observed. Will processes such as typing or oral reading be assessed, or will products such as a typed letter or book report be assessed? In the former case, criteria are needed to judge the pupil's actual performance of targeted criteria; in the latter, criteria are needed to judge the end product of those behaviors. In some cases, both process and product can be assessed. For example, a first grade teacher assessed both process and product when she (1) observed a pupil writing to determine how the pupil held the pencil, positioned the paper, and manipulated the pencil and (2) judged the finished, handwritten product to assess how well the pupil formed his letters. Notice that the teacher observed different things according to whether she was interested in the pupil's handwriting *process* or handwriting *product*. It is for this reason that teachers must know what they want to observe before performance criteria can be identified.

Performance criteria can focus on processes, products, or both.

The key to identifying performance criteria is to break down an overall performance or product into its component parts. It is these parts that will be observed and judged. Consider, for example, a product assessment of eighth graders' written paragraphs. The purpose of the assessment is to judge pupils' ability to write a paragraph on a topic of their choice. In preparing to judge the completed paragraph, a teacher initially listed the following performance criteria:

- First sentence
- Appropriate topic sentence
- Good supporting ideas
- Good vocabulary
- Complete sentences
- Capitalization
- Spelling
- Conclusion
- Handwriting

These performance criteria do identify important areas of a written paragraph, but the areas are vague and poorly stated. What, for example, is meant by "first sentence"? What is an "appropriate" topic sentence or "good" vocabulary? What should be examined in judging capitalization, spelling, and handwriting? If a teacher cannot answer these questions, how can he or she provide suitable examples or instruction for pupils? Performance criteria need to be specific enough to focus the teacher on well-defined characteristics of the performance or product. They must also be specific enough to permit the teacher to convey to pupils, in terms they can understand, the specific features that define the desired performance or product. Once defined, the criteria permit consistent teacher assessments of performance and consistent communication with pupils about their learning.

Following is a revised version of the performance criteria for a well-organized paragraph. Note the difference in clarity and how the revised version focuses the teacher and students on very specific features of the paragraph—ones that are important and will be assessed. Before assigning the task, the teacher wisely decided to share and discuss the performance criteria with the pupils.

- Indents first sentence.
- Topic sentence sets main idea of paragraph.
- Following sentences support main idea.
- Sentences arranged in logical order.
- Uses age-appropriate vocabulary.
- Writes in complete sentences.

- Capitalizes proper nouns and first words in sentences.
- Makes no more than three spelling errors.
- Conclusion follows logically from prior sentences.
- Handwriting is legible.

Cautions in Developing Performance Criteria

Three points of caution are appropriate here. First, it is important to understand that the previous example of performance criteria is not the only one that describes the characteristics of a well-written paragraph. Different teachers might identify varying criteria that they feel are more important or more suitable for their pupils than some of the ones in our example. Thus, emphasis should not be upon identifying the best or only set of criteria for a performance or product, but rather upon stating criteria that are meaningful, important, and can be understood by the pupils.

Very long lists of performance criteria (over 15) become unmanageable and intrusive.

Second, it is possible to break down most school performances and products into many very narrow criteria. However, a lengthy list of performance criteria becomes ineffective because teachers rarely have the time to observe and assess a large number of very specific performance criteria for each pupil. Too many criteria make the observation process intrusive, with the teacher hovering over the pupil, rapidly checking off behaviors, and often interfering with a pupil's performance.

For classroom performance assessment to be manageable and meaningful, a balance must be established between specificity and practicality. The key to attaining this balance is to identify the *essential* criteria associated with a performance or product; 6 to 12 performance criteria are a manageable number for most classroom teachers to emphasize.

Third, the process of identifying performance criteria is an ongoing one that is rarely completed after the first attempt. Initial performance criteria will need to be revised and clarified, based on experience from their use, to provide the focus needed for valid and reliable assessment. To aid this process, teachers should think about the performance or product they wish to observe and reflect on its key aspects. They can also examine a few actual products or performances as bases for revising their initial list of criteria.

The following list shows the initial set of performance criteria a teacher wrote to assess pupils' oral reports.

- Speaks clearly and slowly.
- Pronounces correctly.
- Makes eye contact.
- Exhibits good posture when presenting.
- Exhibits good effort.
- Presents with feeling.
- Understands the topic.
- Exhibits enthusiastic attitude.
- Organizes.

Note the lack of specificity in many of the criteria: "slowly," "correctly," "good," "understands," and "enthusiastic attitude." These criteria hide more than they reveal. After reflecting on and observing a few oral presentations, the teacher revised and sharpened the performance criteria as shown in the following list. Note that the teacher first divided the general performance into three areas (physical expression, vocal expression, and verbal expression) and then identified a few important performance criteria within each of these areas. It is not essential to divide the performance criteria into separate sections, but sometimes it is useful in focusing the teacher and pupils.

The value of performance assessments depends on identifying performance criteria that can be observed and judged.

1. Physical expression
   - Stands straight and faces audience.
   - Changes facial expression with changes in tone of the report.
   - Maintains eye contact with audience.

2. Vocal expression
   - Speaks in a steady, clear voice.
   - Varies tone to emphasize points.
   - Speaks loudly enough to be heard by audience.
   - Paces words in an even flow.
   - Enunciates each word.
3. Verbal expression
   - Chooses precise words to convey meaning.
   - Avoids unnecessary repetition.
   - States sentences with complete thoughts or ideas.
   - Organizes information logically.
   - Summarizes main points at conclusion.

Developing Observable Performance Criteria

The value and richness of performance and product assessments depend heavily on identifying performance criteria that can be observed and judged. It is important that the criteria be clear in the teacher's mind and that the pupils be taught the criteria. The following guidelines should prove useful for this purpose.

Like other writing assignments, good performance criteria need to be revised and clarified over time.

1. *Select the performance or product to be assessed and either perform it yourself or imagine yourself performing it.* Think to yourself, "What would I have to do in order to complete this task? What steps would I have to follow?" It isn't a bad idea to actually carry out the performance yourself, recording and studying your performance or product.
2. *List the important aspects of the performance or product.* What specific behaviors or attributes are most important to the successful completion of the task? What behaviors have been emphasized in instruction? Include important aspects and exclude the irrelevant ones.
3. *Try to limit the number of performance criteria, so they all can be observed during a pupil's performance.* This is less important when one is assessing a product, but even then it is better to assess a limited number of key criteria than a large number that vary widely. Remember, you will have to observe and judge performance on each of the criteria identified.
4. *If possible, have groups of teachers think through the important criteria included in a task.* Because all first grade teachers assess oral reading in their classrooms and because the criteria for successful oral reading do not differ much from one first grade classroom to another, a group effort to define performance criteria will likely save time and produce a more complete set of criteria than that produced by any single teacher. Similar group efforts are useful for other common performances or products such as book reports and science fair projects.

When teachers within a school develop similar performance criteria across grade revels, it is reinforcing to pupils.

5. *Express the performance criteria in terms of observable pupil behaviors or product characteristics.* Be specific when stating the performance criteria. For example, do not write "The child works." Instead, write "The child remains focused on the task for at least four minutes." Instead of "organization," write " Information is presented in a logical sequence."
6. *Do not use ambiguous words that cloud the meaning of the performance criteria. The worst offenders in this regard are adverbs that end in ly.* Other words to avoid are "good" and "appropriate." Thus, criteria such as "appropriate organization," "speaks correct*ly*," "writes neat*ly*," and "performs graceful*ly*" are ambiguous and leave interpretation of performance up to the observer. The observer's interpretation may vary from time to time and from pupil to pupil, diminishing the fairness and usefulness of the assessment.
7. *Arrange the performance criteria in the order in which they are likely to be observed.* This will save time when observing and will maintain primary focus on the performance.

> **Key Assessment Tools 4.3**
>
> # GUIDELINES FOR STATING PERFORMANCE CRITERIA
>
> 1. Identify the steps or features of the performance or task to be assessed by imagining yourself performing it, observing pupils performing it, or inspecting finished products.
> 2. List the important aspects of the performance or product.
> 3. Try to keep the number of performance criteria small so that they can be reasonably observed and judged; a good range to use is 6 to 12 criteria.
> 4. Have teachers think through the criteria as a group.
> 5. Express the criteria in terms of observable pupil behaviors or product characteristics.
> 6. Avoid vague and ambiguous words like "correctly," "appropriately," and "good."
> 7. Arrange the performance criteria in the order in which they are likely to be observed.
> 8. Check for existing performance assessment instruments to use or modify before constructing your own.

8. *Check for existing performance criteria before defining your own.* The performance criteria associated with giving an oral speech, reading aloud, using a microscope, writing a persuasive paragraph, cutting with scissors, and the like have been listed by many people. No one who reads this book will be the first to try to assess these and most other common school performances. The moral here is that one need not reinvent the wheel every time a wheel is needed.

Key Assessment Tools 4.3 summarizes the foregoing guidelines. Regardless of the particular performance or product assessed, clearly stated performance criteria are critical to the success of both instruction and assessment. The criteria define the important aspects of a performance or product, guide what pupils should be taught, and produce a focus for both the teacher and pupil when assessing performance. Clear performance criteria are needed, and the tasks used to teach and assess the desired performance should be aligned to the criteria (McTighe, 1996).

Provide a Setting to Elicit and Observe the Performance

Teachers may observe and assess naturally occurring classroom behaviors or set up situations in which they assess carefully structured performances.

Formally structured performance assessments are needed when teachers are dealing with low-frequency behaviors and making important decisions.

Once the performance criteria are defined, a setting in which to observe the performance or product must be selected or established. Depending on the nature of the performance or product, the teacher may observe behaviors as they naturally occur in the classroom or set up a specific situation in which the pupils must perform. There are two considerations in deciding whether to observe naturally occurring behaviors or to set up a more controlled exercise: (1) the frequency with which the performance naturally occurs in the classroom and (2) the seriousness of the decision to be made.

If the performance occurs infrequently during normal classroom activity, it may be more efficient to structure a situation in which pupils must perform the desired behaviors. For example, in the normal flow of classroom activities, pupils rarely have the opportunity to give a planned 5-minute speech, so the teacher should set up an exercise in which each pupil must develop and give a 5-minute speech. Oral reading, on the other hand, occurs frequently enough in many elementary classrooms that performance can be observed as part of the normal flow of reading instruction.

The importance of the decision to be made from a performance assessment also influences the context in which observation takes place. In general the more important the decision, the more structured the assessment environment should be. A course grade, for example, represents an important decision about a pupil. If performance assessments contribute to grading, evidence should be gathered under structured, formal circumstances so that every pupil has a fair and equal chance to exhibit his or her achievement. The validity of the assessment is likely to be improved when the setting is similar and familiar to all pupils.

Regardless of the nature of the assessment, evidence obtained from a single assessment describes only one example of a pupil's performance. For a variety of reasons such as illness, home problems, or other distractions, pupil performance at a single time may not provide a reliable indication of the pupil's true achievement. To be certain that one has an accurate indication of what a pupil can and cannot do, multiple observations and products are useful. If the different observations produce similar performance, a teacher can have confidence in the evidence and use it in decision making. If different observations contradict one another, more information should be obtained.

Multiple observations of pupil performances provide more reliable and accurate information.

Develop a Score to Describe the Performance

The final step in performance assessment is to score pupils' performance. As in previous steps, the nature of the decision to be made influences the judgmental system used. Scoring a performance assessment can be holistic or analytic, just like scoring an essay question. In situations such as group placement, selection, or grading, holistic scoring is most useful. To make such decisions, a teacher seeks to describe an individual's performance using a single, overall score. On the other hand, if the assessment purpose is to diagnose pupil difficulties or certify pupil mastery of each individual performance criterion, then analytic scoring, with a separate score or rating on each performance criterion, is appropriate. In either case, the performance criteria dictate the scoring or rating approach that is adopted.

Holistic scoring (a single overall score) is good for such things as group placement or grading; analytic scoring (scoring individual criteria) is useful in diagnosing student difficulties.

In most classrooms, the teacher is both the observer and the scorer. In situations where an important decision is to be made, additional observers/scorers may be added. Thus, it is common for performance assessments in athletic, music, debate, and art competitions to have more than a single judge in order to make scoring more fair.

A number of options exist for collecting, recording, and summarizing observations of pupil performance: anecdotal records, checklists, rating scales, and rubrics, and portfolios. The following sections explore these options in detail.

Anecdotal Records, Checklists, and Rating Scales

Anecdotal Records

Written accounts of significant, individual pupil events and behaviors the teacher has observed are called **anecdotal records**. Only those observations that have special significance and that cannot be obtained from other classroom assessment methods should be included in an anecdotal record. Figure 4.1 shows an example of an anecdotal record of pupil Lynn Gregory. Notice that it provides information about the learner, the date of observation, the name of the teacher observing, and a factual description of the event.

Most teachers have difficulty identifying particular events or behaviors that merit inclusion in an anecdotal record. What is significant and important in the life of a pupil is not always apparent at the time an event or behavior occurs. From the hundreds of observations made each day, how is a teacher to select the one that might be important

Anecdotal records are written accounts of significant events and behaviors the teacher has observed in a pupil.

FIGURE 4.1   **Anecdotal Record for Lynn Gregory.**

PUPIL   *Lynn Gregory*   DATE   *9/22/2004*
OBSERVER   *J. Ricketts*

All term Lynn has been quiet and passive, rarely interacting w/classmates in class or on the playground. Today Lynn suddenly "opened up" and wanted continual interaction w/classmates. She could not settle down, kept circulating around the room until she became bothersome to me and her classmates. I tried to settle her down, but was unsuccessful.

enough to write down? It may take many observations over many days to recognize which events really are significant. Moreover, anecdotal records are time-consuming to prepare and need to be written up soon after the event or behavior is observed, while it is fresh in the teacher's mind. This is not always possible. For these reasons, anecdotal records are not used extensively by teachers. This does not mean that teachers do not observe and judge classroom events—we know they do. It simply means that they seldom write down descriptions of these events.

Anecdotal records such as checklists, rating scales, and portfolios are options available to record and collect observations of pupils.

Checklists

A **checklist** is a written list of performance criteria. As a pupil's performance is observed or product judged, the scorer determines whether the performance or the product meets each performance criterion. If it does, a checkmark is placed next to that criterion, indicating that it was observed; if it does not, the checkmark is omitted. Figure 4.2 shows a completed checklist for Rick Gray's oral presentation. The performance criteria for this checklist were presented earlier in this chapter.

A checklist, which is a written list of performance criteria, can be used repeatedly over time to diagnose strengths, weaknesses, and changes in performances.

Checklists are diagnostic, reusable, and capable of charting pupil progress. They provide a detailed record of pupils' performances, one that can and should be shown to pupils to help them see where improvement is needed. Rick Gray's teacher could sit down with him after his presentation and point out both the criteria on which he performed well and the areas that need improvement. Because it focuses on specific performances, a checklist provides diagnostic information. The same checklist can be reused, with different pupils or with the same pupil over time. Using the same checklist more than once is an easy way to obtain information about a pupil's improvement over time.

FIGURE 4.2 **Checklist Results for an Oral Presentation.**

NAME: *Rick Gray*   DATE: *Oct. 12, 2004*

I. Physical Expression

  ✓ A. Stands straight and faces audience.

  _____ B. Changes facial expression with changes in tone of the presentation.

  ✓ C. Maintains eye contact with audience.

II. Vocal Expression

  ✓ A. Speaks in a steady, clear voice.

  ✓ B. Varies tone to emphasize points.

  _____ C. Speaks loudly enough to be heard by audience.

  ✓ D. Paces words in an even flow.

  _____ E. Enunciates each word.

III. Verbal Expression

  _____ A. Chooses precise words to convey meaning.

  ✓ B. Avoids unnecessary repetition.

  ✓ C. States sentences with complete thoughts or ideas.

  ✓ D. Organizes information logically.

  ✓ E. Summarizes main points at conclusion.

There are, however, disadvantages associated with checklists. One important disadvantage is that checklists give a teacher only two choices for each criterion: performed or not performed. A checklist provides no middle ground for scoring. Suppose that Rick Gray stood straight and faced the audience most of the time during his oral presentation, or paced his words evenly except in one brief part of the speech when he spoke too quickly and ran his words together. How should his teacher score him on these performance criteria? Should Rick receive a check because he did them most of the time, or should he not receive a check because his performance was flawed? Sometimes this is not an easy choice. A checklist forces the teacher to make an absolute decision for each performance criterion, even though a pupil's performance is somewhere between these extremes.

A second disadvantage of checklists is the difficulty of summarizing a pupil's performance into a single score. We saw how useful checklists can be for diagnosing pupils' strengths and weaknesses. But what if a teacher wants to summarize performance across a number of criteria to arrive at a single score for grading purposes?

Checklists cannot record gradations in performances.

One way to summarize Rick's performance into a single score is to translate the number of performance criteria he successfully demonstrated into a percentage. For example, there were 13 performance criteria on the oral presentation checklist and Rick demonstrated 9 of them during his presentation. Assuming each criterion is equally important, Rick's performance translates into a score of 69 percent ($9/13 \times 100 = 69\%$). Thus, Rick demonstrated 69 percent of the desired performance criteria.

A second, and better, way to summarize performance would be for the teacher to set up standards for rating pupils' performance. Suppose Rick's teacher set up the following set of standards:

Excellent	12 or 13	performance criteria shown
Good	9 to 11	performance criteria shown
Fair	5 to 8	performance criteria shown
Poor	5 or less	performance criteria shown

These standards allow the teacher to summarize performance on a scale that goes from excellent to poor. The scale could also go from a grade of A to one of D, depending on the type of scoring the teacher uses. The same standard would be used to summarize each pupil's performance. Rick performed 9 of the 13 criteria, and the teacher's standard indicates that his performance should be classified as "good" or "B." Of course, there are many such standards that can be set up and the one shown is only an example. In establishing standards, it is advisable to keep the summarizing rules as simple as possible.

Summarizing performances from a checklist can be done by setting up rating standards or by calculating the percentage of criteria accomplished.

Rating Scales

Although they are similar to checklists, **rating scales** allow the observer to judge performance along a continuum rather than as a dichotomy. Both checklists and rating scales are based upon a set of performance criteria, and it is common for the same set of performance criteria to be used in both a rating scale and a checklist. However, a checklist gives the observer two categories for judging, while a rating scale gives more than two.

Three of the most common types or rating scales are the numerical, graphic, and descriptive scales. Figure 4.3 shows an example of each of these scales as applied to two specific performance criteria for giving an oral presentation. In numerical scales, a number stands for a point on the rating scale. Thus, in the example, "1" corresponds to the pupil *always* performing the behavior, "2" to the pupil *usually* performing the behavior, and so on. Graphic scales require the rater to mark a position on a line divided into sections based upon a scale. The rater marks an "X" at that point on the line that best describes the pupil's performance. Descriptive rating scales, also called **scoring rubrics,** require the rater to choose among different descriptions of actual performance. (We will say more about rubrics in the next section.) (Wiggins and McTighe, 1998; Goodrich, 1997.) In descriptive rating scales, different descriptions are used to represent different levels of pupil performance. To score, the teacher picks the description that comes closest to the pupil's actual performance. A judgment of the teacher determines the grade.

The three most common types of rating scales are numerical, graphic, and descriptive (also called scoring rubrics).

Descriptive rating scales, or scoring rubrics, require the rater to choose among different descriptions of actual performance.

Regardless of the type of rating scale one chooses, two general rules will improve their use. The first rule is to limit the number of rating categories. There is a tendency to think

FIGURE 4.3 **Three Types of Rating Scale for an Oral Presentation.**

Numerical Rating Scale

Directions: Indicate how often the pupil performs each of these behaviors while giving an oral presentation. For each behavior circle **1** if the pupil **always** performs the behavior, **2** if the pupil **usually** performs the behavior, **3** if the pupil **seldom** performs the behavior, and **4** if the pupil **never** performs the behavior.

Physical Expression

A. Stands straight and faces audience

      1   2   3   4

B. Changes facial expression with changes in tone of the presentation

      1   2   3   4

Graphic Rating Scale

Directions: Place an **X** on the line which shows how often the pupil did each of the behaviors listed while giving an oral presentation.

Physical Expression

A. Stands straight and faces audience

| always | usually | seldom | never |

B. Changes facial expression with changes in tone of the presentation

| always | usually | seldom | never |

Descriptive Rating Scale

Directions: Place an **X** on the line at the place which best describes the pupil's performance on each behavior.

Physical Expression

A. Stands straight and faces audience

| **stands straight, always looks at audience** | **weaves, fidgets, eyes roam from audience to ceiling** | **constant, distracting movements, no eye contact with audience** |

B. Changes facial expression with changes in tone of the presentation

| **matches facial expressions to content and emphasis** | **facial expressions usually matches tone; occasional lack of expression** | **no match between tone and facial expression; expression distracts** |

Having too many scales tends to distract the rater from the performance, making the ratings unreliable.

that the greater the number of rating categories to choose from, the better the rating scale. In practice, this is not the case. Few observers can make reliable discriminations in performance across more than five rating categories. Adding a larger number of categories on a rating scale is likely to make the ratings less, not more, reliable. Stick to three to five well-defined and distinct rating scale points, as shown in Figure 4.3.

The second rule is to use the same rating scale for each performance criterion. This is not usually possible in descriptive rating scales where the descriptions vary with each performance criterion. For numerical and graphic scales, however, it is best to select a single

FIGURE 4.4   **Types of Rating Scales.**

NAME: *Sarah Jackson*   DATE: *Nov. 8, 2004*

Directions: Indicate how often the pupil performs each of these behaviors while giving an oral presentation. For each behavior **circle 4** if the pupil **always** performs the behavior, **3** if the pupil **usually** performs the behavior, **2** if the pupil **seldom** performs the behavior, and **1** if the pupil **never** performs the behavior.

   I. Physical Expression

      (4) 3   2   1   A. Stands straight and faces audience

      4   3 (2) 1   B. Changes facial expression with changes in tone of the presentation

      4 (3) 2   1   C. Maintains eye contact with audience

   II. Vocal Expression

      (4) 3   2   1   A. Speaks in a steady, clear voice

      4 (3) 2   1   B. Varies tone to emphasize points

      4   3 (2) 1   C. Speaks loudly enough to be heard by audience

      4 (3) 2   1   D. Paces words in an even flow

      4   3 (2) 1   E. Enunciates each word

   III. Verbal Expression

      4   3 (2) 1   A. Chooses precise words to convey meaning

      4 (3) 2   1   B. Avoids unnecessary repetition

      (4) 3   2   1   C. States sentences with complete thoughts or ideas

      (4) 3   2   1   D. Organizes information logically

      4 (3) 2   1   E. Summarizes main points at conclusion

rating scale and use it for all performance criteria. Using many different rating categories requires the observer to change focus frequently and will decrease rating accuracy by distracting the rater's attention from the performance.

Figure 4.4 shows a complete set of numerical rating scales for Sarah Jackson for an oral presentation. Note that its performance criteria are identical to those on the checklist shown in Figure 4.2. The only difference between the checklist and the numerical rating scales is the way performance is scored.

Whereas checklists measure only the presence or absence of some performance, a rating scale measures the degree to which the performance matches the criteria.

While rating scales provide more categories for assessing a pupil's performance, and thereby provide detailed diagnostic information, the multiple rating categories complicate the process of summarizing performance across criteria to arrive at a pupil's overall score. With a checklist, summarization is reduced to giving credit for checked criteria and no credit for unchecked, criteria. This cannot be done with a rating scale because performance is judged in terms of *degree,* not presence or absence. A teacher must treat ratings of "always," "usually," "seldom, and "never" differently from each other, or there is no point to having the different rating categories.

Numerical summarization is the most straightforward and commonly used approach to summarizing performance on rating scales. It assigns a point value to each category in the scale and sums the points across the performance criteria. For example, consider Sarah Jackson's ratings in Figure 4.4. To obtain a summary score for Sarah's performance, one can assign 4 points to a rating of "always," 3 points to a rating of "usually," 2 points to a rating of "seldom," and 1 point to a rating of "never." The numbers 4, 3, 2, and 1 match the four possible ratings for each performance criterion, with 4 representing the most desirable response and 1 the least desirable. Thus, high scores indicate good performance. Note that before summarizing Sarah's performance into a single score, it is important for the teacher to identify areas of weakness so that Sarah can be guided to improve her oral presentations.

Sarah's total score, 39, can be determined by adding the circled numbers. The highest possible score on the rating scale is 52; if a pupil was rated "always" on each performance criterion, the pupil's total score would be 52 (4 points × 13 performance criteria). Thus, Sarah scored 39 out of a possible 52 points. In this manner, a total score can be determined for each pupil rated. This score can be turned into a percentage by dividing it by 52, the total number of points available (39/52 × 100 = 75%).

Rubrics

Rubrics summarize performance in a general way, whereas checklists and rating scales provide specific diagnostic information about pupil strengths and weaknesses.

Besides numerical summaries, scoring rubrics or descriptive summarizations provide another way to summarize performance on checklists and rating scales. A rubric is a set of clear expectations or criteria used to help teachers and pupils focus on what is valued in a subject, topic, or activity. A rubric describes the level at which a pupil may be performing a process or completing a product. It focuses on academic work and is based on and linked to the teacher's curriculum. A rubric describes what is to be learned rather than on how to teach. It lays out criteria for different levels of performance, which are usually descriptive, rarely numerical. Figure 4.5 lists ways in which rubrics help both the teacher and the pupil.

As with all performance assessments, rubrics are based on clear and coherent performance criteria.

Two Methods of Scoring

There are two basic methods of scoring rubrics, holistic and analytic, similar to essay scoring methods. Holistic scoring is used to assess the overall performance of a pupil across all the performance criteria. Previous examples in this chapter exemplify holistic scoring. The teacher selects the description that most closely matches the pupil's overall performance on the process or product. Analytic scoring is used to assess individually each performance criterion stated in the rubric. Each criterion is rated separately using

FIGURE 4.5 **Rubrics Aid Teachers and Pupils.**

Rubrics help teachers by
- specifying criteria to focus instruction on what is important;
- specifying criteria to focus pupil assessments;
- increasing the consistency of assessments;
- limiting arguments over grading because of the clear criteria and scoring levels that reduce subjectivity; and
- providing descriptions of pupil performance that are informative to both parents and students.

Rubrics help pupils by
- clarifying the teacher's expectations about performance;
- pointing out what is important in a process or product;
- helping them to monitor and critique their own work;
- providing informative descriptions of performance; and
- providing clearer performance information than traditional letter grades provide.

different levels of performance. Figure 4.6 illustrates holistic scoring for foreign language assessment. There are four scoring levels, each including multiple criteria. The assessor selects the scoring level that best describes the pupil's overall language proficiency.

Devising Rubrics

Consider the following set of performance criteria that were developed for a fifth grade book report by one of the author's students.

1. Tell why you chose the book.
2. Describe the main characters of the book.
3. Explain the plot of the book in three to five sentences.
4. Describe the main place or setting of the book.
5. Explain in three sentences how the main characters have changed through the book.
6. Write in complete sentences.
7. Check spelling, grammar, punctuation, and capitalization.
8. Describe whether or not you enjoyed the book and why.

Of course, these criteria could be added to or subtracted from, based on the pupils in a class and what characteristics of a book report the teacher wishes to emphasize. Different teachers might select different performance criteria.

Scoring rubrics for processes and products are developed by stating levels of the performance criteria that indicate different qualities of pupil performance. For example, the scoring rubric constructed for the fifth grade book report contained three levels of performance labeled "excellent," "good," and "poor." Read each description and note how the authors describe different levels of performance for the criteria.

> **Excellent:** Pupil gives two reasons why the book was chosen; all main characters described in great detail; describes the plot in a logical, step-by-step sequence; gives detailed description of the place in which the book takes place; describes how each main character changed during the book in five sentences; all sentences are complete; no more than a total of five spelling, grammar, punctuation, or capitalization errors; states opinion of the book based on book content.

> **Good:** Pupil gives one reason why the book was chosen; all main characters described too briefly; plot described but one main aspect omitted; provides general description of the book setting; briefly describes how most of the main characters changed during the book; a few

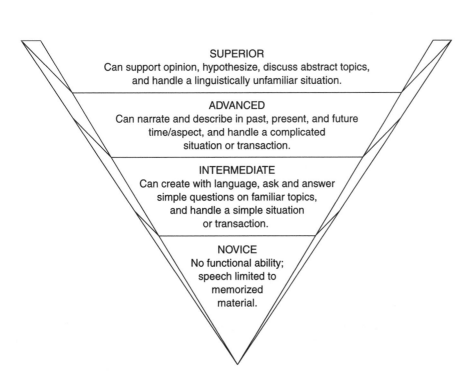

FIGURE 4.6 An Example of Holistic Scoring. ACTFL Proficiency Levels.

Source: Adapted from *Oral Proficiency Interview: Tester Training Manual* (n.p.) by the American Council on the Teaching of Foreign Languages. Copyright 1989 by The American Council on the Teaching of Foreign Languages. Adapted by permission.

SUPERIOR
Can support opinion, hypothesize, discuss abstract topics, and handle a linguistically unfamiliar situation.

ADVANCED
Can narrate and describe in past, present, and future time/aspect, and handle a complicated situation or transaction.

INTERMEDIATE
Can create with language, ask and answer simple questions on familiar topics, and handle a simple situation or transaction.

NOVICE
No functional ability; speech limited to memorized material.

> **Key Assessment Tools 4.4**
> ## GENERAL STEPS IN PREPARING AND USING RUBRICS
>
> 1. Select a process or product to be taught.
> 2. State performance criteria for the process or product.
> 3. Decide on the number of scoring levels for the rubric, usually three to five.
> 4. State description of performance criteria at the highest level of pupil performance (see "excellent" description of the book report rubric).
> 5. State descriptions of performance criteria at the remaining scoring levels (e.g., the "good" and "poor" levels of the book report rubric).
> 6. Compare each pupil's performance to each scoring level.
> 7. Select the scoring level closest to a pupil's actual performance or product.
> 8. Grade the pupil.

nonsentences; more than five spelling, grammar, punctuation, or capitalization errors; states opinion of the book but no reference to the book content.

Poor: Pupil fails to state why book was chosen; not all main characters are described; superficial plot description with key aspects omitted; little information about where the book takes place; incorrectly describes changes in the main characters during the book; a few nonsentences; many spelling, grammar, punctuation, or capitalization errors; no opinion of the book provided.

To score the book report, the teacher would read a pupil's book report, compare it to the three levels, and determine which of the three levels best describes the quality of the pupil's book report. Is it most like the "excellent" description, the "good" description, or the "poor" description? The selected description determines the grade for the pupil's book report. Different rubrics can have different numbers of scoring levels and different descriptions for the levels. Key Assessment Tools 4.4 gives the steps in preparing and using rubrics.

Consider the rubric in Table 4.4 that is used to assess pupils' response journal questions. The rubric has four scoring levels ranging from "excellent" to "poor" performance. After reading the "excellent" scoring level, can you identity the teacher's intended performance criteria? If the criteria are clear you should be able to identify them from the "excellent" rubric.

We can apply the steps in Key Assessment Tools 4.4 to the response journal rubric in Table 4.4:

Step 1: Select a performance process or product: journal response questions.

Step 2: Identify performance criteria based on best pupil performance:
- Answers complete and accurate
- Answers supported with information from readings
- Answers include direct quotations
- Answers show varied and detailed sentences
- Appropriate spelling, capitals, and punctuation

Step 3: Decide on the number of scoring levels: four.

Step 4: State the description of the performance criteria at the highest level: see the "excellent" category in Table 4.4.

Step 5: State descriptions of criteria at the remaining scoring levels: compare the quality of the "excellent" scoring level to the "good," "needs improvement," and "poor" levels.

Step 6: Compare each pupil's performance to the four scoring levels.

Step 7: Select the scoring level that best describes the level of the pupil's performance on the response journal.

Step 8: Assign grade to pupil.

TABLE 4.4   **Scoring Rubric for Fifth Grade Response Journal Questions**

3—Excellent. Answers are very complete and accurate. Most answers are supported with specific information from the reading, including direct quotations. Sentence structure is varied and detailed. Mechanics are generally accurate, including spelling, use of capitals, and appropriate punctuation.

2—Good. Answers are usually complete and accurate. These answers are supported with specific information from the reading. Sentence structure is varied. Mechanics are generally accurate, including spelling, use of capitals, and appropriate punctuations.

1—Needs improvement. Answers are partially to fully accurate. These answers may need to be supported with more specific information from the reading. Sentence structure is varied, with some use of sentence fragments. Mechanics may need improvement, including spelling, use of capitals, and appropriate punctuation.

0—Poor. Answers are inaccurate or not attempted at all. Sentence structure frequently incomplete. Mechanics need significant improvement.

Source: Used with permission of Gwen Airasian.

One important aspect of developing and using rubrics is the construction of scoring levels. The bases for developing good scoring levels are the performance criteria and a set of terms that differentiate levels of pupil performance. For example, go to Table 4.4 and read the four scoring levels. Notice that in each scoring level except the "poor" one, we can see the same aspects of the performance criteria: answers complete and accurate, supported from readings, sentence structure, and mechanics. Even the "poor" level includes three of the four criteria. Note what makes the scoring levels different. It is not the criteria per se. It is the level of performance used to describe each criterion. For example, in the "excellent" level, answers are *very* complete and accurate; in the "good" level, answers are *usually* complete and accurate; in the "needs improvement" level, answers are *partially* accurate; and in the "poor" level, answers are *inaccurate or not attempted.* Try the same analysis with the remaining criteria in the table.

Many common sets of terms are used to describe scoring levels in rubrics. For instance, excellent, good, needs improvement, poor were used in the preceding examples. Other description levels are always, mostly, sometimes, seldom, never; exemplary, competent, inconsistent, lacking; advanced, proficient, basic, in progress; and all, some, few, incomplete. These and many other groups of differentiating labels are used to develop scoring levels.

There are also generic rubrics that can be used to assess a variety of processes and products. Usually, generic rubrics state only the description of the highest level of the scoring rubric. The user must provide his or her own scoring levels to differentiate pupil performance. One example of a description from a generic rubric is "goes beyond expectation, includes extra information, makes no mistakes, demonstrates exceptional grasp of the topic, understands abstract concepts, and finds links among parts." This generic rubric could be applied to many types of performance assessments.

What descriptions for an average and a poor scoring level might follow from the exemplary generic description? For example, if a particular exemplary description is "goes beyond expectation," what phrasing could be used to describe an average or poor level for "goes beyond expectation"? Two possible "average" examples might be "performs adequately" or "exhibits average expectation." A description of a third, poor level of performance might be stated as "performs inadequately" or "exhibits below average expectation." Now, given the generic exemplary description "makes no mistakes," what average and poor level examples can you identify for the generic example? Scoring rubrics may have only two levels or may use up to six, but rarely does the number of scoring levels exceed four or five. Too many scoring levels makes judging the pupil's appropriate level for grading more difficult and unreliable.

More Examples of Rubrics

Rubrics come in various forms to assess various processes and products. A few more examples here will provide a wider glimpse of their usefulness. Figure 4.7 shows a

FIGURE 4.7 **Scoring Rubric Used in First Grade Report Card.**

NOT YET—1	2	DEVELOPING—3	4	ACHIEVING—5	EXTENDING

Such as: May demonstrate one or <u>more</u> of following:
 	
Identifies the topic but does not identify any details from the book.
Cites information incorrectly.
Draws only from personal experience rather than from evidence in the book.
Identifies details but not topic.
		Such as: May demonstrate one or <u>more</u> of following:
		
		Identifies topic and one (1) detail from the book.
		Identifies several details, but needs prompting to clearly state the main topic.
				Criteria: Demonstrates <u>all</u> of following:
				
				Identifies from an informational book:
				  topic of book,
				  two or more supporting details.
				Such as:
				  "This book is about whales. The blue whale is the largest animal on earth. Whales have babies that are born alive—not hatched."
					Identifies main ideas.
					Identifies background knowledge.
					Distinguishes between what she or he already knew and what was just learned.
					Identifies topic and details of an informational book <u>read by student</u>.

Source: Reprinted by permission of the Ann Arbor Public Schools, Ann Arbor, Michigan.

small portion of a first grade report card that is presented as a rubric. The entire report card has a number of such rubrics as well as a cover page sent home to explain the report form to parents. The outcomes reported to parents are the language arts and mathematics outcomes the district has identified as most crucial for teachers to monitor and for students to achieve. Notice that each desired outcome is defined by specific performances or products at each of the three rubric levels: not yet, developing learner, and achieving learner.

Table 4.5 shows a rubric to assess eleventh grade history pupils. There are five scoring levels for each of the two rubrics shown. Can you identify the performance criteria for the two rubrics?

Key Assessment Tools 4.5 shows a general four-level persuasive writing rubric that can be used at varied grade levels. Identify the terms in this rubric that are used to differentiate levels of pupil performance (e.g., "clearly," "consistently," "thoroughly maintained").

Analytic scoring breaks down the general description of a holistic process or product into separate scores for each criterion. For example, consider the persuasive writing rubric. Unlike a holistic score, analytic scoring would provide a score for each of the five performance criteria. Thus, the teacher might score the criteria in the following manner for the first two performance criteria.

Take a position and clearly state their point of view
Completely
Generally
Partially
Not at all

Consistently use facts and/or personal information to develop support for their position
Extensively
Partially
Rarely

Note that analytic scoring can use letters (A, B, C, etc.), numbers (4, 3, 2, 1), and descriptions as in the examples above.

Write analytic scoring forms for the remaining three performance criteria.

TABLE 4.5   California Assessment Program 1990 History–Social Science Grade 11 Scoring Guide: Group Performance Task

	Level I Minimal Achievement	Level II Rudimentary Achievement	Level III Commendable Achievement	Level IV Superior Achievement	Level V Exceptional Achievement
Communication of Ideas 20	(1–4) Position is vague. Presentation is brief and includes unrelated general statements. Overall view of the problem is not clear. Statements tend to wander or ramble.	(5–9) Presents general and indefinite position. Only minimal organization in presentation. Uses generalities to support position. Emphasizes only one issue. Considers only one aspect of problem.	(8–12) Takes a definite but general position. Presents a somewhat organized argument. Uses general terms with limited evidence that may not be totally accurate. Deals with a limited number of issues. Views problem within a somewhat limited range.	(13–16) Takes a clear position. Presents an organized argument with perhaps only minor errors in the supporting evidence. Deals with the major issues and shows some understanding of relationships. Gives consideration to examination of more than one idea or aspect of the problem.	(17–20) Takes a strong, well-defined position. Presents a well-organized, persuasive argument with accurate supporting evidence. Deals with all significant issues and demonstrates a depth of understanding of important relationships. Examines the problem from several positions.
Knowledge and Use of History 30	(1–6) Reiterates one or two facts without complete accuracy. Deals only briefly and vaguely with concepts or the issues. Barely indicates any previous historical knowledge. Relies heavily on the information provided.	(7–12) Provides only basic facts with only some degree of accuracy. Refers to information to explain at least one issue or concept in general terms. Limited use of previous historical knowledge without complete accuracy. Major reliance on the information provided.	(13–18) Relates only major facts to the basic issues with a fair degree of accuracy. Analyzes information to explain at least one issue or concept with substantive support. Uses general ideas from previous historical knowledge with fair degree of accuracy.	(19–24) Offers accurate analysis of the documents. Provides facts to relate to the major issues involved. Uses previous general historical knowledge to examine issues involved.	(25–30) Offers accurate analysis of the information and issues. Provides a variety of facts to explore major and minor issues and concepts involved. Extensively uses previous historical knowledge to provide an in-depth understanding of the problem and to relate it to past and possible future situations.

Source: California Department of Education, 1990. Reprinted with permission.

Involving Pupils in the Use of Rubrics

When using rubrics a teacher should inform the pupils about the criteria that will be used to judge their performance or product *before* assessment takes place. Obviously, the teacher should have identified the criteria before the beginning of instruction and assessment. The criteria—and, ideally, specific examples of good and poor performance—should be described and illustrated for the pupils. Pupils should know what makes a good lab report, oral speech, persuasive essay, "show-your-work" math problem, dissection of a frog, analysis of a poem, bar graph, journal response, or any of a thousand other class-room processes and products.

Knowing the criteria of quality performance before assessment leads to a number of benefits for both pupils and teacher. First, knowledge of performance criteria provides information to pupils about what is expected of their work—what characteristics make the work good work. Second, knowledge of the criteria lends focus and structure to pupils' performances and product. They know what is expected of them and thus can concentrate on learning and demonstrating the desired knowledge and behaviors. This, in turn, saves the teacher time in scoring pupils' products or processes because the criteria narrow the breadth of pupil responses.

Many teachers let pupils help identify the important performance criteria for a class-room process or product. Involving pupils in identifying performance criteria gives them

---

Key Assessment Tools 4.5

GENERIC RUBRIC TO SCORE WRITING TO PERSUADE

When describing observables to incorporate in a rubric to assess student responses to a specific prompt, it is important to address all of the specific criteria that were included in the prompt itself. In addition, we need to consider how skillfully the response was crafted and how effectively it addressed the writer's ability to persuade. To assist you with identifying these factors, the following observables are provided at varying score points.

Students at Level 1:
- Take a position and clearly state their point of view.
- Consistently use facts and/or personal information to develop support for their position.
- Organize details in a logical plan that is thoroughly maintained.
- Consistently enhance what they write by using language purposefully to create sentence variety.
- Incorporate appropriate mechanics (spelling, capitalization, punctuation). Any errors that occur are due to risk taking.

Students at Level 2:
- Take a position and adequately attempt to clarify their point of view.
- Frequently use facts and/or personal information to develop support for their position.
- Organize details in a logical plan that is adequately maintained.
- Frequently support their position by providing sufficient information.
- Frequently enhance what they write by using language purposefully to create sentence variety.
- Incorporate appropriate mechanics (spelling, capitalization, punctuation). Most errors that occur are due to risk taking.

Students at Level 3:
- Take a position and make a limited attempt to clarify their point of view.
- Generally use facts and/or personal information which may or may not support their position.
- Organize details in a plan that may or may not be adequately maintained.
- May or may not support their position by providing sufficient information.
- May or may not attend to mechanics (spelling, capitalization, punctuation).

Student at Level 4:
- Usually provide a position and limited information to support the position.
- Minimally organize details that include some support for the position.
- Seldom take their audience into consideration.
- Occasionally choose vocabulary that sufficiently supports the position.
- Seldom enhance what they write by varying sentence structure and incorporating appropriate mechanics (spelling, capitalization, punctuation).

a sense of ownership of the rubric as well as an early preview of the important characteristics of the process or product they will be working on. Some teachers provide pupils with good and poor examples of the process or product they are teaching and ask pupils to identify what makes a good example. In the process of determining what makes good examples, the pupils are also identifying relevant criteria for the process or product. Figure 4.5 summarized some of the main advantages of rubrics for pupils.

It is very important to understand that there is a learning curve for mastering the construction and use of rubrics. It takes time to learn to use rubrics well. Trial and error as well as practice for both pupils and teachers are needed to help each gain the most out of rubrics. Start with simple and limited performance criteria and scoring levels—perhaps three or four criteria and two or three scoring levels. Explain the rubric process to the pupils: what rubrics are, why we use them, how they can help improve learning and clarify grading. Practice with the pupils. One approach is to have pupils use a rubric to revise their work before passing it in. A teacher should expect to revise a rubric a few times before he or she and the pupils feel comfortable with it.

Portfolios

An important addition to the growing use of classroom performance assessments is portfolio assessment. This assessment method is gaining use in schools and classrooms (Ryan and Miyasaka, 1995). A **portfolio** is a collection of selected student work. The term *portfolio* derives from the collections that models, photographers, and artists assemble to demonstrate their work. In the classroom, portfolios have the same basic purpose: to collect pupil performances to show their work and accomplishments over time. Portfolios do not contain haphazard, unrelated collections of a pupil's work. They contain consciously selected examples of work that is intended to show pupil growth and development toward important curriculum goals. Portfolios support instruction and learning and should be related to teachers' objectives.

A portfolio can be made up of many different pupil performances or it can be made up of a single performance. For example, a multifocused writing portfolio might contain writing samples, lists of books read, journal entries about books read, and descriptions of favorite poems. Conversely, a single-focus portfolio might contain multiple pieces of the same process or product, such as a portfolio containing only book reports, only written poems, or only chemistry lab reports. Key Assessment Tools 4.6 samples the range of materials that can go into a portfolio.

In one first grade class, pupils developed a reading portfolio. Every third week the pupils read a paragraph or two into their audiotape "portfolio." The teacher monitored pupil improvement over time and pupils could play back their pieces to measure their reading improvement. Also, periodically the pupils' reading portfolios were sent home for the parents to listen to their child's reading improvement, an opportunity parents appreciated.

Portfolios can contribute to instruction and learning in many ways:

- Showing pupils' typical work.
- Monitoring pupil progress and improvement over time.

Key Assessments Tools 4.6

WHAT CAN GO INTO A PORTFOLIO

Media: videos, audiotapes, pictures, artwork, computer programs

Reflections: plans, statements of goals, self-reflections, journal entries

Individual work: tests, journals, logs, lab reports, homework, essays, poems, maps, inventions, posters, math work

Group work: cooperative learning sessions, group performances, peer reviews

Work in progress: rough and final drafts, show-your-work problems, science fair projects

> **Key Assessment Tools 4.7**
>
> # PORTFOLIO QUESTIONS
>
> 1. What is the purpose of the portfolio?
> 2. What will go into and be removed from the portfolio during its use?
> 3. Who will select the entries that go into the portfolio: teacher, pupils, or both?
> 4. How will the portfolio be organized and maintained?
> 5. How will the portfolio be assessed?

- Helping pupils self-evaluate their work.
- Providing ongoing assessment of pupil learning.
- Providing diagnostic information about pupil performance.
- Helping teachers judge the appropriateness of the curriculum.
- Facilitating teacher meetings and conferences with pupils, parents, and both pupils and parents.
- Grading pupils.
- Reinforcing the importance of processes and products in learning.
- Showing pupils the connections among their processes and products.
- Providing concrete examples of pupil work.
- Encouraging pupils to think about what is good performance in varied subject areas.
- Focusing on both the process and final product of learning.
- Informing subsequent teachers about pupils' prior work.

Whatever a portfolio's use and contents, it is important that it have a defined, specific purpose that will focus the nature of the information that will be collected in the portfolio. Too often, teachers defer the question of the portfolio's purpose until *after* pupils have collected large amounts of their work in their portfolios. At that time the teacher is likely to be confronted with the question of what to do with a vast, undifferentiated collection of pupil information.

Perhaps the greatest contribution that portfolios provide for learning is that they give pupils a chance to revisit and reflect on the products and processes they have produced. For many pupils, life in school is an ongoing sequence of papers, performances, assignments, and productions. Each day a new batch of paperwork is produced and the previous day's productions are tossed away or lost, both mentally and physically. Collecting pieces of pupils' work in a portfolio retains them for subsequent pupil review, reflection, demonstration, and grading. With suitable guidance, pupils can be encouraged to think about and compare their work over time, providing them an opportunity rarely available in the absence of portfolios. For example, pupils might be asked to reflect on the following questions. Which of these portfolio items shows the most improvement and why? Which did you enjoy most and why? From which did you learn the most and why? In what areas have you made the most progress over the year and what was the nature of that progress? Portfolios allow pupils to see their progress and judge their work from the perspectives of time and personal development.

As noted, there is a great deal more to successful portfolio assessment than simply collecting bunches of pupils' work. Portfolio assessment is a type of performance assessment and thus depends on the same four elements that all types of performance assessment require: (1) a clear purpose, (2) appropriate performance criteria, (3) a suitable setting, and (4) scoring performance. There are a number of questions that must be answered in developing and assessing portfolios. Key Assessment Tools 4.7 lists the main questions that guide classroom use of portfolios.

Purpose of Portfolios

The items that go into a portfolio, the criteria used to judge the items, and the frequency with which items are added to or deleted from the portfolio all depend on the portfolio's purpose. If the purpose is to illustrate a pupil's typical work in various school subjects for a parent's night at the school, the portfolio contents would likely be more wide ranging than if its purpose is to assess the pupil's improvement in math problem solving over a single marking period. In the latter case, math problems would have to be obtained periodically throughout the marking period and collected in the portfolio.

If a portfolio is intended to show a pupil's best work in a subject area, the contents of the portfolio would change as more samples of the pupil's performance became available and as less good ones were removed. If the purpose is to show improvement over time, earlier performances would have to be retained and new pieces added.

Given the many and varied uses of portfolios, purpose is a crucial issue to consider and define in carrying out portfolio assessment. It is important to determine the purpose and general guidelines for the pieces that will go into the portfolio *before* starting the portfolio assessment. It is also critical that all pieces going into a portfolio be dated, especially in portfolios that aim to assess pupil growth or development. Without recorded dates for each portfolio entry, it may be impossible to assess growth and improvement.

To promote pupils' ownership of their portfolios, it is useful to allow pupils to choose at least some of the pieces that will go into their portfolios. Some teachers develop portfolios that contain two types of pieces, those required by the teacher and those selected by the pupil. It is also important that all pupil portfolio selections are accompanied by a brief written explanation of why the pupil feels that a particular piece belongs in her or his portfolio. This will encourage the pupil to reflect on the characteristics of the piece and why it belongs in the portfolio.

It is important to determine the purpose and guidelines for a portfolio's content before compiling it. Is it to grade, group, instruct, or diagnose pupils?

Allowing students to help determine what goes into their portfolios gives them a sense of ownership.

Performance Criteria

Performance criteria are needed to assess the individual pieces that make up a portfolio. Without such criteria, assessment cannot be consistent within and across portfolios. The nature and process of identifying performance criteria for portfolios is the same as that for checklists, rating scales, and rubrics. Depending on the type of performance contained in a portfolio, many of the performance criteria discussed earlier in this chapter can be used to assess individual portfolio pieces.

If pupil portfolios are required for all teachers in a grade or if portfolios are to be passed on to the pupil's next teacher, it is advisable for all affected teachers to cooperate in formulating a common set of performance criteria. Cooperative teacher practice is useful because it involves groups of teachers in the process of identifying important performance criteria. It also helps produce common instructional emphases within and between grades and fosters discussion and sharing of materials among teachers (Herbert, 1992).

It is valuable to allow pupils to help identify performance criteria used for assessing the contents of a portfolio because this can give pupils a sense of ownership over their performance and help them think through the nature of the portfolio pieces they will produce. Beginning a lesson with joint teacher and pupil discussion of what makes a good book report, oral reading, science lab, or sonnet is a useful way to initiate instruction and get the pupils thinking about the characteristics of the process or product they will have to develop.

There is another very important reason why performance criteria are needed for portfolio assessment. The processes or products that will make up a portfolio should, like all forms of assessment, be related to the instruction provided to pupils. Performance criteria are like the teacher's objectives, identifying the important outcomes pupils need to learn. Without explicit criteria, instruction may not provide all the experiences necessary to carry out the desired learning, thereby reducing the validity of the portfolio.

Performance criteria are needed to evaluate each of the individual pieces within a portfolio.

The performance criteria used in evaluating portfolios should align with a teacher's instructional objectives.

Setting

In addition to a clear purpose and well-developed performance criteria, portfolio assessments must take into account the setting in which pupils' performances will be gathered. While many portfolio pieces can be gathered by the teacher in the classroom, others pieces cannot. When portfolios include oral speaking, science experiments, artistic productions, and psychomotor activities, special equipment or arrangements may be needed to properly collect the desired pupil performance. Many teachers underestimate the time it takes to collect the processes and products that make up portfolios and the management and record keeping needed to maintain them. Checking, managing, maintaining, and assessing pupil portfolios is time-consuming but important.

An important dimension of using portfolios is the logistics of collecting and maintaining pupil portfolios. Portfolios require space. They have to be stored in a safe but accessible place. A system has to be established for pupils to add or subtract pieces of their portfolios. Can pupils go to their portfolio at any time or will the teacher set aside special times when all pupils deal with their portfolios? If the portfolio is intended to show growth, how will the order of the entries be kept in sequence? Maintaining portfolios requires time and organization. Materials such as envelopes, crates, tape recorders, and the like will be needed for assembling and storing pupil portfolios.

Scoring

Scoring portfolios is a time-consuming process that involves judging each individual piece and the portfolio as a whole.

Scoring portfolios can be a time-consuming task. Not only does each individual portfolio piece have to be assessed, but the summarized pieces must also be assessed to provide an overall portfolio performance. Depending on the complexity and variety of the contents of the portfolio, assessing may require considerable time and attention to detail, further increasing assessment time.

Summative Scoring

Consider the difference in managing and scoring portfolios that contain varied processes or products compared to portfolios that contain examples of a single process or product. The multifocused portfolio provides a wide range of pupil performance, but at a substantial logistical and scoring cost to the teacher. The single-focus portfolio does not provide the breadth of varied pupil performances of the multifocused portfolio, but can be managed and scored considerably more quickly.

Figure 4.8 is a narrative description of one pupil's writing portfolio. When the purpose of a portfolio is to provide descriptive information about pupil performance for a parent-teacher night or to pass pupil information on to the next year's teacher, no scoring or summarization of the portfolio contents will be necessary. The contents themselves provide the desired information. However, when the purpose of a portfolio is to diagnose, track improvement, assess the success of instruction, encourage pupils to reflect on their work, or grade pupils, some form of summarization or scoring of the portfolio pieces is required.

Performance criteria used to assess an entire portfolio are different from those used to assess individual portfolio items.

The purpose of assessing an entire portfolio, as opposed to the individual pieces, is usually summative—to assign a grade. Such holistic portfolio assessment requires the development of a set of summarizing criteria. For example, improvement in writing might be judged by comparing a pupil's early pieces to later pieces in terms of these performance criteria: (1) number of spelling, capitalization, and punctuation errors, (2) variety of sentence structures used, (3) use of supporting detail, (4) appropriateness of detail to purpose, (5) ability to emphasize and summarize main ideas, (6) link and flow between paragraphs, and (7) personal involvement in written pieces. An alternative approach might be for the teacher to rate earlier written pieces using a general scoring rubric and compare the level of early performances to later performances using the same rubric.

Different portfolios with different purposes require different summarizing criteria. For example, how would you summarize a portfolio containing a number of tape recordings of a pupil's Spanish pronunciation or a portfolio made up of poems a pupil wrote as part of a poetry unit? What criteria would you use to judge *overall* progress or performance?

Scoring the Pieces

Individual portfolio pieces are normally judged using performance criteria that have been assembled into some form of checklist, rating scale, or rubric.

Individual portfolio pieces are typically scored using methods we have discussed: checklists, rating scales, and rubrics. Table 4.6 gives examples. Thus, each story, tape recording, lab report, handwriting sample, persuasive essay, or cooperative group product can be judged by organizing the performance criteria into a checklist, rating scale, or rubric.

Of course, the teacher does not always have to be the one who assesses the pieces. It is desirable and instructive to allow pupils to self-assess some of their portfolio pieces

FIGURE 4.8 Narrative Description of a Pupil's Writing Portfolio.

Date	Genre	Topic	Reason	Length	Drafts
9/??	Self-Reflection	Thinking About Your Writing	Requested	1 page	1 draft
10/17	Narrative/Dramatic	Personal Monologue	Important	1 page	2 drafts
1/16	Response to Literature	On *The Lord of the Flies*	Unsatisfying	1 page	4 drafts
2/??	Self-Reflection	Response to Parent Comments	Requested	1 page	1 draft
2/28	Narrative/Dramatic	"The Tell-Tale Heart"	Free Pick	3 pages	2 drafts
5/22	Response to Literature	On *Animal Farm*	Satisfying	5 pages	2 drafts
6/??	Self-Reflection	Final Reflection	Requested	2 pages	1 draft

As a writer, Barry shows substantial growth from the beginning of the year in his first personal monologue to his last piece, a response to *Animal Farm.* Initially, Barry seems to have little control over the flow and transition of his ideas. His points are not tied together, he jumps around in his thinking, and he lacks specificity in his ideas. By January, when Barry writes his response to *The Lord of the Flies,* he begins a coherent argument about the differences between Ralph's group and Jack's tribe, although he ends with the unsupported assertions that he would have preferred to be "marooned on a desert island" with Ralph. Barry includes three reasons for his comparison, hinges his reasons with transition words, but more impressively, connects his introductory paragraph with a transition sentence to the body of his essay. In the revisions of this essay, Barry makes primarily word and sentence level changes, adds paragraph formatting, and generally improves the local coherence of the piece.   .

By the end of February when he writes his narrative response to Poe's "The Tell-Tale Heart," Barry displays a concern for making his writing interesting. "I like the idea that there are so many twists in the story that I really think makes it interesting." He makes surface-level spelling changes, deletes a sentence, and replaces details, although not always successfully (e.g., "fine satin sheets and brass bed," is replaced with the summary description "extravagant furniture"). Overall, it is an effective piece of writing showing Barry's understanding of narrative form and his ability to manipulate twists of plot in order to create an engaging story.

Barry's last selection in his portfolio is an exceptional five-page, typed essay on Orwell's *Animal Farm.* The writing is highly organized around the theme of scapegoating. Using supporting details from the novel and contemporary examples from politics and sports, Barry creates a compelling and believable argument. The effective intertextuality and the multiple perspectives Barry brings to this essay result largely from an exceptional revision process. Not only does he attempt to correct his standard conventions and improve his word choices, he also revises successfully to the point of moving around whole clumps of text and adding sections that significantly reshape the piece. This pattern of revision shows the control Barry has gained over his writing.

In Barry's final reflection he describes his development, showing an awareness of such issues as organizing and connecting ideas, choosing appropriate words and details, and making his writing accessible to his readers. "I had many gaps in my writing. One problem was that I would skip from one idea to the next and it would not be clear what was going on in the piece. . . . Now, I have put in more details so you don't have to think as much as you would. I also perfect my transitions and my paragraph form. . . . My reading . . . has improved my vocabulary and it helped me organize my writing so it sounds its best and makes the most sense possible. . . . There are many mistakes I have made throughout the year, but I have at least learned from all of them." I agree with him.

Source: P. A. Moss, et al., "Portfolios, accountability, and an interpretive approach to validity," *Educational Measurement: Issues and Practice,* 1992, *11*(3), p. 18. Copyright 1992 by the National Council on Measurement in Education. Used by permission of AERA.

in order to give them practice in critiquing their own work in terms of the performance criteria.

Consider how much more pupil involvement in the writing process portfolios provide, compared to when an assignment is given, passed in to the teacher, graded, returned to the pupil, and soon forgotten. Note also how this kind of assessment encourages pupil reflection and learning.

Allowing students to self-assess their portfolio encourages pupil reflection and learning.

From the teacher's point of view, clearly there are both advantages and disadvantages to performances, product, and portfolio assessments. Table 4.7 summarizes the major trade-offs.

TABLE 4.6 Assessing Individual Portfolio Pieces

Checklist

Selects correct solution method	Yes	No
Draws and labels diagrams	Yes	No
Shows work leading to solution	Yes	No
Gets correct answer	Yes	No

Rating Scale

Selects correct solution method	Quickly	Slowly	Not at all
Draws and labels diagrams	Completely	Partially	Not at all
Shows work leading to solution	Completely	Partially	Not at all
Gets correct answer	Quickly	Slowly	Not at all

Rubric

Selects correct solution method; draws complete, labeled diagrams; shows all work; gets correct answer

Selects correct solution method; draws complete but poorly labeled diagrams; shows partial work; gets partially correct answer

Selects incorrect solution method; neither draws nor labels diagrams; shows very little work; gets incorrect answer

TABLE 4.7 Advantages and Disadvantages of Performance, Product, and Portfolio Assessments

Advantages
- Chart pupil performance over time.
- Conduct pupil self-assessment of products and performances.
- Conduct peer review of products and performances.
- Provide diagnostic information about performances and products.
- Integrate assessment and instruction.
- Promote learning through assessment activities.
- Give pupils ownership over their learning and productions.
- Clarify lesson, assignment, and test expectations.
- Report performance to parents in clear, descriptive terms.
- Permit pupil reflection and analysis of work.
- Provide concrete examples for parent conferences.
- Assemble cumulative evidence of performance.
- Reinforce importance of pupil performance.

Disadvantages

Most disadvantages associated with performance, product, and especially portfolio assessments involve the time they require:
- To prepare materials, performance criteria, and scoring formats.
- To manage, organize, and keep records.
- For teachers and pupils to become comfortable with the use of performance assessments and the change in teaching and learning roles they involve.
- To score and provide feedback to pupils.

Validity and Reliability of Performance Assessments

Since formal performance assessments are used to make decisions about pupils, it is important for them to be valid and reliable. This section describes steps that can be taken to obtain high-quality performance assessments.

Scoring performance assessments is a difficult and often time-consuming activity. The process is often complex and lengthy. Unlike when scoring selection items, teachers' interpretation and judgment are necessary for scoring performances and products. Each student produces or constructs a performance or product that is different from that of other students. This makes scoring difficult; the more criteria to address and the more variation in the products or performances students produce, the more time-consuming, fatiguing, and potentially invalid.

Scoring performance assessments is a difficult, time-consuming activity.

Further, like essays, performance assessments are subject to many ancillary factors that may not be relevant to scoring but may influence the teacher's judgment of the performance assessments. For example, teachers' scoring of products such as essays or reports are often influenced by the quality of a pupil's handwriting, neatness, sentence structure and flow, and knowledge of the pupil being scored. These and similar factors are not key aspects of the product, but they often weigh heavily in scoring. Teachers can rarely be completely unbiased observers of what their pupils do, because they know their pupils too well and have a set of built-in predispositions regarding each one. In each case, there are many irrelevant and distracting factors that can influence the teacher's judgments and the validity and reliability of performance assessments.

Distractions and personal feelings can introduce error into either the observation or judging process, thereby reducing the validity and reliability of the assessment.

The key to improving rating or scoring skills is to try to eliminate the distracting factors so that the assessment more closely reflects the pupil's actual performance. In performance assessments, the main source of error is the observer, who judges both what is happening during a performance and the quality of the performance. Beyond the issue of distractions, teachers can prepare their pupils well and ensure validity and reliability in various other ways.

Preparing Pupils

There are many ways teachers prepare their pupils for performance assessment. First and foremost, they provide good instruction. Pupils learn to set up and focus microscopes, build bookcases, write book reports, give oral speeches, measure with a ruler, perform musical selections, and speak French the same way they learn to solve simultaneous equations, find countries on a map, write a topic sentence, or balance a chemical equation. They are given instruction and practice. Achievement depends upon their being taught the things on which they are being assessed. One of the advantages of performance assessments is their explicit criteria, which focus instruction and assessment.

In preparing pupils for performance assessment, the teacher should inform and explain the criteria on which they will be judged (Mehrens, Popham, & Ryan, 1998). In many classrooms, teachers and pupils jointly discuss and define criteria for a desired performance or product. This helps them to understand what is expected of them by identifying the important dimensions of the performance or product. Another, less interactive way to do this is for the teacher to give pupils a copy of the checklist or rating form that will be used during their assessment. If performance criteria are not made clear to pupils, they may perform poorly, not because they are incapable, but because they were not aware of the teacher's expectations and the criteria for a good performance. In such cases, the performance ratings do not reflect the pupils' true achievement, and the grades they receive could lead to invalid decisions about their learning.

Unless students are informed about the performance criteria upon which they will be judged, they may not perform up to their abilities.

Validity

Validity is concerned with whether the information obtained from an assessment permits the teacher to make a correct decision about a pupil's learning. As discussed previously, either failure to instruct pupils on desired performances or the inability to control personal expectations can produce invalid information. Another factor that can reduce the validity of formal performance assessment is **bias**. When some factor such as race, native language, prior experience, gender, or disability differentiates the scores of one group from those of another (e.g., English-speaking and Spanish-speaking pupils, prior experience and inexperience, hearing disability and no hearing disability) we say the scores are biased. That is, judgments regarding the performance of one group of pupils are influenced by the inclusion of irrelevant, subjective criteria.

When irrelevant, subjective factors differentiate the scores of one group of pupils from another, the scores are said to be biased.

Suppose that oral reading performance was being assessed in a second grade classroom. Suppose also that in the classroom there was a group of pupils whose first language is Spanish. The oral reading assessment involved reading aloud from a storybook written in English. When the teacher reviewed her notes on the pupils' performances, she noticed that the Spanish-speaking pupils as a group did very poorly. Would the teacher be correct in saying that the Spanish-speaking pupils have poor oral reading skills? Would this be a valid conclusion to draw from the assessment evidence? A more reasonable interpretation would be that the oral reading assessment was measuring the Spanish-speaking pupils' familiarity with the English language rather than their oral reading performance. In essence, the assessment provided different information about the two groups (oral reading proficiency versus knowledge of English language). It would be a misinterpretation of the evidence to conclude that the Spanish-speaking pupils had poorer oral reading skills without taking into account the fact that they were required to read and pronounce unfamiliar English words. The results of the assessment were not valid for the teacher's desired decision about oral reading for the Spanish-speaking pupils.

Teachers should select performance criteria and settings that do not give an unfair advantage to any group of students.

When an assessment instrument provides information that is irrelevant to the decisions it was intended to help make, it is invalid. Thus, in all forms of assessment, but especially performance assessment, a teacher must select and use procedures, performance criteria, and settings that do not give an unfair advantage to some pupils because of cultural background, language, disability, or gender. Other sources of error that commonly affect the validity of performance assessments are teachers' reliance on mental rather than written record keeping and their being influenced by prior perceptions of a pupil. The longer the interval between an observation and the written scoring, the more likely the teacher is to forget important features of pupils' performance.

Teachers should write down performance assessments at the time they are observed in order to avoid memory error.

Often, teachers' prior knowledge of their pupils influences the objectivity of their performance ratings. Personality, effort, work habits, cooperativeness, and the like are all part of a teacher's perception of the pupils in his or her class. Often, these prior perceptions influence the rating a pupil is given: the likable, cooperative pupil with the pleasant personality may receive a higher rating than the standoffish, belligerent pupil, even though they performed similarly. Assessing pupils on the basis of their personal characteristics rather than their performance lowers the validity of the assessment. Each of these concerns threatens the validity of teacher interpretations and scores. These concerns are particularly difficult to overcome because of the complexity of performance assessment.

Assessing pupils on the basis of their personal characteristics rather than on their performance lowers the validity of the assessment.

Reliability

Reliability is concerned with the stability and consistency of assessments. Hence, the logical way to obtain information about the reliability of pupil performance is to observe and score two or more performances or products of the same kind. Doing this, however, is not reasonable in most school settings; once a formal assessment is made, instruction turns to a new topic. Few teachers can afford the class time necessary to obtain multiple assessments on a given topic. This reality raises an important problem with the reliability of performance assessments: they may lack generalization. Performances, products, and portfolios are more complex and fewer in number than selection or short-answer assessments. Because of such discrepancies in the quantity of information obtained from particular assessments, the teacher who employs performance assessments sees fewer examples of pupil mastery than when more narrow assessment approaches are used. The teacher's question then becomes how reliable is the limited information I have obtained from pupils? Does a single essay, a few show-your-work problems or a portfolio provide enough evidence that students will perform similarly on other essays, show-your-work problems, or portfolios?

Observing a performance more than once increases the reliability of the assessment but is time-consuming.

An important concern in interpreting performance assessments is the often low generalizability of pupils' performances, products, or portfolios.

Teachers are put on the horns of a dilemma. Because they want their pupils to learn more than facts and narrow topics, they employ performance assessments to ensure deeper, richer learning. However, by employing an in-depth and time-consuming approach, they often diminish the reliability of the assessment. This is a dilemma faced in classroom teachers' own assessments and in more general, statewide pupil assessments. There are few easy ways to overcome the dilemma. However, it is better to use evidence from imperfect performance assessments than to make uninformed decisions about important pupil achievement.

> **Key Assessment Tools 4.8**
> # IMPROVING VALIDITY AND RELIABILITY OF PERFORMANCE ASSESSMENTS
>
> - Know the purpose of the assessment from the beginning.
> - Teach and give pupils practice in the performance criteria.
> - State the performance criteria in terms of observable behaviors and avoid using adverbs such as *appropriately, correctly,* or *well* because their interpretation may shift from pupil to pupil. Use overt, well-described behaviors that can be seen by an observer and therefore are less subject to interpretation. Inform pupils of these criteria and focus instruction on them.
> - Select performance criteria that are at an appropriate level of difficulty for the pupils. The criteria used to judge the oral speaking performance of third-year debate pupils should be more detailed than those to judge first-year debate pupils.
> - Limit performance criteria to a manageable number. A large number of criteria makes observation difficult and causes errors that reduce the validity of the assessment information.
> - Maintain a written record of pupil performance. Checklists, rating scales, and rubrics are the easiest methods of recording pupil performance on important criteria, although more descriptive narratives are often desirable and informative. Tape recordings or videotapes may be used to provide a record of performance, so long as their use does not upset or distract the pupils. If a formal instrument cannot be used to record judgments of pupil performance, then informal notes of its strong and weak points should be taken.
> - Be sure the performance assessment is fair to all pupils.

Reliability is also affected when performance criteria or rating categories are vague and unclear. This forces the teacher to interpret them, and because interpretations often vary with time and situation, this introduces inconsistency into the assessment. One way to eliminate much of this inconsistency is to be explicit about the purpose of a performance assessment and to state the performance criteria and rubrics in terms of observable pupil behaviors. The objectivity of an observation can be enhanced by having several individuals independently observe and rate a pupil's performance. In situations where a group of teachers cooperate in developing criteria for a pupil performance, product, or portfolio, it is not difficult to have more than one teacher observe or examine a few pupils' products or performances to see whether scores are similar across teachers. This is a practice followed in performance assessments such as the College Board English Achievement Essay and in most statewide writing assessments.

Unclear or vague performance criteria increase teacher interpretation, which introduces inconsistency into the assessment.

Having more than one person observe and rate a performance increases the objectivity of the assessment.

Key Assessment Tools 4.8 contains guidelines for improving the validity and reliability of performance, product, and portfolio assessments:

Performance criteria should be realistic in terms of the students' developmental level.

Chapter Summary

- Performance assessments require pupils to demonstrate their knowledge by creating an answer, carrying out a process, or producing a product, rather than by selecting an answer. Performance assessments complement paper-and-pencil tests in classroom assessments.
- Performance assessments are useful for determining pupil learning in performance-oriented areas such as communication skills; psychomotor skills; athletic activities; concept acquisition; and affective characteristics.
- Performance assessments have many uses. They can chart pupil performance over time, provide diagnostic information about pupil learning, give pupils ownership of their learning, integrate the instructional and assessment processes, foster pupils' self-assessment of their work, and assemble into portfolios both cumulative evidence of

performance and concrete examples of pupils' work. Performance assessments can be used in assessing the work of pupils with special needs. The main disadvantage of performance assessments is the time it takes to prepare for, implement, and score them.

- Successful performance assessment requires a well-defined purpose for assessment; clear, observable performance criteria; an appropriate setting in which to elicit performance; and a scoring or rating method.

- The specific behaviors a pupil should display when carrying out a performance or the characteristics a pupil product should possess are called performance criteria. These criteria define the aspects of a good performance or product. They should be shared with pupils and used as the basis for instruction.

- The key to identifying performance criteria is to break down a performance or product into its component parts, since it is these parts that are observed and judged. It is often useful to involve pupils in identifying the criteria of products or performances. This provides them with a sense of involvement in learning and introduces them to important components of the desired performance.

- The number of performance criteria should be small, between 10 and 15, in order to focus on the most important aspects of performance and simplify the observation process. Teacher collaboration on common assessment areas or performances is advisable.

- Ambiguous words that cloud the meaning of performance criteria (e.g., *adequately, correctly, appropriate*) should be avoided; state specifically what is being looked for in the performance or product. Criteria should be stated so explicitly that another teacher could use them independently.

- Performance assessments may be scored and summarized either qualitatively or quantitatively. Anecdotal records and teacher narratives are qualitative descriptions of pupil characteristics and performances. Checklists, rating scales, and scoring rubrics are quantitative assessments of performance. A rubric describes the level at which a pupil may be performing a task. Portfolios may include either qualitative, quantitative, or both kinds of information about pupil performance.

- Checklists and rating scales are developed from the performance criteria for a performance or product. Checklists give the observer only two choices in judging each performance criterion: present or absent. Rating scales provide the observer with more than two choices in judging: for example, always, sometimes, never or excellent, good, fair, poor, failure. Rating scales may be numerical, graphic, or descriptive. Performance can be summarized across performance criteria numerically or with a scoring rubric.

- Portfolios are collections of pupils' work in an area that show change and progress over time. Portfolios may contain pupil products or pupil performances.

- Portfolios have many uses: focusing instruction on important performance activities; reinforcing the point that performances are important school outcomes; providing parents, pupils, and teachers with a perspective on pupil improvement; diagnosing weaknesses; allowing pupils to revisit, reflect on, and assess their work over time; grading pupils; and integrating instruction with assessment.

- Portfolio assessment is a form of performance assessment, and thus involves these four factors: definition of purpose, identification of clear performance criteria, establishment of a setting for performance, and construction of a scoring or rating scheme. In addition to performance criteria for each individual portfolio piece, it is often necessary to develop a set of performance criteria to assess or summarize the entire portfolio.

- To ensure valid performance assessment, pupils should be instructed on the desired performance criteria before being assessed.

- The validity of performance assessments can be improved by stating performance criteria in observable terms; setting performance criteria at an appropriate difficulty level for pupils; limiting the number of performance criteria; maintaining a written record of pupil performance; and checking to determine whether extraneous factors influenced a pupil's performance.

- Reliability can be improved by multiple observations of performance or by checking for agreement among observers viewing the same performance, product, or portfolio and using the same assessment criteria.

Questions for Discussion

1. What types of objectives are most suitably assessed using performance assessment?
2. How do formal and informal performance assessments differ in terms of pupil characteristics, validity and reliability of information, and usefulness for teacher decision making?
3. What are the advantages and disadvantages of performance assessments for teachers? For pupils?
4. How should a teacher determine the validity of a performance assessment?
5. How might instruction differ when a teacher desires to assess pupils' performances and products rather than their responses to selection-type tests?
6. What are some examples of how performance assessment can be closely linked to instruction? For example, how can performance assessment be used to involve pupils in the instructional process?

Activities

1. Select a subject area you might like to teach and identify one objective in that subject matter that cannot be assessed by selection or essay questions. Construct a performance or product assessment instrument for this objective. Provide the following information:
   (a) the objective and a brief description of the behavior or product you will assess and the grade level at which it will be taught.
   (b) a set of at least 10 observable performance criteria for judging the performance or product.
   (c) a method to score pupil performance.
   (d) a method to summarize performance into a single score.
   The assessment procedure used may be in the form of a checklist or a rating scale. A two- to three-page document should adequately provide the needed information. Be sure to focus on the clarity and specificity of the performance criteria and on the clarity and practicality of the scoring procedure.
2. Rewrite in clearer form the following performance criteria for assessing a pupil's poem. Remember, what you are trying to do is write performance criteria that most people will understand and interpret the same way.
   - Poem is original
   - Meaningfulness
   - Contains rhymes
   - Proper length
   - Well-focused
   - Good title
   - Appropriate vocabulary level

Review Questions

1. How do performance assessments differ from other types of assessment? What are the benefits of using performance assessment? The disadvantages?
2. What four steps must be attended to in carrying out performance assessment? What happens at each of these steps?

3. Why are performance criteria so important to performance assessment? How do they help the assessor not only with judging pupils' performance and products but also with planning and conducting instruction?

4. What are the differences between checklists, rating scales, and rubrics? How is each used to assess performance and products?

5. What are the main threats to the validity of performance assessments? How can validity be improved?

6. In what ways are scoring performance assessments similar to scoring essay questions?

7. What makes an effective scoring rubric?

8. What are some pros and cons of portfolios?

References

Arter, J. (1999). Teaching about performance assessment. *Educational Measurement: Issues and Practice, 18*(2), 30–44.

Bartz, D., Anderson-Robinson, S., & Hillman, L. (1994). Performance assessment: Make them show what they know. *Principal, 73,* 11–14.

Brennan, R. L, & Johnson, E. G. (1995). Generalizability of performance assessments. *Educational Measurement: Issues and Practice, 14*(4), 25–27.

Fager, J. J., Plake, B. S., & Impara, J. C. (1997). *Examining teacher educators' knowledge of classroom assessment: A pilot study.* Paper presented at the National Council on Measurement in Education National Conference, Chicago.

Goodrich, H. (1997). Understanding rubrics. *Educational Leadership, 54*(4), 14–17.

Herbert, E. A. (1992). Portfolios invite reflection from both students and staff. *Educational Leadership, 49*(8), 58–61.

Madaus, G. F., & O'Dwyer, L. M. (1999). A short history of performance assessment: Lessons learned. *Phi Delta Kappan, 80*(9), 688–695.

McTighe, J. (1996). Performance-based assessment in the classroom: A planning framework. In R. Blum & J. Arter (eds.), *Student performance assessment in an era of restructuring.* Alexandria, VA: Association for Supervision and Curriculum Development.

Mehrens, W. A., Popham, W. J., & Ryan, J. M. (1998). How to prepare students for performance assessments. *Educational Measurement: Issues and Practice, 17*(1), 18–22.

Quality counts '99. Rewarding results, punishing failure. ***Education Week* (January 11, 1999).**

Ryan, J., & Miyasaka, J. (1995). Current practices in teaching and assessment: What is driving the change? *NAASP Bulletin, 79,* 1–10.

Stiggins, R. (1999). Evaluating classroom assessment training in teacher education programs. *Educational Measurement: Issues and Practice, 18*(1), 23–27.

Swanson, D., Norman, G., & Linn, R. L. (1995).Performance-based assessment: Lessons from the health professions. *Educational Researcher, 24*(5), 5–11, 35.

Wiggins, G. (1992). Creating tests worth taking. *Educational Leadership, 44*(8), 26–33.

Wiggins, G., & McTighe, J. (1998). *Understanding by design.* Alexandria, VA: Association for Supervision and Curriculum Development.

PART THREE

CHAPTER FIVE

Corporate Ethical Leadership
Corporate Culture and Reputation Management

The trouble with the rat race is that, even if you win, you're still a rat.

—LILY TOMLIN

When we speak, we are afraid our words will not be heard, nor welcomed; but when we are silent, we are still afraid. So it is better to speak, Remembering that we were never meant to survive all.

—ANDRE LORDE

Take care to guard against all greed, for though one may be rich, one's life does not consist of possessions.

—LUKE 12: 15

Implications and Accountability: Does Ethics = Value?

Good ethics is good business. Have you heard that before? Did you believe it? Theorists argue about whether ethical decisions lead to more significant profits than unethical decisions. While we are all familiar with examples of unethical decisions leading to high profits, there is general agreement that, in the long run, ethics pays. Lao Tzu in the *Tao Te Ching* contends there is no crime greater than having too many desires and no misfortune greater than being covetous.[1] How would Taoism view the acts and intentions of a profit-maximizing firm in today's market?

Consider from a stakeholder perspective the demise of small bookstores all over the country. In the past several years, large, multipurpose bookstores such as Borders Books and Barnes and Noble have seemed to take over the literary consumption landscape. Chicago alone has seen the collapse of a number of old standbys, bookstores that had been in the city for years serving a specific, sometimes idiosyncratic, population rather than the entire book-purchasing community. These stores (Krochs and Brentanos, Stuart Brent, Guild Books and others) could not survive next to chain superstores that provide a greater selection of low-priced alternatives.

Stuart Brent, a longtime bookseller on prestigious Michigan Avenue in Chicago, in 1996 was forced out of business by competition from Borders and other chain bookstores opening down the street. Brent's store was one where the salespeople could remember your name, where there were large comfy chairs in which to peruse the books, where there were experts available on literary issues and where they knew just the right book for your Uncle Gordy. Brent's sales went down 30% with the opening of a Borders bookstore three blocks away. "Supermarkets," he snorts. "Philistines. My father used to speak of 'men you'd have to stand on tiptoes to talk to.' Where are those men today?" Even Mayor Richard Daley mourned the loss in a telegram sent to Brent on closing day, "Michigan Avenue will miss you, as much as it was enhanced by your fine store and elegant presence."[2] A traditional tale of David and Goliath?

The chain superstores argue that it is not. Instead, these stores contend that they are merely serving the needs of their customers in a more effective, efficient manner and therefore deserve a larger share of the market. "It's no longer simply the big, stupid bestseller stores and the small, elegant, literary bookstores," says shopper and Northwestern University professor Joseph Epstien. "Places like Barnes and Noble and Borders stock the good books, too. I doubt that Stuart Brent had anything these stores don't, except in his specialty of psychoanalytic books."[3] Perhaps these larger bookstores aren't so much predators as they are simply players—answering the needs of the public.

Is there any responsibility of a large chain store entering a small community market? Consider as well the tales of Walgreen stores entering small towns where there is one established pharmacy equipped with a pharmacist who has been serving that public for many years. The pharmacist cannot compete with the economies of scale available to a large firm like Walgreen, so she closes her doors. Is Walgreen to blame? Perhaps. But is it at *fault*? It is using its size to a competitive advantage to reap greater profits for its owners.

Consider what ethical and unethical steps might be taken in the name of profits. Is offering a larger selection, lower prices and a different ambience unethical? Is an act ethical because it results in higher profit or in spite of it? Consider the examples suggested by Jason Lunday and opinion expressed in Al Gini's article. Accountability is directly addressed in the discussion of the Federal Sentencing Guidelines—some ask what better way to encourage ethical behavior than to financially reward those who engage in it and financially punish those who do not? On the issue of accountability, one might also want to check out the perspectives of various consumer and advocacy groups in connection with well-known businesses at any of the following websites:

- www.bankofamericafraud.org
- www.boycottameritech.com
- www.cokespotlight.org
- www.ihatestarbucks.com

- www.noamazon.com
- www.starbucked.com
- www.walmartsurvivor.com

Moreover, though there are many justifications for ethics in business, often the discussion returns to, well, returns—the business case for the return on investment. There is evidence that good ethics is good business; yet the dominant thinking is that, if one can't measure it, it is not important. Consequently, efforts have been made to measure the bottom-line impact of ethical decision making. Persuasive evidence of impact comes from a recent study titled, "Developing Value: The Business Case for Sustainability in Emerging Markets," based on a study produced jointly by SustainAbility, the Ethos Institute and the International Finance Corporation. The research found that, in emerging markets, cost savings, productivity improvement, revenue growth and access to markets were the most important business benefits of sustainability activities. Environmental process improvements and human resource management were the most significant areas of sustainability action. The report concludes that it does pay for businesses in emerging markets to pursue a wider role on environmental and social issues, citing cost reductions, productivity, revenue growth and market access as areas of greatest return for multinational enterprises (MNEs).

In addition, studies have found that there are a number of expected—and measurable—outcomes to ethics programs in organizations. Some look to the end results of firms that have placed ethics and social responsibility at the forefront of their activities, while others look to those firms who have been successful and determine the role that ethics might have played. With regard to the former, consider Johnson & Johnson, known for its quick and effective handling of its experience with tainted Tylenol. J&J had sales in 2001 of $33 billion, almost triple those of the previous decade and representing its 69th year of consecutive sales increases. It has had 17 consecutive years of double-digit earnings increases and 39 consecutive years of dividend increases. Its market value ended in 2001 at more than $180 billion, up from $38 billion in 1991—evidence that a firm that lives according to its strong values and a culture that supports those values not only can survive but can also sustain profit over the long term. CEO Ralph Larsen credits these successes directly to the J&J Credo. "It's the glue that holds our decentralized company together. . . . For us, the credo is our expression of managing the multiple bottom lines of products, people, planet and profits. It's the way we conceptualize our total impact on society."[4]

> There is clear evidence that a good reputation gains a company more customers, better employees, more investors, improved access to credit and greater credibility with government. . . . The difference between a company with ethical capital and one with an ethical deficit—perceived or real—can even determine their "license to operate" in some emerging markets.[5]

> Whether at the World Trade Organization, or at the OECD, or at the United Nations, an irrefutable case can be made that a universal acceptance of the rule of law, the outlawing of corrupt practices, respect for workers' rights, high health and safety standards, sensitivity to the environment, support for education and the protection and nurturing of children are not only justifiable against the criteria of morality and justice. The simple truth is that these are good for business and most business people recognize this.[6]

> We all pay for poverty and unemployment and illiteracy. If a large percentage of society falls into a disadvantaged class, investors will find it hard to source skilled and alert workers; manufacturers will have a limited market for their products; criminality will scare away foreign investments and internal migrants to limited areas of opportunities will strain basic services and lead to urban blight. Under these conditions, no country can move forward economically and sustain development. . . . It therefore makes business sense for corporations to complement the efforts of government in contributing to social development.[7]

> Our findings, both cross-sectional and longitudinal, indicate that there are indeed systematic linkages among community involvement, employee morale and business performance in business enterprises. To the best of our knowledge, this is the first time that such linkages

have been demonstrated empirically. Moreover, the weight of the evidence produced here indicates that community involvement is positively associated with business performance, employee morale is positively associated with business performance and the interaction of community involvement—external involvement—with employee morale—internal involvement—is even more strongly associated with business performance than is either "involvement" measure alone.[8]

Through the readings that follow, this chapter seeks to delineate the nature of an ethical corporation and how one might lead that organization. What is ethical leadership and what are its implications? What is the impact of a corporation's culture; how does one build and sustain an ethical corporate culture and what are the costs of its failure?

Ethical Leadership

The results of a poll conducted by the World Economic Forum released in 2003 suggests that trust is not only declining in institutions worldwide, but also leaders are suffering from an even greater decline in public trust than the companies they lead. Given the scandals of 2000 forward, this finding may not be surprising since the general public blames corporate leadership—correctly in many cases—for the corruption and misdeeds in corporate America. Of the eight leadership categories tested, only the leaders of nongovernment organizations enjoy the trust of a clear majority of their public. In fact, of the eight categories, executives of multinational companies ranked seventh, beating out only leaders of the United States.[9] How does one counteract these perceptions and create instead a perception of ethical leadership?

Another survey may offer insight into these numbers. The results of a survey of 20,000 articles in the U.K press evidence that CEOs of large companies mention ethics or social responsibility issues in only 5% of their communications, compared to 40% that discuss financial matters. (This research was conducted before the collapse of Enron and, in a strange twist of research, the study found that CEOs in the oil and gas sector were the most likely to raise ethical issues!)

Overall, a perception of ethical leadership is most often based on the leaders' communication abilities and opportunities. When employees are satisfied with the way in which their leaders communicate, the results can be significant. These employees are more satisfied with their jobs; they feel that everyone is on the same team and working toward the same goal; they feel confident of their longevity with the firm; and they feel that their companies' products or services are better than their competitors'.[10] To create that perception, corporate leaders must do more than simply putting their values into action. They must learn to disseminate that ethical decision-making process.

The results of a qualitative study of the nature of ethical leadership emphasize the importance of being perceived as a leader with a people orientation, as well as the importance of leaders engaging in visible ethical action. Traits are also important and include receptivity, listening and openness, in addition to the more traditionally considered traits of integrity, honesty and trustworthiness. Finally, being perceived as having a broad ethical awareness and concern for multiple stakeholders, and using ethical decision processes are also important.[11] Those perceived as ethical leaders do many of the things "traditional leaders" do (e.g., reinforce the conduct they are looking for, create standards for behavior, etc.), but within the context of an ethics agenda. People perceive that the ethical leader's goal is not simply job performance, but performance that is consistent with a set of ethical values and principles. And, ethical leaders demonstrate caring for people (employees and external stakeholders) in the process.

However, as mentioned above, all of these traits and behaviors must be visible. If an executive is "quietly ethical" within the confines of the top management team, but more distant employees don't know about it, she or he is not likely to be perceived as an ethical leader. Traits and behaviors must be socially visible and understood in order to be noticed and influence perceptions.[12] People notice when an executive walks the talk and acts on concerns for the common good, society as a whole and the long term because executives are expected to be focused on the financial bottom line and the short-term demands of stock analysts. When they focus on these broader and longer-term concerns, people notice. Finally, making courageous decisions in tough situations represents another way ethical leaders get noticed. Ethical leaders are "courageous enough to say 'no' to conduct that would be inconsistent with [their] values."[13] This type of courageous decision making is certain to garner attention in the organization and to stand out from a neutral or unethical landscape, conveying information about the importance of standing up for what's right.

Corporate Culture

Every organization has a culture, represented by a shared pattern of beliefs, expectations and meanings that influence and guide the thinking and behaviors of the members of an organization or group. Though somewhat ethereal, it is important to consider the cultures of firms because it is the culture that encourages and influences decision making. Consider a firm with a culture to play throughout the day—with Ping-Pong tables in the offices and a cafeteria replete with board games and other distractions, but everyone is also expected to remain in the office until all work is complete for that day, no matter how late that becomes. If you enter that firm with a 9 to 5 attitude, where you intend to give your all to work throughout the day but then to leave as the clock strikes 5, you might not have a "fit." The same might hold true for a firm's values. If you join a firm with a culture that supports other values than those with which you are comfortable, there will be values conflicts—for better or worse.

Some common elements of corporate culture include:

- There are no generically effective or ineffective cultures.
- Culture is self-reinforcing and socially learned.
- Strong, cohesive cultures are double-edged swords.
- Cultures are rooted in successful problem solving and actions.
- Culture's influence operates outside of our awareness.
- Culture is linked to organization performance.
- Cultural change takes time and requires multiple strategies.

A firm's culture can be its sustaining value—that which offers it direction during challenging times. It can, however, also constrain an organization to the common ways of managing issues—"that's how things have always been done here," "that's our prevailing climate." Consider a firm that has lingered for decades under weak management, a lack of any internal corporate controls, little oversight, a sales performance-based significant bonus plan and a product that has been successful because it has suited a need. Now that need has changed slightly and the firm is under pressure to survive. With "the way that we've always done it," employees may have the opportunity—even the imperative—to cut corners and make decisions that would never be tolerated in another culture. "When you've got the incentives [in the form of higher pay cause of bigger profits] to take risks, the system ought to at least throw up some red flags. People are going to overcompete and take risks and sometimes break laws."[14] Given recent downturns in the economy, this is precisely the environment at many organizations—"There is enormous pressure on corporations, never been greater earnings pressure. That will lead people at the top to press down [to workers]—'you will make money for the corporation.' "[15]

Corporate Culture Audits

How do you detect a potentially damaging or ethically challenged corporate culture—sometimes referred to as a "toxic" culture? The first clear sign would be a lack of any generally accepted base values for the organizations. In the absence of other values, the only value is profit—at any cost. Therefore, without additional guidance from the top, a firm is sending a clear message that a worker should do whatever it takes to reap profits. In addition, there are warning signs in the various component areas of the organization. How does the firm treat its customers, suppliers, clients, workers? The management of its internal and external relationships are critical evidence of its values. How does the firm manage its finances? Of course, a firm can be in a state of financial disaster without engaging in even one unethical act (and vice versa), but the manner in which it manages and communicates its financial environment is telling. PricewaterhouseCoopers offers guidance as to early warning signs of an ethically troubled organization that might indicate areas of concern regarding fraud, conflicts of interest, ineffective controls, imbalance of power, inappropriate pressure or other areas, including (but not limited to):

1. Inability to generate positive cash flows despite positive earnings and growth.
2. Unusual pressure to achieve accounting-based financial objectives.
3. Compensation tied closely or only to financial results.
4. Debt covenants violated (or close to being so).
5. Increased liabilities with no apparent source of funding.
6. Off-balance sheet transactions.
7. Complex or creative structures.
8. Ratios/trends that buck expectations or industry trends.
9. Large returns or revenue credits after the close of the period.
10. Large number of nonstandard adjusting entries.
11. History of unreliable accounting estimates.
12. Numerous related-party transactions.
13. Transactions with no/questionable business purposes.

In addition, PwC suggests the following organizational signals:

1. Unusually complex organizational structure; numerous entities with unclear purpose.
2. Insufficient management depth in key positions, especially positions that manage risks.
3. Rapid growth or downsizing placing stress on organizational resources.
4. Resignations of management or board members for reasons other than retirement, health or conflict of interest.
5. Member of board or senior management possibly involved in or aware of financial manipulation (resulting in restatement) still connected with the organization.
6. Finance/accounting staff understaffed.
7. Internal audit department undersized/understaffed.
8. No audit committee or ineffective committee.
9. Management conveys a lifestyle beyond financial means.
10. Scope of internal audit seems too narrow.
11. Failure to address weaknesses in controls or process.

The Institute for Business, Technology and Ethics cites the following eight traits of a healthy organizational culture:

1. Openness and humility from top to bottom of organization.
2. An environment of accountability and personal responsibility.
3. Freedom from risk-taking within appropriate limits.
4. A fierce commitment to "doing it right."
5. A willingness to tolerate and learn from mistakes.
6. Unquestioned integrity and consistency.
7. A pursuit of collaboration, integration and holistic thinking.
8. Courage and persistence in the face of difficulty.

Finally, the Institute of Business Ethics (U.K.) has created a self-assessment checklist for organizations that allows a company to determine where it stands with regard to core issues common to many social or business ethics standards (see Table 5.1).

TABLE 5.1 Self-Assessment Checklist for Businesses

Human Rights and Labor Practices	
Business ethics	Do you have a code of business conduct, ethics or business principles in the company? Is it circulated to all employees and translated as appropriate? Is it available to all stakeholders?
Child labor	Do you comply with ILO conventions prohibiting employment of children under 15 years of age and preventing exposure of staff under 18 years of age to any hazardous conditions?
Suppliers	Do you encourage and/or monitor key suppliers for their compliance with basic workplace standards and human rights? Do you build such information into the selection and review process?
Discrimination, diversity	Do you have an equal opportunities policy? If so, how have you ensured that all staff are aware of your policy? Are salaries, appointments and promotions considered on merit? Is there an objective system of appraisal to enable this?
Freedom of association	Is your workforce freely able to form/join trade unions (or alternative collective units) and to bargain collectively?
Discipline/grievance	Is there a recognized and fair means of discipline in place? Similarly is there a formal and fair grievance process?
Human rights	Are the fundamental principles outlined in the UN Declaration of Human Rights captured in policies of employment and other relevant business practices? Do you have strict codes of conduct for any security personnel employed or contracted?
Health and safety	Do you have a senior manager responsible for ensuring that your product and operations do not pose an unacceptable risk to staff, contractors or visitors? Are all injuries recorded and causes investigated and remedied?
Working hours	Do any of your staff work more than a 48-hour week? If so, do you have systems in place to ensure compliance with the European Working Time Directive?
Remuneration/reward	Do you meet the minimum wage requirements in all of the countries in which you operate? Are all wages sufficient as to ensure staff can meet at least their basic human needs?
Community Involvement	
Consultation	Do you consult communities on business decisions that may have significant impacts upon them before as well as after the event?
Responsibility	Where decisions have an adverse effect on a community, e.g., redundancies, do you take all reasonable steps to work with local communities to minimize these impacts?
Transparency and Accountability	
Stakeholder engagement	Do you engage with external stakeholders? On what basis have you chosen your stakeholders? Do you build stakeholder views into decision making? Do you provide feedback to these stakeholders on your performance or impacts?
Performance measurement	Do you measure and monitor social performance using qualitative or quantitative indicators? Do you set improvement targets? Are such targets built into management objectives?
Disclosure/reporting	Do you publish or disclose your social performance or social impacts, e.g., via a social report, as part of your annual report or on your website? Is this done regularly? Do you invite feedback from readers?
External verification	Is your CSR management system or your social performance externally audited? Are the results of the audit published?
Sustainable development	Do you have an environmental management system in place? Do you regularly evaluate and seek to minimize your environmental impacts?

Consider the messages sent to each and all stakeholders by these behaviors or activities. These are all responsible for creating a culture that permeates the entire organization.

Corporate Missions and Codes

Before articulating the culture through a code of conduct or statement of values, a firm must first determine its mission. A code of conduct then may delineate this foundation both for internal stakeholders such as employees as well as external stakeholders such as customers. The code therefore both enhances corporate reputation and also provides concrete guidance for internal decision making, thus creating a built-in risk management system. When David Packard passed away, his business partner in creating HP, Bill Hewlett, commented, "As far as the company is concerned, the greatest thing he left behind him was a code of ethics known as the HP Way."[16] The vision can be inspiring—should be inspiring. Jim Collins, author of *Built to Last* and *Good to Great,* explains, "Contrary to business school doctrine, we did not find 'maximizing shareholder wealth' or 'profit maximization' as the dominant driving force or primary objective through the history of most of the visionary companies. They have tended to produce a cluster of objectives, of which money is only one—and not necessarily the primary one."[17] By establishing (especially through a participatory process) the core tenets on which a company is built, corporate leadership is effectively laying down the law with regard to the basis and objectives for all future decisions. As is evidenced by the Trevino article in this chapter, however, this is only the first step.

The 1990s brought a proliferation of corporate codes of conduct and mission statements as part of the corporate response to the Federal Sentencing Guidelines (see below)—a 2002 survey found that 75% of these mention the word *ethics.*[18] How successful these codes are depends in large part on the process by which they are conceived and written, as well as their implementation. As with the construction of a personal code or mission, it is critical to first ask yourself what you stand for or what the company stands for. Why does the firm exist, what are its purposes and how will it implement these objectives? Once you make these determinations, how will you share them and encourage a commitment to them among your colleagues and subordinates?

Implementation of a code often requires change—or at least the management of the current environment. Libby Hartman, Senior Director for Organizational Change Management at Cap Gemini Ernst & Young, cautions that one rarely sees change without the prior presence of pain. We don't abandon a current direction unless it is intolerable to continue. So, the first step is to evidence that pain—the basis for the intolerance. Why can't you continue as you are currently? Often the answer is easier if one considers the following image:

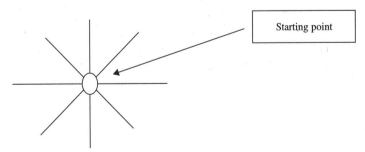

You may be very close in ideology if you're near the center but, if you happen to be on a different line than someone else, as time progresses, you'll grow further apart. It may not appear to be problematic in the beginning; but consider how far apart the two lines will become as the company matures.

The second step in support of this change is the articulation of a clear vision regarding the firm's direction. The Ethics Resource Center provides the following guidelines for writing an ethics code:

1. Be clear about the objectives that the code is intended to accomplish.
2. Get support and ideas for the code from all levels of the organization.

3. Be aware of the latest developments in the laws and regulations that affect your industry.

4. Write as simply and clearly as possible. Avoid legal jargon and empty generalities.

5. Respond to real-life questions and situations.

6. Provide resources for further information and guidance.

7. In all its forms, make it user-friendly because ultimately a code fails if it is not used.

The third step in this process is to identify clear steps as to how this cultural shift will occur. You have a code, but you can't simply "print, post and pray," as Ethics Resource Center president Stuart Gilman has referred to Enron's experience. Do you just post a sign on the wall that says, "Let's make more profits!" Of course not; you need to have processes and procedures in place that support and then sustain that vision. The same holds true for a vision of ethical conduct and the maintenance of an ethical culture.

Finally, to have an effective code that will successfully impact culture, there must be a belief throughout the organization that this culture is actually possible, achievable. If conflicts remain that will prevent certain components from being realized, or if key leadership is not on board, no one will have faith in the changes articulated.

In evaluating the establishment of codes of conduct according to a set of universal moral standards, Wharton professor Mark Schwartz developed a "code of ethics for corporate codes of ethics." Consider how the principles of trustworthiness, respect, responsibility, fairness, caring and citizenship can be embodied in the code creation process and the code, itself.

1. The above six standards should be included in the code, respected by other code content and given priority over bottom line concerns.

2. Code content should be understandable, achievable and justified.

3. All employees should be brought into the code creation process by offering each employee an opportunity to comment on the code.

4. Codes should be widely distributed and made fully accessible to the public.

5. Sufficient training, support and reinforcement should be provided in relation to the code.

6. The board of directors, CEO, president and all senior managers are obligated to demonstrate their support for the code, particularly by acting as role models through their own behavior.

7. Companies should enforce their codes and do so in a consistent and fair manner.

8. Sufficient protections should be provided to employees who report violations of the code.

9. Companies should ensure that a mechanism is in place to monitor and obtain feedback on their codes.[19]

Schwartz explains that the process by which one can change a culture is fluid. Such a transformation "occurs only after you have successfully altered some people's attitudes, which produces a modification in action, which may produce some group benefit for a period of time. People then need to see a connection between the modified behavior and the benefit, which then encourages them to adopt the new attitude, which then modifies their own behavior."[20]

Reputation Management

Several readings in this chapter consider the corporate response to public demands for ethical behavior and the concern for the "appearance of propriety," the corporate reputation. As you review the readings in this section, ponder the following (facetious and sarcastic) recommendations for leadership offered by Gen. Colin Powell as a result of the frustration he experienced during the mishandling of the U.S. hostage crisis in Iran from 1979–81:

1. Release facts slowly, behind the pace at which they are already leaking to the public.

2. Don't tell the whole story until forced to do so.

3. Emphasize what went well and euphemize what went wrong.

4. Become indignant at any suggestion of poor judgment or mistakes.

5. Disparage any facts other than your own.

6. Accuse critics of Monday-morning generalship.

7. Accept general responsibility at the top, thus clearing everybody at fault below.[21]

Why do firms engage in ethical behavior? Earlier chapters have suggested profit motives but, as also discussed, an ethical decision does not always lead to the highest profits possible. Perhaps the firm engages in ethical decision making because "it's the right thing to do," as Sears Roebuck and Co. says in its ethics materials. Perhaps, however, as some of the readings in this section suggest, engaging in ethical behavior, implementing ethics programs, or instituting codes of conduct all contribute both to the internal culture of the firm as well as to the external stakeholders' perceptions of the firm. Is there anything wrong with paying attention to these external perceptions?

Enforcing Culture: The U.S. Sentencing Commission Guidelines

The United States Sentencing Commission, an independent agency in the United States Judiciary, was created in 1984 to regulate sentencing policy in the federal court system. Before that, disparity in sentencing, arbitrary punishments and crime control had been significant congressional issues. In mandating sentencing procedures, Congress through the USSC has been able to incorporate the original purposes of sentencing, bringing some of these challenges under control.

In 1987, the USSC prescribed mandatory sentencing guidelines that apply to individual and organizational defendants in the federal system, bringing some uniformity and fairness to the system. These prescriptions, based on the severity of the offense, assign most federal crimes to one of 43 "offense levels." Each offender also is placed into a criminal history category based upon the extent and recency of past misconduct. The court is then to input this information into a sentencing grid and determine the offender's guideline range (ranges are either in 6-month intervals or 25%, whichever is greater), subject to adjustments.

The relevance of these guidelines to our exploration of ethics and, in particular, to our discussion of the corporate proactive efforts to create an ethical workplace, is that the USSC strived in its guidelines to create both a legal and an ethical corporate environment through these adjustments. The guidelines seek to reward corporations that create an effective compliance system so that they are not penalized (or the penalty is reduced) if they have an effective program but they find themselves in court as a result of a bad apple or two. On the other hand, firms that did not have effective compliance systems would be sentenced additionally to a term of probation and ordered to develop a program during that time.

The relevant language is found in section 8 of the guidelines, which identifies those specific acts of an organization that can serve as "due diligence" in preventing crime. These include:

1. Established effective compliance standards and procedures ("reasonably designed, implemented and enforced so that it will generally be effective in preventing and detecting criminal conduct").[22]

2. Assigned specific high-level person(s) to oversee compliance.

3. Used due care not to delegate important responsibilities to known high-risk persons.

4. Communicated its program effectively to all employees and agents.

5. Monitored and audited program operation and established a retribution-free means for employees to report possible violations to management.

6. Consistently disciplined employee violations.

7. Responded promptly and appropriately to any offenses and remedied any program deficiencies.[23]

Though these steps are likely to lead to an effective program, "[such a program] is more than checking off the seven items on a list. This concept of 'due diligence' is a restless standard, as flexible as changing events reflected in the day's headlines and as creative as the minds of potential wrongdoers."[24] For instance, the Guidelines require an investigation in response to a report of wrongdoing, but they also seem to require more than that. A firm must learn from its mistakes and take steps to prevent recurrences such as follow-up investigation and program enhancements. The USSC also mandates consideration of the size of the organization, the number and nature of its business risks, and the prior history of the organization, mitigating factors such as self-reporting of violations, cooperation with authorities, acceptance of responsibility, as well as aggravating factors such as its involvement in or tolerance of criminal activity, a violation of a prior order or its obstruction of justice. These standards are to be judged against applicable industry standards; however, this requires that each firm benchmark against comparable companies.

In a 1997 survey of members of the Ethics Officers Association, 47% of ethics officers reported that the guidelines were an influential determinant of their firm's commitment to ethics,[25] and another commission study showed that the guidelines influenced 44.5% of these officers to enhance their existing compliance programs.[26]

To provide some context to this exploration, consider which offenses are most likely to reap a fine for an organization. In 2001, the commission received information on 238 organizations sentenced under Chapter 8 (a 21.7% decrease from the previous year). The sentenced organizations had pled guilty in 92.4% of the cases—30% of fines and restitution were issued for cases of fraud, with the next most common crimes to be antitrust and import/export violations (6.7% each). Of those violations that are not included in the fine list, violations of environmental laws with regard to water topped the list at 13%. The mean restitution imposed was $4 million and the mean fine was $2 million.

As you read the following materials, put yourself in the position of someone who is establishing an organization from the ground up. What type of leader would you want to be? How would you create that image or perception? Do you create a mission statement for the firm, a code of conduct? What process would you use to do so? Would you create an ethics and/or compliance program and how would you then integrate the mission statement and program throughout your organization? What do you anticipate might be your successes and challenges?

Application to the Global Business Environment

As discussed with regard to the ethical principles governing global business, there are a number of externally imposed, voluntary codes of conduct. The items refer to global business, while others might be promulgated by professional organizations or accrediting bodies, depending on the organization's industry or the practice involved (i.e., accounting, marketing and so on). Though valuable in many circumstances, the challenges with regard to these voluntary codes are myriad. For instance, based on what values should a global code be developed? Some firms have been accused of imposing American values worldwide, without any sensitivity to the cultural conflicts that might exist in some locations, nor to the sense of colonialism and paternalism that such an imposition creates. In addition, once a firm agrees to either its own codes or that of an outside body, how will the code be enforced? Who will ensure that a firm lives up to the prescribed standards?

With regard to labor codes, and in connection with apparel and footwear manufacturers and brands in particular, an entire industry of monitors has been established. These include internal monitors (firm employees), external monitors (outsiders hired by the firm to monitor its factories or contractors' factories), and external independent monitors (others hired by a third party to monitor according to prior agreement with the manufacturer or brand). The Fair Labor Association, for example, is an industry-supported organization that established a code of conduct and then monitors its signatories to ensure compliance. The signatory might have an entire internal monitoring structure but also will allow FLA monitors to visit their factories or contractor factories.

Critics of these voluntary codes and monitoring regimes claim that they replace effective governmental monitoring or regulation of labor environments. Others see voluntary codes simply as marketing tools, designed to enhance the firm's public relations image. They worry that codes can become mere window dressing and not address the key issues facing workers today, such as the right to organize.

Moral Leadership and Business Ethics

—Al Gini

How do you judge the ethics of a leader? What makes one leader ethical and another unethical? Does it depend on the impact of that leader on her or his followers? Gini identifies the parameters within which we might appropriately judge a leader and the structural restraints imposed upon corporate leadership. Consider the impact of these restraints on the decisions and actions of leaders. Do they justify any (or all) leadership decisions?

How do we judge the ethics of a leader? Clearly, no leader can be expected to be perfect in every decision and action made. As John Gardner has pointed out, particular consequences are never a reliable assessment of leadership.[1] The quality and worth of leadership can only be measured in terms of what a leader intends, values, believes in or stands for—in other words, character. In *Character: America's Search for Leadership*, Gail Sheehy argued, as did Aristotle before her, that character is the most crucial and most elusive element of leadership. The root of the word "character" comes from the Greek word for engraving. As applied to human beings, it refers to the enduring marks or etched-in factors in our personality, which include our in-born talents as well as the learned and acquired traits imposed upon us by life and experience. These engravings define us, set us apart and motivate behavior.

In regard to leadership, said Sheehy, character is fundamental and prophetic. The "issues (of leadership) are those of today and will change in time. Character is what was yesterday and will be tomorrow."[2] For Sheehy, character establishes both our day-to-day demeanor and our destiny. Therefore, it is not only useful but essential to examine the character of those who desire to lead us. As a journalist and longtime observer of the political scene, Sheehy contends that the Watergate affair of the early 1970s serves as a perfect example of the links between character and leadership. As Richard Nixon demonstrated so well, said Sheehy: "The Presidency is not the place to work out one's personal pathology."[3] Leaders rule us, run things, wield power. Therefore, said Sheehy, we must be careful whom we choose as leaders. Because whom we choose, is what we shall be. If, as Heraclitus wrote, "character is fate," the fate our leaders reap will also be our own.

Putting aside the particular players and the politics of the episode, Watergate has come to symbolize the failings and failures of people in high places. Watergate now serves as a watershed, a turning point, in our nation's concern for integrity, honesty and fair play from all kinds of leaders. It is not a mere coincidence that the birth of business ethics as an independent, academic discipline can be dated from the Watergate affair and the trials that came out of it. No matter what our failings as individuals, Watergate sensitized us to the importance of ethical standards and conduct from those who direct the course of our political and public lives. What society is now demanding, and what business ethics is advocating, is that our business leaders and public servants should be held accountable to an even higher standard of behavior than we might demand and expect of ourselves.

Al Gini, "Moral Leadership and Business Ethics." Reprinted by permission. Al Gini is an associate professor of philosophy at Loyola University of Chicago and managing editor of *Business Ethics Quarterly*.

Mutual Purposes and Goals

The character, goals and aspirations of a leader are not developed in a vacuum. Leadership, even in the hands of a strong, confident, charismatic leader remains, at bottom, relational. Leaders, good or bad, great or small, arise out of the needs and opportunities of a specific time and place. Leaders require causes, issues and, most importantly, a hungry and willing constituency. Leaders may devise plans, establish an agenda, bring new and often radical ideas to the table, but all of them are a response to the milieu and membership of which they are a part. If leadership is an active and ongoing relationship between leaders and followers, then a central requirement of the leadership process is for leaders to evoke and elicit consensus in their constituencies, and conversely for followers to inform and influence their leaders. This is done in at least two ways, through the use of power and education.

The term "power" comes from the Latin *posse:* to do, to be able, to change, to influence or effect. To have power is to possess the capacity to control or direct change. All forms of leadership must make use of power. The central issue of power in leadership is not, "Will it be used?" but, rather, "Will it be used wisely and well?" According to James MacGregor Burns, leadership is not just about directed results; it is also about offering followers a choice among real alternatives. Hence, leadership assumes competition, conflict and debate whereas brute power denies it.[4] "Leadership mobilizes," said Burns, "naked power coerces."[5] But power need not be dictatorial or punitive to be effective. Power can also be used in a noncoercive manner to orchestrate, direct and guide members of an organization in the pursuit of a goal or series of objectives. Leaders must engage followers, not merely direct them. Leaders must serve as models and mentors, not martinets. "Power without morality," said novelist James Baldwin, "is no longer power."

For Peter Senge teaching is one of the primary jobs of leadership.[6] The "task of leader as teacher" is to empower people with information, offer insights, new knowledge, alternative perspectives on reality. The "leader as teacher," said Senge, is not just about "teaching" people how "to achieve their vision" but, rather, is about fostering learning, offering choices and building consensus.[7] Effective leadership recognizes that in order to build and achieve community, followers must become reciprocally coresponsible in the pursuit of a common enterprise. Through their conduct and teaching, leaders must try to make their fellow constituents aware that they are all stakeholders in a conjoint activity that cannot succeed without their involvement and commitment. Successful leadership believes in and communicates some version of the now famous Hewlett-Packard motto: "The achievements of an organization are the results of the combined efforts of each individual."

In the end, says Abraham Zaleznick, "leadership is based on a compact that binds those who lead with those who follow into the same moral, intellectual and emotional commitment."[8] However, as both Burns and Rost warned us, the nature of this "compact" is inherently unequal because the influence patterns existing between leaders and followers are not equal. Responsive and responsible leadership requires, as a minimum, that democratic mechanisms be put in place which recognize the right of followers to have adequate knowledge of alternative options, goals and programs, as well as the capacity to choose between them. "In leadership writ large, mutually agreed upon purposes help people achieve consensus, assume responsibility, work for the common good and build community."[9]

■ Structural Restraints

There is, unfortunately, a dark side to the theory of the "witness of others." Howard S. Schwartz in his radical, but underappreciated, managerial text *Narcissistic Process and Corporate Decay,*[10] argued that corporations are not bastions of benign, other-directed ethical reasoning. Nor can corporations, because of the demands and requirements of business, be models and exemplars of moral behavior. The rule of business, said Schwartz, remains the "law of the jungle," "the survival of the fittest," and the goal of survival engenders a combative "us against them mentality" which condones the moral imperative of getting ahead by any means necessary. Schwartz calls this phenomenon "organizational totalitarianism": Organizations and the people who manage them create for themselves a self-contained, self-serving world view, which rationalizes anything done on their behalf and which does not require justification on any grounds outside of themselves.[11] The psychodynamics of this narcissistic perspective, said Schwartz, impose Draconian requirements on all participants in organizational life: do your work; achieve organizational goals; obey and exhibit loyalty to your superiors; disregard personal values and beliefs; obey the law when necessary, obfuscate it whenever possible; and, deny internal or external discrepant information at odds with the stated organizational worldview. Within such a "totalitarian logic," neither leaders nor followers, rank nor file, operate as independent agents. To "maintain their place," to "get ahead," all must conform. The agenda of "organizational totalitarianism," said Schwartz, is always the preservation of the *status quo*. Within such a logic, like begets like, and change is rarely possible. Except for extreme situations in which "systemic ineffectiveness" begins to breed "organization decay," transformation is never an option.

In *Moral Mazes* Robert Jackall, from a sociological rather than a psychological perspective, parallels much of Schwartz's analysis of organizational behavior. According to critic and commentator Thomas W. Norton, both Jackall and Schwartz seek to understand why and how organizational ethics and behavior are so often reduced to either dumb loyalty or the simple adulation and mimicry of one's superiors. While Schwartz argued that individuals are captives of the impersonal structural logic of "organizational totalitarianism," Jackall contends that "organizational actors become personally loyal to their superiors, always seeking their approval, and are committed to them as persons rather than as representatives of the abstractions of organizational authority." But in either case, both authors maintain that organizational operatives are prisoners of the systems they serve.[12]

According to Jackall, all organizations (to be exact, he is specially referring to American business organizations) are examples of "patrimonial bureaucracies" wherein "fealty relations of personal loyalty" are the rule and the glue of organizational life. Jackall argued that all corporations are like fiefdoms of the middle ages, wherein the Lord of the Manor (CEO, President) offers protection, prestige and status to his vassals (managers) and serfs (workers) in return for homage (commitment) and service (work). In such a system, said Jackall, advancement and promotion are predicated on loyalty, trust, politics and personality as much as, if not more than, on experience, education, ability and actual accomplishments. The central concern of the worker/minion is to be known as a "can-do-guy," a "team player," being at the right place at the right time and master of all the social rules. That's why in the corporate world, says Jackall, 1,000 "atta-boys" are wiped away with one "oh, shit!"

As in the model of a feudal system, Jackall maintains that employees of a corporation are expected to become functionaries of the system and supporters of the *status quo*. Their loyalty is to the powers that be; their duty is to perpetuate performance and profit; and their values can be none other than those sanctioned by the organization. Jackall contends that the logic of every organization (place of business) and the collective personality of the workplace conspire to override the wants, desires and aspirations of the individual worker. No matter what a person believes off the job, said Jackall, on the job all of us to a greater or lesser extent are required to suspend, bracket or only selectively manifest our personal convictions.

> What is right in the corporation is not what is right in a man's home or his church. What is right in the corporation is what the guy above you wants from you.[13]

For Jackall the primary imperative of every organization is to succeed. This logic of performance, what he refers to as "institutional logic," leads to the creation of a private moral universe. A moral universe that, by definition, is totalitarian (self-sustained), solipsistic (self-defined) and narcissistic (self-centered). Within such a milieu truth is socially defined and moral behavior is determined solely by organizational needs. The key virtues, for all alike, become the virtues of the organization: goal-preoccupation, problem solving, survival/success and, most importantly, playing by the "house rules." In time, said Jackall, those initiated and invested in the system come to believe that they live in a self-contained worldview which is above and independent of outside critique and evaluation.

For both Schwartz and Jackall, the logic of organizational life is rigid and unchanging. Corporations perpetuate themselves, both in their strengths and weakness, because corporate cultures clone their own. Even given the scenario of a benign organizational structure which produces positive behavior and beneficial results, the etiology of the problem, and the opportunity for abuse that it offers, represents the negative possibilities and inherent dangers of the "witness of others" as applied to leadership theory. Within the scope of Schwartz's and Jackall's allied analysis, "normative" moral leadership may not be possible. The model offered is both absolute and inflexible, and only "regular company guys" make it to the top. The maverick, the radical, the reformer are not long tolerated. The "institutional logic" of the system does not permit disruption, deviance or default. . . .

The term moral leadership often conjures up images of sternly robed priests, waspishly severe nuns, carelessly bearded philosophers, forbiddingly strict parents and something ambiguously labeled the "moral majority." These people are seen as confining and dictatorial. They make us do what we should do, not what we want to do. They encourage following the "superego" and not the "id." A moral leader is someone who supposedly tells people the difference between right and wrong from on high. But there is much more to moral leadership than merely telling others what to do.

The vision and values of leadership must have their origins and resolutions in the community of followers, of whom they are a part, and whom they wish to serve. Leaders can drive, lead, orchestrate and cajole, but they cannot force, dictate or demand. Leaders can be the catalyst for morally sound behavior, but they are not, by themselves, a sufficient condition. Leaders by means of their demeanor and message must be able to convince, not just tell others, that collaboration serves the conjoint interest and well-being of all involved. Leaders may offer a vision, but followers must buy into it. Leaders may organize a plan, but followers must decide to take it on. Leaders may demonstrate conviction and willpower, but followers, in the new paradigm of leadership, should not allow the leader's will to replace their own.[14] To reiterate the words of Abraham Zaleznick: "Leadership is based on a compact that binds those that lead with those who follow into the same moral, intellectual and emotional commitment."

Joseph C. Rost has argued, both publicly and privately, that the ethical aspects of leadership remain thorny. How, exactly, do leaders and collaborators in an influence relationship make a collective decision about the ethics of a change that they want to implement in an organization or society? Some will say, "Option A is ethical," while others will say, "Option B is ethical." How are leaders and followers to decide? As I have suggested, ethics is what "ought to be done" as the preferred mode of action in a "right-vs.-right," "values-vs.-values" confrontation. Ethics is an evaluative enterprise. Judgments must be made in regard to competing points of view. Even in the absence of a belief in the existence of a single universal, absolute set of ethical rules, basic questions can still be asked: How does it impact on self and others? What are the consequences involved? Is it harmful? Is it fair? Is it equitable? Perhaps the best, but by no means definitive, method suited to the general needs of the ethical enterprise is a modified version of the scientific method: (A) *Observation,* the recognition of a problem or conflict; (B) *Inquiry,* a critical consideration of facts and issues involved; (C) *Hypothesis,* the formulation of a decision or plan of action consistent with the known facts; (D) *Experimentation and Evaluation,* the implementation of the decision or plan in order to see if it leads to the resolution of the problem. There are, of course, no perfect answers in ethics or life. The quality of our ethical choices cannot be measured solely in terms of achievements. Ultimately and ethically, intention, commitment and concerted effort are as important as outcome: What/why did leader/followers try to do? How did they try to do it?

Leadership is hard to define, and moral leadership is even harder. Perhaps, like pornography, we only recognize moral leadership when we see it. The problem is, we so rarely see it. Nevertheless, I am convinced that without the "witness" of moral leadership, standards of ethics in business and organizational life will not occur or be sustained. Leadership, even when defined as a collaborative experience, is still about the influence of individual character and the impact of personal mentoring. Behavior does not always beget like behavior on a one-to-one ratio, but it does establish tone, set the stage and offer options. Although it is mandatory that an organization as a whole—from top to bottom—make a commitment to ethical behavior to actually achieve it, the model for that commitment has to originate from the top.[15] Labor Secretary Robert Reich recently stated: "The most eloquent moral appeal (argument) will be no match for the dispassionate edict of the market."[16] Perhaps, the "witness" of moral leadership can prove to be more effective.

Leadership in a Values-Based Organization

—Ralph Larsen

Ralph Larsen was the outgoing Chairman and CEO of Johnson & Johnson at the time that Bentley College invited him to speak at the Sears Lectureship in Business Ethics in February 2002. In his address, Larsen refers not only to ethical leadership embodied by J&J's now-famous response to the Tylenol disaster in Chicago but also to ethical leadership as it is exhibited every day at J&J and in the decisions of its people. Consider the value of the Credo to J&J and ask yourself whether the Credo would work at all firms. What needs to be present in order for a statement like the Credo to be effective?

I am very pleased to be here representing the more than 100,000 people of Johnson & Johnson, people who work so hard each day, not only building our business, but doing it in the right way.

I'm honored to be a part of this lecture series, and so, the first reason I'm here is because you asked. The second reason is that the older I get, the more I like hanging around with people younger than I am, people on the threshold of their careers. You keep us young and nimble. You have a way of distilling and challenging our thought processes. You remind us of what it's all about.

Last year I spoke with a young lady who was serving as a fellow in our corporate communications department. This is a program we have with the Rutgers School of Communications. These master's students work for us as interns for one or two years as they complete their program. I was struck by her story, and I wanted to share it with you today.

Well, somehow our company made an impression on this young girl in India, thousands and thousands of miles away from the headquarters where she ultimately worked. When she came to us she brought with her the expectation that we would be as community-oriented, thoughtful, values-oriented and as upstanding as she had seen on the outside. She also came with the full expectation that she would find an environment where she could express her values and feel encouraged to do the right thing.

Now, I share Sandhya's story with you because I think it's just terrific that a young person can be touched and motivated by our company's values. And I think it's even more encouraging that this motivation meant that she sought out a job with us. You too might have some preconceptions about the kinds of organizations you want to join, and if you do end up someplace with a strong set of core values, I can give you a glimpse of what to expect once you get there.

Obviously, I can speak only from my personal experience which is almost exclusively in Johnson & Johnson. As Chairman and CEO for the past 13 years, I have had the best job in corporate America—of that I am sure. The reason is that leading a company like Johnson & Johnson, with a strong foundation built on values and a heritage based on ethical principles, is very special. There are certain boundaries in place: things

---

This monograph was presented as a lecture in the Sears Business Ethics Lectureship at the Center for Business Ethics at Bentley College on February 7, 2002. Reprinted with permission from the Center for Business Ethics at Bentley College.

you simply don't do, well-accepted management practices that just won't work, changes that just won't stick, parts of our history that simply won't give way to certain new ideas.

Leading a company like this isn't for everybody. It's not a job that goes away at the end of the day. It's a responsibility that sinks into you, because often we wrestle with issues and problems that have no easy answers—no clear right or wrong. For all those challenges . . . challenges I'll go into in more detail in a minute . . . for all those leadership challenges, our core values also make leadership a whole lot easier. You see, values are our greatest point of leverage to get things done . . . achieve all we can achieve. Values are the foundation of our business success.

In his renowned book, *The Fifth Discipline,* Peter Senge uses something called a "trim tab" to explain certain theories of leverage within a system. In this case, how do you get something really big, like an oil tanker ship, to change course? Well, you move the rudder, of course. But the rudder itself is so big that there's water pressure keeping it where it is. So, there is this very small piece (a rudder for the rudder if you will) called a trim tab that compresses the water around the rudder. That action makes it easier for the rudder to move through the water. Easier, therefore, for the rudder to change the direction of the ship. You don't see the trim tab. You probably never even knew it was there, but it makes an incredible difference to the navigation of the ship.

Being bound together around the values . . . around our credo . . . being bound together around values is like the trim tab for leadership at Johnson & Johnson. What I mean is that because it is a deep point of leverage, it makes a huge difference. It's the point of leverage that makes leadership not only possible but also meaningful and enjoyable.

Johnson & Johnson's strong values have been instrumental in our charting a course that has proved successful, and for that I am very thankful.

- Sales last year were $33 billion, almost triple what they were a decade ago, representing our 69th consecutive year of sales increases.
- We've had 17 consecutive years of double-digit earnings increases.
- And we've had 39 consecutive years of dividend increases.
- And our shareowners have done very well. The market value of Johnson & Johnson ended last year at more than $180 billion, up from approximately $38 billion ten years ago.

The point is that our business is healthy and the future looks bright. The challenge is to keep it going and growing. I had the incredibly good fortune to be given the opportunity to lead not only a well-run business, but one that had a very strong guidepost about what we believe in.

At Johnson & Johnson, it's the glue that holds our decentralized company together. It's called our credo, and it is a 60-year-old deceptively simple one-page document. Our credo grew out of General Robert Wood Johnson's (the patriarch of our company) very simple, yet very profound management philosophy. In essence, it says that our first responsibility is to our customers, to give them high-quality products at fair prices. Our second responsibility is to our employees, to treat them with dignity and respect and pay them fairly. Our third responsibility is to the communities in which we operate, to be good corporate citizens and protect the environment. And then, it says that our final responsibility is to our shareholders, to give them a fair return.

In the final analysis, the Credo is built on the notion that if you do a good job in fulfilling the first three responsibilities, then the shareholder will come out all right. That is exactly what has happened over all these years, and that is what we continue to strive for today.

For us, the Credo is our expression of managing the multiple bottom lines of products, people, planet and profits. It's the way we conceptualize our total impact on society. It implicitly tells us what's important: honesty and integrity, respect for others, fairness and straight-dealing. Those are the ethical values on which we operate all over the world.

Johnson & Johnson is a very decentralized company with almost 200 operating companies in 51 countries around the world, selling products in more than 175 countries. These operating companies have their own management boards and are relatively independent. We use this structure because it helps us focus on the markets and people we serve. It's the only way Johnson & Johnson can be such a broadly based health care company.

We are probably best known as a company that is a leader in health care consumer brands you know so well—from Johnson & Johnson Baby Products and Band-Aids to over-the-counter medications such as Tylenol and Motrin.

***

Clearly, as the chief executive officer, I am ultimately accountable for everything that happens, both good and bad. But more than anything else, I am responsible for the tone at the top. To run a good and decent company with good and decent people. I work hard at setting the right tone. I spend a tremendous amount of time developing and selecting credo-based leaders and ensuring that we have the proper systems and controls in place.

But with more than 100,000 people throughout our family of companies, I must rely on all of our company leaders and their teams to do the right thing and work with me to instill credo values throughout their organizations. They share with me the challenge of being responsible for making sure we operate in accordance with our credo values in all that we do.

Coming into my job I had the advantage of knowing that our credo had been translated into dozens of languages. I knew that we had programs in place to help ensure that each new employee had read it and was told of its significance, and I knew that copies of it were prominently displayed in offices and plants all over the world. As a new chief executive officer, I viewed the credo as an important framework for management and a key point of leverage, of differentiation, in today's global marketplace. It gives us the incredible advantage of having a foundation of timeless principles that serve as the "glue" that holds our decentralized organization together through good times and challenging ones.

Now, it has occurred to me that I am making all this sound kind of simple. It is not. In a highly competitive, financially driven world with the tyranny of quarterly earnings and with multiple constituencies, actually living the credo in a meaningful way is a constant challenge. At the end of the day, our credo is all about personal responsibility.

As one read through it, each of the four responsibilities outlined starts with the preposition "to" and that is very important. Said another way, our credo isn't about us being responsible for something. A school child is responsible for her backpack. An assembly line worker is responsible for placing a product in a package. But when you are responsible to, you are responsible "to a person" or "to a group of people." And that's what our credo says . . . we are responsible to our customers, mothers and fathers, doctors and nurses; responsible to employees; responsible to people in communities. This is an intrinsically subjective area precisely because it's personal. It's about owing part of yourself to others. It's a serious responsibility.

I'm no linguist, and so I don't know where the root of the two uses of a particular word in French come together, but I am struck that the word to be physically burdened with lots of luggage, *chargé,* is the same word used to describe a person who has taken on a responsibility. It's part of a title to indicate you're in charge. The idea is simple; when you're in charge, you are responsible. And this responsibility weighs heavily, particularly when you have to balance the interests of different people, all people you are responsible to.

***

Several years ago, we made the decision to close approximately 50 small plants around the world. It involved laying off several thousand people, many in communities and countries in which I knew the people would have a very tough time finding comparable employment. We had never done anything like that before.

I worried about my responsibility to the men, women and their families who would lose their jobs. But our operating costs at these small plants were way out of line, and we were becoming less and less competitive. So yes, I was responsible to our employees in those plants, but I was also responsible to the patients who needed our products to keep them affordable. And I was responsible to all of our other employees around the world to keep the company healthy and growing. The harsh reality was that a great many more would be hurt down the road if I failed to act and we became less and less competitive.

In addition to our employees, I was also responsible to the tens of thousands of stockholders (individuals, retired folks, pension plans and mutual funds) who owned our stock. The facts were clear . . . I knew what had to be done, and we did it as thoughtfully and sensitively as possible. But the decision was hard, because it was personal.

At a deeper level, what became crystal clear was that competing on a global basis with Olympic-class companies had changed the ground rules forever. This new world meant that we could no longer guarantee that if you came to work every day and did your job well, you could count on being employed with us for life. That's the way it used to be, but that was a responsibility that we could no longer fulfill. Rather, we had to focus on making people employable for life. And that's where we put our resources, at life-long development of skill sets that could be used in many different companies and industries.

The bright side to all of this is that being responsible to people has a tendency to become mutual. If I am responsible to you, you are more likely to be responsible to me, and that means I have colleagues I can trust. People are committed to people, not just to paychecks. There's a sense that we are all in it together. In our case, we're all working to get life-saving and life-enhancing products to people who need them. Improving the quality of life and healing and curing disease is our heritage and mission. Being bound together in one purpose makes us able to achieve incredible heights, not only as a group but as individuals.

***

Once inside, new leaders, I think, can grasp what we're all about quite readily because we tend to wear our values on our sleeves and talk openly about them. The credo is part of our daily conversation as we wrestle with decisions of all kinds. This means that for the newcomer there is less confusion, less jockeying and less reticence to make decisions. In our company, it's clear where the lines are, and there's a lot of room to act until you get close to those lines. Our experience is that if we have an executive who tends to bump up against the ethical boundaries time and time again, sooner or later they get themselves, and often the company, in serious trouble and that's the end of their career.

The credo is not a rulebook. It is not a list of do's and don'ts. It outlines fundamental principles that apply to not only our corporate but also our personal behavior as we carry out our business responsibilities. It has proven, over time, to be a guiding force that appeals to the ethical aspirations of all kinds of people, from all kinds of places, from all spiritual and religious backgrounds. That is its magic.

At the highest levels of leadership, the greatest risks are often risks associated with moving into new businesses particularly by acquisition. Mergers and acquisitions are, by their very nature, highly risky endeavors. They can change the fundamental make-up of our business, and they can bring thousands of new people into our company overnight.

I'm often asked if our strong set of values propels or inhibits this process . . . does it scare people off, or make us unapproachable, or make it hard for people from acquired companies to fit in. Not a bit. I think our reputation for being a values-based company is a tremendous asset. It serves as a magnet for smaller companies who do not have the resources to fulfill their potential and want to become a part of the Johnson & Johnson family of companies.

The best evidence of this is that over the last 10 years, we have added more than 50 companies, products or technologies to our company. We've successfully transitioned from a company based heavily on our heritage consumer products to a science-based company on the leading edge of medical technology.

***

Leaders can make values a priority that gets measured and rewarded. We can work hard at making sure that the company's values are well-expressed, well-understood, explicit and visible in all that we do, in all of our programs, policies, products. But the most important thing is to set the proper personal example, the tone at the top.

Our values need to be visible to people like Sandhya, young people who will become the next generation of leaders. The leaders who will wrestle with increasingly complex problems in a complicated world. A world in which often there is no clear answer and where you are not sure of what the "right" thing to do is. Leaders with good judgment who know how to preserve important values and hold fast to them, while at the same time knowing when and how fast to change to meet the challenges of a new world.

If this all sounds interesting to you as you pursue your career, I would urge you to join a company rich in values. There are no perfect people, and there are no perfect companies. We all have our weaknesses and warts. But make sure the company you join has a set of core values that you are comfortable with, that you are proud of, and which will bring out the very best in you.

Venturing Beyond Compliance

—*Lynn Sharp Paine*

Lynn Sharp Paine identifies two strategems to encourage and support an ethical corporate culture: legal compliance and organizational integrity. Consider which might be more effective from a long-term perspective? Which would be easier to implement? Which do you think is more prevalent in the business environment?

How can managers insure that individuals in their companies conduct business in a way that is responsible and ethically sound? This challenge involves organizational design and a number of specific managerial tasks.

Why the Ethics Focus?

In the past decade, a number of factors have brought ethical matters into sharper focus.

Globalization

Global expansion has brought about greater involvement with different cultures and socioeconomic systems. With this development, ethical considerations—such as the different assumptions about the responsibilities of business, about acceptable business practices, and about the values needed to build a cohesive, successful organization—become more important.

Technology

The added capabilities of technology have created a new level of transparency and immediacy to business communication. Now the conduct of businesses around the globe is more exposed than it ever was before.

Competition

Rising competition brings with it added pressure to cut corners. Simultaneously, leaders are looking for new ways to differentiate their companies and move them to a new level of excellence. Some believe that a proactive ethical stance can have a positive impact on the bottom line.

Public Perception and the Law

There is a perceived decline in social ethics that yields uncertainty. Managers are no longer comfortable assuming that employees joining their companies possess the desired ethical values. And public expectations, too, have changed: That which was once deemed acceptable is now more readily scrutinized. New laws and stepped-up enforcement efforts have increased the risk of personal and organizational liability.

Lynn Sharp Paine, "Venturing beyond Compliance," *The Evolving Role of Ethics in Business,* report no. 1141-96-ch, pp. 13–16 (New York: The Conference Board, Inc., 1996). Email: *info@conference-board.org*.

■ Two Strategies Emerge

Most managers are choosing either a *legal compliance* strategy or an *organizational integrity* strategy to support ethics in their companies. These strategies differ markedly in their conception of ethics, human behavior and management responsibility. While the organizational integrity strategy fully acknowledges the importance of compliance with the law, its aim is to achieve right conduct in general. Thus, it is more comprehensive and broader than the legal compliance strategy. Companies that adopt an organizational integrity strategy are concerned with their identity—who they are and what they stand for—and with how they conduct internal and external affairs. These matters are less clear-cut (and hence, more demanding) than those handled by a legal compliance approach.

These strategies differ in several fundamental ways:

Ethos

The legal compliance strategy regards ethics as a set of limits, boundaries over which we must not cross. The compliance approach is externally driven. Here, ethics is viewed as something that *has* to be done.

The organizational integrity strategy defines ethics as a set of principles to guide the choices we make. Companies that adopt this approach choose their own standards for conducting business on an individual and company-wide basis.

Objectives

The compliance approach is geared toward preventing unlawful conduct and criminal misconduct in particular. The integrity approach, by comparison, has a more lofty goal: to achieve responsible conduct across-the-board, even if not required by law.

Leadership

While companies with a compliance approach place lawyers at the helm, the integrity approach is captained by company managers. To insure that their efforts are thorough and effective, these managers are assisted by lawyers, human resources specialists and other experts.

Methods

The compliance focus emphasizes the rules people must not violate. It uses increased oversight and stepped-up penalties to enforce these rules. An integrity approach acknowledges the need for a brake on people's behavior from time to time, but treats ethics as a steering mechanism rather than the brake itself. Here, ethics infuses the organization's leadership, its core systems, and its decision-making processes.

Behavioral Assumptions

Finally, the two approaches rest on very different philosophies of human nature. The compliance strategy's ideas are rooted in deterrence theory—how to prevent people from doing bad things by manipulating the costs of misconduct. The integrity strategy views people as having a fuller, richer set of needs and motivations. While it acknowledges that people are guided by material self-interest and the threat of penalties, it also identifies the other drivers of human nature—individual values, ideals and the influence of peers.

■ Limitations of a Compliance-Based Approach

Why go beyond compliance? While legal compliance is a must, a legal compliance approach to company ethics has several specific limitations:

- Compliance is not terribly responsive to many of the day-to-day concerns that managers and employees face. It follows the law, which is generally backward looking. For a company on the cutting edge of technology, of new financing mechanisms, of new practices, the law is not very helpful as a guide.

- The majority of hot-line calls are not about unlawful or criminal misconduct. They deal with gray areas and with issues of supervisory practice and fair treatment. A legal compliance approach does not provide answers to these types of questions. Therefore, it does not adequately address employees' real concerns and needs.

- The typical legal compliance program runs directly counter to the philosophy of empowerment. Empowerment gives employees discretion, resources and authority, and then trusts them to make good decisions. Compliance programs, though, reduce discretion, increase oversight and tighten controls. If a company tries to put forth an empowerment effort and a compliance-driven ethics program at the same time, the two will cancel each other out. This will result in a lot of employee cynicism.

- A legal compliance program is just not very exciting. Compliance is important, but the law was not designed to inspire human excellence so much as to set a floor for acceptable behavior. Since the law has to apply to everyone, its standards are not as demanding as we might choose for ourselves and for our companies.

Challenges to an Integrity-Based Approach

If one are really interested in organizational effectiveness and organizational development rather than just avoiding liability, an integrity-driven approach is far more promising. But four challenges must be met before an organizational integrity approach can work:

1. *Developing an ethical framework.* Organizational integrity requires a much more robust concept of organizational identity and responsibility than does compliance.
2. *Aligning practice with principles.* This can be very problematic, especially in organizations whose structure, systems and decision processes run counter to the values and principles espoused by senior management.
3. *Overcoming cynicism.* In *The Cynical Americans,* Donald L. Kanter and Phillip H. Mervis' study of cynicism in the United States (San Francisco, Jossey-Bass Publishers, 1989, p. 1), it was revealed that almost 43% of Americans fit the profile of the cynic; that is, one who regards selfishness, dishonesty and fakery as at the core of human behavior. People often adopt cynicism as a self-defense mechanism. This frame of reference often prevents people from seeing reality, and can act as a barrier to instilling ethical values.
4. *Resolving ethical conflicts.* We all have conflicting responsibilities from time to time. If we are very creative, we may be able to solve potential conflicts before they unfold. Sometimes, though, hard trade-offs—between right and right, between two "goods"—must be made.

Navigating with the Ethical Compass

How do you begin to create an ethical compass or a framework for integrity? A useful starting point is to begin by answering some questions related to the four fundamental sources of responsibility.

- Purpose—What is the organization's fundamental reason for being—its ultimate aims?
- People—Who are the constituencies to whom the company is accountable and on whom it depends for success? What are their legitimate claims and interests?
- Power—What is the organization's authority and ability to act?
- Principles—What are the organization's obligations or duties, as well as its guiding aspirations and ideals?

If used as a set of reference points, these questions can help develop a framework against which to benchmark progress on ethical matters (see Figure 5.1).

The framework of ideas is only a start. Putting it into practice is the difficult part. People often wonder why a gap exists between the espoused values and everyday behavior,

FIGURE 5.1   **The Four Points of an Ethical Compass**

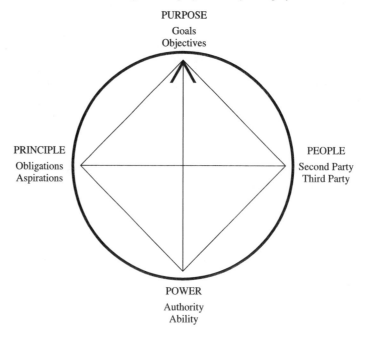

How can managers develop a framework for integrity?

© Lynn Sharp Paine, 1995

when in fact, a gap *should* exist to some degree. If you are fully satisfying your ideals and aspirations, most likely your standards are not high enough. If the gap between principle and practice becomes a chasm, though, it becomes hypocrisy, which is even worse.

▣ Management: Putting It Together

Integrity-based ethics management efforts have contributed to organizational effectiveness in several fundamental ways. Companies that have adopted such programs report fewer and less serious problems of misconduct. Often this is because problems are caught earlier and are dealt with at the onset. In some cases, an integrity approach can yield strengthened competitiveness: it facilitates the delivery of quality products in an honest, reliable way. This approach can enhance work life by making the workplace more fun and challenging. It can improve relationships with constituencies and can instill a more positive mindset that fosters creativity and innovation. And while an organizational integrity approach cannot guarantee bottom-line performance improvements, it is important to understand that ethics is a very practical matter. The purpose of ethics is to enhance our lives and our relationships both inside and outside of the organization.

Clearly, achieving and maintaining integrity requires intense commitment and involvement from managers company-wide. This goes beyond the so-called "tone" set by senior management. It involves specific leadership tasks and behaviors, starting with the development of the integrity framework. Managers must insure that company systems support responsible behavior. Then they must personally model responsible decision making. These leadership tasks are all essential to building the high-integrity organization.

Ethical Business: Survey Results

—Institute of Business Ethics

Every three years, the Institute of Business Ethics (U.K.) surveys larger companies known to have codes of ethics/conduct/business principles about the use they make of them and their views about current business ethics issues. The principal findings follow.

Who is Responsible for Business Ethics?

CEOs turn to a wide spectrum of corporate functions to handle the ethical aspects of company behavior. Comparatively few (16%) retain it in their own department. This is further borne out by the response to a question asking *which department, function or person is responsible for the code.* Table 5.2 sets out the percentage responses in each of three years for which there is data.

Nearly half of respondents look to the legal or compliance function to be responsible for ethical conduct of the organization. The human resources departments seem to be regaining their influence probably because of the rise of human rights issues at the workplace and with particular reference to the conduct of their suppliers. It is, however, the corporate governance functions that still predominate in business ethics. This reflects the attention that was paid in the 1990s to changes of practice following inclusion in the Stock Exchange listing requirements of the provisions of the Hampel Committee's Combined Code.[1]

There is little sign yet that corporate affairs executives are being given increased responsibility for ethical policies following the publication of the Turnbull Report.[2] This requires among other things, that boards of companies assess and report on non-financial risks (i.e., threats to reputation, etc.) as well as the financial ones. It is certainly not too wild to suggest that many corporations will turn to their public affairs staff to advise on, and assume responsibility for, reputation management. It is therefore predicted that by 2004 (when the next survey is due), that function will appear further up the list of those that are responsible for business ethics. The rise in importance of the internal audit department should also be noted.

TABLE 5.2 **Departments Responsible for Codes of Ethics***

	2001	1998	1995
Corporate/External Affairs	10%	11%	1%
Human Resources	20%	12%	7%
Company Secretary and/or Legal Department	46%	44%	14%
Board/Board Committee/CEO	16%	12%	44%
Internal Audit/Finance	14%	7%	—
Other	16%	14%	34%

*Some multiple answers in 2001.

Purpose of a Code

Having an ethics policy now seems to be a well-established feature of the corporate strategy of larger organizations. IBE survey data indicates that in August 2001, 73 of the companies listed in the FTSE100 index either had a code of business ethics or had one in preparation. Others are known to be considering the matter seriously. Previous surveys have shown about the same proportion but the constituents of the index have changed significantly since the last count in 1999. Over half the respondents to the survey have had codes for more than three years, while only 7% have introduced them in the past year. See Table 5.3.

TABLE 5.3 **For How Long Has Your Company Had a Code?**

Less than 1 year	7%
1–3 years	23%
3–5 years	18%
5–10 years	18%
More than 10 years	18%
No answer	16%

It is now seen as part of "good governance" to have and operate such a code.

A question was asked in the survey which sought to find out the motivation or purpose of companies in having an ethics policy. The answers indicate the main benefits that companies expect from the resources they spend on this aspect of their business. See Table 5.4.

TABLE 5.4 **Importance of Codes to Companies (ranked by those giving each first priority)***

Guidance to staff	31
Reduces risk	11
Helps to secure long term shareholder value	10
Helps to guard reputation	7
Shows we are a responsible company	5

*Some multiple answers.

The prime motivation is that of giving guidance to staff on how to respond to ethical dilemmas. This is in sharp contrast to the 1998 survey when "guarding of reputation" was seen as the primary purpose by 75% of respondents whereas in 2001, it was down to 18%. Even if risk reduction is added to reputation protection, employee guidance still predominates as a motive today.

Use of the Code

Having a code is a start, but how is [*sic*] it and its contents made known and what uses are made of it?

Table 5.5a indicates that practically all employees are provided with a copy of the code and increasingly, those outside the company are being informed about the organization's ethical stance.

TABLE 5.5A **Use of the Code**

Circulated	2001	1998
Internally	93%	93%
Externally	46%	33%

The text of the code in the form of a booklet, memorandum or chapter in a staff handbook, or access via the intranet are still the preferred ways to publicize the code (see Table 5.5b). The intranet method was mentioned by a third of respondents compared with just 7% in 1998. Inclusion in new staff induction packs seems to be on the decline which is surprising. There is little evidence of the use of face-to-face briefing as a means of communication. Among methods of promulgating codes of business ethics internally which received only a few mentions were: noticeboards, CD-roms, calendars and videos.

TABLE 5.5B Methods of Internal Publicity of the Code (multiple answers)

	2001	1998
Booklet/circular/staff manual	38	64
Included in induction pack	16	23
Face to face briefing	2	13
Intranet	33	7
Through line management	7	—
Compliance reviews	5	7
Others	13	

As pointed out above, there is less reluctance in 2001 to make companies' codes of ethics available to outsiders. 46% of respondents, compared with 33% in 1998, say they publicize their codes externally (see Table 5.5a). However, Table 5.5c shows that only 13% say they mention it in their annual reports which is a sharp decline compared with 1998. On the other hand, 25% of respondents post their code on their corporate website, which leads to the assumption that they are widely available. Because of this, companies are to some extent making themselves more vulnerable to comparisons of theory and practice as far as behavior is concerned.

TABLE 5.5C External Publicity of the Code

	2001	1998
Annual Report	13%	47%
Given to stakeholders	—	32%
Dedicated report	5%	16%
Posted on website	26%	5%
Briefing to analyst/journalist	0	5%
Other	15%	—

Questions are often asked about the use of codes in overseas locations. Generally a code issued by the Board with the endorsements of the Chairman and for the Chief Executive Officer is applicable throughout the company irrespective of where the business operates. A question was asked for the first time about the translation of codes for use outside the English-speaking world. Table 5.6 sets out the answers.

TABLE 5.6 If You Have Locations Overseas, Do You Translate Your Code for Local Use?

Yes	43%
No	37%
Not applicable	20%

Assuming that the "no" response implies that no translation of the code is undertaken by 37% of companies with non-English speaking staff in the UK or elsewhere, the response indicates that embedding of the code as part of the ethos or culture of the company is not taken very seriously by a significant number of larger businesses.

■ Business Ethics Training

The number of companies with codes who offer training on business ethics has fallen slightly compared with 1998 and remains stubbornly below 50% (Table 5.7).

TABLE 5.7 Do You Offer Training to Members of Staff on the Meaning and Use of Your Code?

	2001	1998
Yes	41%	46%
No	59%	54%

Table 5.7a sets out the principal methods of training provided by companies. They divide into three: 60% refer to staff seminars and 64% to inclusion in house manuals and guides (though how these are used is not clear). Thirdly, the use of the intranet for this type of training is mentioned by more than half of the respondents; in 1998 it was classified within the 20% of "other" methods used.

TABLE 5.7A What Form Does the Training Take? (multiple answers)

	2001	1998
In-house training seminars	60%	50%
Intranet	56%	*
External training	0%	2%
Videos/games etc.	16%	30%
Staff manuals or guides	64%	30%
Other (*included Intranet in 1998)	20%	20%

■■ Implementation of the Code

Apart from the promulgation of the code to all businesses and individuals and the provision of training in relation to it, the main ways to make the code "live" involve reactions of staff to its contents and the use of it made by them.

Table 5.8 sets out responses in the last three surveys on the ways (if any) that are available to employees to raise questions concerning their own or others' conformity to, and interpretation of, their company code.

TABLE 5.8 Is There a Procedure to Raise Questions About the Code?

	2001	1998	1995
Yes	74%	70%	66%
No	26%	30%	34%

Provision of means for issues to be raised has now become a necessary part of any corporate ethics program. It is particularly important in the prevention of what has become known as whistleblowing. Staff are usually driven to make public any behavior which they consider to be harmful, illegal or unethical when there are no adequate procedures in an organization for raising such matters and having them addressed. The law now protects those who do go public on a matter but only if they have failed to get the issue taken seriously within the organization in which they work. The strongest deterrent to "speaking out" is the fear of reprisal. It is therefore interesting to note that in 2001, 91% of respondent companies say they protect the identity of the person raising concerns. This compares with 80% in 1998.

Another indication of how seriously a company takes its ethics program is whether conformity to the code is included in the employees' contracts of employment. Table 5.9 sets out results of a question on this matter.

TABLE 5.9 Is Conformity to Your Code Included in the
Contract of Employment Used by Your Corporation?

	2001	1998	1995
Yes	53%	42%	46%
No	47%	58%	54%

A majority of companies now include conformity to the code in contracts but there is still doubt about this among many respondents. This is partly because it implies that non-conformity would be grounds for dismissal. Clearly this would be the case for any deliberate and clear breaches. But ethical decisions based on conformity to a clause in a code—say, accepting a substantial gift from a supplier—are necessarily a matter of judgment and the reluctance of lawyers to agree to its inclusion in a contract of employment can be understood. Nevertheless, if a board of directors is serious about paying more than lip service to business ethics, a sure way of signalling this is to include it in a contract of employment and making it part of all induction training.

The extent to which codes are taken seriously can also be gauged from their use in corporate disciplinary procedures. It will be seen from Table 5.10 that it is becoming more common.

TABLE 5.10   **Has Your Code Been Used in Disciplinary Procedures in Your Company?**

	2001	1998	1995
Yes	38%	33%	32%
No	62%	67%	68%

38% compared with 33% in 1998 say that the code has been used to enforce the need to conform to standards of business conduct. As reputation risk is seen to be of growing importance, especially among companies with retail brands, anything which is seen to endanger the brand reputation will not be tolerated. This includes unethical conduct. It is likely then, that in future there will be a growth in the inclusion of conformity to a code in contracts of employment.

Some boards of directors have felt that there is not enough information about the way their organizations are seen to behave by those with whom they do business (their stakeholders). Others feel they may be vulnerable to accusations of unethical behavior and need to have assessments of where the weaknesses lie and what can be done to strengthen them. A question was asked about the use of ethical/social audits. The results are set out in Table 5.11.

TABLE 5.11   **Have You Had, or Considered Having, an Ethical/Social Audit of Your Company Carried Out?**

	2001	1998
Have had an ethical/social audit carried out	15%	5%
Have considered an audit	35%	21%
Not interested in such an audit (or no answer)	50%	74%

The answers indicate a growing interest in this type of survey. Its value is that it provides a firm starting base on which to make a policy effective. As long as it includes questions to staff at different levels about their perceptions of the organization's behavior to their customers and other stakeholders as well as themselves, it will provide the ingredients for an ethics policy, including the provision and implementation of a code of business ethics.

As audits of this kind frequently form the basis for an external report for stakeholders, the growth in auditing also reflects a greater interest in using the company's commitment to ethics and social responsibility as part of overall communications.

■ Code Revision

One of the most important ways of keeping a company code of ethics effective is to have a process for its regular review and revision. A question asking if a process was in place to undertake this produced a somewhat surprising result as shown in Table 5.12.

TABLE 5.12 Have You a Process for Revision of Your Code?

	2001	1998	1995
Yes	77%	86%	76%
No	23%	14%	24%

It is not clear why there has been a drop in the number of companies having such a process. It could be because 30% of respondents have had a code for less than three years (see Table 5.3).

For those companies which do have a process, a question was asked about how it was done. Table 5.13 sets out the responses.

TABLE 5.13 How Was the Code Review Process Mainly Undertaken?

	2001	1998
Annual review by board	17%	40%
Decision of chairman/chief executive	30%	25%
Survey of staff	11%	11%
Consultation with stakeholders	15%	9%
Other	27%	15%

While it seems that an annual review by the board is less popular, CEOs are taking more initiative and stakeholders are being included by more companies in the review process, which is likely to be at a less frequent interval than yearly.

Current Business Ethics Issues

Respondents were asked about what ethical issues have been of recent concern to their companies. Most responded with more than one issue (see Table 5.14).

TABLE 5.14 Which Ethical Issues Have Recently Been of Concern to Your Organization? (multiple answers)

	Cited by
Supply chain issues/sourcing	38%
Bribery and corruption	32%
Remuneration of senior staff or board	30%
Work/life balance issues	28%
Product safety	25%
Other	18%
No answer	18%

Media attention in recent years on issues such as use of child labor, health and safety issues and other human rights matters in the organizations overseas where goods are sourced has raised important issues for importing companies. Some reputations have been severely tarnished when it was reported that companies had not taken into account these matters in their purchase and supply policies. It is not surprising, therefore, that this heads the list of current concerns. Bribery and board remuneration issues have continued to cause concern but work/life balance (better: work/home balance!) is a recent issue to appear in a list of corporate concerns.

Managing Ethics and Legal Compliance

What Works and What Hurts

—Linda Klebe Trevino, Gary R. Weaver,
David G. Gibson and Barbara Ley Toffler

Some ethics programs work and others do not. What are the differences between the two groups?

A survey of employees at six large American companies asked the question: "What works and what hurts in corporate ethics/compliance management?" The study found that a values-based cultural approach to ethics/compliance management works best. Critical ingredients of this approach include leaders' commitment to ethics, fair treatment of employees, rewards for ethical conduct, concern for external stakeholders and consistency between policies and actions. What hurts effectiveness most are an ethics/compliance program that employees believe exists only to protect top management from blame and an ethical culture that focuses on unquestioning obedience to authority and employee self-interest. The results of effective ethics/compliance management are impressive. They include reduced unethical/illegal behavior in the organization, increased awareness of ethical issues, more ethical advice seeking within the firms, greater willingness to deliver bad news or report ethical/legal violations to management, better decision making because of the ethics/compliance program and increased employee commitment.

Ten years ago, a Business Roundtable report titled *Corporate Ethics: A Prime Business Asset* suggested that "there are no precise ways to measure the end results of the widespread and intensive efforts to develop effective corporate ethics programs. Despite this difficulty in measuring their accomplishments, corporate ethics and legal compliance programs have become even more widespread over the last decade. Companies are investing millions of dollars on ethics and compliance management. A recent survey of Fortune 1000 firms found that 98% of responding firms address ethics or conduct issues in formal documents. Of those firms, 78% have a separate code of ethics, and most distribute these policies widely within the organization. Many employees also receive ethics training and have access to a telephone line for reporting problems or seeking advice. Much of this activity has been attributed to the 1991 U.S. Sentencing Commission's Guidelines for organizational defendants. The Guidelines prescribe more lenient sentences and fines to companies that have taken measures to prevent employee misconduct.

"Managing Ethics and Legal Compliance: What Works and What Hurts," by Linda Klebe Trevino, Gary R. Weaver, David G. Gibson, and Barbara Ley Toffler. Reprinted from *California Management Review* (Winter 1999), with permission of the University of California, Walter A. Haas School of Business.

What do these ethics and legal compliance programs actually accomplish? A firm's approach to ethics and legal compliance management has an enormous impact on employees' attitudes and behaviors. In this study, we found that specific characteristics of the formal ethics or compliance program matter less than broader perceptions of the program's orientation toward values and ethical aspirations. What helps the most are consistency between policies and actions as well as dimensions of the organization's ethical culture such as ethical leadership, fair treatment of employees and open discussion of ethics in the organization. On the other hand, what hurts the most is an ethical culture that emphasizes self-interest and unquestioning obedience to authority, and the perception that the ethics or compliance program exists only to protect top management from blame.

In order to investigate what works and what hurts in ethics and compliance management, we administered a survey to over 10,000 randomly selected employees at all levels in six large American companies from a variety of industries. The companies varied in their ethics/compliance program approaches. Because we were relying on employees' perceptions, we had to be concerned about socially desirable responses—having employees tell us what they thought we wanted to hear rather than the truth. We took a number of steps to guard against such biased responding. Surveys were completely anonymous, they were sent to employees' homes and they were returned directly to the researchers for analysis.

***

What Influences Ethics/Compliance Program Effectiveness?

There are several key organizational and program design factors that are associated with ethics/compliance management effectiveness. . . .

1. Program Orientation

Ethics/compliance programs can be designed with very different goals and orientations. Previous research has referred to two types of approaches, a compliance-based approach and an integrity or values-based approach. According to [L. S.] Paine ["Managing for Organizational Integrity," *Harvard Business Review,* March/April 1994, pp. 106–17], a compliance approach focuses primarily on preventing, detecting and punishing violations of the law, while a values-based approach aims to define organizational values and encourage employee commitment to ethical aspirations. She asserts that the values-based approach should be more effective than a compliance-based approach because a values-based approach is rooted in personal self-governance and is more likely to motivate employees to behave in accordance with shared values. She argues that compliance approaches can be counterproductive because they emphasize avoiding punishment instead of self-governance. They define ethics in terms of legal compliance rather than ethical aspirations, and they implicitly endorse a "code of moral mediocrity."

A recent study of Fortune 1000 firms was conducted in part to determine the orientations of their ethics/compliance management efforts. The survey found that the compliance and values-based approaches are not mutually exclusive. Rather, most firms' approaches to ethics/compliance management combine these orientations in some way. Nevertheless, the compliance approach predominated over the values-based approach in over half of the firms. The U.S. Sentencing Guidelines (implemented in late 1991) contribute to the development of compliance approaches because fines and sanctions for companies convicted of crimes vary dramatically depending upon management's cooperation and whether the firm has a legal compliance program in place.

Given that a compliance-based approach predominates in most firms, our study needed to test the contention that a values-based approach is "better" (achieves more positive outcomes) than a compliance-based approach. Also, many companies hope to maintain or improve their public image and relationships with external stakeholders by adopting an ethics/compliance program. Therefore, we identified an orientation toward satisfying external stakeholders (customers, the community, suppliers) as a third approach in our study. Alternatively, employees sometimes suspect that an ethics/compliance program is introduced in part to protect top management from blame for ethical failures or legal problems. In fact, Paine associated this suspicion with a compliance-based program, suggesting that skeptical employees may see a compliance-oriented program as "nothing more than liability insurance for senior management." Another of Badaracco and Webb's interviewees put it this way: "I'm cynical. To me, corporate codes of conduct exist to cover the potential problems companies may have. It provides deniability. It gives the employers an excuse. . . . The top officers can say, 'These employees messed up. They violated our way of doing business' " [L. Badaracco and A. P. Webb, "Business Ethics: A View from the Trenches," Winter 1995, pp. 8–28]. Therefore, we also assessed the impact of a "protect top management from blame" orientation.

2. A Values Orientation Is the Most Effective Single Orientation

Across the six firms in this study, employees perceived the presence of each of the four orientations (compliance-based, values-based, external stakeholder and protect top management) to varying degrees, and all of them were important in influencing outcomes. However, it is clearly most important to have a program that employees perceive to be values-based. In these six companies, if employees perceived a values-based program, each of the seven outcomes studied was significantly more positive and the relationships were quite strong. Unethical/illegal behavior was lower, awareness of ethical/legal issues was higher, and employees were more likely to look for advice within the firm, to be willing to deliver bad news to management, and to report ethical violations. They also were more committed to the organization and more likely to believe that decision making was better because of the ethics/compliance program.

3. Compliance and External Orientations Are Also Helpful

Outcomes were also more positive if employees perceived a compliance or an external stakeholder orientation. Contrary to Paine's argument, if employees perceived a compliance-based program, all of the outcomes were significantly more positive. However, the relationships were not as strong as with the values orientation. If employees perceived an external stakeholder orientation, once again the same outcomes were significantly more positive. However, the relationships were even weaker than those for compliance orientation.

4. Combining These Orientations May Be Effective

The data also supported the idea that these orientations are not mutually exclusive. For example, values orientation is highly correlated with compliance orientation (correlation = .60) and with external stakeholder orientation (correlation = .53). So, it is clearly possible to design a program that combines these different orientations, while also emphasizing a values-based approach. A values orientation can be backed up with accountability systems and discipline for violators. Values can include a concern for customers, suppliers and the community as well as shareholders and internal stakeholders such as employees. The ideal mix of orientations likely depends on specific organizational circumstances, such as the organization's culture, product and industry.

5. "Protect Top Management" Is Clearly a Harmful Approach

Not surprisingly, where employees perceived that the ethics/compliance program was oriented toward protecting top management from blame, all of the important outcomes were significantly more negative. These relationships were particularly strong and negative for commitment to the organization, for the perception that it's okay to deliver bad news to management and that employees would report ethical/legal violations to management. In addition, unethical/illegal behavior was higher, employees were less aware of ethical issues and they were less likely to seek advice about ethical concerns. Furthermore, they did not believe that decision making was better because of the ethics/compliance program.

Summary of Program Orientation Findings

A key finding of this study is the importance of designing an ethics program that is perceived by employees to be first and foremost about shared organizational values and about guiding employees to act on their ethical aspirations. Such programs motivate employees to be aware of ethical or legal issues, report bad news to management, report ethical or legal violations and refrain from engaging in unethical or illegal conduct. In addition, unethical/illegal behavior is reduced, employee commitment is higher and employees believe that decision making in the organization is better because of the ethics program.

This values-based approach can be supplemented with an orientation toward legal compliance and satisfying external stakeholders. Valuing external stakeholders such as customers and the community has a positive impact on all outcomes, as does holding employees accountable for their behavior through monitoring and disciplinary systems. Discipline for rule violators serves an important symbolic role in organizations—it reinforces standards, upholds the value of conformity to shared norms, and maintains the perception that the organization is a just place where wrongdoers are held accountable for their actions.

Finally, a program must avoid conveying the message to employees that it exists to protect top management from blame. Having a program that is perceived in this way by employees may be worse than having no program at all. Recall Paine's proposal that employees were likely to associate a compliance approach with this "protect top management from blame" orientation. Our data did not support this contention. There was little association between employees' perceptions of the program as compliance-oriented and their perceptions of the program as being oriented toward protecting top management from blame. However, this protect-top-management orientation was even less likely to be associated with a program that employees perceived to be values-based. Perhaps the most important message to executives is that this protect-top-management perception is real. Employees judge top management's motives in implementing an ethics/compliance program. Also, it is important that they perceive it to be a sincere attempt to have all employees do what's right rather than just an attempt to create legal "cover" for executives in case of a legal mishap.

Formal and Informal Ethics/Compliance Program Characteristics

With regard to specific ethics/compliance program and organizational characteristics, we asked employees about formal characteristics including the official policies, procedures, offices and supporting structures (e.g., telephone hotline). We also asked for employees' perceptions of the more informal ways ethics and compliance concerns are handled every day (e.g., how well the company "follows through" on its policies).

Formal Program Characteristics are Relatively Unimportant

All six companies in the study had the "basics" of a comprehensive ethics/compliance program: an ethics/compliance office and officer, a formal code of conduct and a telephone hotline. Despite the existence of these formal program characteristics, employees may be more or less aware of them and more or less likely to use them. Therefore, we asked employees how familiar they were with the code's contents and how frequently they referred to the code for guidance. Interestingly, these factors had little impact on the outcomes, especially unethical conduct. It simply did not matter much whether employees were familiar with or referred frequently to the company's code of conduct. We also asked employees whether their company has a formal mechanism for raising ethical and legal compliance issues and concerns and whether ethics is a formal part of performance evaluation in the company. Both of these program characteristics are dynamic, requiring some kind of ongoing attention from the organization; whereas a code can be drafted, distributed and forgotten. To the extent that employees perceived the company to have a formal mechanism for raising concerns and to make ethics a formal part of performance appraisal, all of the outcomes were significantly more positive.

Program Follow-Through is Essential

With regard to program follow-through, we asked employees whether the company works hard to detect violators, whether the company follows up on ethical concerns raised by employees and whether there is consistency between ethics/compliance policies and actual organizational practices. Follow-through tells employees that a focus on ethics and legal compliance represents a sincere commitment on the part of management.

The more that employees in our study perceived the organization to be following through, the more positive were all of the outcomes. Further, employees' perceptions of follow-through were much more important than their perceptions of the formal characteristics. Employees' perception that the company's actions are consistent with its policies were particularly important. Employees need to perceive that policies are not just "window dressing" and that the company follows words with actions. Therefore, an approach that goes beyond the mere establishment of formal programs is necessary if employees are to be convinced that the organization really means what it says.

Ethical Culture in the Organization

Managing ethics in organizations is not just about managing formal ethics/compliance programs. Researchers have suggested that the broader ethical context in an organization—referred to as the ethical climate or culture—is particularly important, perhaps more important than specific ethics/compliance program goals or characteristics. The elements of ethical culture that guide employee thought and action include leadership, reward systems, perceived fairness, ethics as a topic of conversation in the organization, employee authority structures and an organizational focus that communicates care for employees and the community.

Executive and Supervisory Leadership

A decade ago, the Business Roundtable report *Corporate Ethics: A Prime Business Asset* referred to the crucial role of top management. "To achieve results, the Chief Executive Officer and those around the CEO need to be openly and strongly committed to ethical conduct, and give constant leadership in tending and renewing the values of the organization."

We were interested in the role of executive leadership because executives play a crucial role in creating, maintaining and changing ethical culture. We also wanted to investigate the role of supervisory leadership. Leaders at every level serve as role models, and employees have more daily contact with their supervisors than they do with executive leaders. Supervisors are responsible for rewards and punishments and they carry the message of how things are really done in the organization. Therefore, in separate sets of questions we asked employees for their perceptions of executive and supervisory ethical leadership.

Perceptions of these two groups were highly related (correlation = .78), suggesting that employees don't think differently about supervisors and executive leaders with regard to their attention to ethics and legal compliance. Essentially, if executive leaders value and pay attention to ethics, so do supervisory leaders.

Leadership was a key ethical culture factor—one of the most important factors in the study. Where employees perceived that supervisors and executives regularly pay attention to ethics, take ethics seriously and care about ethics and values as much as the bottom line, all of the outcomes were significantly more positive. Employees paint all leaders with the same broad ethical brush. When it comes to ethics, leaders are leaders, and the level (supervisory or executive) doesn't seem to matter much to employees.

Fair Treatment of Employees

We also explored a less obvious aspect of ethical culture—employees' perceptions of general fair treatment in the organization. Why should general fair treatment of employees be related to ethics-related outcomes? First, the word *ethics* can mean different things to different people or groups. Kent Druyvesteyn, former ethics officer at General Dynamics, said that when managers say "ethics," employees hear "fairness." To most employees, ethics means how the organization treats them and their coworkers. This helps to explain why so many calls to ethics hotlines concern human resources issues of fair treatment in hiring, layoffs, performance appraisals and promotions. Also, recent research has highlighted the importance of fair treatment for ethics-related outcomes such as employee theft. When employees feel that they are treated unfairly, they may try to "balance the scales of justice" by engaging in unethical behaviors such as stealing from the organization. Some companies have acknowledged this connection between fair treatment and ethics management. For example, we know of a company that sees the elimination of executive dining rooms and other perks as important to making their ethics programs work. Employees see that rules apply to everyone because every employee, up to the CEO, has to have expense reports signed. "That sends a good message [to employees]. . . . Nobody is above the rules and code of conduct. . . . A high level person could get dismissed if they violated [a rule] as much as another person." Another company pegged executive pay to employee pay because of similar concerns about the implications of fair and consistent employee treatment for ethics management.

It is important to note that the survey questions concerning fair treatment had nothing to do with the ethics/compliance program. Rather, they were general questions that asked whether employees think of the company as fair in terms of rewards and punishments (do employees get the rewards and punishments they deserve), whether employees are treated fairly in general and whether supervisors treat employees with courtesy, dignity and respect. Employees' perception of fair treatment was strongly related to all outcomes and was one of the most important factors in the study. It had the strongest correlation with employee commitment and with the perception that it's acceptable to deliver bad news to management.

Companies demonstrate their good ethics to employees primarily through fair treatment. If a company passes the "fair treatment test," employees are more likely to be open to ethics and legal compliance initiatives and to cooperate in making them successful.

Ethics in Discussions and Decisions

We also asked employees whether people in the company talk openly about ethics and values and whether ethics and values are integrated into decisions. One of the ways ethics and values get "baked into" the corporate culture is to make these sorts of discussions the norm. Our previous experience with one company provides an example of how this should not be done. An oil company employee asked if he could bring an ethical problem to a meeting of divisional presidents. Their immediate response was, "If he wants to talk ethics, let him talk to a priest or a psychiatrist. The office is no place for it." Imagine what employees would think of a formal ethics/compliance program in such an environment.

In our study, perceptions that ethics is talked about and integrated into decision making were important for all outcomes. Open discussion of ethics and values in the company was particularly important for employee commitment, the perception that it's acceptable to deliver bad news, the belief that employees would report an ethics violation and that decision making is better because of the ethics/compliance program.

Reward Systems that Support Ethical Conduct

Good managers know that people do what's rewarded and avoid doing what's punished. Therefore, an ethical culture should include a reward system that supports ethical conduct. We asked employees whether ethical behavior is rewarded and unethical behavior is punished in their organizations. Perceptions of both of these dimensions were important for all outcomes. However, employee perceptions that ethical behavior is rewarded were more important than were perceptions that unethical behavior is punished. The belief that ethical behavior is rewarded was particularly important for employees' commitment and their perceptions that it's okay to deliver bad news to management and that employees would be likely to report ethical violations.

Unquestioning Obedience to Authority

An ethical organizational culture must emphasize each individual's accountability and responsibility for his or her own actions and an obligation to question authority when something seems wrong. An unethical culture is more likely to require unquestioning obedience to authority—"Just do as I say and don't ask any questions." In this study, we found that where employees perceived a structure that expects unquestioning obedience to authority, all outcomes were significantly more negative. Most affected were employee commitment to the organization, willingness to report an ethical or legal violation and willingness to deliver bad news to management.

Organizational Focus

Research on ethical climate has found that employees' perceptions of the organization's focus are associated with both unethical behavior and employee commitment. In this study, we considered three types of focus: employee focus (where employees perceive an organizational focus on what's best for them and their coworkers); community focus (where employees perceive an organizational focus on what's best for customers and the public); and self-interest focus (where employees perceive that everyone in the organization is simply out for himself or herself).

Where employees perceived the organization to be focused on what's best for employees (employee focus) or for customers and the public (community focus), all of the outcomes were significantly more positive. However, where employees perceived that people in the organization were mostly out for themselves (self-interest focus), all outcomes were significantly more negative.

Summary of Ethical Culture Findings

As a set, the ethical culture factors emerged as the most important influential factors. Of these factors, leadership, fairness perceptions, the perception that ethics is discussed in the organization and the perception that ethical behavior is rewarded were the most significant factors in the study. As to "what hurts" in ethics/compliance management, two culture factors were quite harmful. Outcomes were more negative where employees perceived an expectation of unquestioning obedience to authority, and where they perceived a focus on self-interest rather than concern for employees and/or the community.

What Works and What Hurts in Ethics/Compliance Management: Prescriptions for Action

What should firms be doing if they want to achieve the most positive outcomes from their ethics/compliance management efforts? What should they avoid doing?

1. Tap the Trenches—Employee Perceptions Matter

Badaracco and Webb recently presented "a view from the trenches" in a report that summarized the results of in-depth interviews with recent graduates of the Harvard MBA program. These young managers reported pressures to be unethical, insufficient help from formal ethics programs and executives who were "out-of-touch" on ethical issues. The authors recommended in-depth interviews with lower-level employees to learn more about employee perceptions. While few companies have the resources to conduct in-depth interviews with a large number of employees, they can conduct surveys and focus groups to learn what their employees are thinking. Employees can tell a company a great deal about what's going on in its trenches. Our survey suggests that they are willing to report both the positive and the negative, such as the extent to which they perceive strong ethical leadership, employee fair treatment and consistency between words and actions, or the extent to which they perceive a focus on self-interest and unquestioning obedience to authority. Obviously, asking these questions may make ethical issues more salient to employees. Therefore, asking the questions assumes that you want to know the answers and that you are willing to take corrective action.

2. Build a Solid Ethical Culture

The ethics officer in a Fortune 500 company once stated, "I have a hard time when people [ask] me, 'Tell me about your company's ethics plan.' I want to tell them about everything we do. Because in my mind, everything we do is part of it." This quote demonstrates that ethics/compliance management is first and foremost a cultural phenomenon. As noted, ethical culture factors were among the most powerful factors in this study. It is not enough to have formal policies and programs. To achieve desired outcomes, concerns for ethics and legal compliance must be baked into the culture of the organization. Therefore, attention to the ethical culture should come first in any corporate ethics/compliance effort. Executive leaders and supervisors must regularly show they care about ethics and shared values (including demonstrating that values are as important as the bottom line), and they must show that they care through words and consistent actions. Consider employees' reactions when the CEO of a major bank who preached responsible use of corporate resources sent a corporate plane to California to pick up a pair of shoes for his wife. This CEO didn't understand that his actions spoke louder than his words.

3. Create a Values-Based Program That Incorporates Accountability and Care for Stakeholders

When it comes to creating a formal ethics/compliance program, managers need not choose between values-based and compliance-based approaches. Rather, these approaches are complementary. They are further complemented by an approach that is concerned about external stakeholders. However, to be most effective, formal efforts to manage ethics and legal compliance should be oriented primarily toward values. A values approach can include valuing customers and the community, as well as employee accountability for ethical conduct.

4. Focus on Formal Program Follow-Through

Some companies approach ethics/compliance management with the idea that all they need to do is check off the U.S. Sentencing Commission's seven requirements for due diligence by appointing an ethics officer, writing and distributing a formal code of conduct, communicating standards via codes and training programs and setting up hotlines and investigative procedures. The results of this study suggest that simply putting formal staff, structures and procedures into place does little to influence important outcomes. More important were employees' perceptions that the company follows through on its formal codes, policies and procedures by working hard to detect violators and by following up on ethical concerns raised by employees. Most important was the perception that actual practice is consistent with formal policies. Again, actions speak louder than words.

***

■ Conclusion

Contrary to the Business Roundtable's decade old statement, our study found that there are ways to measure the end results of corporate ethics and compliance programs. There are a number of important outcomes that can be measured reliably via employee surveys and that can be linked to key program and organizational influences.

A values-based cultural approach to ethics/compliance management works best. This approach requires the sincere commitment of leadership at all levels, including ongoing attention to key issues such as fair treatment of employees, rewards for ethical conduct, concern for external stakeholders and consistency between words and actions. The ethics/compliance program itself should be values-based, motivating employees to aspire to ethical conduct, encouraging them to question authority when ethics are at stake and holding them accountable for rule violations. The results of such an approach are impressive. They produce highly committed employees who are aware of ethics and compliance issues, who seek advice within the organization and who are willing to deliver bad news to their managers or report ethical/legal violations. Results also include less unethical/illegal behavior in the organization and better decision making because of the organization's ethics/compliance efforts.

Corporate Codes of Conduct

—International Labour Organization,
Bureau for Workers' Activities

Corporate codes of conduct have no globally accepted definition. The concept usually refers to companies' policy statements that define ethical standards for their conduct; however, there is great variance in the ways these statements are drafted. The following document prepared by the International Labour Organization offers an in-depth discussion of the origins of corporate codes of conduct, their various formats, transparency, monitoring and enforcement.

▌▌ Background

Defense Industry Scandals

Worldwide interest in corporate conduct was initially awakened in the 1980s by scandals in the defense industry and on Wall Street. Companies viewed business ethics as a way of promoting self-regulation and deterring government intervention and regulatory action. Corporate interest quickly led to the "institutionalization" of business ethics programs, consisting largely of codes of conduct, ethics officers and ethics training. (See, KPMG, *The Age of Ethics.* KPMG is the abbreviation for the names of the founding members: Klynveld, Peat, Marwick, Goerdeler. KPMG is a business services firm operating in 155 countries.)

Among the first companies to establish codes of conduct were General Electric, General Dynamics, Martin Marietta (now Lockheed Martin), and other defense contractors. These companies had all experienced procurement scandals (although General Dynamics and Martin Marietta were not formally charged with wrongdoing). Now, the defense sector actively polices itself. In 1986, 17 contractors signed the Defense Industry Initiative on Business Ethics and Conduct, which declares that each of the companies will review its ethical practices annually.

Naturally, corporate codes of conduct existed prior to the movement of the 1980s. For example, Johnson & Johnson's *Credo* was published in 1943. As early as 1935, General Robert Wood Johnson urged his fellow industrialists to embrace what he termed "a new industrial philosophy." Johnson defined this as the corporation's responsibility to customers, employees, the community and stockholders. According to Johnson & Johnson, the corporation has drawn heavily on the strength of the *Credo* for guidance through the years—at no time was this more evident than during the Tylenol® crises of 1982 and 1986, when the company's product was adulterated with cyanide and used as a murder weapon. (Johnson & Johnson's home page: http://www.j&j.com.)

Following the pricing scandals that rocked the defense industry in the 1980s, General Electric became a prime example of an American corporation in need of an image overhaul. In response, the company created a corporate ombudsman's office, originally for the

---

Reprinted with permission of the International Labour Organization
(http://www.ictilo.it/english/actrav/telearn/global/ilo/ code/main.htm).

purpose of examining its government defense contracts. The company also drew up a summary of in-house rules on ethical concerns, called "Integrity: The Spirit & the Letter of Our Commitment," which is 80 pages long and is available in most languages that are spoken in the General Electric worldwide network, including Arabic and Urdu. In early 1993, the office started a network of toll-free help lines for each business unit in the United States. Employees can call the hot lines anonymously to ask questions about the guidelines and to report suspected violations.

***

Consumer Power

While the long arm of the law is a factor in business decision making, sometimes the arm of ethics is longer still. Consumer power is increasingly being wielded to affect company behavior. The boycott mechanism has long been a means for political protest; for many years, a significant number of consumers avoided buying South African products. Recently, however, boycotts have been called to protest against the actions of specific companies. Nestlé's sales suffered from the boycott protesting about its policy on selling baby formula in the third world, and Shell was forced to change its plans for disposal of the Brent Spar oil platform when German consumers stopped buying Shell petrol. A 1995 poll of 30,000 consumers in the UK showed that one in three had boycotted stores or products in the past because of concerns about ethical standards, and 6 in 10 were prepared to boycott in the future. Almost two in three of those surveyed were more concerned about ethical issues now than five years ago. (See, International Society for Business, Economics and Ethics, *How Ethical Auditing Can Help Companies Compete More Effectively at an International Level?*)

Pressure groups are growing more professional and more vociferous. While in the past, unethical behavior by a company might have been kept quiet through skilled public relations, there is now a greater likelihood that employees from within a company will alert relevant pressure groups, as loyalty to employers has lessened while concern for the public good has grown. It is also more likely now than in the past that the pressure group will be successful in generating significant publicity about the incident. (International Society for Business, Economics and Ethics, *How Ethical Auditing Can Help Companies Compete More Effectively at an International Level?*)

In response to consumer pressure, a whole sector of ethical corporations has arisen in recent years. Some companies have made principled withdrawals from countries where they could otherwise manufacture profitably—this was the course taken by Levi Strauss in China. Levi Strauss has adopted a strong "good guy" image, because of its refusal to use subcontractors that exploit workers in developing countries. Protest from outraged consumers may force companies manufacturing in India or Thailand to sack the underage children they were previously employing. Codes prohibiting child labor have been introduced, especially among apparel manufacturers, merchandisers and retailers. (See the apparel company codes in the list of company codes.)

Globalization

Consciousness of the growing interdependence of all people on the earth—globalization—calls for more uniform treatment of people and their environment in every corner of the world. Globalization is one factor that has pushed multinationals to initiate uniform standards of conduct in all countries in which they operate. It may have seemed acceptable decades ago for Shell to apply lower environmental standards to its drilling in Ogoniland than those applied in Europe or North America, but in an era of acute consciousness of the interdependence of the world ecosystem, the same standards are rightly expected on every continent.

In 1986, Frederik Philips (former President of Philips Electronics) and Olivier Giscard d'Estaing (Vice-Chairman of INSEAD) founded the Caux Round Table of business leaders from Europe, Japan and the United States. Caux is committed to energizing the role of business and industry as a vital force for innovative global change. At the urging of Ryuzaburo Kaku, Chairman of Canon Inc., the Round Table has focused attention on the importance of global corporate responsibility in reducing social and economic threats to world peace and stability. Caux Round Table Principles for Business were drafted by a committee composed of Japanese, European and U.S. business representatives, and include a relatively long section on workers' rights.

Number of Codes

Although, a number of surveys have been carried out on corporate codes of conduct, it is difficult to estimate how common they actually are. Certainly, codes are very common among those companies that respond to surveys, but the rate of response tends to be low. For example, only 264 companies out of 1,900 responded to the Conference Board survey in 1991.

However, this survey is important, because it is the only international survey that follows up on the results of a previous survey, conducted in 1987. By and large, the participants were the same companies that had participated in the earlier survey, from the United States (186 companies), Canada (34 companies) and Europe (40 companies). Most of the companies surveyed were large, with median annual sales of the participants at $1 billion.

In 1991, 82% of the responding companies had codes of conduct. As was the case in 1987, companies in the financial sector were less likely to have codes (57%). Nearly half of the codes discussed or submitted by survey respondents had been enacted since the last study was published (45%). Codes were much more typical of U.S. companies than of European companies. (The Conference Board, *Corporate Ethics Practices,* 1992.)

KPMG surveyed 1,000 Canadian companies in 1996, but only 251 responded. Of these, 83% indicated that they have a published mission statement, and 66% reported having a code of conduct. (See KPMG, *1997 Business Ethics Survey Report.*)

In an International Center for Human Rights and Democratic Development (ICHRDD) survey in 1996, the proportion of Canadian companies that had codes of conduct was much smaller. Only one in five of the 43 Canadian companies that responded reported having adopted a code of conduct for international operations. A total of 98 companies were surveyed. (See, ICHRDD, *Canada's Largest Corporations Lack Codes of Conduct on Treatment of Workers Overseas.*)

Formats of Codes

In the Conference Board survey, the *compliance code* was the most common code type in all regions. Over 90% responded that their company's statement requires particular types of employee or company behavior. Three-fourths of the responding organizations with codes said their statement is a credo that explains the company's accountability to its key constituencies (e.g., employees, customers and suppliers). *Management philosophy declarations* are the least common format—still, more than half of the companies with codes use this type of statement. Canadian firms are more likely to use philosophy declarations than are U.S. or European firms. (The Conference Board, *Corporate Ethics Practices,* 1992.)

Survey responses indicated that most codes are hybrids of more than one type. Of the three types, the compliance code is likely to have been in existence the longest. The median date of adoption for compliance statements is 1985.

The reports of 1987 and 1991 indicate that code drafting is a dynamic process. Nearly two-thirds of the compliance codes were revised between the two surveys.

In the KPMG survey (251 Canadian companies in 1996), 79% of companies with a published code of conduct said that the code is appropriately described as a set of "Guiding Principles," while 32% felt that "Rules and Regulations" was a fitting label.

In a U.S. Department of Labor survey, which focused on child labor in the apparel industry, 33 of 42 companies that provided reportable responses had corporate codes of conduct, statements of principles, or compliance certificates specifically addressing child labor in overseas production. Twelve further respondents did the same through contract requirements contained in purchase orders, letters of credit, or buying agent agreements.

Nine respondents used a combination of both types of policy, while six had no policy on overseas child labor. (See United States Labor Department, The Apparel Industry and Codes of Conduct, Chapter E: Development of Apparel Industry Codes of Conduct.)

A comparison of the codes of conduct . . . provides an idea of how differently codes can be formulated. An example of a specific and clear format is Halliburton's code, in which concepts and scope are well defined. Administration of the code is clear and unambiguous, including such issues as allocations of responsibility, delegation of substantial discretionary authority, communication of policies, monitoring and auditing, the reporting system, investigation of violations and disciplinary measures. Under each issue regulated by the code, there are sections regarding the purpose, policy and procedures related to the issue. However, this code seems to be an exception. Most codes are rather brief and general statements, which leave a good deal of room for interpretation and contain no administrative details.

***

Content of Codes

All Issues

The Conference Board questionnaire identified 13 issue areas dealt with in corporate codes. Most codes include some formal statement of the company's fundamental principles. Nine specific issues in codes were named by more than 66 companies. Among these, six relate in some degree to the employee's contract with the company.

Purchasing guidelines and security of proprietary information—issues focused on employee honesty—were the only specific areas of concern cited by over half the code companies. Of the remaining human resource-oriented issues, three acknowledge company commitments to the employee (workplace safety, confidentiality of employee records and employee privacy), and one focuses on employee obligations (intellectual property safeguards). The three remaining major subject areas relate to corporate social accountability—for example in environmental, marketing and product safety responsibility.

There were few regional variations in subject matter. Codes in the United States are more likely to include sections on the security of proprietary information. Workplace safety is a more frequent subject of European ethics statements.

Over the period between the 1987 and 1991 surveys, 20% of the European companies had added environmental responsibility to their codes. Among U.S. companies, the most common addition was fundamental guiding principles of company. Among Canadian companies, the most common additions related to intellectual property and marketing.

Besides fundamental guiding principles, environmental responsibility was the only issue added in over 10% of the codes. (For examples of environmental accountability statements, see the codes of Nestlé and Waste Management.)

The interest in environmental problems has grown in the last ten years especially among chemical companies. Member companies of the Chemical Manufacturers' Association have adopted six codes of management practices under the Responsible Care initiative, which was launched in 1988: Community Awareness and Emergency Response, Pollution Prevention, Process Safety, Distribution, Employee Health and Safety and Product Stewardship.

In the KPMG survey of 251 Canadian companies in 1996, participants were first asked to score for importance seven issue areas in their codes of conduct. The scoring was on a scale of 1 to 4, and the criteria for scoring was [sic] the potential risk to their business posed by the issue area in question. The most important categories identified by the respondents were employee and workplace issues and the handling of company assets.

Next, the companies were asked to rank individual issues as to their associated risk factor. Worker health and safety was the second most important issue in rank.

***

◼◼◼ Transparency of Codes

Dissemination

According to the Conference Board report, companies were more willing to discuss their codes openly in 1991 than in 1987, when only a handful of respondents returned a copy of their code with a completed questionnaire. In 1991, more than one-third of companies with ethics statements supplied them with the questionnaire.

According to the KPMG survey of 251 Canadian companies in 1996, external distribution of the code was reported by less than 30% of respondents that had codes of conduct.

The ICHRDD survey of 43 Canadian companies in 1996 indicated that Canadian companies are reluctant to speak about their relations with workers abroad. Even companies that report having codes of conduct are reluctant to share them with the public. The study suggests that "Canadian business places a very low priority on communicating its response to issues it confronts in its overseas operations to the non-governmental sector. A large number of firms expressed no . . . interest in the subject."

According to the U.S. Department of Labor survey of 42 U.S. apparel companies in 1996, a few companies made an effort to communicate information on their codes of conduct and monitoring programs to the general public, including their shareholders: Levi Strauss and The Gap have sections on their codes of conduct in their annual reports to shareholders.

Distribution

Within the Company

According to the Conference Board report, there is a clear trend in favor of distributing the company's code to all employees. In 1987, nearly two-thirds of the responding code companies gave it to all their employees. Among 1991 survey participants, 77% followed this practice. The figure for Canada (83%) was slightly higher than that in the United States or Europe. Of companies that have codes, 22% limited distribution to top and middle management (down from over one-third in 1987), and just three companies gave the code only to top managers.

Distribution to employees in overseas divisions is common, but not universal—72% of survey participants engaged in this practice. Canadian companies were somewhat less likely to distribute codes in this manner than were U.S. or European companies.

European companies were more likely to modify their documents for use outside the home country (25%) than were U.S. (14%) or Canadian companies (13%). In fact, nearly half of all European companies had branches, subsidiaries or divisions with their own codes (45%). This practice is much less common in U.S. and Canadian firms.

The KPMG survey (251 Canadian companies in 1996) revealed that just over 80% of companies with a published mission statement believed that "the average employee is likely to be aware of it." A lower proportion of those with mission statements (73%) indicated that the mission statement was often referred to in policies and other statements. A published code of ethics, practice or conduct was somewhat less common. Of those who had a published code of conduct, all but 4% indicated that the codes were widely distributed internally.

To Contractor Companies

According to the U.S. Department of Labor survey (42 U.S. apparel companies in 1996), only a very few respondents indicated that they have tried to ensure that production workers in overseas facilities know about their code or policy by specifically requiring that copies of such statements be posted. Only three companies stated that they unconditionally require contractors to post their code. The Gap requires that its code, which has been translated into 39 languages, be posted in each contractor facility. Liz Claiborne, which has translated its Standards of Engagement into more than 10 different languages, requires all contractors to post the Standards in the local language in common areas, such as cafeterias or locker rooms, of every facility where Liz Claiborne products are made. Phillips-

Van Heusen stated that it insists that every facility post its "PVH Shared Commitment" poster, which contains guidelines and standards on worker's rights. The poster is printed in English and Spanish, and is sent to Asia with instructions for it to be translated into local languages. Nike and Sara Lee stated that their codes are posted at some facilities. Nike indicated that its code is posted in all its footwear contractors' factories in two or three languages, but this is not necessarily the case for its apparel contractors. Nike stated that its footwear contractors produce exclusively for Nike, while its apparel contractors often produce for many other companies. Nike often uses individual apparel contractors for only a short period of time. Sara Lee indicated that it posts notices of employees' rights at its wholly owned facilities in English and the host language.

Managers of two-thirds (47 out of 70) of surveyed plants that currently export to U.S. apparel companies indicated that they were aware of codes of conduct issued by their U.S. customers. Based on company visits, awareness among managers about codes of conduct was highest in El Salvador (all eight companies visited knew about the codes) and Guatemala (six out of nine companies knew). In three other countries visited—the Dominican Republic, Honduras and the Philippines—managers interviewed were more evenly divided between those who were aware and those who were not. In India, only two out of seven producers visited were aware of the codes of conduct of their U.S. customers. However, only 34 of the 47 companies that indicated they were aware of codes of conduct had available a copy of the code (or contractual provision) that they could show and discuss with the visiting Department of Labor official. Thus, managers at less than half of the plants visited were able to produce a code of conduct upon request.

The plant visits by Department of Labor officials suggest that while posting of a U.S. garment importer's codes of conduct seems to be common practice in El Salvador, it is not the norm in the garment industries of the other countries visited. In all, 21 of the 70 plants visited by the officials had posted a code of conduct of a U.S. customer, and seven of these were in El Salvador (out of eight total plants visited in that country). Elsewhere, two plants visited in the Dominican Republic had codes of conduct posted, one plant in Honduras, two in Guatemala, two in India and seven in the Philippines.

Although a significant number of suppliers knew about the U.S. corporate codes of conduct, meetings with workers and their representatives in the six countries visited suggested that relatively few workers were aware of the existence of codes of conduct, and even fewer understood their implications.

The lack of awareness on the part of workers about codes of conduct may be attributable in part to the relatively low level of effort on the part of producers to inform their workers about the codes. Management regards codes of conduct—and compliance with labor law—as a management problem, and approaches the monitoring and supervision of these matters as management responsibilities. Workers are not seen by management as having a role in these activities.

Managers in 22 of the companies visited told the Department of Labor officials that they informed workers about codes of conduct—13 companies indicating they do so orally, and only 9 stating that they do so both orally and in writing. Of all the plants that were visited in the six countries, there was only one example of a producer that had an explicit policy of informing workers about the code of conduct of its U.S. customer. (For more detailed, company specific, information, see United States Department of Labor, The Apparel Industry and Codes of Conduct, section Transparency.)

***

◼◼ Monitoring of the Codes

Just over 40% of the participants in the KPMG survey (251 Canadian companies in 1996) indicated that there was a senior-level manager whose role specifically includes the implementation, monitoring or assurance of the ethics program. Of the 102 companies with such a senior manager, 16 reported that this manager had the title "Compliance Officer," while three indicated that the title of this manager was "Ethics Officer." Most often (in 22 cases), the "Human Resources Manager" was indicated as having this responsibility.

Of the 251 responses, 76 indicated there was a position within the firm that had responsibility for enabling "upstream communication" and equitable resolution of ethics or compliance problems. Of these, 14 reported that this role is a full-time assignment. In companies that reported this type of "ombudsperson" role, almost two-thirds had established the position three or more years prior to the survey.

In 78% of the responding companies, there was no formal policy to protect employees that report ethics violations or non-compliance with the law or with company policies. Of the 54 companies that indicated they did have such a policy, over half said that the policy was supported by a confidential hot-line or similar procedure.

A specific policy on conflicts of interest and specific guidelines in this regard were reported by 58% of all respondents. Of these, three-quarters require a compliance sign-off, and almost half have reviewed or updated the policy within the last year.

Over 60% of the respondents reported that they had never undertaken a comprehensive review of their ethics-related policies and performance. Over half of the companies that have undertaken such a review indicated that it was completed within the year prior to the survey.

According to the U.S. Department of Labor survey (42 United States apparel companies in 1996), eight companies had no monitoring system to implement their codes of conduct. A further 28 companies had developed internal monitoring systems, using local or regional company personnel or employees from United States corporate offices to monitor labor practices. Internal monitoring may be used by companies that are reluctant to grant access to their facilities, procedures and business practices to outside monitors. It is most common among large, vertically integrated companies (i.e., those in which the corporation owns or directly controls all stages of the production process). Internal monitoring is less common for companies, particularly retailers, that do not own or control the factories that make the products they sell. Some retailers internally monitor only those plants producing private-label merchandise, which they import directly. United States retailers and manufacturers who use hundreds or thousands of foreign contractors may find it a logistical or financial hardship to monitor all of the facilities from which they source.

Buying agents were relied on to monitor compliance with corporate codes by 12 companies in the survey. This procedure avoids the financial and logistical burden of monitoring, but also removes the U.S. corporation from the direct line of control in implementing its policy. Only four companies used an outside auditor, and only two an NGO for the monitoring of their codes. (For more detailed, company specific, information, see United States Department of Labor, The Apparel Industry and Codes of Conduct, Implementation of Apparel Industry Codes of Conduct.)

All 70 of the plants exporting garments to the United States that were visited by Department of Labor officials confirmed that they are subject to regular visits by their U.S. customers or their agents to verify product quality and to coordinate production and delivery schedules. About 90% of the companies visited stated that monitors or inspectors verifying product quality generally also examined working conditions in the plant, with emphasis on safety and health issues (climate control, ventilation systems, fire escapes, etc.).

Whether monitoring visits are announced or unannounced differs widely from company to company. In 41 of the companies interviewed (58%), monitoring visits by the U.S. importer, its agent or its representatives were announced in advance. In 13 companies (18%) they were unannounced, while there were both announced and unannounced visits in 16 companies (23%).

While monitoring for product quality and even for health and safety conditions is customary in the garment industry, the field visits by Department of Labor officials suggest that monitoring for compliance with labor-related provisions of the U.S. garment importer's codes of conduct is not. This applies particularly to child labor. Where such monitoring does occur, the degree to which it extends to all labor standards addressed by the codes—as opposed to exclusively safety and health issues—seems to vary widely across suppliers. Foreign suppliers that are wholly owned by a U.S. corporation, or contract directly with a U.S. corporation with a presence abroad, seem to be subject to the most frequent and most thorough monitoring of codes of conduct, including those related to child labor and other labor standards.

Monitoring the implementation of child labor provisions of codes of conduct is very challenging. Generally, the closer the relationship between a U.S. garment importer and the actual producer of the items, the greater the ability of the U.S. company to influence labor practices in the production process, including prohibitions on child labor. Conversely, it is more complex and challenging to implement labor policies in longer chains of procurement and production—in one example drawn from the Philippines, there were five steps between producer and final buyer. With more levels of buying agents, contractors and subcontractors, the U.S. importer has less ability to influence labor practices.

The field visits also revealed numerous instances of contractual monitoring of codes of conduct. Contractual monitoring is most prevalent in the case of U.S. retailers, which do not have a significant presence abroad.

In these situations, the burden of monitoring compliance with the U.S. importer's child labor policies rests with the foreign agent, contractor or subcontractor, typically through a self-certification process. In these instances, the role of the U.S. importer in monitoring compliance of its code of conduct is minimal. In Honduras, Fabena Fashions is required by Macy's and Wal-Mart to sign a contract including a no-child-labor clause. In Tirupur, India, the producer Chenduran Textiles exports about one-half of its output to the United States. Its main U.S. customer is Tropic Textiles of New York City, a supplier to Wal-Mart. Tropic requires Chenduran to certify that no slave or child labor is used in the production of goods through a paragraph in the contract or bill of lading. Tropic accepts Chenduran's self-certification of the clause and does not have any in-country monitoring, education, implementation or enforcement programs. Also in India, Pankaj Enterprises is an exporter of mid-grade apparel items based in New Delhi that exports to the United States. Pankaj's U.S. buyers require that no child labor be used in the manufacture of garments. Pankaj buys its fabric, and guarantees that no child labor is used in the production of garments through a self-certification process. There is no monitoring by the importer or its agents.

In some instances, U.S. importers use a combination of contractual and active monitoring, using auditors from the importer itself or its agents to verify compliance. In the Philippines, Liz Claiborne has a policy of monitoring and supervising its contractors, which must certify that they are in compliance with the code of conduct. In addition, contractors are subject to frequent visits from Liz Claiborne's Philippines office, which monitors implementation of the code of conduct as well as quality control. Warnaco requires that contractors certify that child labor has not been used, and also audits suppliers in Honduras for full compliance with its child labor policies, including age verification. Macy's, Wal-Mart and The Limited have checked personnel records at Fabena Fashions to verify the age of workers. In India, Zoro Garments supplies 75% of its production to the U.S. market. Zoro's major U.S. customers are Rustic River, Quick Silver, Blue Print and JCPenney, while Phillips-Van Heusen is a former customer. According to Zoro's management, representatives of U.S. customers have visited Zoro's factory occasionally for quality control inspections. Most of these visits were walk-throughs with some general questions raised about the use of child labor, but no checklist of requirements was administered. Phillips-Van Heusen had previously raised the subject of codes of conduct with Zoro's management and asked the company to fill out a questionnaire. When Zoro was producing for Phillips-Van Heusen, there was a clause in its contract related to child labor. Primo Industries in El Salvador, a contractor for Liz Claiborne, Lands' End, Polo and JCPenney, met with Liz Claiborne several years ago to discuss and sign the Liz Claiborne code of conduct. The plant manager told Department of Labor officials that Liz Claiborne is "the toughest on child labor." He also said that American inspectors visit the plant approximately twice a month to check on quality control and see whether their rules and regulations are being implemented.

Based on field visits, it appears that most monitoring conducted by U.S. corporations primarily covers quality control issues. As such, there seems to be relatively little interaction between monitors on the one hand, and workers and the local community on the other. It also appears that monitors have a technical background in production and quality control and are relatively untrained with regard to the implementation of labor standards. (For more detailed, company-specific information, see United States Department of Labor, The Apparel Industry and Codes of Conduct, chapter E: Monitoring.)

■ Enforcement of the Codes

None of the surveys discussed above dealt with the issue of enforcement of codes internally within the companies themselves, in cases where management or employees of the company may violate the code. A quick overview indicates that most codes do not include any enforcement provisions or are not specific regarding enforcement measures. For example, the Boeing code states simply that "violations of the company standards of conduct are cause for appropriate corrective action including discipline."

However, there are also codes that are specific regarding disciplinary measures. A good example is Halliburton's code, which states that:

1. The Company shall consistently enforce its Code of Business Conduct through appropriate means of discipline. Pursuant to procedures adopted by it, the Executive Committee shall determine whether violations of the Code of Business Conduct have occurred and, if so, shall determine the disciplinary measures to be taken against any employee or agent of the Company who has so violated the Code of Business Conduct.

    The disciplinary measures, which may be invoked at the discretion of the Executive Committee, include, but are not limited to, counseling, oral or written reprimands, warnings, probation or suspension without pay, demotions, reductions in salary, termination of employment and restitution.

    Persons subject to disciplinary measures shall include, in addition to the violator, others involved in the wrongdoing such as (i) persons who fail to use reasonable care to detect a violation, (ii) persons who if requested to divulge information withhold material information regarding a violation and (iii) supervisors who approve or condone the violations or attempt to retaliate against employees or agents for reporting violations or violators.

2. Documentation. Subject to the applicable document retention program, the Company shall document its compliance efforts and results to evidence its commitment to comply with the standards and procedures set forth above.

According to the U.S. Department of Labor survey (42 U.S. apparel companies in 1996), companies that pass the screening process and become contractors of U.S. corporations may face a range of corrective measures should they fall short in complying with the code of conduct.

In Guatemala, although garment contractors and subcontractors were unable to articulate the U.S. companies' policies to address violations of their codes of conduct, they expressed great concern about the possibility of losing their contracts if they were found to have child labor problems. A representative of Phillips-Van Heusen stated that in May 1996, his company had identified three young workers (under 15 years of age) in a plant operated by a subcontractor in San Pedro de Sacatepequez. Upon learning of their presence, Phillips-Van Heusen required the company to dismiss the three young workers immediately.

In the Dominican Republic, many companies stated that U.S. clients had requested changes in the physical conditions of the factories during their visits to the companies. These changes often included requirements for eating facilities, restrooms and more lighting or ventilation. In most cases, changes affecting working conditions were related to safety and health issues. Most of the companies that had contracts with Levi Strauss in the Santiago Zona Franca said that all companies were requested to reinforce, move or rebuild wooden mezzanines—where sewing machines were stationed—as a fire safety precaution.

Undergarment Fashions mentioned that JCPenney, in addition to performing periodic visits to the plant, also had a rating system to evaluate the contractor's performance. Under this rating system, a company must receive at least 50 points in order to maintain its current contract. If the company does not obtain a satisfactory rating, it is put on probation and given a reasonable period of time to make the requested changes.

High Quality Products, located in Zona Franca Los Alcarrizos, a contractor for the Jones Apparel Group, said that Jones Apparel terminated a contract with Bonahan Apparel (in Zona Franca Bonao) because of Bonahan's refusal to recognize the establishment of a union in its plant.

In Honduras, Rothschilds made a number of recommendations regarding clean toilets, lighting, ventilation, drinking water and hours of work for 14- and 15-year-old workers at Global Fashions.

In part because of the priority to improve quality, but also because of a concern about violations of labor standards (and child labor provisions in particular), U.S. garment importers have cut back sharply on subcontracting and also reduced the number of their foreign suppliers. From the point of view of foreign garment producers, the streamlining of suppliers in the U.S. garment industry has resulted in clear winners and losers.

On the one hand, suppliers to the United States market that can meet the considerations of quality and timeliness of product while complying with codes of conduct have been rewarded with continued orders. They have also received additional orders which have been diverted to them from producers that rely on subcontracting schemes.

On the other hand, marginal suppliers—in terms of quality and timeliness of output, physical plant or ability to comply with labor standards—have lost their contracts with United States importers. They have had to resort to sales to other, less profitable markets, including their own domestic market.

Continued access to the U.S. market is a very large incentive for overseas garment producers to meet quality and timeliness requirements and to comply with codes of conduct. Thus, the prospect of continued ability to ship to the United States reinforces compliance with appropriate standards. Foreign countries also have a great deal at stake, as unused import quota allocations translate into the loss of export revenue in the short term and loss of the import quota in the longer term. (For more detailed, company specific, information, see United States Department of Labor, The Apparel Industry and Codes of Conduct, chapter F: Enforcement.)

Profitable Ethical Programs

—Jason Lunday

In response to a previous e-mail to a listserver on teaching business ethics, Jason Lunday identifies some apparently successful ethical business practices from the annals of business history.

. . . Some apparently successful ethical business practices:

(In some cases, the companies claim a very direct bottom-line effect to certain ethical practices. Others claim that their ethical practices contribute to an overall corporate climate which cuts waste, encourages efficiency, promotes community/marketplace goodwill, allowing the company a healthy bottom line.)

1. 3M—through its Pollution Prevention Program (3P), initiated in the mid-1970s, the corporation claims to have decreased its production and emission of air, solid and water pollutants by billions of pounds AND saved the company over $500 million during its first 15 years. It did so by using its expertise in innovation to find new ways of manufacturing which led to fewer pollutants. To qualify for the 3P program, ideas had to meet three of four measures, only one of which was cost savings. [See Alfred Marcus, *Business and Society: Strategy, Ethics and the Global Economy,* Irwin, Chicago, 1996.]

While 3M was considered the first, I understand that a large number of companies have successfully accomplished similar environmental initiatives, reducing pollutants and saving money. Contact the Management Institute for Environment and Business, Washington, DC, for examples.

2. Levi Strauss—with a strong history of employee goodwill, LSCO has worked for numerous years to insure that its employee policies demonstrate respect for workers and their lives. It has consistently paid workers at the top of the industry and granted benefits uncommon among its competitors (like year-round employment). Further, it has encouraged strong employee communication and idea-sharing. It has expected that such treatment would create mutual respect. This apparently came true when a South American operation effectively communicated one of its new product launches to headquarters during a time of overall lagging sales. The idea, Dockers, became the biggest product introduction in U.S. history and reinvigorated the company. [See Jeffrey Edwards and Jason Lunday, *Levi Strauss & Co.: The South Zarzamora Street Plant,* Darden Graduate Business School Case Bibliography.]

There are other stories of how factory employees have taken pay cuts, done without raises, and accepted other risks at certain times because of the company's fair treatment and with an expectation that such a well-managed company will overcome periodic difficulties.

3. South Shore Bank—the company came up with the great idea to help its local community, a depressed area of Chicago, where few could get bank loans. In finding ways to grant credit where other banks would not, South Shore not only helped a community pick itself back up, it increased bank earnings.

Jason Lunday, "Profitable Ethical Programs," e-mail, June 18, 1996. Reprinted by permission of the author.

[Sorry, don't have a reference handy. South Shore has won Business Ethics Magazine's annual award in recent years, so a past edition of the magazine will overview the company's story.]

4. Johnson & Johnson—need we say more on this one? For a treatment of this, see *Managing Corporate Ethics,* Francis Aguilar, Oxford University Press, New York, 1994.

5. Delta Air Lines—Delta also has a strong history of employee relations, to the extent that, for years, it was the only non-unionized airline. This allowed the carrier flexibility during recessions to move workers around in order to maximize manpower in key areas. It also traditionally allows the airline to have employees perform multiple tasks so that it does not have to hire additional workers. The airline had, for many years, consistently been at the top of the Department of Transportation's lowest complaint list. It generally is still there, occasionally being beat out by Southwest. Employee goodwill because of the company's treatment also helps the company keep a very low employee/seat miles ratio. Some years back, because of exceptional treatment, the employees chipped in and bought the company a passenger jet. Delta has also ended up as one of the country's most admired companies for many years. [Personal unpublished research—if you want article references, just ask. I've got a lot.]

6. Lincoln Electric—arc welding. Company claims that strong employee orientation has allowed it to earn exceptional profits. [See *Managing Corporate Ethics,* Francis Aguilar, Oxford University Press, New York, 1994.]

7. Honda—attention to customer quality allowed it strong entrance into U.S. market. [*Business and Society,* Alfred Marcus, Irwin, Chicago, 1996.]

8. BFI—effort to help New York rid itself of corruption in the trash hauling business gave the company early entry into a lucrative market. [See recent *Fortune* cover story.]

9. Socially responsible companies Body Shop, Ben & Jerry's, Tom's of Maine, etc.: each claims that their orientation to meeting stakeholder needs—in a variety of forms— allowed them to become large players in their respective markets. [See *Body and Soul,* Anita Roddick, *The Soul of a Business,* Tom Chappell, don't know Ben & Jerry's book.]

10. Merck—another company at the very top of Fortune's Most Admired Companies. The company ended up paying millions of dollars to formulate, manufacture and distribute a drug which cures river blindness, which is generally found in poor regions of lesser developed countries. The goodwill alone from this has apparently, like J&J and Tylenol, given it many consumers' trust. Granted, it would be difficult to quantify how much that is worth, but I doubt that Vagelos or the current chairman would deny it has been worth a lot.

11. Sears, Roebuck—when questions arose about possible inappropriate sales practices of product warranties, which, by the way, were making BIG money for the retailer, they retrained their associates to ensure that the warranties were not being pushed on customers or otherwise sold unethically. Expecting a drop in warranty sales, they instead were hit with a sizeable increase. [See *Ethikos* back issue, can't remember the date. Also, personal consulting experience with them.]

Business ethics books are generally filled with cases of companies which have gotten into trouble. We don't see enough of the good stories since, I suppose, we simply expect this. However, the positive examples can go a long way in encouraging prosocial behavior, which, like deterrence theory, is another aspect of business ethics.

Corporate Codes and Ethics Programs

—Michael C. Deck

In the following selection, Michael Deck explains research conducted to gather and to analyze 200 codes of conduct. The researcher found that while many firms have codes, they are not always communicated to stakeholders, nor are they always adhered to. Consider whether any firm you have worked for has had a code and whether you felt it was completely integrated into the decision-making functions of the firm.

Stakeholder Theory

Our research program has examined more than 70 Canadian corporations over the last 10 years. As we studied the data, it became clear that the managers of successful companies no longer regard shareholders as the sole and necessarily most important stakeholders in the corporation. The concept of shareholders endowed with a right to the maximization of profits is being replaced by the concept of stakeholders, of which shareholders comprise only one group. The shareholder is no longer the preeminent stakeholder, to be rewarded at the expense of other stakeholders. . . .

What this research shows is that when management or the board of a company favor one group of stakeholders at the expense of other primary stakeholder groups, difficulties always develop. When shareholders are favored unfairly, when maximizing the bottom line takes full priority, customers or employees or suppliers invariably will be short-changed. . . .

Managing Ethics in the Workplace

If we agree that values, ethics and moral principles are essential to sound decision making, how does a manager go about managing that aspect of the organization?

In looking for an answer to that question, we thought it would make sense to begin looking for the values, ethics and moral principles of an organization in its Code of Ethics. Beginning three years ago, our Centre undertook to gather and to analyze 200 corporate codes. We learned that while corporations do indeed have values, ethics and moral principles, these are not always communicated in a code of ethics and may in fact be quite different from what the code might lead one to believe.

While it would be ingenuous to think that ethical behavior within an organization can be changed simply by posting a list of high sounding principles, it is equally naive to imagine that the ethics of an organization "just happens and there's nothing to be done about it."

Every organization, as Steven Brenner points out, has an ethics program, whether it knows it or not.[1] The ethics program is that set of factors both explicit and implicit which

---

Michael C. Deck, "Corporate Codes and Ethics Programs," www.kpmg.ca/ethics/eth_clks.htm First presented at "Business Practices under NAFTA: Developing Common Standards for Global Business," University of Colorado–Denver, December 8–10, 1994. Reprinted by permission of the author.

communicate corporate values, define parameters of decision making and establish the ground rules for behavior. This is similar to what Robert Jackall has described as "institutional logic." An effective ethics program encourages behavior consistent with corporate principles.

Explicit elements of a corporate ethics program include the things which an organization says it believes in, and the efforts made to communicate those principles directly. The centerpiece of the explicit components is the corporate code. In order to evaluate the effectiveness of a corporate code, the purpose of the code must be considered. Corporate codes can serve a variety of purposes: from "image enhancing" to "due diligence defense," from guidance for employees who want to "do the right thing" to helping an employee resist pressure from a superior. The corporate code and its implementation can raise issues of ethics to a conscious level and legitimate discussion.[2]

Our research on about 200 corporate codes revealed some interesting details about their nature and purpose.[3] Using the Stakeholder Model, we sorted out the statements made in these codes according to which stakeholder's interests were being addressed. One observation is that most of the text in these codes is concerned with the duty and responsibility of the employee to the company. Put more strongly, it seems that the most common purpose of a corporate code is to protect the firm from its employees. This is borne out by the observation that the most frequently cited "reason why" for ethical behavior is that violations will hurt the company. The problem with this approach is that if the possibility of getting caught (and incurring the penalty) is apparently small, then the reason for ethical behavior evaporates. . . .

The analysis of these codes also looked at the "approach" used for each statement, categorizing each as Guiding Principle, Act & Disclose, Seek Advice or Rule. These categories lie along a scale which we describe as "Source of Control."

. . . This analysis [made it] clear that there were really three basic types of codes, differentiated by the source of control.

The terms "*Code of Ethics*," "*Code of Conduct*" and "*Code of Practice*" are often used interchangeably. It is useful, however, to distinguish among these terms in order to establish a basic typology. Each basic code type has a different intent and purpose.

Codes of Ethics are statements of values and principles which define the purpose of the company. These codes seek to clarify the ethics of the corporation and to define its responsibilities to different groups of stakeholders as well as defining the responsibilities of its employees. These codes are expressed in terms of credos or guiding principles. Such a code says: "This is who we are and this is what we stand for," with the word "we" including the company and all its employees, whose behavior and actions are expected to conform to the ethics and principles stated in the code.

Codes of Practice are interpretations and illustrations of corporate values and principles, and they are addressed to the employee as individual decision maker. In effect they say: "This is how we do things around here." Such a code seeks to shape the expression of the corporation's stated values through the practices of its employees. Codes of practice tend to rely on guidelines for decision making, using such rules of thumb as "act and disclose" or "seek advice." This approach takes a view of ethics as "what we do because it is our character."

Codes of Conduct are statements of rules: "This is what one must (or must not) do," as distinct from the code of ethics, which is stating: "This is how we expect one to behave." Codes of Conduct typically are comprised of a list of rules, stated either affirmatively or as prohibitions. Penalties for transgressions may be identified and systems of compliance and appeal defined. Potential conflicts of interest are often described, with appropriate rules for guidance. This approach takes a view of ethics as what is not to be done (or seen not to be done) in view of the consequences.

In practice, corporate codes tend to include elements of all three types, but for analytical purposes it is helpful to consider these three basic types as benchmarks. Each of the three types is useful and each can be appropriate or necessary in particular business and organizational settings. For example, in a divisionalized corporation, it would be appropriate to draft a Code of Ethics in order to enunciate the company's overall purpose and the guiding principles and ethics that govern its actions and behavior. At the divisional and functional area levels, different and divisionalized Codes of Conduct and Practice are appropriate, so long as the rules, examples and guidelines are not in conflict with the statement of the corporation's guiding principles and ethics. . . .

Have Ethics Programs Failed?

It is interesting to note at this point that recent research has found no significant correlation between corporations having a code of ethics and a reduction in ethical violations.[4] Is the problem that the code was badly written? Probably not. Is there a problem with implementation? A more likely suspect, since, of the 90% of companies that have codes, only 28% do any training. There is, however, another factor which, I would suggest, accounts for these findings. I referred earlier to the implicit components of an ethics program. It may well be that the failure of the explicit components to produce results is the result of their having to fight an uphill battle against the implicit components.

If the goal is to produce behavior which is in line with the explicit values, principles and ethics of the organization, then congruency between the explicit and implicit components of the ethics program is essential.

To evaluate the potential effectiveness of an ethics program we propose several criteria which can be applied to the explicit components, beginning with the published code of ethics/practice/conduct. Assuming that the corporate code is satisfactory, the next step is to evaluate implementation efforts. Ultimately, the success and effectiveness of the program will depend on the next step, which is an honest and objective audit of the "implicit" components.

One danger of using a phrase such as "ethics program" is that it might suggest a requirement for a large scale, disruptive and expensive process. Just the opposite is true. As I said at the beginning of this section, every corporation already has an ethics program. What is proposed here is a framework for looking at the effectiveness of what is already in place and for identifying what, if any, aspects need strengthening or modification. The ethical ground rules, values and practices of an organization develop incrementally over time and will require time to change.

Notes

1. Brenner, S. N., "Ethics Programs and Their Dimensions," *Journal of Business Ethics,* Vol. 11: 391, 399, 1992.
2. Metzger, M., D. R. Dalton, and J. W. Hill, "The Organization of Ethics and the Ethics of Organizations: The Case for Expanded Organizational Ethics Audits," *Business Ethics Quarterly,* Vol. 3, Issue 1, 1993, pp. 27–43.
3. The details of this research are expanded in M. B. E. Clarkson and M. C. Deck, "Applying the Stakeholder Management Model to the Analysis and Evaluation of Corporate Codes," in *Business and Society in a Changing World Order,* pp. 55–76 (Best Papers volume of the 1992 Conference of the International Association for Business and Society), Dean C. Ludwig, Editor. Edwin Mellen Press, New York. 1993.
4. Rich, A. J., C. S. Smith, and P. H. Mihalek: 1990, "Are Corporate Codes of Conduct Effective?" *Management Accounting* (September), pp. 34–35.

Do Codes of Conduct Deliver the Goods?

—Maureen Quigley

Mission statements are constantly and consistently developed by firms, though there is only some conclusive evidence of their impact. Maureen Quigley asks the questions that many corporations therefore would like answered!

Companies adopt a range of ways and means to tackle ethical problems found within their supply chains, such as abuse of safety standards in factories in developing countries. Each approach has inherent strengths and pitfalls, yet each represents a step in a process of improving conditions. Companies most commonly start by adopting codes of conduct and internal monitoring systems. But are such steps enough? Experiences of the Pentland Group suggest that companies facing the difficult and complex demands of ethical trading will need more than formulaic codes or monitoring.

A code can be an essential first step. It defines key principles and aspirations, and companies can often use their purchasing power to urge suppliers' compliance with it. Yet such leverage is limited in scope because:

- It hinges on a buyer committed to taking a large percentage of a supplier's production.
- It offers no advantage to smaller companies that lack significant purchasing power.
- It could be used unfairly to discriminate against small to medium-sized enterprises.
- It is piecemeal, tackling issues on factory-by-factory basis rather than addressing larger root causes.
- It may be used cosmetically to guard corporate reputations rather than improve conditions.

A second, more progressive phase is where a company implements a code of conduct, either by imposing it on suppliers or by more collaborative means, then works to integrate the principals of the code into its own supply chain management and other management systems. The blending together of principals and actions is essential to sustainable ethical trading.

Nonetheless, the roots of the problems and dilemmas found in manufacturing are too complex to be sorted out on a factory-by-factory basis. Tackling problems found in worker health and safety involves looking at external forces and conditions, such as the capacity of civic institutions to regulate, enforce and provide essential services to businesses and workers. The route to lasting improvement is to overcome contextual barriers, inefficiencies and inequalities commonly associated with underdevelopment, that impede sustainable change. Companies that seek to be a positive force for change need to take a developmental approach that is characterized by (although not limited to):

- Local ownership of issues.
- Collaborative relationships with suppliers.

- Multi-sectoral partnerships.
- Capacity building of institutions.

These values define a long-term strategy that fuses integrated management systems with partnership development. Traces of this method have been found traditionally within extractive industries. However, it is an option and an opportunity for companies of varying size and in all sectors. Strategic partnerships enable small companies to overcome vast resource requirements of a developmental approach by complementing partners' expertise and material contributions. Partnerships cannot be limited to suppliers and workers, but must include competitors, local and foreign governmental institutions and NGOs if they are to build a comprehensive strategy for change.

Debate within ethical trading circles remains steeped in issues of how best to monitor and to evaluate company codes. As more companies develop codes, it is clear that codes represent only part of a process. Given the vast effort expended on monitoring, one must question whether resources might be better applied to treating the root causes of problems rather than to monitoring symptoms. Advocates for ethical trading must be aware of the risk of failing to see the forest for the trees. The challenge for corporations, nongovernmental organizations, unions and governments is to develop viable, collaborative programs to root out the causes of human rights abuses and unsatisfactory working conditions.

Hoffman-LaRoche Case

A Sentencing Guidelines Milestone

—Jeffrey M. Kaplan

When the corporate sentencing guidelines went into effect in November 1991, prosecutors, compliance officers and others noted that fines under the new law could reach as high as $290 million or even greater. After the Daiwa Bank prosecution in 1996—which resulted in a $340 million criminal fine—punishment beyond the $290 million figure was no longer just a theoretical possibility. Later that year, a Delaware court, in the Caremark decision, raised the prospect of individual liability for a fine under the corporate sentencing guidelines, by permitting shareholders to sue directors personally for losses arising from failure to ensure that their company had put in place "an effective program to prevent and detect violations of law," which is the guidelines' articulation of a meaningful compliance program.

Now, another sentencing guidelines milestone has been reached. In May 1999, F. Hoffman-LaRoche, Ltd.—a large Swiss pharmaceutical company—was convicted of an antitrust conspiracy and fined $500 million. This is the largest criminal fine in the history of American law.

According to documents filed in court and other accounts, Hoffman-LaRoche, BASF AG (a German firm) and Rhone Poulenc SA (of France), engaged in a conspiracy from 1990 to 1999 to control the price and sales volume of a wide range of vitamins used as nutritional supplements or to enrich human food and animal feeds (including vitamins A, B2, B5, C, E and beta carotene). The conspiracy involved annual meetings to plan production, divide the market and fix prices, with follow-up sessions to enforce compliance. One member of the cartel referred to it as "Vitamins, Inc."

U.S. Assistant Attorney General for Antitrust, Joel Klein, said that "[t]his conspiracy has affected more than $5 billion of commerce in products found in every American household." According to some estimates, prices of vitamins were pushed up by 15–40%.

In addition to the record fine against Hoffman-LaRoche, BASF AG will pay a fine of $225 million, which is also one of the largest financial penalties ever imposed in a criminal case. Rhone Poulenc, on the other hand, was not prosecuted at all. Because it brought evidence of the conspiracy to the government's attention, it was a beneficiary of the Antitrust Division's amnesty program. According to Gary Spratling, Deputy Assistant Attorney General, Rhone Poulenc's cooperation "led directly to the charges and the decision of the defendants" to plead guilty.

The fines will likely not be the only costs to the companies for their offenses. They also face class action lawsuits from businesses that bought vitamins. Hoffman-LaRoche and BASF have announced that they will attempt to settle the cases, but doing so may be costly in light of the admission of liability. Additionally, Karel Van Miert, the EU Competition Commissioner, declared after the U.S. prosecutions were announced, "This

Jeffrey M. Kaplan, "Hoffman-LaRoche Case: A Sentencing Guidelines Milestone," *Ethikos and Corporate Conduct Quarterly* 13, no. 1 (July/August 1999), pp. 1–11. Reprinted with permission of *Ethikos and Corporate Conduct Quarterly.*

kind of cartel needs to be fined very heavily. It needs to be punished." Indeed, authorities in Canada, Europe and Australia have begun their own investigations into the matter.

In addition, the former head of Roche's global marketing division, Dr. Kumo Sommer, was charged with participating in the conspiracy and with lying to government investigators. He agreed to plead guilty, serve four months in prison, and pay a $100,000 fine. (The extent of *individual* financial liability under the sentencing guidelines is often underappreciated. In one recent antitrust case, an executive was fined $10 million.)

Hoffman-LaRoche is clearly an important prosecution. But looking beyond the headlines, what are the implications of this case for those engaged in business ethics and compliance work?

■■ Lesson 1: The Need for Strong Antitrust Compliance

Many of the largest fines under the corporate sentencing guidelines have involved antitrust violations. In addition to the penalties against Hoffman-LaRoche and BASF, at least three other companies have been fined $100 million or more in the past few years. Indeed, there are apparently about 35 federal grand juries investigating price-fixing in a variety of industries. The number of *state* investigations is harder to ascertain but could also be large, given the increasing emphasis on antitrust enforcement at the state level (as evidenced, among other ways, by the participation of many state attorneys general in the *Microsoft* case).

Despite this, many companies—particularly those that are moving from purely regulated into more entrepreneurial endeavors—have not adopted meaningful antitrust compliance measures. The risk of such inaction is great, given that the Antitrust Division has been on record for several years in setting forth the types of steps it expects to see in compliance programs. These include, according to Deputy Assistant Attorney General Spratling, "both regular and unannounced audits of price changes, discount practices and bid sheets, conducted by those familiar with the firm's past and present business practices and trained in recognizing questionable divergence, [and] [b]oth regular (scheduled) and unannounced audits of front-line pricing and bidding personnel to test their level of understanding of the antitrust laws and their degree of compliance with a program's requirements and standards relating to prevention and detection, backed up by disciplinary mechanisms and potential penalties for failures."

Spratling has also emphasized that "the elements of a compliance program, particularly the audit elements, should be 'customized'—that is, designed and targeted to the firm's specific organization, operation, personnel and business practices."

In the face of this clear guidance and the dramatically escalating penalties for noncompliance, any company's failure to take meaningful antitrust compliance measures will likely be inexplicable to the government, shareholders and others.

■■ Lesson 2: The Value of Self-Reporting

The importance of *timely* self-reporting could not be more starkly apparent than from the results of the vitamin price-fixing conspiracy. Two firms—Hoffman-LaRoche and BASF—will pay fines totaling $725 million. Yet the third conspirator—Rhone Poulenc—avoided prosecution altogether, because it was the first to report the crime to the government.

While the value of such cooperation may be most dramatically evident in the antitrust area (given the amnesty program), the same general principle applies to virtually every other risk area as well. Indeed, the *Daiwa Bank* case, involving a $340 million fine under the corporate sentencing guidelines, was premised largely on the defendant's *late* reporting of a crime by one of its employees.

Yet self-reporting requires more than good intentions (or, in the case of some companies, a formal self-reporting policy). Unless companies have the means to *uncover* internal wrongdoing it is unlikely that they will receive the type of early warning that is often the key to prompt self-reporting. For this and other reasons, compliance auditing—emphasized in Spratling's recommendations—should not be limited to the antitrust area.

***

■■■ Lesson 5: The Worst is Likely Yet to Come

Assistant Attorney General Klein announced that with the Hoffman-LaRoche and BASF pleas, the Antitrust Division had "already secured more than $900 million in criminal fines in this fiscal year," which, he said, is "more than three times our previous annual record; in fact, more than the total amount of fines in the entire history of U.S. antitrust enforcement."

But records are clearly made to be broken, and it is likely that some prosecutors are already looking for a way to top the $500 million mark. Indeed, as great as the penalties were against Hoffman-LaRoche, they actually could have been worse. Spratling noted that the sentencing guidelines would have permitted a fine of as high as $1.3 billion.

Which company will make history with the first *billion* dollar fine? It will likely be one whose executives fail to heed the lessons of *Hoffman-LaRoche.*

So Then Why Did You Do It?

—John Dunkelberg and Debra Ragin Jessup

What causes unethical behavior and what can we learn from those individuals who have had spectacular ethical lapses? The profiles of several prominent individuals, including Dennis Levine and Charles Keating, are examined in the following article to try to provide some insight into what might lead them down the slippery slope to criminal and unethical behavior. What was found was that all those examined certainly knew they were breaking the law and that most went to extraordinary lengths to cover up what they were doing. Additionally, the authors found that each individual had attained a position of authority that enabled them to break the law without being seriously challenged by others who knew, or suspected, what was being done. Each person was highly compensated for their efforts; yet they chose to engage in unethical and illegal activities in the pursuit of lust, a little more money or power.

A recent study examined the background and environment of 129 individuals who either pled guilty or were found guilty of a crime that generated an article in *The Wall Street Journal* between January 1, 1990, and December 31, 1997. No general pattern emerged from that paper of the variables studied that could explain their criminal activity. The current paper, however, will delve into a deeper examination of some of these individuals in an attempt to see what lessons can be learned from their stories. They range from a man with very little education who became the CEO of a large defense contractor to a couple of attorneys with a privileged upbringing who worked for the most prestigious law firms in Chicago. What led these people down the slippery slope to criminal activity and what penalties did they pay? More importantly, what can we learn from their mistakes?

The individuals presented in this paper include: Dennis Levine who pled guilty to four felony charges of insider trading, Charles Keating who was found guilty of 73 counts of racketeering and fraud involving Lincoln Savings and Loan, Robert Fomon who was the CEO of E. F. Hutton during its rise as a lending brokerage firm and subsequent demise caused by unethical leadership . . . and Robert Citron who pled guilty to six felony counts of securities fraud involving the loss of $1.64 billion in Orange County funds. . . .

▇▇ Dennis Levine—Insider Trading

Dennis Levine was born and raised as the youngest of three brothers, in a Jewish middle class area of Queens. His father sold aluminum and vinyl siding to support his family and Dennis admired his work ethic. Dennis, however, aspired to a higher standard of living. From an early age, he wanted to be a Wall Street player and he seemed dazzled by expensive clothes, cars and large estates. He was not, however, willing to work hard to achieve his goals and did not excel as a student or as an athlete in high school. He went on to graduate from Baruch College with an undistinguished record. He obtained a job with Citicorp and, after not getting a promotion, moved to Smith Barney. Within a year, he was sent to

Paris and soon set up a Swiss bank account. To Dennis the Swiss bank account meant that he was "playing like the big boys now." On his return to the New York office he talked his way into the mergers and acquisition department. Within his team he was noted for his dismal math skills and an inflated view of his skills and contributions, but he was part of a group that worked on the details of mergers before they were known to the public.

Dennis saw the price of stocks moving up before mergers were announced and was convinced that everybody was getting rich on insider information but him. During his Citicorp days, Dennis had met and become friends with Robert Wilkis. Wilkis had an excellent education, Harvard, then Stanford Business school, and who spoke five languages fluently. Within a week of his move to Smith Barney, Dennis had called Wilkis with a stock tip and Wilkis purchased a couple of hundred shares. The stock rose dramatically and the beginning of a partnership that would end in jail sentences, large fines and public humiliation was formed. Dennis and Wilkis agreed to trade only on the other's information, never share tips with anyone else, and to use code names when calling the other partner. The knowledge and monetary benefits gained from one "friend" proved insufficient to satisfy Dennis Levine's dreams and he soon recruited a ring of associates. As a group they worked for almost all of the major firms engaged in the merger and acquisition practice during a time when this business was very lucrative. They traded information gathered as part of their confidential work with these firms. Using this information, Dennis Levine's trading profits grew to over $11.6 million in less than five years. He even had an arrangement with Ivan Boesky in which Levine would be paid a percentage of any "profits" Boesky made with the "tips" he received from Levine. The revelation of this insider trading ring would make national headlines and shake the faith of the financial system as it had been rarely shaken before.

After his arrest, Dennis agreed to cooperate with the government, implicating all the people with whom he had traded information, even placing calls that were recorded by the government investigators to those with whom he had conspired. In pleading guilty, he agreed to pay restitution to the Securities Exchange Commission of the $11.6 million in alleged trading profits. He was allowed to keep his Park Avenue co-op, his personal effects, including a BMW and personal savings, but lost all of his real estate investments, retirement account, Drexel shares and his beloved Ferrari Testarossa (with only 3,847 miles on it). He was sentenced to two years in prison. The night before going to prison, he tried to explain to his five-year old son why he would be away for the next couple of years. He said that there are rules for big people just like there are rules for children and that he had broken those rules and now must pay. His son listened and then said, "Daddy, did one know what one were doing was wrong?" Dennis answered, "Yes." His son then replied: "So then, why did you do it?"

Dennis had indeed known the rules. He had used cash to fly to Geneva, and later to a bank in the Bahamas, where he set up secret bank accounts under coded names. He used code names in dealing with his co-conspirators, photocopied secret documents and agreed to a formula providing cash payments for his tips to Ivan Boesky. On one occasion, he even stole his father's passport and photocopied it for a trip to Nassau. He knew he was to blame for his own actions but he had a huge desire for fast, easy money. "Money became the way you gauged your level of success, compared to those about you," and the more money the better. "When I was an associate, I wanted to be a Vice-President, when I was a VP, I wanted to be a Senior VP, and when I was a Senior VP, I wanted to be a managing director." On another occasion Dennis noted that when "I was earning $20,000, I wanted $100,000; when I was making $100,000, I wanted $200,000; when I was making $200,000, I wanted $1 million, and then $3 million." There was never any satisfaction.

Insider trading reached its peak in the late 1980s. The scandal brought national attention to such infamous names as Mike Milken, who paid a fine of over $1 billion and spent time in jail, and Martin Revson, of Revlon fortune fame, who traded tips with a group of his well-known socialite friends known as the Southhampton Seven. Why were these men, and dozens of others, willing to trade their good reputations for the small additional marginal utility of a little more money? Maybe because they did not think that if they broke the rules sooner or later they would have to answer the question, "So then why did you do it?"

■■ Charles Keating—Savings and Loan Scandal

Charlie Keating was raised in very modest conditions. His father, who had managed a local dairy, became disabled when Charlie was seven by Parkinson's disease. He received a Jesuit school education and was known as an excellent student. However, he flunked out of the University of Cincinnati and then enlisted in the Navy as a fighter pilot but he never saw combat. After World War II, he went back to college, received a liberal arts degree, and won gold medals in the NCAA and Pan American Games in the breaststroke. After college he earned a law degree and later started working for Carl Lindner, Jr., a well-known multimillionaire in Cincinnati. During this time, he built a national reputation for his hatred of pornography and in one year flew over 200,000 miles around the country giving talks on the subject. He kept lots of pornography around just to show people how bad it was. Interestingly, at least twelve of his secretaries had breast enlargements, allegedly because Charlie loved to walk around and look down their blouses.

In 1976, Charlie Keating and Carl Lindner parted company. Charlie moved to Phoenix, Arizona, and took over American Continental Corporation (ACC), a home building business with assets of half a million and liabilities of over $110 million. By 1983 the firm was in the black and building over eight homes a day. During this turn-around, Charlie hired all employees and almost all the men were white, tall and blue-eyed. The women were blond, good-looking and buxom. He fired people easily and often but paid those that he kept excellent wages. The offices of ACC were all white, the carpeting, walls and even the desks, and the desktops were always utterly clear of any material.

In September of 1983, Keating bought Lincoln Savings and Loan for $54 million, although its net worth was $34 million. Lincoln had $1.2 billion in assets of which $250 million were judged to be "risky ventures." By 1984, assets had grown to $2.5 billion and the risky ventures had grown to $1.6 billion. Much of the growth in assets had come from brokered loans. (Brokered loans are those sold by brokers who obtain the highest yield possible from the competing financial institutions for these FDIC-insured deposits. Thus the U.S. Government became the insurer of these very risky loans.) Ultimately these brokered loans would total about $5 billion of Lincoln's assets.

With this money, Charlie went on a spending spree. He built or refurbished hotels in Detroit and Phoenix, spending hundreds of millions of dollars on the finest décor. A residential real estate scheme in the desert outside of Phoenix included plans for thousands of homes, a PGA-caliber golf course and a huge clubhouse. Over $100 million of these federally insured deposits went in Ivan Boesky's investment schemes and hundreds of millions into Mike Milken's junk bonds. There were over 52 large real estate deals that never had a credit check and the real estate appraisals were grossly inflated. Files on these loans would be brought "up-to-date" months after the loan was made and corrected to existing regulations.

Charlie Keating gave generously, of money from ACC, to charitable groups. He was proud of his Catholic faith and gave millions to Mother Teresa, in India, and Father Bruce Ritter, in New York. To live in style, Keating had a $2 million home in Phoenix, a $5 million home in Florida, and a fabled retreat in the Bahamas. The care and feeding of his pilots and aircraft was over $35 million. Parties for his staff were first class with one Christmas party costing over $460,000. Since he saw himself as a business tycoon, he spent like one with one meal for four at Le Cirque in Manhattan costing over $2,495 and a single stop to buy a few sports jackets and slacks at Giorgio's on Rodeo Drive totaling $7,694. He and his family flew often and all over the world. In addition, he kept the regulators at bay by giving large sums to political campaigns including five senators (John Glenn, John McCain, Dan Riegle, Dennis DeConcini and Alan Cranston) all later known as the Keating Five. With all the money flowing to others, Charlie also paid himself and his top staff extremely well. He and his family were paid $34 million over five years. In 1987, he had over $5 million in income, but no personal donations to charity.

With spending like this the end was, of course, in sight. ACC used very creative accounting to show a profit and thus kept Charlie Keating going. With over 54 subsidiaries, ACC would buy properties from one subsidiary and sell to another and book the profit. Upstreaming is another example of the schemes used to keep this giant cash machine going. In this scheme, Lincoln would loan money to an individual who would use the money to purchase an asset. The asset would be sold at a higher price and the profits were booked. Since these two transactions were linked, the buyer is a straw buyer, not a real buyer, and this makes the deal a felony. However, with the spending out of control, even schemes of this type could not keep ACC viable.

In September of 1989, ACC declared bankruptcy. The corporation showed $6 billion in assets, but a couple billion was missing. The next day the U.S. Government took over Lincoln Savings and Loan. The case was the largest bank fraud case ever. Lincoln was charged with using straw buyers, sham land sales, inside stock deals, upstreaming of money and fraudulent loans. Charlie Keating was charged with 73 counts of fraud but he claimed he was innocent. Instead he became the poster boy for all that went wrong with the S&L failures in the late 1980s. He was tried, found guilty and sentenced to 10 years in prison and required to pay a fine of $250,000. The judge in this case described Charlie Keating's treatment of Lincoln as "an adult taking candy from a helpless child." Judge Sorkin also wondered how the accountants and the law firms involved with ACC and Lincoln could not have seen the problems. At the time of sentencing Keating was sixty-six years old.

Why did a man who publicly made so much of love of his family and his Catholic religion, his hatred of pornography and drugs, use fraudulent techniques to enrich himself, his family and his friends? His motivation seemed not to be the money but the power and acceptance that money brings. He was earning his way into a club that he coveted, the Boesky, Milken, Lindner club. As a swimmer he had been driven to win because he liked the applause. As the CEO of a company it was the power and seduction and control of people and events.

■ Robert Fomon—Chairman of the Board of E. F. Hutton

Wall Street probably has never occupied so prominent a place in the public's consciousness as it did during the 1980s. A great bull market was in progress and many individuals were amassing fortunes buying and selling, both stocks and corporations. The news media made several of these individuals virtual heroes and extolled their financial and business acumen. Unfortunately too many of these heroes later turned out to be frauds who made money through unlawful manipulations. Others skirted just inside the law but employed dubious ethical tactics to accumulate wealth during this time. When money comes so easily to so many, few are willing to stop and critically examine how the money is being made. As a result, several corporations became spectacular failures during this time but all these failures were preventable. E. F. Hutton was but one of these firms and its demise is worth examining (Stevens, 1989 and Sterngold, 1990).

E. F. Hutton started in 1904, on April Fool's Day, and grew into a brokerage powerhouse using such famous marketing lines as: "I'm J. Paul Getty and E. F. Hutton is my broker," and "When E. F. Hutton talks, people listen." In the 1970s and the first six years of the 1980s, Hutton was led by Robert Fomon a short, paunchy man who was adept at manipulating images and people. Bob Fomon's early life was one of little joy and less love. His mother died of cancer when he was four. His father, a physician, had very little desire to have the responsibility of raising children, so he sent his three sons to be raised by his wife's spinster sister. He visited his sons no more than twice a year, at Christmas and during his summer vacation. Bob Fomon was a prankster throughout his school years and was thrown out of a Catholic high school and then a public high school just before graduation. He went to the University of Southern California and graduated, with a very undistinguished record, in 1947 with a fine arts degree. After a brief fling in law school he dropped out and tried to determine what he should do with his life.

Through his fathers' connections, Fomon had met many people from the moneyed side of society and he liked the life they led. He saw the stock brokerage business as one that could be quite lucrative. After being rejected by Merrill Lynch and Dean Witter, a friend of his father helped him get a job with E. F. Hutton. Although he demonstrated little in the way of investment acumen, he had a remarkable knack of selling himself to the country club set and they eagerly handed him their business. After building a power base in California, he rose to be the CEO of Hutton through a mixture of charm and double-cross. The charm included a mixture of hard drinking with other brokers in his office and tales of his prowess as a seducer of women.

During his tenure as CEO, E. F. Hutton grew through the raiding of top brokers from other firms and the purchase of other brokerage firms to become one of the nation's most well regarded brokerage houses. Although in an industry that preferred to maintain a rather staid image, Bob Fomon retained his notorious personal behavior of hard drinking and womanizing. When he was in his fifties, he was dating young women in their late teens and early twenties. He also contributed to this rakish behavior with scandalous public statements. For example, he once was quoted describing women as objects of decoration, better seen than heard. Interestingly, his second marriage was to Sharon Kay Ritchie, a former Miss America. Although Hutton did little business in Paris, Fomon had Hutton open an office there, which was overseen by girlfriends from California. Another girlfriend, a young lady in her twenties, was given the job as head of advertising although she had no training of any kind in this field. He also had Hutton pick up the hotel tab for guests at his daughter's wedding and his son charged over $100,000 in expenses in just one year.

Encouraged by E. F. Hutton's culture and to maintain the profit growth, the firm started several questionable practices that would later not only be embarrassing but lead to its ultimate demise. One of these practices was the selling of products, such as tax shelters, that were notable more for the high commissions generated for Hutton brokers than the tax benefits generated for their customers. To help secure public finance business (selling tax-exempt bonds) in various states, Hutton entertained some state officials at brothels. Several brokerage units found money laundering to be profitable business and, in one case, a customer regularly paid for his security purchases with a gym bag full of small bills. To obtain the lucrative commissions from selling bonds, Hutton underwrote some "junk" bonds with the par value guaranteed, thus if the bonds' ratings slipped, Hutton could, and did, lose millions of dollars. Hutton also entered into the risky second mortgage business charging up to eighteen percent interest, plus up-front fees that pushed the rates closer to forty percent. All of these practices paled before the grand scheme that gained Hutton much unneeded notoriety—check kiting.

By 1980, E. F. Hutton was looking for new ways to make profits; and many of its brokerage units across the United States wrote large checks against uncollected balances to create a float for Hutton and inflate its bank balances. Hutton engaged in an illegal practice known as "pinwheeling." A pinwheel occurred when multiple checks were passed from one Hutton account to another to earn interest on the float. This is a felonious action and Hutton's accountants, Arthur Andersen, had warned management about it. Playing the float was too lucrative a practice to be stopped and became Hutton's most profitable product, earning $95.9 million in one year. The end, however, was in sight.

In 1985 Hutton pled guilty to over 2,000 felony counts of defrauding its banks of several million dollars, and customers started fleeing the company in large numbers. Several of the tax shelters defaulted, the junk bonds were down-rated and Hutton had to buy them back at par value, costing the firm additional millions. The Providence, Rhode Island, office was charged with laundering money for organized-crime figures and entertaining customers in a notorious call-girl ring involving several Brown University coeds. With its capital almost gone, Hutton put itself up for sale. Shearson purchased the once proud firm, in what amounted to a fire sale, in December of 1987. In the aftermath, 8,000 of Hutton's 18,000 employees lost their jobs, but Bob Fomon and the directors of the firm were rewarded handsomely for their stewardship. For example, Bob Fomon sold his 230,000 shares of Hutton stock before the problems at the firm became public knowledge. His golden parachute gave him $4 million in cash, $500,000 a year for seven years, plus a pension of $612,450 for life. The directors also gave him an additional 76,000 shares of stock worth about $3 million.

Of all the individuals studied in this paper, only Bob Fomon was never charged with a crime, yet he presided over a firm that had an impeccable reputation before his arrival and was notorious for its sordid activities at the end. His unethical behavior led the firm to its demise and cost many of his employees their livelihood.

***

Robert Citron

Robert Citron had been the Orange County Treasurer-Tax Collector for over 24 years when he was indicted for securities fraud. As treasurer, he was responsible for investing billions of dollars in county tax revenue. His investment record was amazing in that he had consistently matched or outperformed managers in other counties. Why did his investment empire crumble before his eyes, landing Orange County in the largest municipal bankruptcy in U.S. history?

Citron was born in Los Angeles and grew up in Burbank. He never finished college and had been married to the same woman for 39 years and lived in the same house for 22 years. As treasurer, Citron was responsible for the county's investment pool. His investment record showed an average return of 9.03% during the ten years just prior to the bankruptcy, which was double what comparable pools made. Citron was known as one of the best county finance officers in the nation and once received an award naming him one of the top five best government investors nationwide.

Citron's strategy was simple, he used the investment pool's U.S. treasury bill and bonds as collateral to borrow short-term loans at low interest rates. He then invested the borrowed funds in mid-term corporate bonds and securities that paid a higher rate of return. This type investment strategy can result in large returns if the interest rates stay low and stable. However, if interest rates rise, the entire investment strategy collapses.

The public was forewarned about the potential problems with Citron's investment strategy when he ran for reelection in 1994. John Moorlach, his political opponent, questioned his investment practices. Of course, this criticism fell on deaf ears because Citron had been singled out as one of the best county finance officers in the nation. He had also received an award for one of the five best government investors nationwide. Nevertheless, Moorlach persisted throughout the campaign, accusing Citron of "overly risky strategy that left the county's investment pool vulnerable to rising interest rates."

It appears that Moorlach had a crystal ball. When interests rates went up, Citron's world collapsed. On December 6, 1994, Citron resigned due to reports that the county's investment fund had lost $1.5 billion in value due to rising interest rates and risky investment transactions. In fact, the interest rate increases wiped out, on paper, almost one of every five dollars in the fund. Citron gave no reason for his resignation; however, his lawyer said that "no one shares the county's pain more than Mr. Citron."

After his resignation, someone who knew Citron said that his successful investments made him believe he was infallible, that he started to believe his own press. Others said that Citron loved to be praised and he spoke often of his own accomplishments.

Citron was charged with defrauding investors and misappropriating public money in connection with the county's investment pool. He pled guilty and the evidence showed that he diverted over $100 million in other agencies' money into the county's account. Prior to sentencing, Citron's attorney sought information that would implicate others involved, stating that they were "more sophisticated and knowledgeable about matters concerning securities and accounting." He also said that Citron "relied on financial and legal experts." Everyone was shocked to discover in court, that two of the "experts" were a mail-order astrologer and a psychic. The psychics were right about one thing: Citron was told that December of 1994 would be a bad month, but after that, his money worries would be over.

Citron was sought and was given leniency by the judge for his cooperation with the prosecutors. The judge sentenced Citron to one year in the county jail and a fine of $100,000. He was also placed on probation for five years, ordered to perform 1,000 hours of community service and undergo psychological counseling.

Citron reported to the county jail on January 10, 1997, and stayed 20 minutes, then went home. The sheriff agreed to let him serve his time by doing clerical work during the day and returning home at night. What do you know, the psychics were right again, they said he wouldn't go to jail.

***

Conclusion

The objective of this paper was to provide a detailed look at individuals whose level of illegal or unethical behavior brought them national attention in order to learn something about what caused them to fall into their destructive pattern of action. A possible common thread seems to be an addictive behavior that started with a simple, almost insignificant, act that grew into an uncontrollable habit of unethical and illegal behavior. The drive for this irrational behavior seems to be a feeling of power that comes from having more control over others, more money, or a higher status position.

All of these individuals share common characteristics even though they all took different paths to success. They all had attained a level of success in their field that was enviable by others yet they decided to break the rules, risking and then losing everything. So why did they do it? They were all driven by a desire to have more power, more money or more recognition. They were driven to the point of obsession and lacked the ability to rationally assess their conduct. Specifically, all of the individuals studied, acted as though they believed they were above the rules. Add the autonomy that came with their jobs and you have the perfect combination for disaster.

What can we learn from these ethical lapses? We offer these suggestions. First, create an ethical environment that encourages and rewards ethical behavior. This can be done in a variety of ways. Professor Robin discusses this issue in his book, *Questions & Answers about Business Ethics* (1999). He tells us to combat unethical behavior,

> the company must constantly support and develop the culture. The culture should make it clear that peers will find unethical behavior unacceptable and will report it, thus, the perceived probability of getting caught increases. When ethical misdeeds are detected, the company should punish the individual fairly but openly.

Thus, it is imperative that companies implement policies and procedures that make it clear that unethical conduct will be detected and the employee punished. The punishment should be direct, publicized and long-lasting. The company must send a message that unethical conduct will not be tolerated.

Additionally, Professor Robin tells us that "employees entering the workplace are looking for guidelines for acceptable behavior." New employees will look to role models and mentors to set the standard for ethical behavior. The "ethical tone" of the business must be set by top management and trickle down to the entry-level employees. If the ethics of top management is beyond reproach, this sends a clear message that ethical conduct and success go hand in hand.

Secondly, these individuals have taught us that there must be balance between power and autonomy. The desire to commit unethical acts is nothing without the autonomy to do so. Autonomy is the factor in the equation that sends intelligent successful people over the ethical edge. They believe they are invincible because no one is looking over their shoulder. We certainly cannot assume that all highly successful people would behave unethically; however, we can guard against the possibility by refraining from giving an individual complete autonomy over their duties.

In conclusion, ethical behavior within the business structure has to be a priority, right up with making a profit. Ethical business environments do not miraculously appear. The ethical business environment must be meticulously cultivated and failure to do so can result in great loss to the company, the profession, and society.

■■ References

Binstein, M., and C. Bowden: 1993, *Trust Me: Charles Keating and the Missing Billions* (Random House, New York).

Frantz, D.: 1987, *Levine & Company: Wall Street's Insider Trading Scandal* (Henry Holt and Company, New York).

Robin, D.: 1999, *Questions & Answers about Business Ethics: Running an Ethical and Successful Business* (Thomson Learning, Cincinnati, OH).

Sterngold, J.: 1990, *Burning Down the House: How Greed, Deceit, and Bitter Revenge Destroyed E. F. Hutton* (Summit Books, New York).

Stevens, M.: 1989, *Sudden Death: The Rise and Fall of E. F. Hutton* (NAL Books).

Stewart, J.: 1991, *Den of Thieves* (Simon & Schuster, New York).

Traub, J.: 1990, *Too Good to Be True, The Outlandish Story of Wedtech* (Doubleday, New York).

Endnotes

1. Lao Tzu, *Tao Te Ching,* Book 2, XLVI: 105.

2. Jeff Lyon, "For Starters," *Chicago Tribune Sunday Magazine,* January 14, 1996, p. 6.

3. John Blades, "Staying Alive," *Chicago Tribune,* March 20, 1996, sec. 5, pp. 1, 4.

4. Ralph Larsen, "Leadership in a Values-Based Organization," Sears Lectureship in Business Ethics, Bentley College, February 7, 2002.

5. J. Nelson/The Prince of Wales Business Leaders Forum, *Business as Partners in Development: Creating Wealth for Countries, Companies and Communities* (London: The Prince of Wales Business Leaders Forum, 1996), pp. 47, 52.

6. Thomas d'Aquino, CEO of Canada's Business Council on National Issues, quoted in C. Forcese, "Profiting from Misfortune? The Role of Business Corporations in Promoting and Protecting International Human Rights," MA Thesis, Norman Paterson School of International Affairs, Carleton University, Ottawa (1997), referred to in C. Forcese, *Putting Conscience into Commerce: Strategies for Making Human Rights Business as Usual* (Montreal: International Centre for Human Rights and Democratic Development, 1997).

7. J. Ayala II, "Philanthropy Makes Business Sense," *Business Day* (Bangkok), September 25, 1995, and J. Ayala II, "Philanthropy Makes Business Sense," *Ayala Foundation Inc.* 4, no. 2 (July–September, October–November 1995), p. 3.

8. D. Lewin and J. M. Sabater, "Corporate Philanthropy and Business Performance," *Philanthropy at the Crossroads* (Bloomington, IN: Indiana University, 1996), pp. 105–26.

9. World Economic Forum, "Declining Public Trust Foremost a Leadership Problem," press release, January 14, 2003.

10. Institute for Global Ethics, *Ethics Newsline* 5, no. 13 (April 1, 2002), citing Maritz Research Poll (January 14–17, 2002).

11. L. Trevino, M. Brown and L. Hartman, "A Qualitative Investigation of Perceived Executive Ethical Leadership: Perceptions from Inside and Outside the Executive Suite," *Human Relations* 56, no. 1 (January 2003), pp. 5–37.

12. *Ibid.*

13. *Ibid.*

14. Kenneth Bredemeier, "A Rogue within the Ranks," *Washington Post,* March 25, 2002, p. E1.

15. *Ibid.*

16. James Collins and Jerry Porras, "Building Your Company's Vision," *Harvard Business Review,* September/October 1996.

17. Mark Satin, "We Need to Alter the Culture at Places Like Enron—Not Just Pass More Laws," *Radical Middle Newsletter,* March/April 2002, http://www.radicalmiddle/com.

18. American Management Association Report, *2002 Corporate Values Survey.*

19. Mark Schwartz, "A Code of Ethics for Corporate Codes of Ethics," *Journal of Business Ethics,* no. 41 (2002), pp. 27–43.

20. *Ibid.*

21. Colin Powell and Joseph Persico, *My American Journey* (New York: Random House, 1995) p. 250.

22. USSC, *Guidelines Manual,* sec. 8A1.2, comment (n. 3(k)) (2000).

23. *Ibid.*

24. Joseph Murphy, "Lost Words of the Sentencing Guidelines," *Ethikos,* November/December 2002, p. 5.

25. Ethics Officers Association, "1997 Member Survey," 2000, p. 9.

26. USSC, "Corporate Crime in America: Strengthening the 'Good Citizen' Corporation," 123–91 (1995).

Moral Leadership Article

1. John W. Gardner, *On Leadership* (New York: The Free Press, 1990), p. 8.

2. Gail Sheehy, *Character: America's Search for Leadership* (New York: Bantam Books, 1990), p. 311.

3. *Ibid.,* p. 66.

4. James MacGregor Burns, *Leadership* (New York Harper Torchbooks, 1979), p. 36.

5. *Ibid.,* p. 439.

6. For Senge the three primary tasks of leadership include: leader as designer; leader as steward; leader as teacher.

7. Peter M. Senge, *The Fifth Discipline* (New York: Double/Currency Books, 1990), p. 353.

8. Abraham Zaleznik, "The Leadership Gap," *Academy of Management Executive* (1990), V.4, N.1, p. 12.

9. Joseph C. Rost, *Leadership for the Twenty-First Century,* p. 124.

10. Howard S. Schwartz, *Narcissistic Process and Corporate Decay* (New York: New York University Press, 1990).

11. Howard S. Schwartz, "Narcissism Project and Corporate Decay: The Case of General Motors," *Business Ethics Quarterly,* V.1, N.3, p. 250.

12. Thomas W. Norton, "The Narcissism and Moral Mazes of Corporate Life: A Commentary on the Writings of H. Schwartz and R. Jackall," *Business Ethics Quarterly,* V.2, N.1, p. 76.

13. Robert Jackall, *Moral Mazes* (New York: Oxford University Press, 1988), p. 6.

14. Garry Wills, *Certain Trumpets,* p. 13.

15. Dolecheck, *"Ethics: Take It From the Top,"* p. 14.

16. William Pfaff, "It's Time for a Change in Corporate Values," *Chicago Tribune,* January 16, 1996, p. 17.

Ethical Business: Survey Results Article

1. *The Hampel Report, Committee on Corporate Governance:* Final Report, 1998

2. *Internal Control, Guidance for Directors on the Combine Code (aka the Tumbull guidance)* ICAEW, September 1999.

CHAPTER SIX

Ethics in Practice

This chapter highlights several firms that have been cited as among the best in the business community.[1] These firms are noted for their general business performance and behavior as well as for their commitment to ethical behavior. Included are The Boeing Company, a project management firm; Hewlett-Packard, a high-technology company; and Johnson & Johnson, a consumer products producer.

This chapter also examines actions taken by five other firms. Each action has been selected to represent one of the following types of ethical issues: bribery, coercion, deception, theft, and unfair discrimination. Using the modified Velasquez et al. model, this chapter examines the ethical dimension of the decision. Where the action is judged to be unethical, the focus is on what went wrong, what may have led to the unethical behavior, and how top management could have acted to encourage ethical behavior, rather than what actually occurred.

Ethical Companies

The Boeing Company

Boeing has been widely recognized as a well-run, successful, ethical organization. The firm, which began operations in 1916, is the world's largest producer of commercial aircraft. Other primary business activities include military aircraft, helicopters, and aerospace equipment. The firm grew significantly in the 1990s by acquiring Rockwell International Corporation's aerospace and defense units in 1996 and merging with the McDonnell Douglas Corporation in 1997.

Boeing's strong set of values can be traced back to William Allen, the CEO who took the reins at the end of World War II. Allen faced the formidable challenge of transforming Boeing from a wartime producer to a peacetime aircraft manufacturer. He is remembered for his sincerity, honesty, and integrity. The night he agreed to serve as company president, Allen developed a list of resolutions that reflected his personal values:

Must keep temper—always—never get mad.

Be considerate of my associates' views.

Don't talk too much . . . let others talk.

Don't be afraid to admit that you don't know.

Don't get immersed in detail—concentrate on the big objectives.

Make contacts with other people in industry—and keep them.

Try to improve feeling around Seattle toward the company.

Make a sincere effort to understand labor's viewpoint.

Be definite; don't vacillate.

Act—get things done—move forward.

Develop a postwar future for Boeing.

Try hard, but don't let obstacles get you down. Take things in stride.

Above all else be human—keep your sense of humor—learn to relax.

Be just, straightforward; invite criticism and learn to take it.

Be confident. Having once made a move, make the most of it. Bring to the task great enthusiasm, unlimited energy.

Make Boeing even greater than it is.[2]

Boeing became known as an ethical, reputable company under Allen's guidance. In 1964, Allen created an ethics committee comprised of upper management and members of the board that reported directly to the board of directors.[3] At the same time, Boeing drafted and implemented an ethics policy that reinforced the company's commitment to high values.

Allen's successor, T. A. Wilson, carried on the tradition of high standards established by Allen. The firm experienced continuing success until the commercial and military airplane markets collapsed in 1969–1970. During the next few years, Boeing downsized its labor force by two-thirds. Wilson's efforts became totally focused on maintaining the viability of Boeing.

Unknown to Wilson, several Boeing employees were engaged in foreign payments that came to light in the aircraft industry foreign payments scandals of 1974.[4] Such payments were in direct violation of Boeing standards. It became clear that the high standards of operation established during the Allen years had deteriorated. Wilson took immediate action. Boeing thoroughly reviewed its sales policies, developed sales training programs that reinforced the company's standards, and developed an auditing mechanism to insure compliance.

In 1981 Boeing began an effort to upgrade its ethics program. This led to a presentation in 1984 by the vice president of contracts and general counsel entitled "Pressures on Your Ethical Barometer."[5] The presentation discussed the competitive and internal organizational pressures that could lead to ethics violations. It also stressed the importance of managing the company's ethical culture. Only days after the presentation, Boeing Computer Services Company (BCS) was notified by the Department of the Interior that it had access to government inside information prior to submitting a bid to construct a financial system for the National Park System.[6] Because this was a violation of federal procurement rules, BCS's Federal Systems Group (FSG) was suspended from further business with any branch of the federal government. FSG worked on many government contracts held by Boeing; thus, the entire Boeing company was affected.

BCS quickly located the offending employees and took disciplinary action. It also made plans to initiate a major ethics program and thus got the suspension lifted. The program consisted of revising marketing procedures, implementing an employee-training program, appointing an ethics adviser whom employees could contact to report ethics violations, and creating internal audit procedures for screening all future government proposals. The BCS transgression underlined the need for management to manage the ethical climate of the organization.

Three lessons were learned from the foreign payments and the insider information incidents. First, the ethics involved when dealing with government agencies differs from the ethics of dealing with commercial firms. Second, employees who deal with outside parties require special attention so that they do not become ethical liabilities. Third, maintaining high ethical standards can be central to a firm's survival.[7]

Work continued on the ethics program and in 1985 Boeing revised and consolidated its ethics policy statements into a booklet entitled "Business Conduct Guidelines."[8] Business conduct was divided into five areas: marketing practices; offering of business courtesies; conflict of interest; acceptance of business courtesies; and the use of company time, materials, equipment, and proprietary information. The current edition added four additional areas: marketing to the U.S. government sector, relationships with suppliers, former U.S. government employees—conflict of interest, and buying and selling securities—insider trading.[9] In addition, training programs in a number of operating divisions were implemented. In 1986 Boeing added the Office of Business Practices to its corporate headquarters.[10] Boeing continues to upgrade its ethics program. Over the years, the program has been principle and value based rather than policy or rule focused.

Boeing states that the purpose of the program is to:

1. Communicate the Boeing values and standards of ethical business conduct to employees.
2. Inform employees of company policies and procedures regarding ethical business conduct.
3. Establish companywide processes to assist employees in obtaining guidance and resolving questions regarding compliance with the company's standards of conduct and the Boeing values.
4. Establish companywide criteria for ethics education and awareness programs and to coordinate compliance oversight activities.[11]

The Ethics and Business Conduct Committee, whose members are appointed by The Boeing Company Board of Directors, has oversight responsibility for the program. Members of the committee include the company chairman and chief executive officer, the president and chief operating officer, the presidents of the operating groups, and the senior vice presidents. The vice president of ethics and business conduct administers the program.

On June 16, 1992, Raymon L. Pedersen, a rivet supervisor in the manufacturing department of The Boeing Commercial Airplane Group, was indicted on charges of mail fraud, interstate travel to promote commercial bribery, and extortion.[12] Pedersen was accused of accepting $46,500 from VSI Corporation and $22,000 from Huck Manufacturing to promote the use of their aerospace fasteners. The latter payment was extorted from Huck using the threat of stopping the installation of Huck parts on Boeing aircraft. He was also accused of receiving $35,000 for supplying VSI with confidential business information about one if its competitors.[13] The indictment came 11 days after the president and two former top executives of VSI pleaded guilty to providing prostitutes, cash payments, and other gifts to win business from Boeing and other aerospace companies.[14] You can be sure that Pedersen is no longer employed by Boeing.

Recent events have cast a shadow on Boeing's ethics program. The Project on Government Oversight cited Boeing as being involved in 36 cases of misconduct between 1990 and 2003, resulting in fines, penalties, and settlements of $358 million.[15] It should be noted that in the murky world of federal contract rules not every dispute is the result of unethical actions. There may be honest disagreements over what is covered and what is not. In addition, a number of the cases were inherited with the recent acquisitions and merger. However, the name on the cases today is still Boeing.

The latest case to come to light involved a contract competition between Boeing and Lockheed to build a new Air Force rocket known as the EELV. Boeing's Huntington Beach, California, rocket division, part of McDonnell Douglas prior to the merger in August 1997, won the competition in 1998, giving it 19 out of 28 planned launches valued at $1.88 billion.[16] The remaining nine launches were given to Lockheed. Following the competition, it was discovered that Boeing had in its possession 25,000 pages of confidential Lockheed documents describing Lockheed's EELV project.[17] The Air Force subsequently punished Boeing by shifting seven of the launches previously awarded to Boeing to Lockheed and giving Lockheed three additional launches that had yet to be awarded.[18] That cost Boeing approximately $1 billion. It also suspended three Boeing space subsidiaries from receiving new government contracts for at least 60 to 90 days.

Boeing was extremely apologetic, running a full-page ad in major newspapers, admitting its shortcomings and promising to make amends. Boeing has also admitted to receiving 8,800 pages of confidential Lockheed documents pertaining to its competition with Lockheed to build satellites for New Skies Satellites N.V. of the Netherlands.[19] On July 30, 2003, Boeing held a mandatory four-hour ethics training program for approximately 75,000 employees at its St. Louis Boeing Integrated Defense System.[20] It also appointed former Senator Warren B. Rudman to conduct an independent review of company ethics policies and competitive information handling.

Boeing's rapid growth beginning in the mid 1990s via mergers and acquisitions may have contributed to its ethical lapses. It acquired Rockwell's aerospace and defense business in 1996 with 21,000 employees.[21] It merged with McDonnell Douglas in 1997, adding 64,000 more people.[22] In 2000, Boeing purchased Hughes Space and Communications with 9,000 people, Jeppesen Saunders Inc. with 1,400 people, and Hawker deHavilland of Australia with 950 people.[23] The result was 96,000 people coming from five different organizational cultures. Folding these disparate cultures into the Boeing culture could not be accomplished overnight. It should be noted that the majority of the cases of misconduct cited previously came to light after the acquisitions began and involved some personnel from the acquired firms. Hopefully, through its training programs and renewed emphasis upon ethics, Boeing can recover its reputation for integrity.*

Hewlett-Packard Company

Hewlett-Packard Company (HP) was founded in 1939 by William Hewlett and David Packard. The direction of the company was set in the 1950s when objectives were developed that provided the foundation for the core values of the organization:[24]

- Recognize that profit is the best measure of a company's contribution to society and the ultimate source of corporate strength;
- Continually improve the value of the products and services offered to customers;
- Seek new opportunities for growth, but focus efforts on fields in which the company can make a contribution;
- Provide employment opportunities that include the chance to share in the company's success;
- Maintain an organizational environment that fosters individual motivation, initiative, and creativity;
- Demonstrate good citizenship by making contributions to the community;
- Emphasize growth as a requirement for survival.

The core values formed the basis of what has become known as "The HP Way," described by Bill Hewlett as follows:

> I feel that in general terms it is the policies and actions that flow from the belief that men and women want to do a good job, a creative job, and that if they are provided the proper environment they will do so. But that's only part of it. Closely coupled with this is the HP tradition of treating each individual with consideration and respect, and recognizing personal achievements.[25]

Employees see the values and ethics of the company evidenced in the behavior of the company's managers and executives. The values are part of the strong culture, which is reinforced on a daily basis.

The core content of HP's values has been reflected in three documents. The primary document, "Corporate Objectives" developed in 1957, provides a summary of HP's approach that was developed for managers who no longer have day-to-day contact with top management due to size and geographic remoteness. The Corporate Objectives document was organized into the following sections: profit, customers, fields of interest, growth, our people, management, and citizenship.[26] This document and the lessons communicated by the corporate culture provided the primary communication of organizational values. Two lesser documents included "Communicating the HP Way" and the "Standards

---

*As this book went to press, two significant events occurred at Boeing. CFO Michael Sears was dismissed along with a senior executive in the company's missile defense unit, Darleen Druym. Boeing learned that Sears had talked with Druym about potential employment at Boeing while she was working as an acquisitions officer in the Pentagon for the Air Force. Her work involved Boeing business, most notably negotiations involving the leasing of 100 Boeing 767 aerial tankers. A few days later, as reported in The Wall Street Journal, December 2, 2003, CEO Phil Condit resigned stating that "the controversies and disturbances of the past year were obscuring the great accomplishments of this company."

of Business Conduct." Ethics was not prominently labeled in any of the documents, but moral values were clearly communicated. Values relating to employee treatment were highly visible.

HP is currently reinventing itself and is thus creating a new set of guiding documents. The corporate objectives have been revised to include the following sections: customer loyalty, profit, market leadership, growth, employee commitment, leadership capability, and global citizenship.[27] The new document is designed to reflect the continuing values of the organization while adapting them to the changed environment in which the company operates. There is also a document entitled "Business Ethics" that focuses upon integrity and the dedication to the principles of honesty, excellence, responsibility, compassion, citizenship, fairness, and respect.[28] This more overt declaration of ethics appears to be a response to the times.

HP has recently completed its first "Social and Environmental Responsibility Report."[29] The report focuses upon the workplace, the environment, and sustainability. The firm is developing significant programs to reduce material and energy usage. It is also developing a number of recycling programs focusing upon "end-of-life" issues.

In keeping with the changing business environment, HP has developed a "Supplier Code of Conduct" that all of its suppliers must follow.[30] The code requires suppliers to adhere to all laws protecting the environment, worker health and safety, and labor and employment practices in the countries in which they operate. In addition, they must establish management systems that insure compliance with the laws and regulations.

The firm's confidence in and respect for its employees continues to be constantly stressed. Employees are given a great deal of freedom. They select which eight-hour shift they want to work, beginning at 6, 7, or 8 a.m. HP does not use time clocks. Employees are given specific job objectives and may negotiate with their supervisor to determine how the objectives will be met.

Open communication is stressed. Everyone in the firm is on a first-name basis. Company offices are created using low partitions so that one may talk to the person in the next office simply by leaning over the partition. Management strongly encourages open communication both up and down the levels in the firm. HP also has an "Open Door Policy," which is described in company documents in these words:

> All employees have the right, if in their opinion they feel such steps are necessary, to discuss their concerns with the level of management they feel is appropriate to handle the situation. Any effort to prevent an employee from going to higher-level managers, through intimidation or any other means, is absolutely contrary to company policy and will be dealt with accordingly. Using the open door policy will not in any way impact any evaluations of employees or subject them to any other adverse consequences.[31]

HP advocates employee sharing of benefits and responsibilities. Equal sharing of rewards through a profit-sharing plan and a stock-purchase plan is stressed. Offices are generally the same size, with supervisors sharing offices with their secretaries. Carpeting is a rarity and parking spaces are generally unassigned. The company fosters a sense of teamwork and partnership in its everyday business operations. Decisions are generally made through consensus and persuasion in small work groups.

HP demonstrates a strong concern for the individual employee. It has gone to great lengths to avoid layoffs. Growth has been deliberately slowed at times so the firm could manage expansion without subsequent layoffs. The firm has been able to get voluntary agreements from employees to take a pay and hour cut to avoid laying off part of its workforce. While jobs come and go, management has generally been able to accommodate the workforce via shifts. The company takes the position that it provides employment security, not job security.[32] Thus, if a worker's job disappears, HP will offer to provide training for another position within the firm. In addition, the firm strongly encourages employee development. The company promotes from within and provides extensive training and educational opportunities.

Honesty and integrity are basic HP core values. HP does not tolerate dishonesty among its employees. The "Standards of Business Conduct" cites four areas of employee obligations: obligations to HP, to customers, to competitors, and to suppliers.[33] Obligations to

HP include avoiding conflicts of interest, maintaining the confidentiality of company information, and reporting and avoiding payments to foreign sales agents or government officials. Customer obligations encompass trade practices, price discrimination, unfair methods of competition, government procurement, and confidentiality of information. Competitor obligations include competitor relations, obtaining competitive information, and commenting about competitors. Supplier obligations encompass honoring confidential information and discriminating among suppliers on relevant bases. General managers are responsible for their employees' familiarization with the standards.

HP's internal audit department has developed an audit program to monitor employee awareness of the standards, to uncover any violations of the standards, and to make sure steps are taken to rectify the deficiencies. The audit team also has an extensive annual interview with each of the top managers from each work group.

In September 1987, company officials were alarmed by rumors of drug use at its Santa Clara, California, sales office. At 5 a.m. on Friday, September 18, a team of private security guards with two golden retrievers and one Labrador retriever entered the sales office.[34] The guards and dogs searched the building, including management offices, looking for drugs. No locked files, desks, or offices were opened. As the 300 employees arrived for work, they were asked to open their handbags and parcels. No drugs were found and employees were upset by the invasion of privacy and lack of trust. However, in March 1987 drugs were found in a shipping and receiving office in Boise, Idaho. Twenty employees were fired.

In July 1999, Carly Fiorina was chosen as the first outside president and chief executive of HP.[35] On May 3, 2002, she won a hard-fought battle to merge HP with Compaq Computers to create the second largest computer company. The merger has resulted in eliminating more than 15,000 people from the combined workforce.[36] Layoffs of that magnitude appear to fly in the face of the HP Way. As Fiorina continues to bring change to HP, it will be interesting to see what those changes will be and how they will impact the firm and the venerable HP Way of doing business.

Johnson & Johnson

Johnson & Johnson was founded in 1887 in New Brunswick, New Jersey.[37] It has become one of the world's largest manufacturers of health care products with major business interests in consumer, professional, and pharmaceutical products. Johnson & Johnson is a highly decentralized company with a strong organizational culture. The formation of this culture can be traced back to General Robert Wood Johnson, son of one of the founders, who became head of the firm in 1932.[38] The General set out to change Johnson & Johnson and succeeded in creating a series of independent operating companies that were diversified in both products and geography. This was contrary to the conventional wisdom that advocated centralization to achieve economies of scale. The General also bucked the trend by exhibiting a strong concern for his employees' welfare. He published a list of general principles for business success that began with this statement: "Accept attainment of a decent living for all as the fundamental goal of business." His belief in fair employee treatment, decentralization, and product quality was set forth in 1944–45 in a document entitled "An Industrial Credo."[39]

The original Credo has been revised over the years with the title changed to its current "Our Credo" in 1948.[40] In the 1950s the document was revised to clarify wording. In 1972 the Credo was featured in the annual report. Dinner meetings were held with over 4,000 of the firm's managers to strengthen their beliefs.[41] The Credo itself is a deceptively simple document to guide the operations of a major firm. It is less than one page in length! It is written in plain language that relates to the everyday concerns of the manager. The current Credo is shown in Figure 6.1.

During the mid-1970s, the media carried numerous stories of improper political payments being made by firms. Corporate codes were being offered as an answer to such behavior. When the issue was raised at Johnson & Johnson, management saw no need to develop a code. They already had their Credo. However, the discovery of several incidents of improper payments being made in their foreign operations, with records being altered

FIGURE 6.1   Johnson & Johnson Credo

Our Credo

We believe our first responsibility is to the doctors, nurses and patients,
to mothers and fathers and all others who use our products and services.
In meeting their needs everything we do must be of high quality.
We must constantly strive to reduce our costs
in order to maintain reasonable prices.
Customers' orders must be serviced promptly and accurately.
Our suppliers and distributors must have an opportunity
to make a fair profit.

We are responsible to our employees,
the men and women who work with us throughout the world.
Everyone must be considered as an individual.
We must respect their dignity and recognize their merit.
They must have a sense of security in their jobs.
Compensation must be fair and adequate,
and working conditions clean, orderly and safe.
We must be mindful of ways to help our employees fulfill
their family responsibilities.
Employees must feel free to make suggestions and complaints.
There must be equal opportunity for employment, development
and advancement for those qualified.
We must provide competent management,
and their actions must be just and ethical.

We are responsible to the communities in which we live and work
and to the world community as well.
We must be good citizens — support good works and charities
and bear our fair share of taxes.
We must encourage civic improvements and better health and education.
We must maintain in good order
the property we are privileged to use,
protecting the environment and natural resources.

Our final responsibility is to our stockholders.
Business must make a sound profit.
We must experiment with new ideas.
Research must be carried on, innovative programs developed
and mistakes paid for.
New equipment must be purchased, new facilities provided
and new products launched.
Reserves must be created to provide for adverse times.
When we operate according to these principles,
the stockholders should realize a fair return.

Johnson & Johnson

to protect the company, raised a red flag. The Credo was not being supported to the extent thought. Thus, the president, James Burke, decided to hold a series of meetings with top management to determine if the Credo was still a valid document. These meetings, subsequently known as the Credo challenge meetings, took place between 1975 and 1978 and involved more than 1,200 managers.[42] The sessions, consisting of no more than 25 managers each, took place over two days and were headed by either Burke or David Clare, who succeeded Burke. The main issues addressed were whether the Credo was still applicable, whether any changes should be made, and how it should be implemented in the management of the Johnson & Johnson companies. The meetings uncovered a strong belief in the principles contained in the Credo and a general agreement that it was very difficult to balance the responsibilities derived from it. The meetings had another beneficial effect. When a manager would question whether the company would really support one tenet of the Credo, a manager from a different area would often provide an example of such support. The value of the meetings can be shown by the comments of a president of one of Johnson & Johnson's companies:

> At the Credo challenge meetings you discover, listening to your peers, that it [the Credo] has crept into everyone's value system. Finding that out is really beneficial. You come away with a healthy respect for the document and what it says, and you pass that on in your own company.[43]

Some say that the Credo describes a way of doing business. James Burke asserts that "It tells us what our business is about."[44] The Credo challenge meetings have become a regular event held twice a year for new top managers. Company presidents are also encouraged to hold their own Credo challenge meetings for their top management. In 1979, the Credo underwent another revision to keep it current with changing company and social conditions. The revised Credo was introduced in a World Wide Managers Meeting in New York.[45] The fact that top managers are rarely all brought together emphasizes the importance the firm places on the Credo.

In 1986 Johnson & Johnson began a Credo survey. The purpose was to determine how the employees view Johnson & Johnson's Credo performance. The survey, along with quality audits, safety performance records, and reports of consumer/customer complaints, is taken very seriously by the firm's executive committee. When the reports are reviewed by the committee, company presidents are in attendance and must be prepared to talk about the reports for their organizations. The company does not look kindly on violations of the Credo. For example, some very senior executives were discovered to have expense-account improprieties. The transgressions involved use of frequent-flyer coupons, personal expenses listed on company expense accounts, expenses from an outside business venture charged to the company, and changing previously approved personal benefits. Although the amounts were not large, the executives were fired immediately. A letter was sent to all senior management indicating that senior management had committed the offenses, the exact nature of the offenses, and that such actions were in violations of the Credo.[46]

While Johnson & Johnson runs a very decentralized company, it fosters a strong culture to guide management's actions via the Credo, which serves as the compass for managers. This was evident in the Tylenol crisis. Larry Foster, vice president for public relations, said they had no choice but to pull Tylenol from the market. Not to do so would have been a violation of the Credo. "It would have been hypocrisy at its best or worst."[47]

On January 11, 1995, Johnson & Johnson pleaded guilty to charges of obstructing justice in federal court in Newark, New Jersey.[48] The company agreed to pay a $5 million fine plus $2.5 million in court costs. The penalty resulted from the dermatology and public-relations divisions of Johnson & Johnson's Ortho Pharmaceutical unit destroying files relating to the firm's promotion of Retin-A, an acne drug. The federal government was investigating the promotion of the drug as a wrinkle-reducing product, a use not yet approved by the Food and Drug Administration. In 1992, Johnson & Johnson notified the U.S. Justice Department that it had discovered that files relevant to the case were destroyed a year earlier. As a result, three senior employees were fired.

The Batting Average

Each of these three major companies—Boeing, HP, and Johnson & Johnson—has a history of exemplary ethical behavior. They were selected to represent a cross-section of business activity. Yet each has and continues to experience ethical transgressions. Boeing is having a particularly difficult time as it blends a number of different organizational cultures into the Boeing culture. Hopefully, they can make the transition successfully. As a firm becomes large, it employs a large number of people. In that firm, many thousands of significant decisions are made each year by many different people. Just as you and I have made decisions that we are not particularly proud of, so have companies. The important thing is how the results of the bad decisions are handled and the ratio of the good to the bad. In effect, we are talking about a batting average. Even the best people experience poor judgment at times. The important question is how they handle the results and what action they take to prevent repetitions.

It should be noted that the firms just described are a small sample of the ethical companies operating in the world. They do not usually make headlines for doing what they do right. It is expected! Instead, we hear about their negative actions with no mention of their positive acts, which would provide a more accurate picture of the organization. Boeing is a current case in point.

The Ethics of Actions

Bribery

AB Bofors is one of Sweden's oldest companies. It was purchased in 1880 by Alfred Nobel, who is better known for the Nobel prize and the invention of dynamite.[49] Bofors's main business is to produce arms for the Swedish army. Although not a large arms supplier according to world standards, just making the top 50, it has been manufacturing howitzer cannons since 1936.[50] Swedish weapons are considered to be of high quality and users report a high level of satisfaction.[51]

Sweden has long been a neutral country following a policy of "armed neutrality." The country has preferred to rely on its own arms suppliers—a practice that has led to an expansion of its domestic weapons industry. Although accounting for an average of 50 percent of Bofors's business, Swedish military orders have fluctuated widely. In some years, they have accounted for as much as 75 percent of the business, while in other years they have dropped to as little as 30 percent.[52] Swedish law prohibits the sale of arms outside its borders. However, in order to survive, the firm must have outside customers. The government has decided that to maintain a domestic weapons industry, it must make exceptions and issue export licenses to countries it considers outside "areas of conflict."[53]

Bofors had a recent history of financial difficulties. In 1983, Bofors laid off hundreds of workers from its Karlskoga plant when missile orders from Sweden's armed forces ran out. In addition, orders from its explosives subsidiary, Nobel Kemi, had to be canceled when undercover smuggling was discovered. Bofors and Karlskoga were both concerned about their survival.

Imagine the joy the people of Karlskoga felt on April 1, 1986, when Martin Ardbo, then head of Bofors, announced that Bofors had signed a contract with the Indian army for $1.3 billion worth of artillery.[54] It was the largest export contract in Bofors's history. Four hundred 155mm howitzers were to be shipped at the rate of 14 per month.[55] This order guaranteed employment for the company's 5,000 workers for at least the coming four years.

Olof Palme, prime minister of Sweden at the time, was known for his pursuit of peace and nuclear disarmament. He spent a great deal of time building bridges with the third world. However, he apparently was talking more than peace and disarmament in talks with his friend Rajiv Gandhi, prime minister of India, in a series of meetings that took place in early 1986 prior to the signing of the Bofors's contract. Palme was offering India significant state export credits to buy the Bofors's cannons rather than competing French artillery.[56] In the past, Sweden had prohibited the use of export credits in arms deals. Palme was attempting to create jobs for Karlskoga which was in danger of going under. He was also trying to save a defense firm that was considered important to Sweden.

One other incentive was provided in the arms deal, although it did not come to light until later. Apparently, Bofors transferred 188 million Swedish kronor ($26 million U.S.

in 1986) to a coded Swiss bank account.[57] The beneficiary of the account was a Panama-registered company known as Svenska. When the Swedish central bank questioned the transfers, Bofors replied that Svenska was "an Indian who has been an agent for Bofors for 10–15 years."[58] The final recipients of the funds are unknown.

The sale of the howitzers was sealed with state concessions of export credits and large hidden payments to unknown Indian officials. The question is: Given the conditions, was the decision to sell the cannons to India an ethical act? The decision support model will help answer this question.

You will remember that the first step in the model is to collect information. This includes identifying the relevant stakeholders and determining the positive and negative impacts on the stakeholders. The stakeholders affected by the sale to India include Bofors's employees; Bofors's stockholders; the town of Karlskoga; the Swedish government; the Indian army; the Indian government; Svenska; and the French weapons supplier's employees, community, and stockholders.

The sale would create business and thus create work for Bofors's employees. It would, in turn, create profits or reduce losses for Bofors's stockholders. Karlskoga would benefit from the employment of its citizens, who would bring money into the community and provide additional tax revenues. The sale would help the Swedish government meet its goals of maintaining a viable defense industry and minimizing unemployment as well as increasing tax revenues. The Indian army would neither gain nor lose, assuming that the French guns performed as well as the Swedish cannons. The Indian government would gain only if the Swedish export credits made the deal more attractive than the French offer. If this were the case, there would have been no reason to make the secret payment. However, someone in India gained 188 million Swedish kronor! The negative consequence would be that the French manufacturer would lose the business from the contract. This in turn would result in fewer jobs for the French employees, lower profits for the French stockholders, and put less money in the French local community. The French government would lose tax revenue and unemployment would be higher.

There would be no significant reaction from any stakeholder as long as the payment was kept secret. However, if the payment came to light, the Swedish government would likely prosecute and the Swedish people could be expected to react negatively, which could have political consequences. The Indian government would also probably prosecute those who accepted payment and the Indian people might react negatively, which could have political consequences. Although the French stakeholders would probably be upset, they would not have much leverage to take any action.

Now that we know the stakeholders and how they are affected by the decision, we must determine whether the decision to sell the weapons using the hidden payment (bribe) violated ethical norms. Historically, bribery cases in all three countries have resulted in public condemnation; thus, the moral values of the cultures do not support bribery. We can assume community norms prohibit the paying of bribes. Given consistent support by norms in all three countries, the Bofors's payment is clearly unethical.

It is instructive to examine why the three countries condemn bribes. Bribery raises questions of fairness, which invoke principles of justice. Justice requires fair treatment; it applies to competition by requiring honest representation and dealing. The payment made by Bofors was kept secret and thus the French were not given a chance to compete. This provided an unfair advantage to Bofors and thus violated the principles of justice.

The payment apparently was made to influence government officials. The officials receiving the payments were benefiting only because they were responsible for making the weapons decision. The state paid the officials to make the decision, yet the officials were gaining additional benefits not available to their peers who were performing other equally necessary government business. Thus, the payment created an unfair situation in which some officials received extra rewards for doing their job that were not available to others doing equally important work. This is a violation of the principles of justice. In addition, the payment created a conflict of interest for the government employees. Although they were employed to represent the interests of the Indian government, the payment indebted them to represent Bofors's interests. Thus, the payment of the 188 million

Swedish kronor must be judged as unacceptable. This seems to be the position taken by both the Indian and Swedish people.[59]

The payment of a bribe to influence government officials is considered unethical by most cultures of the world and thus may be a hypernorm. Apparently the bribe was paid to keep Bofors from failing. Bofors was in financial difficulty because the country's weapons needs could not support a defense contractor its size. That raises the question of whether Bofors was really needed. One solution might be to downsize Bofors so it could be profitable meeting the country's weapons needs. However, downsizing does not take care of the wide swings in demand. If the Swedish government believes that it needs to maintain Bofors as a domestic weapons contractor, it has the obligation to subsidize the firm to guarantee its financial solvency. Otherwise, Bofors should be allowed to compete on the open market and fail if it cannot compete.

Apparently, top management was aware of the bribe being offered. If it was not, it is incompetent. Top management has only two choices if it wants to encourage ethical behavior. It must convince the government to provide subsidies to make up for the business revenue its military does not provide, or it must obtain approval to compete on the world market. A third alternative is to dissolve the firm.

Coercion

Maxine Munford was hired as assistant collections manager for the James T. Barnes Company on January 28, 1976, and reported to work the following day. During the morning, her new boss, Glenn Harris, asked her to go with him to the 25th floor to get office supplies. On the way, Harris made overt sexual suggestions to Munford. She immediately rejected his proposition. Harris then threatened her with the loss of her job if she did not submit to his demands.[60]

During the next few days, Harris made numerous sexual suggestions and propositions to Munford, both verbal and written. He harassed her by leaving sexually oriented cartoons on her desk. She repeatedly told him that she was not interested in any relationship with him. Finally, she told him that she had had enough and that if he did not stop, she was going to report his behavior to his boss, Robert Zulcosky. Harris said that if she reported him, she would only succeed in getting herself fired because Zulcosky was his friend.[61]

On February 12, 1976, Harris called Munford to his office. He told her that she was to go with him on an overnight business trip to Grand Rapids, Michigan, where he would book a motel room for the two of them. After they had finished work the first day, they would spend the night together in the room and have sexual relations. Munford agreed to accompany him on the trip, but said she would not stay in the same room or have sexual intercourse with him.[62] Harris repeated his demands the following day, but Munford held her ground. Harris then fired her.

Munford immediately went to Zulcosky, told him what had happened, and asked for her job back. Zulcosky backed Harris and told Munford that she no longer had a job. Not willing to drop the matter, Munford arranged a meeting with Harris, Zulcosky, company owner James T. Barnes, and attorneys representing the various parties. The company made no effort to come to her aid.[63]

The stakeholders in this case are Munford, Harris, and the James T. Barnes Company. The decision by Harris to pursue a sexual liaison with Munford created a potential benefit for Harris at the expense of Munford. Harris could gain sexual satisfaction, but Munford would be used as an object and not as a person of value; she would lose her personal dignity. The Barnes company could experience a deterioration in work performance due to Harris's actions. The time Harris spent harassing Munford was certainly not productive for the firm. If Harris was successful, Munford would likely be less productive due to her decline in self-esteem. If Munford decided to pursue the case in court, both Harris and the company would be exposed to significant financial damages. In fact, that is what happened.

Coercion raises questions of human rights. It violates the core human right of personal freedom, a hypernorm supported by the United Nations Universal Declaration of Human

Rights (see Appendix B). In order to keep her job, Munford would have to submit to Harris's sexual advances. This action violates her right to life and safety, for, if she submits to Harris, she becomes a sex slave. She loses her freedom, and she is also in danger from potential abuse and/or disease. Thus, Harris's coercive acts are clearly unethical as well as illegal. His behavior is unacceptable.

Harris is not fulfilling the requirements of his job. He is acting unprofessionally and is using company time in an attempt to obtain personal benefits. The firm apparently has no clear policy on relationships among employees. One suspects that Harris may have overstepped his bounds before without any consequences. The responsibility to resolve the problem lies with company owner James T. Barnes. He must establish a clear policy that prohibits sexual harassment and coercion in the workplace. To do less indicates incompetent management. Harris may have to become the first casualty of the policy. Munford should be rehired.

Deception

Volvo was incorporated as a ball-bearing manufacturer in 1915.[64] The company began exporting automobiles in volume to the U.S. market in 1957. It built its reputation on safety and reliability. Volvo pioneered the laminated windshield in the 1950s, introduced the first three-point seat belts in 1959, and incorporated front disk brakes in the 1960s. In 1966 the Volvo 140 series automobile was introduced with standard safety features that included a dual braking system, energy-absorbing front and rear ends, a divided steering shaft, and safety locks.[65] Volvo was promoting safety long before it was popular among car buyers. Volvo cars rank very high in crash tests performed by the National Highway Traffic Safety Administration, and the accident statistics published by the Insurance Institute for Highway Safety support these findings.

In November 1988, the Arthritis Foundation of Vermont held a monster truck event as a fund-raiser.[66] A number of different automobiles were parked in a line and the monster truck was driven over the automobiles. All of the cars were crushed except a Volvo station wagon, which came through the ordeal in relatively good shape. An account executive at Scali, McCabe, and Sloves, Volvo Cars of North America's advertising agency for the past 23 years, heard about the event. Subsequent discussion in the agency resulted in the idea to shoot a commercial re-creating the scene.[67]

The shooting took place on June 12, 1990, in Austin, Texas. A local resident, Dan White, went to the Texas Exposition & Heritage Center that day hoping to pick up a Volvo for parts. As he walked around the area, he discovered a man cutting the roof support pillars from all the cars except the Volvos. Later in the day, he discovered a Volvo wagon being reinforced with steel C-channel supports welded inside the car. He also discovered another Volvo with a 2-by-4 wood framework support inside the car.[68] White took pictures of what he saw and alerted the Texas attorney general's office. The first ad showing the doctored re-creation appeared in *Forbes* in late September and began to run on cable TV on October 8 (see Figure 6.2). Volvo was notified on October 24 that the state of Texas planned to file a suit.[69] State law requires that a notice of intent to file must be given five days prior to the actual filing of a suit. Both print and TV spots were voluntarily discontinued on October 31. Volvo reached a settlement with the state of Texas on November 5. They admitted no wrongdoing but agreed to run corrective ads in the state of Texas and pay the state $316,250 in investigative costs.[70] The firm asked to appear with the Texas attorney general at his press conference announcing the settlement. In addition, Volvo decided to run the corrective ads in the *Wall Street Journal*.

The question of who decided to doctor the cars is still unanswered. Volvo Cars of North America's president and chief executive, Joseph L. Nicolato, apologized in national newspaper ads, stating that Volvo first learned of the alterations to the automobiles on October 30, 1990.[71] The company insisted that the ads were supposed to re-create faithfully the actual event as it happened. Scali's Chairman-CEO Marvin Sloves stated that the ad agency did not authorize any alterations of vehicles at the shooting location.[72] Both Volvo and Scali had representatives at the shooting site in Austin. The actual filming was done by Perretti Productions, a New York production studio.

FIGURE 6.2   **Volvo Advertisement**

AB Volvo, the parent Swedish company, took control of the internal investigation. Perretti was accused of being uncooperative in their investigation. Pehr Gyllenhammar, AB Volvo chairman, called the ads ". . . an offense against our company and what we represent and an insult to all Volvo owners."[73] Both Volvo and Scali agreed to a proposed consent agreement with the Federal Trade Commission (FTC). The agreement required each firm to pay a $150,000 fine and to abide by the FTC truth-in-advertising standards without admitting any violation of the law.[74] Scali resigned from the $40 million Volvo account.

The Volvo case provides an interesting case of deception. A questionable act was committed, but we do not know who was responsible. Volvo already had a reputation for safe automobiles and thus did not need to use deception to gain an advantage. Scali had been having a bad year, but it was in no danger of losing its largest account, Volvo.[75]

Let's assume that Perretti Productions made the decision to alter the automobiles and that it was strictly a production decision. They were simulating an event that actually happened. Making a commercial is a time-consuming event with many retakes. One may want to re-create the Vermont scene, but running the monster truck over a line of automobiles would be difficult to repeat a number of times trying to get the right shot. Maybe the automobiles would not collapse the first, second, or third time like they did in Vermont, or maybe the Volvo would collapse. It would be very expensive to shoot a number of crushings until the right combination worked because many automobiles would have to be destroyed. Perhaps someone wanted to help it along a little to make sure the right effect was obtained the first time. How? By weakening the other cars and strengthening the Volvo, one would decrease the time and cost of filming the commercial while faithfully reproducing the original result.

The stakeholders involved include Volvo of North America and AB Volvo, Scali et al., Perretti Productions, and potential Volvo buyers. How are the stakeholders affected? Perretti would probably gain the most by alterations that would significantly reduce the time and cost of filming the commercial. Scali would be unaffected because their contract with Volvo called for production costs to be passed through to Volvo with no markup.

Potential customers are unlikely to be affected because the car's reputation for safety is well known. Volvo and its parent company would benefit about the same as they would from any other ad. Thus, nobody would lose, assuming that the ad replicated an actual event and knowledge of the tampering did not become public. However, local resident Dan White got the word out, and his information raised suspicions that the ad did not represent an actual event. Volvo's reputation became tarnished when potential buyers as well as current owners questioned the integrity of the firm.

Deception raises the issue of an individual's right to truth. If this is not a hypernorm, it is likely to be a community norm in most local communities. Based on our assumption that the ad was re-creating an actual event, the commercial is portraying the truth. Whether it was filmed the first time using doctored cars or the 25th time using unaltered cars, the communication effect is the same. Thus, while we may be a little uncomfortable with the alterations and judge the action to be marginally acceptable, it is not violating any rights. The other cars were actually crushed in the event; they are not being misrepresented.

To increase our comfort level with the decision, we will apply two other ethics principles. Focusing on the commercial, we conclude that nothing is being done unfairly. The event is portrayed exactly as it happened. The details of how the portrayal was created do not match the event, but that is not the issue. Thus, justice principles do not appear to be violated. From a utilitarian standpoint, the fact that the alterations resulted in more efficient production argues for doctoring the cars. Fewer resources are required for the same output. Thus, there does not appear to be anything unethical about the alterations. The cost savings probably move the alternative from marginal to an acceptable level.

However, there is one important point in this case: While the alterations are not unethical, they may be illegal under U.S. law. In a communication with Volvo, the company pointed out that such deception has not been ruled illegal in proven case law. Volvo elected not to resolve the issue in the courts. The company stated it had not desired nor intended for the ad to be produced in such a manner and accepted full responsibility. The firm voluntarily withdrew the ad and offered to settle with the authorities. Volvo stated, "The ad as it was executed violated *our* principles." Thus, Volvo and Scali paid fines and Scali lost a major customer.

Theft

The Low family acquired controlling interest in Ka Wah Bank of Hong Kong in 1974. Family members were previously employed in banks in Malaysia and Singapore. Low Chung Song became chief executive; his brother Low Chun Seng was executive director; and a third brother, Low Chang Hian, was a director.[76] In 1980 Chang Ming-thien, chairman of the Overseas Trust Bank, sold his interest in Ka Wah. In late 1984, Ka Wah Bank announced that it was expanding into the U.S. market with branches in New York and Los Angeles.[77] An advertisement for the bank claimed that it was using state-of-the-art computers and communications in its modern management style. It claimed to have avoided the many property financing pitfalls that befell numerous financial institutions in Southeast Asia over the last few years.[78]

In June 1985, Chang Ming-thien's Overseas Trust Bank failed due to massive fraud by management and had to be rescued by the Hong Kong government.[79] The bank failure caused a significant drop in the stock market. The resulting loss of confidence in the financial community led to a run on the Ka Wah Bank. The government, concerned about the financial stability of the British colony, secretly arranged to guarantee a $128 million emergency line of credit from the British-owned Hong Kong & Shanghai Banking Corporation and the Communist-owned Bank of China.[80] The Hong Kong banking commissioner stressed that there was "no management problem at the bank."[81]

In January 1986, Ka Wah Bank was rescued from the verge of collapse by the Chinese government's International Trust & Investment Corporation.[82] Although the Hong Kong government may have to provide from $130 to $260 million to cover bad loans, it maintained that the failure was due to circumstances beyond the bank's control. It claimed that the bank was solidly managed.[83]

Let's examine an indicator of that management. In November 1983, Ka Wah Bank loaned Compact Investment & Finance Ltd. of Hong Kong $10.8 million. The firm's paid-up capital at the time was $1.9 million.[84] Compact provided as collateral shares of the Taiwan Hotel Company, a firm building a hotel in Taipei, Taiwan. The fact was that the Taiwan Hotel shares were worthless and Ka Wah Bank knew it! The company had been dissolved two years earlier by its shareholders' meeting in the Ka Wah Bank building. According to public records, the three Low brothers and three other members of Ka Wah Bank management were stockholders of the Taiwan Hotel as of 1981. Most of them were at the meeting that dissolved the Taiwan Hotel.[85] Two directors of the Taiwan Hotel were Malaysian associates of the Lows. On July 1, 1985, when Ka Wah was in financial difficulty, Ka Wah's management renewed the loan. Compact was dissolved in July 1986 by a Hong Kong High Court order, leaving Ka Wah little chance of recovering any of its funds.

The stakeholders involved were the bank management, the bank depositors, the Hong Kong government, and Compact. Compact can be discounted because it was only a shell. The bank management, specifically the Lows and their associates, gained millions of dollars at the expense of the depositors. In an effort to protect the depositors, the Hong Kong government lost millions of dollars; the exact amount is still unknown.

This is an obvious case of theft, the taking of private property without the owner's consent. The right to property ownership is a hypernorm that has obviously been violated. Private property, depositors' funds, was given to the Lows and their accomplices to protect and put to productive use. Instead, management substituted shares of a worthless company and took the money for its use and its associates' use. Property of no value, shares of a worthless company, were substituted for property of value, deposits. This action violates the depositors' right to own private property and is clearly unethical behavior. It is an unacceptable act. It is also unethical under the utilitarian principle—private gain at the expense of public good—and it violates the justice principle of equals being treated equally.

The documentation on this and many other fraudulent acts by the bank management lead us to believe that acquiring Ka Wah Bank was part of a plan to bilk depositors out of millions of dollars. The bank management was able to gain control of Ka Wah Bank because of lax banking regulations. This type of theft can only be controlled by government's exercising closer control over banks. Top management *is* the problem and would have no reason to solve it. In fact, the culprits quickly left the country after the failure, apparently having accomplished their mission. Several governments have cooperated in arresting many of the bank officials and extraditing them back to Hong Kong.

Unfair Discrimination

Mr. Barber worked for Guardian Royal Exchange Assurance Group of England, which provides comprehensive investment services in the United Kingdom and throughout the world. With the exception of industrial life, all principal classes of insurance are offered, as are investments in stocks, shares, loans, and property. In addition, Guardian is in the property-development and fund-management business.

Guardian contracts with an outside vendor to maintain and administer a pension plan for its employees. The pension is wholly funded by Guardian. Under the terms of the plan, employees in Mr. Barber's employment category could retire and begin receiving pension payments at age 62 for males and 57 for females.[86] That was more generous than the state social security system that began making payments at 65 for males and 60 for females. Special provisions were made for employees who were laid off. Under the section of the pension contract entitled "GRE Guide to Severance Terms," an employee who was laid off prior to retirement was entitled to immediate pension payments if he or she had reached an age of 55 for males and 50 for females.[87]

Mr. Barber was "made redundant with effect from December 31, 1980, when he was aged 52," the British wording for laid off.[88] He was given the cash payments required under the severance terms, the statutory payment required for being laid off, and an *ex gratia* payment. He also was entitled to begin receiving a pension when he reached age

62. If he were a woman, he would have been immediately eligible to begin receiving pension payments. Believing that the difference in the age requirements discriminated unfairly against him, Mr. Barber took his case to an industrial tribunal.[89]

The stakeholders of interest in this case are Mr. Barber, Guardian Royal Exchange Assurance Group, the company that is handling the pension fund, and the current female and male employees of Guardian. Mr. Barber and the current male employees are obtaining fewer pension benefits by being forced to work to an older age before beginning to collect their pensions. This has a double impact because males tend to have shorter life spans than females. The pension company is unlikely to be affected because it is simply administering the fund. Guardian has to pay less money into the fund for males because men become eligible for benefits five years later than women.

There appears to be a community norm operating that provides benefits at an earlier age to females than to males. Thus, from an Integrative Social Contracts Theory perspective, the payments decision is ethical. The community norm does not violate a hypernorm, and males are free to leave the community if they don't want to be bound by its norms. However, Barber has the right to attempt to alter the community norm, which is what he seeks to do. Consider the arguments he might use.

The issue seems to be one of fairness: Are equals being treated as equals? Guardian created the pension to replace the state system for its employees. The pension age clearly favors women over men; thus, it violates the distributive justice principle and so does the country's social security system. Although the plan discriminates in favor of women, it does allow employees to begin drawing a pension at an earlier age.

However, unfair discrimination did take place, which is the major argument to be used in attempting to change the norm. This, in fact, is the argument Mr. Barber used, although it took a series of appeals before he won his case.[90]

Summary

This chapter began with a discussion of several companies that have earned a reputation for ethical behavior. They were chosen to represent a variety of types of business: project management, high technology, and consumer products. Even among these companies, lapses do occur. Controlling such lapses appears to be more difficult during times of company expansion through mergers and acquisitions. Merging cultures of organizations is one of the most difficult challenges faced by management. Maintaining continuity across a succession of top managers is also a difficult process.

Modern corporations are very complex organizations oftentimes employing thousands of people. Because humans are not perfect, one would expect that mistakes will be made. One would only hope that they will not be frequent and will be minor rather than major. The important point is how a firm handles the mistakes. We would like to see the batting average highly in favor of ethical behavior with the errors being of small magnitude.

The chapter closed with an examination of actual ethical dilemmas encountered by five firms. They were chosen to represent the five types of ethical issues on which this book is based: bribery, coercion, deception, theft, and unfair discrimination. Each dilemma was examined using the decision support model. These examples are provided to assist the reader in applying the model to help resolve ethical dilemmas in his/her work environment in a positive manner.

Final Comments

Even highly ethical companies from time to time find employees engaging in unethical behavior. Such behavior is relatively isolated and quickly corrected. These companies' cultural values permeate their firms and create an environment where ethical behavior is expected. It is the norm, not the exception. Unethical behavior may be more likely when a merger or acquisition takes place and the new employees have not

Your firm has fallen on hard times and there is talk that half of the people working on the line will be laid off. You are a successful salesperson with a couple of prospects that could bring in enough work to get your firm back on track. The prospects are interested in a new model your firm is bringing out that is scheduled to be available the first of the year. However, you happen to know that development work has fallen behind schedule, and the new model will not be available until May.

Your two prospects are eager to obtain the new model because they believe it will give them a significant edge over their competition. You could tell them about the delay and hope that they would be willing to wait instead of going to a competitor. However, one of your competitors is working on a new model scheduled to be available in March that will match the performance of your new model.

You can make the sale based upon the expected January delivery date. You believe you can string your prospects along until May, given that they have made their commitment. But they may lose the competitive advantage they are counting on if they have to wait. Would you try to make the sale based upon the January delivery date? Why or why not? What are the risks involved in making or not making the sale? Who gets hurt?

fully assimilated into the culture of their new employer. Worse yet, there is a danger that the culture of the former employer(s) may modify the culture of the acquiring firm in the wrong direction.

We hope that by examining real ethical issues that occurred in different types of firms in different countries, you have developed an understanding of how to approach decisions that contain ethical dimensions. The model provides a framework with which to structure your thinking about the issues. You also have a set of tools to use when examining the ethical dimension of a decision. The decisions are now yours.

Throughout this book, we have argued that ethics is important, that ethical behavior makes business more productive and certainly more pleasant. We do not discount the importance of business strategy and tactics. However, we believe, as we hope you now do, that ethics is a necessary but not a sufficient condition for business success.

Discussion Questions

1. What is meant by an ethical batting average?
2. Why do the decisions of some companies tend to be more ethical than the decisions of others? What is different?
3. If you were recently appointed CEO of a firm, what steps would you take to promote a high level of ethical performance within the organization?
4. How is it possible for firms operating ethically in one country to take actions that firms operating in another country consider unethical? Does the Barber case provide an example?
5. How can you tell a hypernorm from a community norm?
6. Why might it sometimes be difficult to determine the priority rules that pertain to a decision involving community norms?
7. Would employees at Hewlett-Packard or General Motors tend to be more upset with the firm bringing in dogs to search for drugs? Why?
8. Which of the five ethical issues—bribery, coercion, deception, theft, or unfair discrimination—do you consider to be the most important? Why?
9. What community norms would you like to see changed in your country? Industry? Company?

Endnotes

1. All three firms are cited in "Corporate Ethics: A Prime Business Asset," James Keogh, ed. (New York: The Business Roundtable, 1988), and Thomas J. Peters and Robert H. Waterman, Jr., *In Search of Excellence: Lessons from America's Best-Run Companies* (New York: Harper & Row, Publishers, 1982). The latter two are cited in Robert Levering, Milton Moskowitz, and Michael Katz, *The 100 Best Companies to Work for in America* (Reading, MA: Addison-Wesley Publishing Company, 1984); and Milton Moskowitz and Carol Townsend, "100 Best Companies for Working Mothers," *Working Mother,* October 1993, pp. 27–69.

2. Harold Mansfield, *Vision: A Saga of the Sky* (New York: Madison Publishing Associates, 1986).

3. Keogh, "Corporate Ethics A Prime Business Asset."

4. Ibid.

5. Ibid.

6. Ibid.

7. Ibid.

8. Ibid.

9. "Business Conduct Policy and Guidelines," The Boeing Company, 1998.

10. Letter to Boeing employees from President Frank A. Shrontz, June 2, 1986.

11. Boeing Internet website: www.boeing.com/companyoffices/aboutus/ethics/ index.htm.

12. "Former Boeing Supervisor Indicted," *Seattle Post-Intelligencer* 129, no. 145 (June 17, 1992), p. B5.

13. Steve Miletich, "Former Execs of Plane-parts Firm Guilty," *Seattle Post-Intelligencer* 129, no. 145 (June 17, 1992), p. B5.

14. "Former Boeing Supervisor Indicted."

15. Bill Virgin, "Boeing May Not Practice the Ethics It Preaches," *Seattle Post-Intelligencer,* July 31, 2003, p. C1.

16. Anne Marie Squeo and Andy Pasztor, "Space Case: U.S. Probes Whether Boeing Misused a Rival's Documents—At Issue in the Investigations: A Rocket Scientist Hired Away from Lockheed—Mr. Branch's 43 Business Trips," *Wall Street Journal,* May 5, 2003, p. A1.

17. Renae Merle, "U.S. Strips Boeing of Launches; $1 Billion Sanction over Data Stolen from Rival," *Washington Post,* July 25, 2003, p. A1.

18. Ibid.

19. Andy Pasztor and Anne Marie Squeo, "Leading the News: Boeing Ex-Employee's Suit Adds to Strife on Lockheed Documents," July 18, 2003, p. A3.

20. "Boeing Acts Fast to Repair Damage," *Satellite News,* Potomac, August 4, 2003, p. 1.

21. Annual Report, The Boeing Company, 1996.

22. Annual Report, The Boeing Company, 1997.

23. Annual Report, The Boeing Company, 2000.

24. Annual Report, Hewlett-Packard, 2001.

25. "Communicating the HP Way," Hewlett-Packard, 1989.

26. "Corporate Objectives," Hewlett-Packard, 1989.

27. "HP Corporate Objectives," Hewlett-Packard website, 2003.

28. Business Ethics," Hewlett-Packard website, 2003.

29. "Social and Environmental Responsibility Report," Hewlett-Packard website, 2003.

30. "HP Supplier Code of Conduct," Hewlett-Packard website, 2003.

31. "Communicating the HP Way," Hewlett-Packard, 1989.

32. Ibid.

33. "Standards of Business Conduct," Hewlett-Packard, 1989.

34. David Sylvester, "H-P Cracks Down on Drug Use, Searches Office," *San Jose Mercury News,* September 19, 1987, NewsBank EMP 88:G11, microfiche.

35. John Markoff, "Hewlett-Packard Picks Rising Star at Lucent as Its Chief Executive," *New York Times,* July 20, 1999, p. C1.

36. "HP Says Merger May Cause More Job Cuts, Layoffs," *San Jose Mercury News,* October 2, 2001, p. 1C.

37. Katz, *The 100 Best Companies to Work for in America,* p. 161.

38. "Corporate Ethics: A Prime Business Asset."

39. Ibid.

40. Ibid.

41. Ibid.

42. Ibid.

43. Ibid.

44. Ibid.

45. Ibid.

46. Ibid.

47. "Business Ethics," Arthur Andersen video.

48. Elyse Tanouye, "J & J to Admit to Shredding Retin-A Papers," *Wall Street Journal* 132, no. 7 (January 11, 1995), pp. B1, B5.

49. Karen DeYoung, "Swedish Arms Scandals Mar Peacemaking Image," *Washington Post* 110, no. 274 (September 5, 1987), pp. A1, A30.

50. "Bofors: Hoist by Its Own Petard," *The Economist* 304, no. 7516 (September 19, 1987), p. 82.

51. "The Gun That Can Kill at Four Years' Range," *The Economist* 313, no. 7619 (September 9, 1989), pp. 35–36.

52. "Bofors: Hoist by Its Own Petard."

53. DeYoung, "Swedish Arms Scandals Mar Peacemaking Image."

54. "Bofors: Hoist by Its Own Petard."

55. Pranay Gute, "Rhetoric and Reality in the Iranian Arms Trade," *Forbes* 140, no. 8 (October 19, 1987), pp. 32–35.

56. Ibid.

57. "In the Soup over Bofors," *The Economist* 313, no. 7624 (October 14, 1989), pp. 37–38.

58. Ibid.

59. "The Gun That Can Kill"; DeYoung, "Swedish Arms Scandals Mar Peacemaking Image."

60. *Maxine Munford* v. *James T. Barnes Co., Glenn D, Harris,* 441 F. Supp. 459 (1977).

61. Ibid.

62. Ibid.

63. Ibid.

64. "Volvo: A Company on a Fast Roll Upward," *Automotive News* 5099 (October 30, 1985), p. 404.

65. Ibid.

66. Raymond Serafin and Gary Levin, "Ad Industry Suffers Crushing Blow," *Advertising Age* 61, no. 47 (November 12, 1990), pp. 1, 76.

67. Raymond Serafin and Jennifer Lawrence, "Volvo Parent Seizes Control of Inquiry," *Advertising Age* 61, no. 48 (November 19, 1990), pp. 1, 54.

68. "How Volvo's Bogus Advertisements Were Discovered," *Automotive News* 5367 (November 19, 1990), pp. 3, 11.

69. Ibid.

70. Jennifer Lawrence, "How Volvo's Ad Collided with the Truth," *Advertising Age* 61, no. 47 (November 12, 1990), p. 76.

71. Jim Henry, "Volvo Stained by Monster Truck Ad Flap," *Automotive News* 5366 (November 12, 1990), pp. 1, 41.

72. Serafin and Lawrence, "Ad Industry Suffers Crushing Blow."

73. Jim Henry, "Volvo Digs into Ad Fiasco," *Automotive News* 5367 (November 19, 1990), p. 3.

74. "Volvo Agrees to $150,000 Penalty for 'Monster Truck' Ads," *Automotive News* 5408 (August 26, 1991), p. 35.

75. Gary Levin, "Volvo Loss Worsens Tailspin at Scali," *Advertising Age* 61, no. 48 (November 19, 1990), pp. 2, 54.

76. Cheah Cheng Hye, "Records Indicate Abuse by Management Pushed a Hong Kong Bank to the Brink," *Wall Street Journal* 209, no. 4 (January 7, 1987), p. 24.

77. "Expansion Plans by Ka Wah Bank," *New York Times* 134, no. 46219 (November 5, 1984), p. D8.

78. Ibid.

79. Francine C. Brevetti, "British, Peking-Owned Banks Join in a Hong Kong Rescue," *American Banker* 150, no. 119 (June 19, 1985), pp. 2, 11.

80. Ibid.

81. Ibid.

82. "China Acts to Rescue Ailing Hong Kong Bank," *Journal of Commerce* 367, no. 26140 (January 10, 1986), pp. 1A, 5A.

83. Ibid.

84. Ibid.

85. "Records Indicate Abuse by Management Pushed a Hong Kong Bank to the Brink."

86. "Contracted-out Pensions Fall within EC Sex Equality Provision," *Times* (London), 63, no. 709 (May 18, 1990), p. 42.

87. Ibid.

88. Ibid.

89. *Barber* v. *Guardian Royal Exchange Group* (Case C-262/88).

90. Ibid.

PART FOUR

Creativity and Innovation*

After completing this chapter, you should be able to

1. Describe the creative process.
2. Identify the traits or characteristics that are related to individual creativity.
3. Explain the difference between creativity and innovation.
4. Describe the stages and the different types of innovation.
5. Gain insight into the key issues associated with the management of creativity and innovation processes.
6. Understand the interplay among human behavior, group behavior, creativity, and innovation.

Key Terms and Concepts

Adaption–innovation model

Administrative innovation

Creative process

Creativity

Creativity-relevant skills

Domain-relevant skills

Dual ladders

Emotional intelligence

Incremental innovation

Innovation

Innovation process

Person-oriented approach

Process innovation

Process-oriented approach

Product innovation

Product-oriented approach

Radical innovation

System-maintaining innovation (SMI)

System-transforming innovation (STI)

Task motivation

*This chapter was revised and modified in collaboration with Dr. Carol Sexton, Pepperdine University. We are grateful to Dr. Sexton.

Chapter Outline

Chapter Preparation

Activity 7.1:

Exploring Creativity in an Organizational Setting: 3M's Post–it Note Pads

Objectives:

a. To explore the organizational context for creativity and innovation.

b. To identify the variety of skills and competencies involved in triggering and facilitating creativity.

Task 1 (Homework):

Students are to read the following case, 3M Post-it Note Pads and respond to the question at the end of the case.

Task 2:

Individuals are to share the answers in small groups. Each group is to develop a shared response, which will be presented and discussed with the class.

■ Case: 3M's Post-it Note Pads*

In 1922 Minnesota Mining and Manufacturing inventor Francis G. Okie was dreaming of ways to increase sandpaper sales, the company's major product at the time, when a novel thought struck him. Why not sell sandpaper as a replacement for razor blades? The idea was that people could rub their cheeks smooth. The idea never caught on, but Okie went on at 3M and eventually developed a waterproof sandpaper that became a major staple in the auto industry. Okie's failure is as much legend at 3M as is his successful idea.

The 3M Company was founded at the turn of the century by a doctor, a lawyer, two railroad executives, and a meat market manager on the shores of Lake Superior. Their purpose was to mine corundum, an abrasive used in sandpaper. Unfortunately, the corundum mine yielded a mineral of no value to the sandpaper industry. Most of the original investors left, and those who remained turned to inventing. Their first success was an abrasive cloth used in metal polishing. Then Okie's wet or dry sandpaper came along. Since then, 3M has never stopped.

William L. McKnight is the legendary spiritual father of the company. McKnight worked himself up from bookkeeper through sales to chairman and chief executive. As a salesman he pitched his products directly to furniture makers on the factory shop floors rather than to the purchasing agents.

This became the 3M approach—get close to the customer. Both Scotch tape and masking tape were developed to meet individual customers' needs. Part of McKnight's manifesto was, "If management is intolerant and destructively critical when mistakes are made, I think it kills initiative." In addition to tolerating mistakes, the company rarely hires from outside (never at the senior level). The turnover rate among managers and other professionals is less than 4 percent. Divisions are kept small so that division managers are on a first-name basis with their staffs. 3M continues to spend more than $1 billion annually in research, development, and related expenses for new products and to improve the performance of their existing products operationally and environmentally.

---

*Source: Background on 3M was drawn from "Masters of Innovation," *BusinessWeek,* April 10, 1989, pp. 58–63, and the corporate website, *http://www.3m.com/about3m/century/index.jhtml*. This case is a shorter and modified version of "3M's Little Yellow Note Pads: Never Mind I'll Do It Myself," in P. R. Nayak and J. M. Kerrengham (eds.), *Breakthroughs!* (New York: Rawson Associates, 1988), pp. 50–73. Used by permission.

New-Product Development

A 3Mer comes up with an idea for a new product. He or she forms an action team by recruiting full-time members from technical areas, manufacturing, marketing, sales, and finance. The team designs the product and figures out how to produce and market it. Then the team develops new uses and line extensions. All members of the team are promoted and receive raises as the project develops. As sales grow, the product's originator can go on to become project manager, department manager, or division manager. There's a separate track for scientists who don't want to manage. The result is that there are 42 divisions. Each division must follow the 25 percent rule: A quarter of a division's sales must come from products introduced within the past five years. In addition, there is a 15 percent rule. Virtually anyone at the company can spend up to 15 percent of the workweek on anything he or she wants to as long as it's product related. Managers do not carefully monitor their scientists' use of this 15 percent rule. If this policy were enforced rigidly, such action would undermine its intent and inhibit the creative energy of researchers. This practice (called "bootlegging" by members of the company) and the 25 percent rule are at the heart of one of 3M's most famous innovations, the yellow Post-it Note.

The Post-it Note

Unlike many of the incremental improvements and innovations made in product lines, the Post-it Note pad was unique, a product entirely unrelated to anything that had ever been developed or sold by 3M. Post-it Notes are ubiquitous in modern business because they do something no product ever did before. They convey messages in the exact spot where people want the messages, and they leave no telltale sign that the message was ever there at all.

This small but powerful idea was begun by a 3M chemist, Spencer Silver, refined by two scientists named Henry Courtney and Roger Merrill, and nurtured from embryo to offspring by Arthur L. Fry. Post-it revenues are estimated at as much as $300 million per year.

Post-it Notes started out as another oddball idea—an adhesive that didn't form a permanent bond—with no perceptible application. In 1964 Silver was working in 3M's central research labs on a program called Polymers for Adhesives. 3M regularly sought ways to improve its major products. Tapes and adhesives were 3M's primary product lines, and adhesives that created stronger bonds were actively sought. Silver found out about a family of monomers that he though might have potential as ingredients for polymer-based adhesives, and he began exploring them.

In the course of this exploration, Silver tried an experiment, just to see what would happen with one of the monomers, and then to see what would happen if a lot more of the monomer was added to the reaction mixture, rather than the amount dictated by conventional wisdom. This in itself was irrational, as in polymerization catalysis, the amounts of interacting ingredients were controlled in tightly defined proportions according to theory and experience. Silver says, "The key to the Post-it adhesive was doing the experiment. If I had sat down and factored it out beforehand, and thought about it, I wouldn't have done the experiment. If I had really seriously cracked the books and gone through the literature, I would have stopped. The literature was full of examples that said you can't do this." To Silver, science is one part meticulous calculation and one part fooling around.

Silver describes what happened with the unusual concoction as a "Eureka moment"— the emergence of a unique, unexpected, previously unobserved and reliable scientific phenomenon. "It's one of those things you look at and you say, This has got to be useful! You're not forcing materials into a situation to make them work. It wanted to do this. It wanted to make Post-it adhesive."

The adhesive became Silver's baby. Silver started presenting this discovery to people who shared none of his perceptions about the beauty of his glue. Interested in practical applications, they had only a passing appreciation for the science embodied in Silver's adhesive. More significantly, they were "trapped by the metaphor" that insists that the ultimate adhesive is one that forms an unbreakable bond. In addition, Silver was immersed in an organization whose lifeblood was tape of all kinds. In this atmosphere imagining a piece of paper that eliminated the need for tape is an almost unthinkable leap into the void.

Silver couldn't say exactly what it was good for. "But it has to be good for something," he would tell them. "Aren't there times," Silver would ask people, "when you want a glue to hold something for a while but not forever? Let's think about those situations. Let's see if we can turn this adhesive into a product that will hold tight as long as people need it to hold but then let go when people want it to let go."

From 1968 to 1973, support for Silver's idea slipped away. The Polymers for Adhesives program ran out of funding and support, and the researchers were reassigned. Silver had to fight to get the money to get the polymer patented because there was no commercial application immediately present.

Silver was a quiet, well-behaved scientist with an amazing tolerance for rejection. Spencer Silver took his polymer from division to division at 3M, feeling that there was something to be said for such a product. He was zealous in his pursuit because he was "absolutely convinced that this had some potential." The organization never protested his search. At every in-house seminar no one ever said to Silver, "Don't try. Stop wasting our time." In fact, it would have violated some very deeply felt principles of the company to have killed Silver's pet project. As long as Silver never failed in his other duties, he could spend as much time as he wanted fooling around with his strange adhesive.

The best idea Silver could come up with on his own was a sticky bulletin board, not a very stimulating idea even to Silver. But 3M did manufacture them, and a few were sold, though it was a slow-moving item in a sleepy market niche. Silver knew there had to be a better idea. "At times I was angry because this stuff is so obviously unique," said Silver. "I said to myself, Why can't you think of a product? It's your job!"

Silver had become trapped by a metaphor. The bulletin board, the only product he could think of, was coated with adhesive—it was sticky everywhere. The metaphor said that something is either sticky or not sticky. Something "partly sticky" didn't occur to him.

Silver and Robert Oliveira, a biochemist whom Silver met in his new research assignment, continued to try selling the idea. Geoff Nicholson, who was leading a new venture team in the commercial tapes division, agreed to see them. Nicholson knew nothing about adhesives and had just taken the position in commercial tapes. Silver and Oliveira were literally the first people to walk through his door. Nicholson says that he was "ripe for something new, different, and exciting. Most anybody who had walked in the door, I would have put my arms around them." Nicholson recruited a team to work on an application for the five-year-old discovery. One of these people, Arthur Fry (a chemist, choir director, and amateur mechanic), would make the difference. Fry had "one of those creative moments" while singing in the choir of his church. "To make it easier to find the songs we were going to sing at each Sunday's service, I used to mark the places with little slips of paper. Inevitably the little slips would flutter to the floor." The idea of using Silver's adhesive on these bookmarks took hold of him at one of these moments. Fry went to 3M, mixed up some adhesive and paper, and invented the "better bookmark." Fry realized that the primary application for the adhesive was not to put it on a fixed surface, such as the bulletin board, but on the paper itself. It was a moment of insight that contemplation did not seem to generate. Fry now has his own lab at 3M and often speaks to large groups of businesspeople about the climate for creativity at 3M. Silver is still in 3M's basement, working out of a cramped, windowless office in a large lab—a place where experimental ferment and scientific playfulness still reign.

The product was not perfected at the moment of Fry's discovery. It still took two more scientists on the Nicholson team—Henry Courtney and Roger Merrill—to invent a paper coating that would make the Post-it adhesive work. Silver said, "Those guys actually made one of the most important contributions to the whole project, and they haven't got a lot of credit for it. The Post-it adhesive was always interesting to people, but if you put it down on something and pulled it apart, it could stay with either side. It had no memory of where it should be. It was difficult to figure out a way to prime the substrate, to get it to stick to the surface you originally put it on. Roger and Hank invented a way to stick the Post-it adhesive down. And they're the ones who really made the breakthrough discovery because once you've learned that, you can apply it to all sorts of different surfaces."

To get the product to manufacturing, Fry brought together the production people, designers, mechanical engineers, product supervisors, and machine operators and let them describe the many reasons why something like that could not be done. He encouraged them to speculate on ways that they might accomplish the impossible. A lifelong gadgeteer, Fry found himself offering his own suggestions. "Problems are wonderful things to have, especially early in the game, when you really should be looking for problems," said Fry.

In trying to solve the problem of one difficult phase of production, Fry assembled a small-scale basic machine in his own basement, which was successful in applying adhesive to paper in a continuous roll. The only problem was that it wouldn't fit through his basement door. Fry accepted the consequences and bashed a hole through the basement wall. Within two years Fry and 3M's engineers had developed a set of unique, proprietary machines that are the key to Post-it Notes' consistency and dependability.

Discussion Questions

1. Describe the creative process that resulted in the Post-it Note pads as we know them today.
2. Identify the factors that fostered and hindered the creative process.
3. Describe the characteristics of Spencer Silver.

Introduction

Most companies are dependent on development driven by creative ideas, designs, products or services, and innovative solutions. Creativity and innovation are processes that provoke continuing interest among managers and researchers alike.[1] At the surface level, individual creativity is not the same as organizational creativity or organizational innovation. We can relatively easily identify creative individuals and innovative organizations. Yet, while we can decipher what it takes to facilitate creative behavior at the individual level, organizational innovation is a more complex and baffling phenomenon. *Organizational creativity and innovation* are viewed as processes by which individuals working together in a complex social system create a valuable, useful new product, service, idea, procedure, or work process.[2] As such, they play a central role in the long-term survival of organizations and are key processes that must be managed.

We introduced the subject of environmental turbulence as the backdrop against which to understand the rapidly expanding use of behavioral science technology in the world of entrepreneurship and corporations. Alvin Toffler described this growing turbulence in *Future Shock* in 1970, which was followed by *Third Wave* in 1980. In 1990 he completed his trilogy with *Powershift,* which claims that the accelerated dissemination of information has resulted in a shift of power and wealth.[3] During the 1990s and early 2000 era, we have seen the effect of information, information technology, and globalization. From the old smokestack era with mass production of individual models requiring timely planning and changeovers, we have moved into the new computer-driven economies that make possible designer production and services tailored to specific client needs. The power vested in the stable financial institutions, which existed with the old industrial giants, has been diluted by the shift to designer financial systems and currencies, making a multitude of new enterprises powerful in a global production market. Adding to this mix are the economic and political turbulence (resulting, for example, from the manipulation of budget deficits as special interest groups assert power with the aid of modern media methods) and the social turbulence, arising from changing population demographics and a highly pluralistic society.

There seems to be little question that you and your peers will experience environmental change at an augmented rate never before experienced by humankind. Similarly, organizations in all phases of their lifecycles will experience this whirlpool-type environment.

In the past, organizational behavior practitioners spoke of "coping with change" as a primary viewpoint for meeting this challenge, but more recently they broadened this view to include a more proactive strategy of **innovation,** which emphasizes finding new products and new methods to enable organizations to maintain the lead in competitive endeavors. At present the buzzwords *creativity* and *innovation* fill the work world vocabulary. Organizations such as Asian Brown Bovery (ABB), General Electric, Ford, IBM, Intel, and Coca-Cola send their employees to training programs where they learn techniques for becoming more creative in their thinking. Numerous games and software are now available to teach people how to become more creative. But let us turn first to defining and exploring the relevant concepts. Next we present a summary of some of the literature that describes strategies being used in organizations to attain a competitive edge regarding creativity and innovation. We begin by discussing creativity as an aspect of individual effectiveness and then move on to describing innovation as an aspect of organizational effectiveness.

What Is Creativity?

In the early 1990s, an interactionist model of creative behavior was proposed.[4] The interactionist view suggests that **creativity** is the complex product of a person's behavior in a given situation. The situation is characterized in terms of the contextual and social influences that either facilitate or hinder creative accomplishments. The person brings to the situation his or her cognitive abilities, personality traits, and noncognitive abilities. The interactionist view provides an integrative framework that combines important elements of personality, cognitive style and abilities and social psychology elements such as leadership dynamics, group dynamics, motivation, organizational elements such as work and organization design, and technology and information technology. Figure 7.1 captures the interactionist model of organizational creativity.

It is probably most useful to start with the view of cognitive psychology that the brain is a creative entity, continuously processing data for problem solving, understanding, and responding, mostly at the unconscious level. We are all creative because the brain is creative. Creative in this sense means processing data to come up with an answer, whether it be "get out of the way of that oncoming truck" (an unconscious response) or arithmetic reasoning (a primarily but not entirely conscious process). There is some evidence that individuals may be either right-brain or left-brain dominant. Right-brain dominant people tend to be more intuitive in their response to problem solving and learning, and left-brain dominants more logical and rational. Right-brain dominants were thought to be more creative, but more evidence suggests that both sides must work together. Test your own brain dominance at *http://www.mindmedia.com/interact/specials/brain.jsp.*

Webster's dictionary defines *creativity* as "the ability to bring something new into existence." Early experiments by Wolfgang Koehler add the element of "insight" to creativity.[5] Koehler placed a piece of fruit outside a chimpanzee's cage and beyond the reach of a stick in the chimp's hand. He placed a longer stick in the vicinity of the fruit. The chimp tried without success to reach the fruit with the short stick. After an extended pause, the chimp suddenly used the short stick to drag the longer one to him and then used the longer stick to haul in the fruit. This sudden flash of insight into the right answer has been referred to as the *aha process* or the *eureka process.*

Scientists long ago[6] developed a process to exploit the "insight" mechanism, and they show up on TV talk shows from time to time to tell about it. When confronted with a difficult problem, they systematically go through several stages:

1. Studying the problem area to realize its different aspects.
2. Saturating the brain with all available data.
3. Allowing incubation time during which the cognitive process at the unconscious level reform and reshape the data.
4. Awaiting enlightenment (insight).
5. Testing hypotheses.

FIGURE 7.1 **Conceptual Links among Creative Persons, Processes, Situations, and Products**

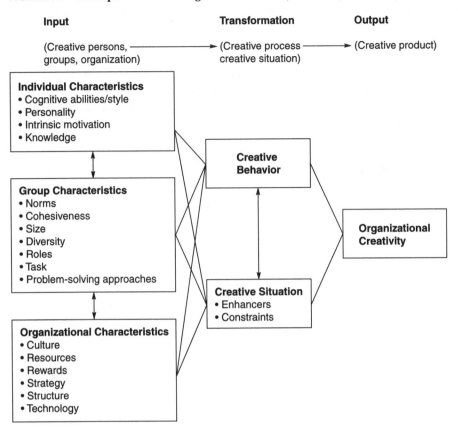

Source: R. W. Woodman, J. E. Sawyer, and R. W. Griffin, "Toward a Theory of Organizational Creativity," *Academy of Management Review* 18, no. 2 (1993), p. 309.

This process is used in many professions. Engineers are intensely aware of this inventive approach. Judges most often do not give decisions until time for incubation is allowed. Architects work and rework designs. All of us do this naturally, but awareness and practice can augment our effectiveness in both our personal and our work lives. (The next time you write a term paper, follow this procedure. After time for incubation, you will be surprised how much better than expected the material will fall into meaningful form so that you can write an excellent paper.) For more information and models of the creative process and how you use it, go to *http://members.ozemail.com.au/ ~caveman/Creative/Brain/process.htm.*

Defining creativity as we have used it refers to brain functions of acquiring and processing data for purposes of problem solving, whether it be responses, answers, actions, or new ideas. This involves both unconscious and conscious processes.

As we have seen, the interactionist view would advocate the need to stress that in working organizations, everyone has the potential for creativity—to solve problems and to give new ideas. Executives and managers with whom we have worked almost always are looking for "creative people," assuming that "you've either got it (creativity) or you haven't." The implication is that very few have it. Yet most consultant firms readily admit that their recommendations in managerial and organizational effectiveness surveys come primarily from internal sources: the employees they have interviewed. (Of course, these firms have performed the important function of judging the merits of each recommendation.)

There is further support for this idea. In Sternberg's studies, unskilled workers in a milk-processing plant always developed operating procedures that required the least physical efforts. The author reviewed other studies consistent with these findings and concluded, "Beneath the surface of adaptation, however, lie continuing acts of creativity—the invention of new ways of handling old and new problems. Since creativity is a term ordinarily reserved for exceptional individuals and extraordinary accomplishments, recognizing it in the practical problem-solving activities of ordinary people introduced a new perspective from which to grasp the challenge of the ordinary."[7]

Carrying this idea one step further, there is additional evidence for widespread creativity in the multitude of unique ways in which disgruntled workers can come up with methods to resist or even sabotage management.

We know that some people have more new ideas than others have, but we also want to point out that the widespread (and self-fulfilling) expectation system of management overlooks the major contributions that the whole body of the employee system has to offer.[8]

Distringuishing between Creativity and Innovation

Sociologists have long used concepts related to these subjects. Invention represents a completely new idea, often related to technology, that has an impact on societal institutions. Innovation is the reforming or reworking of old ideas to come up with something new. Both of these ideas would be included in our recent definition of creativity. We mention this here because the term *innovation* is currently being used in organizational settings in a trendy way to mean many things. In much of the literature discussing applications of creativity and innovation, the words are used loosely and often interchangeably. Current usage in organizational behavior defies definition of innovation as a concept. However, J. J. Kao's distinction between creativity and innovation is adequate for our purposes.[9] If creativity implies the vision of what is possible, then the term *innovation* suggests the implementation process by which inspiration leads to the practical results. Creativity involves problem solving that may lead to a useful idea. The term *innovation* is more suitably applied to decision-making processes: the decision to search for a new, useful idea; the decision to select the most useful idea; and the decision of how to implement the chosen idea.

Although creativity depends on many uncontrollable factors (such as the degree of knowledge available; the characteristics, skills, and motivation of the person or persons involved; and a good dose of chance or luck), innovation requires organizational choice and change that can be planned. Finally, an innovation when defined as implementation is not necessarily unique. Successful innovation may result from imitation or adoption of an innovation from another source.

Many people use the term *invention* when they are distinguishing creativity from innovation. However this distinction can be misleading about the nature of creativity. Most of us think of an invention as a tangible, usually technical, product or an idea that can be readily translated into a useful product. This is too limiting a view of creativity. Creativity involves characteristics of the individual exhibiting creative behavior and a process as well as a product.

Creativity can be defined from the person-oriented, process-oriented, and product-oriented perspectives. The **person-oriented approach** to creativity studies patterns of personality traits and characteristics observed in individuals who exhibit creative behavior. Such creative behavior might include the activities of inventing, designing, contriving, composing, and planning.[10] The **process-oriented approach** to creativity examines the development of a new and valuable idea or product through the unique interaction of the individual with the available resources, settings, people, and situations. The **product-oriented approach** to creativity focuses on the production of novel and useful ideas by an individual or a small group of individuals working together. A full understanding of creativity requires an integration of these orientations. An agreement seems to exist that the creative behavior, the creative interaction, and the creative idea need not be successful, commercial, nor applied.

Innovation, in contrast, generally refers to the successful application of a new idea to the firm. Success in this case refers to the actual translation of the idea into a useful product or process. An innovation may or may not be profitable or beneficial to the firm. Innovation is a process of developing and implementing a new idea, whether it is a new technology, product, or organizational process. Obviously, creativity can be a part of this implementation process.[11] It may involve recombining old ideas in a new way, a scheme that challenges the present order, or an approach perceived as new by those involved.[12] Note that the idea need not be a breakthrough idea such as superconductivity or a completely new organizational model; it need only be new, or perceived as new, to the organization. Given these distinctions between creativity and innovation, we next examine people's orientation toward creativity.

The Creative Person

The stereotyped image we have of the creative person originates from the mad scientist, the crazy artist, the computer nerd, or the absent-minded professor. We typically think of a collection of personality traits that immediately sets the individual apart from others. Do such stereotypes hold? Outstanding creative people have been studied across fields to try to determine the common traits. Unfortunately, the common traits do not come in a precise package that would help you to immediately identify a creative person.

The intelligence level has been of major interest. Exceptionally creative architects, mathematicians, scientists, and engineers usually score no higher on intelligence tests than their less creative peers do. Testing suggests that a certain level of intelligence is related to creativity, but the correlation between the two factors disappears when the person's IQ is above 120. This lack of correlation is particularly important to know in a work setting because managers tend to believe that only the brightest people are apt to be creative. (Refer to our previous discussion of creativity being widespread among workers.)

In general, the literature tends to show that expertise and intrinsic motivation are essential components of creativity—which is another way of saying that the individual has to know the field and want to do something about an issue or a problem. The following characteristics also have been related to creativity: high energy level, dedicated and effective work habits, a persistent and high level of curiosity, interest in reflective thinking, relatively little tie to reality, low level of sociability, unusual appreciation of humor, facility for producing humor, need for adventure, need for variety, self-confidence, tolerance of ambiguity, introversion, high need for autonomy, self-direction, and an impulsive personality. Emotional intelligence has recently been linked to effective creativity.

Emotional Intelligence and Creativity

Leadership and personality play critical roles in shaping human behavior at the workplace. As of late, one of the growing areas that seems to attract attention centers around the role that emotional intelligence plays in leadership and organizations.[13] **Emotional intelligence** is defined as the ability to sense, understand, and effectively apply the power and acumen of emotions as a source of human energy, information, trust, creativity, and influence.[14] In a recent book, R. Cooper and A. Sawaf attempt to demonstrate ". . . how the science of emotional intelligence has enabled manager after manager, company after company, to begin capturing the single most powerful source of human energy, authenticity, and drive."[15] While the topic of emotional intelligence is beyond the scope of this chapter, and more empirical research is needed, we want to make the following points:

1. Creativity is one of the 21 scales that map out emotional intelligence.
2. Creativity seems to be influenced by the person's emotional intelligence level.
3. Creativity seems to be influenced by the supervisor/leader/coach's level of emotional intelligence.
4. The emotional intelligence level of the leaders influence the workplace context and dynamics.

Additional links for further investigation of emotional intelligence include the following: *http://www.qmetricseq.com* and *http://www.a2zpsychology.com/articles/emotional_ intelligence1.htm*. You can explore your own emotional intelligence at http://etesting. modwest.com/tests.php.

The Organizational Context Of Creativity

Creativity involves a special kind of problem-solving. In organizational settings, attempts have been made to identify potentially creative people by observing the problem-solving behavior. Yet as we have seen, individual creativity is a function of antecedent conditions (that is, part reinforcement history), cognitive style and ability (that is, divergent thinking), personality, relevant knowledge, motivation, social influences, and group, unit, and organizational actors.[16]

The Adaption–Innovation Model

The **adaption–innovation model**—and others—identify two types of people within organizations: adaptors and innovators.[17] *Adaptors* prefer structured situations, seek answers to the problem at hand, and are perceived by innovators as being rigid, conforming, "safe" people. *Innovators,* on the other hand, appreciate an unstructured work environment, seek to answer questions that have not yet been asked, and are perceived by adaptors as being impractical, abrasive risk takers. Although both types can be found in and are needed in all organizations, research has found that both are capable of generating original creative solutions but from different problem-solving orientations (see Figure 7.2).[18]

Motivation and Creativity

We have argued that the personality traits associated with creativity are not enough to guarantee creative behavior. What motivates a person to be creative? The process is complex and involves both intrinsic and extrinsic motivation as well as skills and abilities. The components of individual creativity are shown in Figure 7.3.[19] The framework clusters three components of individual creativity: domain-relevant skills, creativity-related skills, and task motivation.

Domain-relevant skills are the general skills in the area (or domain) an individual must bring to the situation. If a person is working on the problem in microelectronics, then he or she must be knowledgeable, talented, and trained, for example, in electrical engineering.

Creativity-relevant skills are the "something extra" that makes the difference in creative performance. The individual's cognitive style is characterized by the ability to break out of old ways of thinking. The individual also depends on a *heuristic* (a general strategy that helps in approaching problems or tasks). A creative heuristic might be "when all else fails, try something counterintuitive" or "make the familiar strange." Finally, the individual's working style must be conducive to creativity. For example, persistence, a long attention span, and the ability to venture off in a new direction when the well-worn direction is not leading to a new idea are all characteristics of a creative work style. Creativity-relevant skills depend on training, experience, and the personality characteristics mentioned earlier.

Regardless of the individual's skill level, it is **task motivation** that determines if these skills will be fully utilized. If a person is not motivated to do something, no amount of skills can compensate for the lack of motivation. The individual's attitude toward the task is simply the person's natural inclination either toward or away from the task—do I want to do this or not? The individual's perception of his or her motivation, however, depends on factors in the social and work environments. If an individual feels that there are extrinsic motivational factors in the environment intended to control his or her performance of the task (for example, surveillance, evaluation, deadlines, competition, rewards, and restricted choices), his or her motivation to generate new ideas is likely to suffer. In contrast, if the person does not feel pressures to perform in a certain way or if the person is able to minimize or ignore such pressures, he or she is likely to have a higher level of motivation, even a "passion" for the project.

Creativity and Commitment

One additional element that may be related to the degree of intrinsic motivation is the individual's *commitment* to the organization (the degree to which an employee's personal

Implications	Adaptors	Innovators
For problem solving	Tend to take the problem as defined and generate novel, creative ideas aimed at "doing things better." Immediate high efficiency is the keynote of high adaptors.	Tend to redefine generally agreed on problems, breaking previously perceived restraints, generating solutions aimed at "doing things differently."
For solutions	Generally generate a few well-chosen and relevant solutions that they generally find sufficient but that sometimes fail to contain ideas needed to break the existing pattern completely.	Produce numerous ideas, many of which may not be either obvious or acceptable to others. Such a pool often contains ideas, if they can be identified, that may crack hitherto intractable problems.
For policies	Prefer well-established, structured situations. Best at incorporating new data or events into existing structures of policies.	Prefer unstructured situations. Use new data as opportunities to set new structures or policies accepting the greater attendant risk.
For organizational "fit"	Essential to the ongoing functions, but in times of unexpected changes may have some difficulty moving out of their established role.	Essential in times of change or crisis, but may have some trouble applying themselves to ongoing organizational demands.
For potential creativity	Capable of generating original, creative solutions that reflect their overall approach to problem solving.	Capable of generating original, creative solutions that reflect their overall approach to problem solving.
For collaboration	High adaptors do not get along easily with innovators. Middle adaptors may act as bridges.	High innovators do not get along easily with adaptors. Middle innovators may act as bridges.
For perceived behavior	Seen by innovators as sound, conforming, safe, predictable, relevant, inflexible, wedded to the system, and intolerant of ambiguity.	Seen by adaptors as unsound, impractical, risky, abrasive, often shocking their opposites and creating dissonance.

FIGURE 7.2

Characteristics of Adaptors and Innovators

Source: Adapted with permission from M. J. Kirton, "Adaptors and Innovators: Problem Solvers in Organizations," in K. Gronhaug and G. Kaufmann (eds.), *Innovation: A Cross-Disciplinary Perspective* (Oslo, Norway: Norwegian University Press, 1988), p. 72.

Domain-Relevant Skills	Creativity-Relevant Skills	Task Motivation
Includes	*Includes*	*Includes*
Knowledge about the domain	Appropriate cognitive style	Attitudes toward the task
Technical skills required	Implicit or explicit heuristics for generating novel ideas	Perceptions of own motivation for undertaking the task
Special domain-relevant "talent"	Conducive work style	
Depends on	*Depends on*	*Depends on*
Innate cognitive abilities	Training	Initial level of intrinsic motivation to the task
Innate perceptual and motor skills	Experience in idea generation	Presence or absence of salient extrinsic constraints in the social environment
Formal and informal education	Personality characteristics	Individual ability to cognitively minimize extrinsic constraints

FIGURE 7.3   **Components of Individual Creativity**

Source: Adapted with permission from T. M. Amabile, "From Individual Creativity to Organizational Innovation," in K. Gronhaug and G. Kaufmann (eds.), *Innovation: A Cross-Disciplinary Perspective* (Oslo, Norway: Norwegian University Press, 1988), p. 149.

goals are aligned with the organization's goals). Some authors have suggested that (1) there is a direct connection between level of commitment and motivation to engage in creative behaviors and (2) highly ideological organizations will produce more highly committed individuals.[20]

Creativity and Social Influence

What are the external influences that can operate on the individual, encouraging the display and development of creative potential in the organization? What can be done to increase creative behavior within the organization, that is, to turn a potentially creative person into an actively creative person? We have described some of the factors that can inhibit creativity, but several factors have been identified that have a positive effect on creative behavior. These factors can be organized into the general areas of freedom, support, and participation.[21]

Freedom: Freedom from external constraints can lead to creative behavior. The notion of freedom includes the following managerial actions:

1. Provide freedom to try new ways of performing tasks.
2. Permit activities or tasks to be different for different individuals.
3. Allow an appropriate amount of time for the accomplishment of tasks.
4. Allow time for non-task-related thinking and development of creative ideas.
5. Encourage self-initiated projects.
6. Respect an individual's need to work alone.
7. Encourage divergent activities by providing resources and room.

Support: Noncontrolling support can be given in the following ways:

1. Support and reinforce unusual ideas and responses of individuals.
2. Communicate confidence in the individuals.
3. Tolerate complexity and disorder.
4. Provide constructive feedback.
5. Reduce concern over failure.
6. Create a climate of mutual respect and acceptance among individuals.
7. Encourage interpersonal trust.
8. Listen to individuals.

Participation: Involving the individual in the decision-making process as well as the problem-solving process (participation) provides motivation that encourages creative behavior. Participation can be enhanced in the following ways:

1. Encourage individuals to have choices and to be part of the goal-setting process.
2. Encourage involvement of those interested in the problem—don't limit involvement across jobs, departments, and divisions.
3. Challenge individuals to find new tasks and problems.
4. Encourage questioning.
5. Encourage a high quality of interpersonal relationships including a spirit of cooperation, open confrontation of conflicts, and the expression of ideas.

Freedom, support, and participation can be implemented in a variety of ways, depending on the situation. The application of these factors can reduce the extrinsic motivational factors that have a negative effect on creative performance.

Developing The Creative Process Within The Organization

The ways of increasing creativity listed previously make up the organizational environment in which the creative process is to take place. The organization must introduce into this context a learning model for operational use. Individuals and teams must be made aware of the **creative process,** which we described in our discussion at the beginning of the chapter, and they must make a systematic effort to allow it to work. Thus in stage 1 the problem is defined in all its dimensions and decisions are made regarding who will be involved, who has the expertise, and what support is needed. Management needs to select people for participation who have the required domain-relevant skills and task motivation ensuring high-level involvement. In stage 2, data are collected and all available sources are explored. Again, domain-relevant skills and creativity-relevant skills are essential. Stage 3 allows a time lapse for the incubation of ideas and the injection of new data, with the recognition that there will be periods of no progress, that consultation and dialogues may be needed, and that dropping the effort temporarily may be useful. In stage 4, insight (hopefully) comes to the individual or the team in terms of useful ideas or solutions.

Finally, in stage 5 some testing and verification are conducted to find out whether the idea will be useful and whether its implementation is possible.

Throughout the creative process, two types of thinking have been identified: divergent thinking and convergent thinking. *Divergent thinking* is creative thinking. By using divergent thinking, the individual creates new connections between ideas (as in making metaphors) and thinks of many possibilities and alternatives (as in brainstorming). In this type of thinking, a person's built-in censor is temporarily turned off. *Convergent or critical thinking* involves comparing and contrasting, improving and refining, screening, judging, selecting, and making decisions. In the creative process, the individual moves back and forth between these types of thinking. In group settings, different individuals may be valued for their divergent or convergent skills.

Team Creativity

We have focused primarily on the role of the individual in creativity. Team problem solving and decision making were discussed. We noted that under certain conditions teams can achieve *synergy*—a group solution superior to that of the most accurate member's solution. One reason for this superior group solution was that the pool of knowledge in the group was usually greater than that of any individual. Another reason was creativity: Individuals built on others' ideas and produced new ideas. Many factors were at work. There seems to be little doubt that the interactive group process can facilitate or hinder team creativity. However, managers must examine the conditions under which teams can be expected to be more creative or solve problems better than individuals. If team creativity is viewed as a team capability that is needed, designing the appropriate work context, content and process that will facilitate the appropriate interaction patterns between team members is critical.

A recent published study identifies three operating principles to guide the management of team creativity, based on the successful experiences at BMW:

1. *Protect the creative team*—the need to shield the team from the commentaries of others in the company, such that the creative process is allowed to emerge in its natural course.
2. *Safeguard the artistic process*—the need to establish barriers around the product development such that time-to-market pressures and other time constrains do not disrupt the process.
3. *Develop an inventive communication*—managing at the intersection of known and unknown, routine and nonroutine, art and commerce means translating the creative language to the language of the company.[22]

The research results to date are not conclusive, yet they suggest that conditions such as the actual design of the work space, interaction patterns, member expertise, time, openness, and communication tend to influence team creativity.[23]

From Creativity to Innovation

Once a creative idea has been developed and verified, how does it become meaningful to the organization? The creative process described previously is commonly perceived as the first step in the process of innovation. It is a necessary first step to innovation, whether the innovation is a groundbreaking internal discovery or an idea brought to the organization from the outside. How the process unfolds is a function of the type of innovation, the innovation process itself, and key elements that influence innovation. Innovation is rarely the work of one individual. As we saw in the 3M case, many people, from scientists to managers, were involved in bringing that creative idea to commercial fruition.

Organizational Innovation

Types of Innovation

At the beginning of this chapter, we defined *innovation* as the successful application of a new idea to the firm. The idea may be a new technology, a new product, or a new organizational or administrative process. The innovation may be an imitation of a product, a person, or an idea used elsewhere, which becomes unique because it is placed within a new context.

We tend to think most often of innovations as **radical innovations** (discontinuous break-throughs in technology).[24] Often, however, there is an **incremental innovation** (an improvement of a technology, product, or process). A series of incremental innovations can lead to radical innovation, as in the 3M case where Silver discovered the Post-it Note adhesive while experimenting on improving traditional adhesives. Another distinction is between process and product innovations. A zero-defect quality control system is an example of a **process innovation.** **Product innovations** are usually the more visible of the two types, but not necessarily the more important. A product innovation can require process innovation.

Administrative innovations often affect the organization as much or more than technological innovations. New incentive systems and new communication network systems are just two examples of administrative innovations, as are new marketing and sales techniques. Finally, it is important to make a distinction between **system-maintaining innovation (SMI)** and **system-transforming innovation (STI).** SMI refers to new ideas that enhance or improve some aspect of the business without changing the overall nature of how the organization operates. STI refers to a new idea that affects the fundamental aspects of organizing, requiring change in several of the subsystems or segments of the organization in order to fully implement the innovation.

Stages of the Innovation Process

Although there are many types of innovation, it is generally agreed that the **innovation process** for each is similar. Descriptions of the innovation process have been borrowed from many fields. Group development and problem-solving models,[25] decision process models,[26] and organizational change models[27] have all been applied to the innovation process. These models as well as innovation process models have traditionally viewed the innovation process as occurring in a linear fashion in a series of discrete stages, generally from idea generation to adoption to implementation.[28] Although these activities occur in innovation, there is little empirical evidence for their occurrence in discrete stages. More recent research has found that the process is more "fluid" than stage theories would suggest.

The Minnesota Innovation Studies Program has been one of the most comprehensive research projects seeking to understand the process of innovation. Based on an in-depth review of longitudinal development of seven major innovations, the researchers of this study made six important observations about the process:

1. An initial shock to the organization precedes innovation. This shock may be new leadership, a product failure, a budget crisis, lack of market share, opportunity, or dissatisfaction of some kind.
2. Ideas proliferate.
3. While ideas are proliferating, setbacks and surprises are likely to occur.
4. These setbacks and surprises provide opportunities for trial-and-error learning and the blending of old and new ideas.
5. Restructuring of the organization at some or all levels occurs.
6. A hands-on approach of top management is evident all the way through the process.[29]

It is evident that this view of the innovation process is not a neat, step-by-step, easily planned activity. How the process unfolds is determined by the elements described next.

Key Elements That Influence The Innovation Process

Key Players and Roles

The previous description of the innovation process emphasized the important role of top management in influencing innovation. Top management not only provides resources for innovation but also provides a vision of the organization and its members as innovative. In addition, several roles required in the innovation process have been described. As early as 1931, the phenomenon of innovation was being studied by J. Schumpeter, an economist.[30]

His basic "one-man theory" described characteristics of the "dynamic entrepreneur." This figure is still evident in small and new organizations. However, in larger organizations it makes sense to view a variety of individuals who participate by playing different roles.

The *product champion* is the one who promotes the innovation and overcomes resistance to change. The product champion may or may not have formal power and influence within the organization, but this person has top-management support, which is necessary for success.[31]

The *technical innovator* is the inventor or the person who makes the most significant technical contribution to the innovation. In the 3M case this role may have been shared by Silver and Fry.[32]

The *technological gatekeeper* has been identified as the person who has both technical know-how and formal influence channels to other parts of the organization.[33]

Atmosphere or Climate

The organizational factors that were discussed as positively influencing creativity—freedom, support, and participation—also influence innovation, which is reasonable because creativity and innovation are viewed as parts of the same process. The climate or culture of the organization (the visions and goals, strategies, style of leadership, work setting, characteristics of the individuals, type of work, way people organize to get the work done, qualitative features of the context, and the values and norms of the people) may promote or inhibit innovation. How to measure the creative climate of the organization has been problematic. Using questionnaires and interviews, researchers have had some success discriminating between working climates that are more or less favorable to innovative outcomes.[34]

Organization Design

Managing work and the organization design process were discussed. However, the relationship between organization design and innovation is not definite. An early study of organizational innovation identified organic versus mechanistic organizations as likely to encourage innovation.[35] Bureaucracy, with its formal hierarchical levels, has often been identified as the mechanistic organization, whereas the organic organization has been described as flat. However, other researchers have argued that no one form of organization is superior to another in terms of being conducive to innovation; rather, it is the links for collaboration and problem solving throughout the organization that are important.[36] Reorganization during the process of innovation is likely to result in different designs as well as structures.

Incentives, Rewards, and Evaluation

We have seen that expected evaluation has been found to have a detrimental effect on creativity and that external incentives must stimulate intrinsic motivation. It is not so clear how reward systems contribute to creative and innovative effort. One view is that rewards based on seniority rather than performance tend to inhibit innovation and creativity, whereas merit-based systems, in which individual performance is rewarded, stipulate creativity. However, in Japan, where lifetime employment systems and seniority-based reward systems in large organizations are the norm, long-range thinking appears to be promoted, and there seems to be less necessity to resist new ideas (and freedom to fail) because a person's promotion and rewards are not based on short-term performance.[37] Innovative firms generally have innovative incentive and reward systems, which acknowledge both individual and group efforts in non-threatening ways.

Job Design, Job Rotation, and Careers

Jobs that offer intrinsic motivation to perform well, that involve the employee, and that provide variety and autonomy tend to increase innovative levels of activity. Recently, career planning involving **dual ladders** has gained a lot of attention. In a dual-ladder system, a high-performing individual may choose to climb the managerial or technical ladder, depending on his or her own personal preferences and goals. Companies such as 3M, Monsanto, Eastman Kodak, and General Mills have successfully implemented dual-ladder systems, which they have found lead to more open communications, are an aid in recruiting, and provide better advancement opportunities for people at all levels.[38] To be successful, the dual-ladder system requires the full commitment of management.

Management's Challenge

A challenge that most managers and companies face is how to create an organization that allows activities to be effectively performed, while creativity and innovation are given opportunities to flourish. If creativity and innovation are both parts of a process that is becoming a greater and greater necessity in today's organizations, then managers must become aware of how this process can be managed. Organizational creativity and innovation process frequently requires making order out of chaos or working in between known and unknown domains.[39] Creativity and innovation imply change, although not all change is an innovation or creative. Just as there is no one way to organize, there is no one way to encourage organizational creativity and innovation. Innovation is risky, and the manager's role in this process can be likened to a balancing act. On the one hand, he or she must provide the stability, support, and security that free employees from the fear of failure. On the other hand, the manager must encourage risk taking, which is likely to result in new ideas that are beneficial to the organization as a whole.

Part of this challenge is to hire, train, and develop a set of individuals with not only a variety of specialized and technical skills and abilities but also skills in problem solving, communication, conflict resolution, and team building. Another part of the challenge is to retain these employees not only through innovative reward and incentive systems but also by providing the vision, resources, autonomy, and support they need.

Another part of the challenge is to develop organizational learning mechanisms that foster learning climate.[40] A variety of learning mechanisms can be created that can facilitate creativity and innovation. A recent study that focused on organizational creativity in a pharmaceutical research and development organization demonstrated that both learning mechanisms and individual motivation (intrinsic and extrinsic) are highly correlated to creativity. Furthermore, the climate of information sharing was found to serve as a catalyst for creativity.[41]

As we have seen in this chapter, the management task is not easy. Innovative environments are turbulent, and the innovation process requires the management of change as an integral part of organizational and managerial routines. In addition to providing a free, supportive, and participative environment to encourage creative thinking, management must also deal with resistance to change, which is likely to occur in some parts of the organization when an innovation is developed. All of these elements demand that the manager be involved in an ongoing, creative problem-solving process. Creativity and innovation rely on creative and innovative management processes.

Cautions on Creativity

When expectations for creativity and innovation in the work world are high, there are bound to be counterproductive excesses. Young people may feel they will not be regarded as having high potential if they are not offering new ideas, and managers can feel they are not providing a supportive climate if they do not try new ideas. A "change for the sake of change" approach can be disruptive and must be guarded against. "If it's not broken, don't fix it" is often good advice.

Summary

In this chapter we have examined the organizational process that begins with creativity at the individual or team level and culminates in an innovation that contributes to the success of the organization as a whole. We have defined *creativity* as the brain functions of acquiring and processing data for the purposes of problem solving, whether it be responses, answers, actions, or new ideas. Creativity involves both unconscious and conscious processes. A five-stage process for the individual to utilize in producing creative reactions was given. *Innovation,* in contrast, was defined as the implementation process through which creative ideas are transformed into practical applications in the organization.

Study Questions

1. Creativity and innovation are different parts of the same process. Can an innovation occur without creativity? Discuss why or why not.

2. "The creative person is born, not made." Do you agree or disagree? Why?

3. Charlie likes to wrestle with a problem for several days or weeks, looking at it from all sides. Janet focuses on solving the problem efficiently and doesn't worry if she has considered all possible solutions. Which of the two is likely to be more creative? Why?

4. Sam loves his job because it is open ended and he decides what to do each day. He works hard, often forgetting to quit at 5 P.M. Discuss Sam's motivation.

5. List the five steps in the creative process. Identify the skills required at each step.

6. Think of an innovation that you would consider radical. How does it differ from an incremental innovation?

7. Mr. Jones has just returned from a short course on innovative management and has decided to reorganize his firm to increase innovation. He has isolated the scientists and design engineers in one building so they won't be disturbed by the production people and the marketing and sales forces. Is Mr. Jones' plan likely to increase innovative activity? Why?

8. Two employees of a high-tech firm began their careers with the firm as design engineers. Both are highly skilled, creative workers. Employee A now manages the production research department. Employee B has a private lab in the basement. Both are very satisfied. Discuss career choices and personal and organizational factors that led to this situation.

9. You are designing a new incentive and reward system for a R&D lab. All the employees have advanced engineering degrees, and the market for their skills is very competitive. How would you structure such a system?

10. Mrs. White has just been hired to run a large, nationwide, temporary employee company. The former CEO suggests to her that she might be interested in attending a seminar on managing innovation. Mrs. White laughs and says, "Why would I want to do that? We're not concerned with innovation around here. That's something for managers of high-tech companies." Do you agree or disagree with Mrs. White? Explain your answer.

Activity 7.2: Downsizing and Creativity

Objectives:

To examine the relationship between company restructuring and creativity.

Task 1 (Individual):

Read the following section, connect to the 3M website, and answer the questions at the end of the section.

Task 2:

Class discussion.

▪▪ Current Events at 3M Company

In spite of 3M's legendary history of fostering entrepreneurial innovation within the company, 1988 revenues were flat. Projections of dependable earnings were down 3 percent. The slowdown of the Asian economies cost the company hundreds of millions in lost profits. Even though 30 percent of sales have come from products released in just the past four years, entrepreneurial freedom has caused some experiments to lie dormant in the lab for years. According to *U.S. News and World Report* (December 21, 1998, p. 50), the company's new product portfolio for the 1990s was "horrendous."

3M has introduced a new program call Pacing Plus, designed to identify high-potential products earlier and release them faster and to drop underperforming products. It hopes to reduce the workforce by 6 percent in response to slower growth, but through attrition rather than layoffs. In addition, 3M has increased the number of partnerships by 36 percent, abandoning its "go-it-alone" mindset. However, 3M continues to resist radical restructuring.

Continue to search for current information about 3M. You can connect to 3M at *www.3M.com*.

Questions:

1. What do you think is the effect of radical restructuring on creativity and the innovation process?
2. The pressure to innovate has increased at 3M. How will this environment affect the creativity and innovation process?

**Activity 7.3:
Organizational
Innovation: Learning
from the WWW**

Objectives:

Reflecting on organizational innovation by learning from information on the WWW.

Task 1 (Individual):

Go to the Innovation Network website on articles and reports on organizational innovation: *www.thinksmart.com*. What are some of the skills most critical to the organizations that were 1998 Land Award winners for innovation?

Task 2 (Team):

Each team is to share its learning and prepare a three-minute presentation based on its collective learning.

Activity 7.4:
Making a Metaphor

Objectives:

To explore individual paradigms that affect individual creativity. A metaphor is a figure of speech in which we liken two objects or concepts that do not appear to be alike. Through metaphor we can make connections and discoveries that did not previously exist. We can make the familiar strange and thus challenge our way of thinking. In the 3M case, metaphors had to be changed so people could break through old mental sets.

Task 1:

Complete the following metaphors, choosing from one of the options given or making up your own.

Eating a fine dinner is like

a. Throwing a javelin a long distance.
b. Watching an hourglass drip sand.
c. Reading a popular novel at the beach.
d. Putting nail polish on your toes.

Raising a child is like

a. Driving from Seattle to New York.
b. Weeding your garden.
c. Building a fire and watching it burn.
d. Fishing for rainbow trout.

Playing a piano recital is like

a. Investing in the stock market.
b. Growing orchids.
c. Driving through rush hour traffic with your gas gauge on empty.
d. Fasting for three days.

Finding truth is like

a. Making banana nut bread.
b. Walking into a room and forgetting the reason why.
c. Navigating a sailboat through a violent thunderstorm.
d. Taking a test that has no wrong answers.

Task 2:

Share your metaphors with your group. Explain why you chose the metaphor you did. The instructor will facilitate a class discussion on the use of metaphors and creativity.

Source: This activity is adopted with permission from R. von Oeck, *A Kick in the Seat of the Pants* (New York: Warner Books, 1986), p. 72.

Endnotes

1. See, for example, R. J. Sternberg, "The Concept of Creativity: Prospects and Paradigms" in R. J. Sternberg (ed.), *Handbook of Creativity* (Cambridge, UK: Cambridge University Press, 1999), pp. 45–56; T. Amabile, C. N. Hadley, and S. J. Kramer, "Creativity Under the Gun," *Harvard Business Review,* August 2002, pp. 52–61; S. G. Scott and R. A. Bruce, "Determinants of Innovative Behavior: A Path Model of Individual Innovation in the Workplace," *Academy of Management Journal* 37, no. 3 (1994), pp. 580–607; R. J. Sternberg, L. A. O'Hara, and T. I. Lubart, "Creativity as Investment," *California Management Review* 40, no. 1 (1997), pp. 8–21; and C. J. Nemeth, "Managing Innovation: When Less Is More," *California Management Review* 40, no. 1 (1997), pp. 59–74.

2. See, for example, D. Bohm, *On Creativity* (London, UK: Routledge, 2000); K. Unsworth, "Unpacking Creativity," *Academy of Management Review* 26, no. 2 (2001), pp. 289–97; R. W. Woodman, J. E. Sawyer, and R. W. Griffin, "Towards a Theory of Organizational Creativity," *Academy of Management Review* 18, no. 1 (1993), pp. 293–321; and J. D. Couger, *Creativity and Innovation* (Danvers, MA: Boyd & Fraser, 1996).

3. A. Toffler and H. Toffler, *Powershift* (New York: Bantam Books, 1990); T. M. Amabile, "The Motivation to Be Creative," in S. Isaksen (ed.), *Frontiers of Creativity Research: Beyond the Basics,* (New York: Bearly Limited, 1987), pp. 223–54.

4. See R. W. Woodman and J. F. Schoenfeldt, "An Interactionist Model of Creative Behavior," *Journal of Creative Behavior* 24 (1990), pp. 279–90; and R. W. Woodman and J. E. Sawyer, "An Interactionist Model of Organizational Creativity," paper presented at the annual Academy of Management Meeting, Miami, 1991. For an example of how this interaction might work among co-workers and supervisors, see J. Zhou, "When the Presence of Creative Coworkers Is Related to Creativity: Role of Supervisor Close Monitoring, Developmental Feedback, and Creative Personality," *Journal of Applied Psychology* 88, no. 3 (2003), pp. 413–22.

5. W. Koehler, *The Mentality of Apes* (London: Pelican, 1925/1957).

6. G. Wallas, "Stages of Control," in *The Art of Thought* (New York: Harcourt Brace Jovanovich, 1926).

7. R. J. Sternberg, *The Nature of Creativity: Contemporary Psychological Perspectives* (New York: Cambridge University Press, 1988); and R. J. Sternberg, and R. K. Wagner, *Practical Intelligence* (New York: Cambridge University Press, 1986).

8. D. Leonard and S. Straus, "Putting Your Company's Whole Brain to Work," *Harvard Business Review,* July–August 1997, pp. 111–21.

9. J. J. Kao, *Managing Creativity* (Englewood Cliffs, NJ: Prentice-Hall, 1991); D. Bohm and F. D. Peat, *Science, Order, and Creativity* (New York: Bantam Books, 1987); and J. R. Evans, *Creative Thinking* (Cincinnati, OH: South Western, 1991).

10. J. P. Guilford, "Creativity," *American Psychologist* 14 (1950), pp. 469–79; J. P. Guilford, "Creativity Research: A Quarter Century of Progress," in I. A. Taylor and J. W. Getzels (eds.), *Perspectives in Creativity* (New York: Aldine, 1975).

11. E. Rogers, *The Diffusion of Innovations,* 3rd ed. (New York: Free Press, 1983); and A. H. Van de Ven, "Central Problems in the Management of Innovation," *Management Science,* May 1986, pp. 590–607.

12. G. Zaltman, R. Duncan, and J. Holbek, *Innovations and Organizations* (New York: Wiley-Interscience, 1973).

13. P. Salovey and J. Myer, *Emotional Development and Emotional Intelligence* (New York: Basic Books, 1997); and H. Weisinger, *Emotional Intelligence at Work* (San Francisco: Jossey-Bass, 1997).

14. D. Goleman, R. Boyatzis, and A. McKee, *Primal Leadership: Realizing the Power of Emotional Intelligence* (Boston: Harvard Business School, 2002); and R. Cooper, "Applying Emotional Intelligence in the Workplace," *Training & Development,* December 1997, pp. 31–38.

15. R. Cooper and A. Sawaf, *Executive EQ: Emotional Intelligence in Leadership and Organizations* (New York: Grosset/Putman, 1998).

16. Woodman, Sawyer, and Griffin, "Towards a Theory of Organizational Creativity," p. 296.

17. M. J. Kirton, "Adaptors and Innovators: Cognitive Style and Personality," in S. Isaksen (ed.) *Frontiers of Creative Research* (New York: Bearly Limited, 1987), pp. 282–304.

18. M. J. Kirton, "Adaptors and Innovators: Problem Solvers in Organizations," in K. Gronhaug and G. Kaufmann *Innovation: A Cross-Disciplinary Perspective* (Norway: Norwegian University Press, 1988), p. 72.

19. Amabile, "The Motivation to Be Creative," pp. 223–54.

20. R. L. Kuhn and G. T. Geis, "A Cross-Organization Methodology for Assessing Creativity and Commitment," in Y. Ijiri and R. Kuhn (eds.), *New Directions in Creative and Innovative Management* (Cambridge, MA: Ballinger, 1988), pp. 303–22.

21. S. G. Isaksen, "Educational Implications of Creativity Research: An Updated Rationale for Creative Learning," in Isaksen (ed.) *Frontiers of Creativity Research,* p. 149.

22. C. Bangle, "The Ultimate Creativity Machine: How BMW Turns Art into Profit," *Harvard Business Review,* January 2001, pp. 5–11.

23. See, for example, G. Vissers and B. Dankbaar, "Creativity in Multidisciplinary New Product Development Teams," *Creativity & Innovation Management* 11 (2002), pp. 31–43; S. F. Kylen and A. B. Shani, "Triggering Creativity in Teams: An Exploratory Investigation," *Creativity & Innovation Management* 11 (2002), pp. 17–41; and Amabile, Hadley and Kramer, "Creativity Under the Gun."

24. M. Tushman and D. Nadler, "Organizing for Innovation," *California Management Review,* Spring 1986, pp. 74–92; and J. Galbraith, "Designing the Innovating Organization," *Organizational Dynamics,* Winter 1982, pp. 5–25.

25. K. Lewis, "Frontiers in Group Dynamics," *Human Relations* 1 (1947), pp. 5–41; and R. F. Bales and F. L. Strodtbeck, "Phases in Group Problem-Solving," *Journal of Abnormal and Social Psychology* 46 (1951), pp. 485–95.

26. J. G. March and H. Simon, *Organizations* (New York: John Wiley & Sons, 1958); and M. D. Cohen, J. G. March, and J. P. Olsen, "A Garbage Can Model of Organizational Choice," *Administrative Science Quarterly* 17 (1972), pp. 1–25.

27. G. W. Dalton, P. R. Lawrence, and L. E. Greiner, *Organizational Change and Development* (Homewood, IL: Dorsey Press, 1970).

28. W. J. Abernathy and J. M. Utterback, "Patterns of Industrial Innovation," in M. Tushman and W. Moore (eds.), *Readings in the Management of Innovation* (Boston: Pitman 1975), pp. 97–150; M. Jelinek and C. Bird-Schoonhoven, *Innovation Marathon: Lessons from High Technology Firms* (Oxford, UK: Basil Blackwell, 1990); and R. M. Kanter, "Innovation—The Only Hope for Times Ahead?" *Sloan Management Review,* Summer 1984, pp. 51–55.

29. R. Schroeder, A. H. Van de Ven, G. D. Scudder, and D. Polley, "The Development of Innovative Ideas," in A. H. Van de Ven, H. Angle, and M. Poole (eds.), *Research on the Management of Innovation: The Minnesota Studies* (New York: Harper & Row, 1990), pp. 107–34.

30. J. Schumpeter, *Theorie der wirtschaftlichen Entwicklung. Eine Untersuchung uber Unternehmergewinn, Kapital, Kredit, Zins und den Konjunkturzyklus,* 3rd ed. (Munich, Germany: Duncker & Humblot, 1931).

31. A. K. Chakrabarti, "The Role of Champions in Product Innovation," *California Management Review* 17 (Winter 1974), pp. 58–62; and K. Gronhaug, and G. Kaufmann, *Innovation: A Cross-Disciplinary Perspective* (Oslo, Norway: Norwegian University Press, 1988).

32. T. J. Allen and S. I. Cohen, "Information Flow in Research and Development Laboratories," *Administrative Science Quarterly* 14 (1969), pp. 12–19.

33. G. Ekvall and Y. T. Andersson, "Working Climate and Creativity: A Study of an Innovative Newspaper Office," *Journal of Creative Behavior* 20 (1986), pp. 215–25; R. M. Burnside, T. M. Amabile, and S. S. Gryskiewicz, "Assessing Organizational Climates for Creativity and Innovation: Methodological Review of Large Company Audits," in Y. Ijiri and R. Kuhn (eds.), *New Directions in Creative and Innovative Management* (Cambridge, MA: Ballinger Publishing Co., 1988), pp. 169–86.

34. T. Burns and G. M. Stalker, *The Management of Innovation* (London: Tavistock Publications, 1961).

35. J. L. Pierce and A. L. Delbecq, "Organization Structure, Individual Attitudes, and Innovation," *Academy of Management Review* 2, (January 1977), pp. 27–37.

36. Jelinek and Schoonhoven, *Innovation Marathon.*

37. T. Kono, *Structure of Japanese Enterprises* (London: Macmillan, 1984).

38. M. F. Wolff, "Revamping the Dual Ladder at General Mills," *Research Management* (November 1979), pp. 8–11.

39. M. Sundgren and A. Styhre, "Managing Organizational Creativity" in N. Adler, A. B. Shani, and A. Styhre (eds.), *Collaborative Research in Organizations: Foundations for Learning, Change and Theoretical Development* (Thousand Oaks, CA: Sage, 2004), pp. 237–53; and Y. Cheng and A. H. Van de Ven, "Learning the Innovation Journey: Order out of Chaos?" *Organization Science* (November/December 1996), pp. 593–615.

40. A. B. Shani and P. Docherty, *Learning by Design: Building Sustainable Organizations* (London, UK: Blackwell, 2003).

41. M. Sundgren, E. Dimenas, J.-E. Gustasson, and M. Selart "Drivers of Organizational Creativity: A Path Model of Creative Climate in Pharmaceutical R&D" *Strategic Management Journal* (in press).

CHAPTER EIGHT

What Is Critical Thinking?

When Arthur was in the first grade, the teacher directed the class to "think." "Now, class," she said, "I know this problem is a little harder than the ones we've been doing, but I'm going to give you a few extra minutes to think about it. Now start thinking."

It was not the first time Arthur had heard the word used. He'd heard it many times at home, but never quite this way. The teacher seemed to be asking for some special activity, something he should know how to start and stop—like his father's car. "Vroom-m-m," he muttered half aloud. Because of his confusion, he was unaware he was making the noise.

"Arthur, please stop making noises and start thinking."

Embarrassed and not knowing quite what to do, he looked down at his desk. Then, out of the corner of his eye, he noticed that the little girl next to him was staring at the ceiling. "Maybe that's the way you start thinking," he guessed. He decided the others had probably learned how to do it last year, that time he was home with the measles. So he stared at the ceiling.

As he progressed through grade school and high school, he heard that same direction hundreds of times. "No, that's not the answer, you're not thinking—now *think!*" And occasionally, he would hear from particularly self-pitying teachers given to talking to themselves aloud: "What did I do to deserve this? Don't they teach them anything in the grades anymore? Don't you people care about ideas? Think, dammit, THINK."

So Arthur learned to feel somewhat guilty about the whole matter. Obviously, this thinking was an important activity that he'd failed to learn. Maybe he lacked the brain power. But he was resourceful enough. He watched the other students and did what they did. Whenever a teacher started in about thinking, he screwed up his face, furrowed his brow, scratched his head, stroked his chin, stared off into space or up at the ceiling, and repeated silently to himself, "Let's see now, I've got to think about that, think, think (I hope he doesn't call on me), think." Though Arthur didn't know it, that's just what the other students were saying to themselves.

Your experience may have been similar to Arthur's. In other words, many people may have told you simply to think without ever explaining what thinking is and what qualities a good thinker has that a poor thinker lacks. If that is the case, you've got a lot of company. Extensive, effective training in thinking is the exception rather than the rule. This fact and its unfortunate consequences are suggested by the following comments from accomplished observers of the human condition:

> The most interesting and astounding contradiction in life is to me the constant insistence by nearly all people upon "logic," "logical reasoning," "sound reasoning," on the one hand, and on the other their inability to display it, and their unwillingness to accept it when displayed by others.[1]

> Most of our so-called reasoning consists in finding arguments for going on believing as we already do.[2]

Clear thinking is a very rare thing, but even just plain thinking is al-most as rare. Most of us most of the time do not think at all. We believe and we feel, but we do not think.[3]

Mental indolence is one of the commonest of human traits.[4]

What is this activity that everyone claims is important but few people have mastered? Thinking is a general term covering numerous activities, from daydreaming to reflection and analysis. Here are just some of the synonyms listed in *Roget's Thesaurus* for *think:*

appreciate	consult	fancy	reason
believe	contemplate	imagine	reflect
cerebrate	deliberate	meditate	ruminate
cogitate	digest	muse	speculate
conceive	discuss	ponder	suppose
consider	dream	realize	weigh

All of those are just the *names* that thinking goes under. They really don't explain it. The fact is, after thousands of years of humans' experiencing thought and talking and writing about thinking, it remains in many respects one of the great mysteries of our existence. Still, though much is yet to be learned, a great deal is already known.

Mind, Brain, or Both?

Most modern researchers use the word *mind* synonymously with *brain,* as if the physical organ that resides in the human skull were solely responsible for thinking. This practice conveniently presupposes that a problem that has challenged the greatest thinkers for millennia—the relationship between mind and physical matter—was somehow solved when no one was looking. The problem itself, and the individuals who spent their lives wrestling with it, deserve better.

Neuroscience has provided a number of valuable insights into the cognitive or thinking activities of the brain. It has documented that the left hemisphere of the brain deals mainly with detailed language processing and is associated with analysis and logical thinking, that the right hemisphere deals mainly with sensory images and is associated with intuition and creative thinking, and that the small bundle of nerves that lies between the hemispheres—the *corpus callosum*—integrates the various functions.

The research that produced these insights proved that the brain is *necessary* for thought, but it has not shown that the brain is *sufficient* for thought. In fact, many philosophers claim it can never show that. They argue that the mind and the brain are demonstrably different. Whereas the brain is a physical entity composed of matter and therefore subject to decay, the mind is a *metaphysical* entity. Examine brain cells under the most powerful microscope and you will never see an idea or concept—for example, beauty, government, equality, or love—because ideas and concepts are not matter and so have no physical dimension. Where, then, do these nonmaterial things reside? In the nonmaterial mind.[5]

The late American philosopher William Barrett observed that "history is, fundamentally, the adventure of human consciousness" and "the fundamental history of humankind is the history of mind." In his view, "one of the supreme ironies of modern history" is the fact that science, which owes its very existence to the human mind, has had the audacity to deny the reality of the mind. As he put it, "the offspring denies the parent."[6]

The argument over whether the mind is a reality is not the only issue about the mind that has been hotly debated over the centuries. One especially important issue is whether the mind is *passive,* a "blank slate" on which experience writes, as John Locke held, or *active,* a vehicle by which we take the initiative and exercise our free will, as G. W. Leibnitz argued. This book is based on the latter view.

Critical Thinking Defined

Let's begin by making the important distinction between thinking and feeling. *I feel* and *I think* are sometimes used interchangeably, but that practice causes confusion. Feeling is a subjective response that reflects emotion, sentiment, or desire; it generally occurs spontaneously rather than through a conscious mental act. We don't have to employ our minds to feel angry when we are insulted, afraid when we are threatened, or compassionate when we see a picture of a starving child. The feelings arise automatically.

Feeling is useful in directing our attention to matters we should think about; it also can provide the enthusiasm and commitment necessary to complete arduous mental tasks. However, feeling is never a good substitute for thinking because it is notoriously unreliable. Some feelings are beneficial, honorable, even noble; others are not, as everyday experience demonstrates. We often "feel like" doing things that will harm us—for example, smoking, sunbathing without sunscreen, speaking our mind to our professor or employer, or spending the rent money on lottery tickets.

In contrast, thinking is a conscious mental process performed to solve a problem, make a decision, or gain understanding.* Whereas feeling has no purpose beyond expressing itself, thinking aims beyond itself to knowledge or action. This is not to say that thinking is infallible; in fact, a good part of this book is devoted to exposing errors in thinking and showing you how to avoid them. Yet for all its shortcomings, thinking is the most reliable guide to action we humans possess. To sum up the relationship between feeling and thinking, feelings need to be tested before being trusted, and thinking is the most reasonable and reliable way to test them.

There are two broad categories of thinking: creative and critical. The focus of this book is the latter. The essence of critical thinking is *evaluation*. Critical thinking, therefore, may be defined as the process by which we test claims and arguments and determine which have merit and which do not. In other words, critical thinking is a search for answers, a *quest*. Not surprisingly, one of the most important techniques used in critical thinking is asking probing *questions*. Where the uncritical accept their first thoughts and other people's statements at face value, critical thinkers challenge all ideas in this manner:

Thought	*Question*
Professor Vile cheated me in my composition grade. He weighted some themes more heavily than others.	Did he grade everyone on the same standard? Were the different weightings justified?
Before women entered the workforce, there were fewer divorces. That shows that a woman's place is in the home.	How do you know that this factor, and not some other one(s), is responsible for the increase in divorces?
A college education isn't worth what you pay for it. Some people never reach a salary level appreciably higher than the level they would have reached without the degree.	Is money the only measure of the worth of an education? What about increased understanding of self and life and increased ability to cope with challenges?

Critical thinking also employs questions to analyze issues. Consider, for example, the subject of values. When it is being discussed, some people say, "Our country has lost its traditional values" and "There would be less crime, especially violent crime, if parents and teachers emphasized moral values." Critical thinking would prompt us to ask:

1. What is the relationship between values and beliefs? Between values and convictions?
2. Are all values *valuable?*
3. How aware is the average person of his or her values? Is it possible that many people deceive themselves about their real values?

---

*Some informal definitions of thinking include daydreaming. It is excluded from this definition because it is a passive mental state over which we exercise little or no control. It is therefore of little use in evaluating ideas.

4. Where do one's values originate? Within the individual or outside? In thought or in feeling?

5. Does education change a person's values? If so, is this change always for the better?

6. Should parents and teachers attempt to shape children's values?

Characteristics of Critical Thinkers

A number of misconceptions exist about critical thinking. One is that being able to support beliefs with reasons makes one a critical thinker. Virtually everyone has reasons, however weak they may be. The test of critical thinking is whether the reasons are good and sufficient.

Another misconception is that critical thinkers never imitate others in thought or action. If that were the case, then every eccentric would be a critical thinker. Critical thinking means making sound decisions, regardless of how common those decisions are.

A third misconception is that critical thinking is synonymous with having a lot of right answers in one's head. There's nothing wrong with having right answers, of course. But critical thinking involves the process of finding answers when they are not so readily available.

Yet another misconception is that critical thinking cannot be learned, that one either "has it" or does not. On the contrary, critical thinking is a matter of habit. The most careless, sloppy thinker can become a critical thinker by developing the characteristics of a critical thinker.

We have already noted one characteristic of critical thinkers—skill in asking appropriate questions. Another is control of one's mental activities. John Dewey once observed that more of our time than most of us care to admit is spent "trifling with mental pictures, random recollections, pleasant but unfounded hopes, flitting, half-developed impressions."[7] Good thinkers are no exception. However, they have learned better than poor thinkers how to stop that casual, semiconscious drift of images when they wish and how to fix their minds on one specific matter, examine it carefully, and form a judgment about it. They have learned, in other words, *how to take charge of their thoughts,* to use their minds actively as well as passively.

Here are some additional characteristics of critical thinkers, as contrasted with those of uncritical thinkers:

Critical Thinkers...	*Uncritical Thinkers...*
Are honest with themselves, acknowledging what they don't know, recognizing their limitations, and being watchful of their own errors.	Pretend they know more than they do, ignore their limitations, and assume their views are error-free.
Regard problems and controversial issues as exciting challenges.	Regard problems and controversial issues as nuisances or threats to their ego.
Strive for understanding, keep curiosity alive, remain patient with complexity, and are ready to invest time to overcome confusion.	Are impatient with complexity and thus would rather remain confused than make the effort to understand.
Base judgments on evidence rather than personal preferences, deferring judgment whenever evidence is insufficient. They revise judgments when new evidence reveals error.	Base judgments on first impressions and gut reactions. They are unconcerned about the amount or quality of evidence and cling to their views steadfastly.
Are interested in other people's ideas and so are willing to read and listen attentively, even when they tend to disagree with the other person.	Are preoccupied with themselves and their own opinions, and so are unwilling to pay attention to others' views. At the first sign of disagreement, they tend to think, "How can I refute this?"

Recognize that extreme views (whether conservative or liberal) are seldom correct, so they avoid them, practice fairmindedness, and seek a balanced view.	Ignore the need for balance and give preference to views that support their established views.
Practice restraint, controlling their feelings rather than being controlled by them, and thinking before acting.	Tend to follow their feelings and act impulsively.

As the desirable qualities suggest, critical thinking depends on mental discipline. Effective thinkers exert control over their mental life, direct their thoughts rather than being directed by them, and withhold their endorsement of any idea—even their own—until they have tested and confirmed it. John Dewey equated this mental discipline with freedom. That is, he argued that people who do not have it are not free persons but slaves:

> If a man's actions are not guided by thoughtful conclusions, then they are guided by inconsiderate impulse, unbalanced appetite, caprice, or the circumstances of the moment. To cultivate unhindered, unreflective external activity is to foster enslavement, for it leaves the person at the mercy of appetite, sense, and circumstance.[8]

The Role of Intuition

Intuition is commonly defined as immediate perception or comprehension of something—that is, sensing or understanding something *without the use of reasoning.* Some everyday experiences seem to support this definition. You may have met a stranger and instantly "known" that you would be partners for life. When a car salesman told you that the price he was quoting you was his final, rock-bottom price, your intuition may have told you he was lying. On the first day of a particular course, you may have had a strong sense that you would not do well in it.

Some important discoveries seem to have occurred instantaneously. For example, the German chemist Kekule found the solution to a difficult chemical problem that way. He was very tired when he slipped into a daydream. The image of a snake swallowing his tail came to him—and that provided the clue to the structure of the benzene molecule, which is a ring, rather than a chain, of atoms.[9] The German writer Goethe had been experiencing great difficulty organizing a large mass of material for one of his works when he learned of the tragic suicide of a close friend. At that very instant, the plan for organizing his material occurred to him in detail.[10] The English writer Samuel Taylor Coleridge (you may have read his *Rime of the Ancient Mariner* in high school) awoke from a dream with 200–300 lines of a new and complex poem clearly in mind.

Such examples seem to suggest that intuition is very different from reasoning and is not influenced by it. But before accepting that conclusion, consider these facts:

> Breakthrough ideas favor trained, active minds. It is unusual for someone totally untrained in a subject to make a significant new discovery about it. Thus, if Kekule had been a plumber, Goethe a bookkeeper, and Coleridge a hairdresser, they would probably not have received the intuitions for which they are famous.

> Some intuitions eventually prove to be mistaken. That attractive stranger may turn out to be, not your lifelong partner, but a person for whom you develop a strong dislike. The car saleman's final price may have proved to be exactly that. And instead of doing poorly in that course, you may have done well.

> It is difficult to make an overall assessment of the quality of our intuitions because we tend to forget the ones that prove mistaken.

These facts have led some scholars to conclude that intuition is simply a consequence of thinking. They would say that something about the stranger appealed to you, something the salesman said or did suggested insincerity, something about the professor frightened you. In each case, they would explain, you made a quick decision—so quick, in fact, that you were unaware that you'd been thinking. In the case of the breakthrough ideas, the scholars would say that when people become engrossed in problems or issues, their unconscious minds often continue working on them long after they have turned their attention elsewhere. Thus, when an insight seems to come "out of nowhere," it is actually a delayed result of thinking.

Which view of intuitions is the correct one? Are they different from and independent of thinking or not? Perhaps, for now, the most prudent answer is sometimes they are independent and sometimes they are not.

Basic Activities in Critical Thinking

The basic activities in thinking are investigation, interpretation, and judgment, in that order. The following chart summarizes each activity in relation to the other two:

Activity	Definition	Requirements
Investigation	Finding evidence—that is, data that will answer key questions about the issue	The evidence must be both relevant and sufficient.
Interpretation	Deciding what the evidence means	The interpretation must be more reasonable than competing interpretations.
Judgment	Reaching a conclusion about the issue	The conclusion must meet the test of logic.

As we noted previously, irresponsible thinkers first choose their conclusions and then seek out evidence to justify their choices. They fail to realize that the only conclusion worth drawing is one based on a thorough understanding of the problem or issue and its possible solutions or resolutions. Is it acceptable to speculate, guess, and form hunches and hypotheses? Absolutely. Such activities provide a helpful starting point for the thinking process. (Besides, we couldn't avoid doing so even if we tried.) The crucial thing is not to let hunches and hypotheses manipulate our thinking and dictate our conclusion in advance.

Critical Thinking and Writing

Writing may be used for either of two broad purposes: to discover ideas or to communicate them. Most of the writing you have done in school is undoubtedly the latter kind. But the former can be very helpful, not only in sorting out ideas you've already produced but in stimulating the flow of new ideas. For some reason, the very act of writing down one idea seems to generate additional ideas.

Whenever you write to discover ideas, focus on the issue you are examining and record all your thoughts, questions, and assertions. Don't worry about organization or correctness. If ideas come slowly, be patient. If they come suddenly, in a rush, don't try to slow the process down and develop any one of them; simply jot them all down. (There will be time for elaboration and correction later.) Direct your mind's effort, but be sensitive to ideas on the fringes of consciousness. Often they, too, will prove valuable.

If you have done your discovery writing well and have thought critically about the ideas you have produced, the task of writing to communicate will be easier and more enjoyable. You will have many more ideas—carefully evaluated ideas—to develop and organize.

Critical Thinking and Discussion[11]

At its best, discussion deepens understanding and promotes problem solving and decision making. At its worst, it frays nerves, creates animosity, and leaves important issues unresolved. Unfortunately, the most prominent models for discussion in contemporary culture—radio and TV talk shows—often produce the latter effects.

Many hosts demand that their guests answer complex questions with simple "yes" or "no" answers. If the guests respond that way, they are attacked for oversimplifying. If, instead, they try to offer a balanced answer, the host shouts "You're not answering the question" and proceeds to answer it himself. Guests who agree with the host are treated warmly; others are dismissed as ignorant or dishonest. Often as not, when two guests are debating, each takes a turn interrupting while the other shouts "Let me finish." Neither shows any desire to learn from the other. Typically, as the show draws to a close, the host thanks the participants for a "vigorous debate" and promises the audience more of the same next time.

Here are some simple guidelines for ensuring that the discussions you engage in—in the classroom, on the job, or at home—are more civil, meaningful, and productive than what you see on TV. By following these guidelines, you will set a good example for the people around you.

Whenever possible, prepare in advance.

Not every discussion can be prepared for in advance, but many can. An agenda is usually circulated several days before a business or committee meeting. And in college courses, the assignment schedule provides a reliable indication of what will be discussed in class on a given day. Use this advance information to prepare for discussion. Begin by reflecting on what you already know about the topic. Then decide how you can expand your knowledge and devote some time to doing so. (Fifteen or twenty minutes of focused searching on the Internet can produce a significant amount of information on almost any subject.) Finally, try to anticipate the different points of view that might be expressed in the discussion and consider the relative merits of each. Keep your conclusions very tentative at this point, so that you will be open to the facts and interpretations others will present.

Set reasonable expectations.

Have you ever left a discussion disappointed that others hadn't abandoned their views and embraced yours? Have you ever felt offended when someone disagreed with you or asked you what evidence you had to support your opinion? If the answer to either question is yes, you probably expect too much of others. People seldom change their minds easily or quickly, particularly in the case of long-held convictions. And when they encounter ideas that differ from their own, they naturally want to know what evidence supports those ideas. Expect to have your ideas questioned, and be cheerful and gracious in responding.

Leave egotism and personal agendas at the door.

To be productive, discussion requires an atmosphere of mutual respect and civility. Egotism produces disrespectful attitudes toward others—notably, "I'm more important than other people," "My ideas are better than anyone else's," and "Rules don't apply to me." Personal agendas, such as dislike for another participant or excessive zeal for a point of view, can lead to personal attacks and unwillingness to listen to others' views.

Contribute but don't dominate.

If you are the kind of person who loves to talk and has a lot to say, you probably contribute more to discussions than other participants. On the other hand, if you are more reserved, you may seldom say anything. There is nothing wrong with being either kind of person. However, discussions tend to be most productive when everyone contributes ideas. For this to happen, loquacious people need to exercise a little restraint, and more reserved people need to accept responsibility for sharing their thoughts.

Avoid distracting speech mannerisms.

Such mannerisms include starting one sentence and then abruptly switching to another; mumbling or slurring your words; and punctuating every phrase or clause with audible pauses ("um," "ah,") or meaningless expressions ("like," "you know," "man"). These annoying mannerisms distract people from your message. To overcome them, listen to yourself when you speak. Even better, tape your conversations with friends and family (with their permission), then play the tape back and listen to yourself. And whenever you are engaged in a discussion, aim for clarity, directness, and economy of expression.

Listen actively.

When the participants don't listen to one another, discussion becomes little more than serial monologue—each person taking a turn at speaking while the rest ignore what is being said. This can happen quite unintentionally because the mind can process ideas faster than the fastest speaker can deliver them. Your mind may get tired of waiting and wander about aimlessly like a dog off its leash. In such cases, instead of listening to the speaker's words, you may think about her clothing or hairstyle, or look outside the window and observe what is happening there. Even when you are making a serious effort to listen, it is easy to lose focus. If the speaker's words trigger an unrelated memory, you may slip away to that earlier time and place. If the speaker says something you disagree with, you may begin framing a reply. The best way to maintain your attention is to be alert for such distractions and to resist them. Strive to enter the speaker's frame of mind and understand each sentence as it is spoken and to connect it with previous sentences. Whenever you realize your mind is wandering, drag it back to the task.

Judge ideas responsibly.

Ideas range in quality from profound to ridiculous, helpful to harmful, ennobling to degrading. It is therefore appropriate to pass judgment on them. However, fairness demands that you base your judgment on thoughtful consideration of the overall strengths and weaknesses of the ideas, not on your initial impressions or feelings. Be especially careful with ideas that are unfamiliar or different from your own because those are the ones you will be most inclined to deny a fair hearing.

Resist the urge to shout or interrupt.

No doubt you understand that shouting and interrupting are rude and disrespectful behaviors, but do you realize that in many cases they are also a sign of *intellectual insecurity*? It's true. If you really believe your ideas are sound, you will have no need to raise your voice or to silence the other person. Even if the other person resorts to such behavior, the best way to demonstrate confidence and character is by refusing to reciprocate. Make it your rule to disagree without being disagreeable.

Avoiding Plagiarism[12]

Once ideas are put into words and published, they become "intellectual property," and the author has the same rights over them as he or she has over a material possession such as a house or a car. The only real difference is that intellectual property is purchased with mental effort rather than money. Anyone who has ever wracked his or her brain trying to solve a problem or trying to put an idea into clear and meaningful words can appreciate how difficult mental effort can be.

Plagiarism is passing off other people's ideas or words as one's own. It is doubly offensive in that it both steals and deceives. In the academic world, plagiarism is considered an ethical violation and is punished by a failing grade for a paper or a course, or even by dismissal from the institution. Outside the academy, it is a crime that can be prosecuted if the person to whom the ideas and words belong wishes to bring charges.

Some cases of plagiarism are attributable to intentional dishonesty, others to carelessness. But many, perhaps most, are due to misunderstanding. The instructions "Base your paper on research rather than on your own unfounded opinions" and "Don't present other people's ideas as your own" seem contradictory and may confuse students, especially if no clarification is offered. Fortunately, there is a way to honor both instructions and, in the process, to avoid plagiarism.

Step 1: When you are researching a topic, keep your sources' ideas separate from your own. Begin by keeping a record of each source of information you consult. For an Internet source, record the Web site address, the author and title of the item, and the date you visited the site. For a book, record the author, title, place of publication, publisher, and date of publication. For a magazine or journal article, record the author, title, the name of the publication, and its date of issue. For a TV or radio broadcast, record the program title, station, and date of transmission.

Step 2: As you read each source, note the ideas you want to refer to in your writing. If the author's words are unusually clear and concise, copy them *exactly* and put quotation marks around them. Otherwise, paraphrase—that is, restate the author's ideas in your own words. Write down the number(s) of the page(s) on which the author's passage appears.

If the author's idea triggers a response in your mind—such as a question, a connection between this idea and something else you've read, or an experience of your own that supports or challenges what the author says—write it down and put brackets (not parentheses) around it so that you will be able to identify it as your own when you review your notes. Here is a sample research record illustrating these two steps:

> Adler, Mortimer J. *The Great Ideas: A Lexicon of Western Thought* (New York: Macmillan, 1992) Says that throughout the ages, from ancient Greece, philosophers have argued about whether various ideas are true. Says it's remarkable that most renowned thinkers have agreed about what truth is—"a correspondence between thought and reality." 867 Also says that Freud saw this as the *scientific* view of truth. Quotes Freud: "This correspondence with the real external world we call truth. It is the aim of scientific work, even when the practical value of that work does not interest us." 869 [I say true statements fit the facts; false statements do not.][13]

Whenever you look back on this record, even a year from now, you will be able to tell at a glance which ideas and words are the author's and which are yours. The first three sentences are, with the exception of the directly quoted part, *paraphrases* of the author's ideas. The fourth is a direct quotation. The final sentence, in brackets, is your own idea.

Step 3: When you compose your paper, work borrowed ideas and words into your own writing by judicious use of quoting and paraphrasing. In addition, give credit to the various authors. Your goal here is to eliminate all doubt about which ideas and words belong to whom. In formal presentations, this crediting is done in footnotes; in informal ones, it is done simply by mentioning the author's name.

Here is an example of how the material from Mortimer Adler might be worked into a composition. (Note the form that is used for the footnote.) The second paragraph illustrates how your own idea might be expanded:

> Mortimer J. Adler explains that throughout the ages, from the time of the ancient Greeks, philosophers have argued about whether various ideas are true. But to Adler the remarkable thing is that, even as they argued, most renowned thinkers have agreed about what truth is. They saw it as "a correspondence between thought and reality." Adler points out that Sigmund Freud believed this was also the scientific view of truth. He quotes Freud as follows: "This correspondence with the real external world we call truth. It is the aim of scientific work, even when the practical value of that work does not interest us."

> This correspondence view of truth is consistent with the commonsense rule that a statement is true if it fits the facts and false if it does not. For example, the statement "The twin towers of New York's World Trade Center were destroyed on September 11, 2002" is false because they were destroyed the previous year. I may sincerely believe that it is true, but my believing in no way affects the truth of the matter. In much the same way, if an innocent man is convicted of a crime, neither the court's decision nor the world's acceptance of it will make him any less innocent. We may be free to think what we wish, but our thinking can't alter reality.[1]

---

[1] Mortimer J. Adler, *The Great Ideas: A Lexicon of Western Thought* (New York: Macmillan, 1992), pp. 867, 869.

Applications

1. Think back on your previous schooling. How closely has your experience matched Arthur's?

2. Reflect on your powers of concentration. Do you find it difficult to ponder important matters? Are you able to prevent the casual, semiconscious drift of images from interrupting your thoughts? Do you have less control in some situations than in others? Explain.

3. Rate yourself on each of the seven characteristics of good thinkers that are listed on pp. 19 and 20. Which are you strongest in? Which weakest? If your behavior varies from situation to situation, try to determine what kinds of issues or circumstances bring out your best and worst mental qualities.

4. Consider how you approach problems and issues. Is there any pattern to the way you think about a problem or an issue? Does an image come to mind first? Or perhaps a word? What comes next? And what after that? If you can't answer these questions completely, do this exercise: Flip half a dozen pages ahead in this book, pick a sentence at random, read it, and note how your mind deals with it. (Such thinking about your thinking may be a little awkward at first. If it is, try the exercise two or three times.)

5. Read each of the following statements carefully. Then decide what question(s), if any, a good critical thinker would find it appropriate to ask.

   a. Television news sensationalizes its treatment of war because it gives us pictures only of injury, death, and destruction.

   b. My parents were too strict—they wouldn't let me date until I was sixteen.

   c. It's clear to me that Ralph doesn't care for me—he never speaks when we pass in the hall.

   d. From a commercial for a news network: "The news is changing every minute of the day, so you constantly need updating to keep you informed."

   e. The statement of an Alabama public elementary school teacher who had students recite the Lord's Prayer and say grace before meals: "I feel part of my job as a teacher is to instill values children need to have a good life."

A Difference of Opinion

The following passage summarizes an important difference of opinion. After reading the statement, use the library and/or the Internet and find what knowledgeable people have said about the issue. Be sure to cover the entire range of views. Then assess the strengths and weaknesses of each. If you conclude that one view is entirely correct and the others are mistaken, explain how you reached that conclusion. If, *as is more likely,* you find that one view is more insightful than the others but that they all make some valid points, construct a view of your own that *combines* the insights from all sides and explain why that view is the most reasonable of all. Present your response in a composition or an oral report, as your instructor specifies.

> **Should colleges require students to live in coed housing?** As recently as thirty years ago most colleges would not *permit* students to live in coed housing. But times have changed and now some colleges *require* it. In 1997 two young Yale undergraduates asked the administration for permission to live off-campus rather than in a coed dormitory because sharing bath and shower facilities with women would violate their Orthodox Jewish faith. (Incidentally, it would also violate tenets of Islam, Orthodox Christianity, and Catholicism.) The college denied their request, saying, in effect, "Coed dorms are part of the Yale experience and if you don't like it, you can leave." Many people support Yale's disposition of the case, believing that the requirement of coed housing is reasonable. Many others regard that requirement as an outrage.

Endnotes

1. Chester I. Barnard, *The Function of the Executive* (Cambridge, Mass.: Harvard University Press, 1938), p. 303.

2. James Harvey Robinson, in Charles P. Curtis, Jr., and Ferris Greenslet, eds., *The Practical Cogitator, or the Thinker's Anthology* (Boston: Houghton Mifflin, 1945), p. 6.

3. Leonard Woolf, quoted in Rowland W. Jepson, *Clear Thinking,* 5th ed. (New York: Longman, Green, 1967 [1936]), p. 10.

4. Percey W. Bridgman, *The Intelligent Individual and Society* (New York: Macmillan, 1938), p. 182.

5. For a remarkably clear discussion of this complex subject, see Mortimer J. Adler, *Intellect: Mind over Matter* (New York: Macmillan, 1990).

6. William Barrett, *Death of the Soul from Descartes to the Computer* (Garden City, N.Y.: Doubleday, 1986), pp. 10, 53, 75.

7. John Dewey, *How We Think* (New York: Heath, 1933), p. 4.

8. Dewey, *How We Think,* pp. 88–90.

9. R. W. Gerard, "The Biological Basis of Imagination," *The Scientific Monthly,* June 1946, p. 477.

10. Gerard, "Biological Basis," p. 478.

11. Copyright © 2002 by MindPower, Inc. Used with permission.

12. Copyright © 2002 by MindPower, Inc. Used with permission.

PART FIVE

Global Standards/
Global Village[1]

Our experience with the Global Compact over the past four years has shown conclusively that voluntary initiatives can and do work. But we have also learned that they have to be made to work. Governments have to do the right thing: to govern well, in the interests of all their people. Business must restrain itself from taking away, by its lobbying activities, what it offers through corporate responsibility and philanthropy. And civil society actors need to accept that the business community is not a monolithic bloc; that it has leaders and laggards; and that leaders should be encouraged when they take positive steps, even though they may occasionally stumble, and not to be frightened off from trying in the first place . . .

The Compact's core comparative advantages are the universality of its principles, the international legitimacy that only the United Nations embodies, and the Compact's potential to be a truly global platform with great appeal not only in the industrialized countries, but also in the developing world. The Compact's new strategic concept must therefore give special emphasis to the potential for links, synergies and mutual support between the global and local levels of our activities.

Kofi Annan, Secretary General, United Nations, June 23, 2004

Global and Local Standards

Many companies will want to—and should—develop their own codes of conduct, ethical principles, operating standards, and core values to reflect their unique purpose, customer groups, and internal values. In developing these internal principles, companies can define what they stand for and what their standards of integrity are. Yet it is clear that internally developed standards will have to satisfy the external scrutiny of increasingly sophisticated stakeholders and meet the foundation standards articulated in documents like the United Nations' Global Compact, the Global Sullivan Principles, the CERES environmental principles, and the United Nations' Code of Conduct for Multinationals. To cope effectively with all these principles, companies need to ensure that their own standards are at least meeting the minimum standards set by various industry, governmental, nongovernmental (NGO), and coalition groups.

The processes of globalization and the explosion of connectivity engendered by the World Wide Web have made obvious that some standards and principles of action need to be global. Further, implementation of these standards can help corporate citizens avoid free ridership, externalities, and prisoners' dilemma problems that place some companies and countries at a disadvantage to others. Emerging standards and principles are therefore based on end values that attempt to ensure balance among the spheres of human activity and with nature, and to provide for respect for basic human dignity.

Global standards and principles are typically established through consensus-building processes set up by international bodies, sometimes industry organizations, and frequently coalitions of various interested stakeholders. Despite the vast diversity and pluralism of societies in the world, the emergence of these statements of principles and codes of conduct is testimony to the fact that, after all is said and done, we live one world.

To cope with the recent proliferation of standards and accountability measures, this chapter will explore the emergence of standards in all three of the spheres of human civilization as well as those that have emerged with respect to the natural environment. In this exploration, we will see that although global accountability measures are still in the early stages of development, more and more agreement is being generated about the standards to which global companies will have to adhere.

As public attention shifts from topic to topic, global brands are often targets of exposés and activist pressures.[2] Among other incidents, religious groups spearheaded a consumer boycott of the Nestlé Corporation for its sales of infant formula in developing nations in the late 1970s; the boycott culminated in Nestlé's appointment of an internal infant formula audit commission. Combined with a global boycott of products from companies operating in South Africa, these and similar forms of consumer activism vividly demonstrate the usefulness of consumer movements to attempt to change corporate behavior and hold companies accountable.

Another source of increasing pressure for corporate accountability is the social or ethical investing movement, which is now estimated by the Social Investment Forum to include some $2 trillion in equities screened on social criteria in the United States alone. Although social investing is yet to become fully mainstream, there is enough investor interest, with about one of every eight dollars invested in screened equities,[3] that even major investment houses like Smith Barney and large pension funds like TIAA-CREF have begun to create social funds. By the late 1990s, corporate governance activists had also become sophisticated in their use of shareholder resolutions targeted at specific corporate practices.[4]

Outsourcing, strategic and other alliances, and just-in-time inventory management systems began to blur the boundaries between companies and their suppliers and customers during the 1980s and 1990s. Outsourcing created new global supply chains, often in developing nations, and human rights, labor, and environmental activists became concerned about corporate practices in the increasingly long supply chains of consumer goods, clothing, and toy companies.[5] Boundaries between multinational companies and their suppliers, clear perhaps in the eyes of managers, have been much less clear to activists wanting to create corporate accountability.

The Gap between the Ideal and the Real

Demands for greater corporate transparency and accountability, as well as anti-corruption measures, are fostering significant new accountability, reporting, and transparency initiatives among coalitions of business, labor, human rights, investor, and governmental bodies. Indeed, a database created by the International Labor Organization and available over the Internet lists nearly 450 Web sites of industry and business associations; corporate, NGO, and activist groups; and consulting organizations that have developed and are promulgating a wide range of relevant policy initiatives. These initiatives include a mix of transparency and reporting initiatives, codes of conduct, principles, and fair trade agreements.[6] Responses to these demands are varied. Many companies, particularly those under NGO and social activist pressures to reform labor and human rights abuses in their supply chains, have formulated their own codes of conduct. Notable among these companies are Levi Strauss, Nike, and Reebok, all significant targets of activism.

The array of emerging standards suggests that there is a gap between growing public expectations from a variety of stakeholders and actual company performance. Pressures from a wide range of stakeholders appear to be pushing companies toward a common set of guidelines of what *ought* to be and away from the stark and not always pleasant realities of global competition.[7]

Foundation Principles

Corporate critics might ask whether a company that employed 180 forced laborers yesterday and only 160 today could really be considered to be a leading corporate citizen. The company has shown improvement, but its basic practice of forced labor—slavery—is reprehensible. It violates a fundamental value inherent in responsible practice. Such baseline-level behaviors, practices, and values are foundation principles. *Foundation principles are generally agreed-on standards that provide a floor of acceptable practice below which it is ethically and managerially problematic to go.* Business ethicists Thomas Donaldson and Thomas Dunfee term such general principles or values "hypernorms" and suggest that a relatively universal consensus must be reached for them to exist at all. They define hypernorms as "principles so fundamental to human existence that they serve as a guide in evaluating lower level moral norms."[8]

General agreement by businesses on a common set of foundation principles—a baseline or a moral minimum for operating practice—is important to providing a level playing field for companies. One author argues that a set of universal moral standards would include trustworthiness, respect, responsibility, fairness, caring, and citizenship; such standards could underpin the development of codes and principles themselves.[9] Agreement on foundation principles could help companies avoid the information overload and code mania that some are currently experiencing as the number and types of initiatives grow, as well as disparities between developed and developing nations.[10]

Donaldson and Dunfee provide a framework for core values, built on the need for system integrity that builds trust and the mutual respect that emerges from the philosopher Immanuel Kant's categorical imperative.[11] Donaldson argues that these basic principles of respect are useful aids for searching out foundation values:

- Respect for core human values, which determine the absolute moral threshold for all business activities.
- Respect for local traditions.
- Respect for the belief that context matters when deciding what is right and wrong.[12]

From these guiding principles, Donaldson articulates three core values, all involving the critical element of respect. Core or foundational principles seemingly need to emphasize what leadership theorists James McGregor Burns terms end values,[13] which ultimately respect:

- Human dignity.
- Basic rights.
- Good citizenship (which involves working together to support and improve the institutions on which the community depends).[14]

These guiding principles negotiate the tension that exists in treating people as ends, not means, and treating each individual as unique and deserving of respect and dignity, while simultaneously holding valuable the context of community or common good that makes societies work.

Spheres and Related Values

The three spheres of human civilization and the ecological surround provide a useful framework for considering the range of possible foundation principles. As discussed earlier, core purposes within each of these spheres differ; hence, there are likely to be foundation principles associated with each sphere, though these will clearly merge into other spheres as well. To the extent that foundation principles exist, chances are they exist within broad-based consensus documents, generated not from theory but from agreements by the nations of the world, such as those promulgated by the United Nations (UN), perhaps the longest-existing multilateral global enterprise. Although a few nations may not agree with principles articulated in these broad-based consensus documents (e.g., China on human rights), they nonetheless represent the world's best efforts to date to find agreed-on values.

Indeed, the recent development of the UN's Global Compact, launched in 1999 by Secretary-General Kofi Annan, provides significant insight into the relatively few values that may have achieved the status of global agreement that may serve as candidate for actual hypernorms. Four principles deal with labor rights and can be said to fall within the economic sphere. Two principles deal with human rights, which fall within the civil society sphere, and three are ecological principles within the environmental sphere that underpins human civilization. A tenth anti-corruption principle, which falls most dominantly within the governmental sphere, was added in 2004 at a summit of leaders engaged in Global Compact activities. In the following sections we will explore foundation principles associated with each of the spheres before moving to a discussion of accountability.

The Global Compact

At the World Economic Forum, held in Davos, Switzerland, in January 1999, UN Secretary-General Kofi Annan challenged world business leaders to "embrace and enact" a Global Compact, both in their individual corporate practices and by supporting appropriate public policies. The principles articulated by Annan include human rights, labor standards, the natural environment, and corruption (see Table 9.1). The Global Compact initially involved establishing a coalition of businesses, business associations, workers' or labor organizations, national governments, and other types of organizations that are attempting to establish standards for business and industry. It is an effort by Annan to establish a standard for corporate citizenship by developing global companies into model corporate citizens who voluntarily agree to operate in accordance with a core set of principles that establish standards with respect to labor, human rights, and environmental practices.

Not everyone greeted Annan's attempt with cheers. Indeed, many NGO leaders believe that the Global Compact puts the UN's credibility at risk because it too closely aligns the UN with corporate forces.[15] In part, the critiques arise because the 50 or so companies that had signed on with the Global Compact by the end of 2000 had done so voluntarily.

TABLE 9.1 Principles of the Global Compact

Source: The Global Compact, www.unglobalcompact.org/Portal/Default.asp (accessed July 2, 2004).

> The Global Compact's ten principles in the areas of human rights, labor, the environment, and anti-corruption enjoy universal consensus and are derived from:
>
> - The universal Declaration of Human Rights
> - The International Labour Organization's Declaration
> - The Rio Declaration on Environment and Development
>
> The Global Compact asks companies to embrace, support and enact, within their sphere of influence, a set of core values in the areas of human rights, labor standards, and the environment. The principles are as follows.
>
> **Human Rights**
>
> *Principle 1*: Businesses should support and respect the protection of internationally proclaimed human rights, and
> *Principle 2*: make sure that they are not complicit in human rights abuses.
>
> **Labor Standards**
>
> *Principle 3*: Businesses should uphold the freedom of association and the effective recognition of the right to collective bargaining,
> *Principle 4*: the elimination of all forms of forced and compulsory labor,
> *Principle 5*: the effective abolition of child labor, and
> *Principle 6*: the elimination of discrimination in respect of employment and occupation.
>
> **Environment**
>
> *Principle 7*: Businesses should support a precautionary approach to environmental challenges,
> *Principle 8*: undertake initiatives to promote greater environmental responsibility, and
> *Principle 9*: encourage the development and diffusion of environmentally friendly technologies.
>
> **Anti-Corruption**
>
> *Principle 10*: Businesses should work agains all forms of corruption, including extortion and bribery.

Additionally, there is little or no external monitoring of their activities on the three main areas covered by the principles and little enforcement power of the standards. Clearly, corporations hoping to live up to the principles embedded in the Global Compact, as well as some of the other standards noted below, have a long way to go before their activities are fully transparent to NGOs and activists and before they can be held fully accountable.

Beyond Economizing: Economic Sphere Foundation Principles

Businesses operate within the economic sphere with the dominant goal of economizing. Since it is employees who produce the work of organizations, labor standards are certainly one important arena in which foundation principles are needed. Economizing means using resources, including human resources, in the most efficient way. In the economic sphere, principles derived from International Labor Organization (ILO) standards and the UN Declaration on Human Rights are particularly relevant.[16] The International Labor Standards of the ILO were developed with government policy in mind, targeting the development of national labor laws. Companies, of course, are subject to labor laws in countries where they have a presence, but the International Labor Standards do not generally specifically target companies. Such standards involve the fundamental principles of respect for humans as ends, not means, and, fundamentally, for human dignity at work.[17]

The International Labor Standards cover a broad range of areas and lack universal acceptance in their entirety; thus, they lack key traits necessary to serve as a foundation for economic sphere principles. Specifically with respect to labor standards, one analysis of existing global labor standards (building on the concept of human dignity and rights identified as fundamental by Donaldson and Dunfee) has demonstrated that there *are* certain basic labor rights that are relatively universally acknowledged.[18] These minimal labor rights are derived from the UN Declaration on Human Rights; the UN International Convention on Economic, Social and Cultural Rights; the Caux Round Table Principles; and the International Labor Organization labor standards. They are operationalized by the SA 8000 labor standards, as well as being found in many corporate and business association codes of conduct. The following foundation principles may represent the minimal set of conditions and standards to which all companies' labor standards should adhere:

- Just and favorable working conditions, including a limit to the number of hours a human should have to work each day and a healthy working environment.
- Minimum age and working conditions for child labor.
- Nondiscrimination requirements regarding the relative amount that a worker should be paid and the right to equal pay for equal work.
- Freedom from forced labor.
- Free association, including the right to organization and to bargain collectively in contract negotiations.[19]

Beyond Power Aggrandizing: Governmental Sphere Foundation Principles

Sustaining the integrity of the business and economic system demands *trust* in the system, particularly at the intersection between government (with its power to regulate and create the rules by which businesses operate) and business. Trust is the key to sustainable nations and a sustainable economic system. Governments have the capacity to use coercive power (or power-aggrandizing tendencies) to create the system under which other types of entities exist. System integrity is fundamentally undermined by corruption and bribery, which have the tendency to make both the economic and political systems untrustworthy. Accountability in corrupt systems is nonexistent, and companies that participate in corruption work against system integrity and the necessary foundation of trust. Transparency International (TI) and the World Bank, two global organizations working at the country level on the issue of corruption, have highlighted the need for foundational principles built on the concept of system integrity, and the UN Global Compact added a tenth anticorruption principle in 2004 to deal with this important issue.

As stated on the TI Web site (www.transparency.org), there are several reasons for fostering system integrity, integrity that structures business-government relationships and ultimately fosters democracy. The reasons are:

- Humanitarian, as corruption undermines and distorts development and leads to increasing levels of human rights abuse.
- Democratic, as corruption undermines democracies and in particular the achievements of many developing countries and countries in transition.
- Ethical, as corruption undermines a society's integrity.
- Practical, as corruption distorts the operations of markets and deprives ordinary people of the benefits which should flow from them.[20]

TI's core principles form the foundation of possible baseline principles with respect to the interactions of business and government, as well as providing some guidance for business transactions and reporting. Interestingly, TI's core principles are similar to the ethical principles of the numerous business initiatives aimed at improving management practice analyzed by Jeanne Liedtka, suggesting their broad applicability. TI's mission statement articulates its foundation principles as:

- Participation.
- Decentralization.
- Diversity.
- Accountability.
- Transparency.[21]

The UN Global Compact's tenth principle states the core value very simply: Business should work against corruption in all its forms, including extortion and bribery.[22]

Making Civilizing Real: Civil Society Sphere Foundation Principles

Basic human rights are possible candidates for fundamental principles associated with the civil society sphere, which is the realm of social organizations: family, church, schools, NGOs, and so on. Foundation principles related to human rights are most well known from their promulgation in the UN Declaration on Human Rights, first written in 1948 and more recently updated to include basic environmental concerns as well as human rights. Based on this declaration and other sources, Donaldson and Dunfee suggest that there is significant cross-cultural agreement on the following principles, all of which respect the dignity and humanity of individuals:

- The right to freedom of physical movement.
- The right to ownership of property.
- The right to freedom from torture.
- The right to a fair trial.
- The right to nondiscriminatory treatment.
- The right to physical security.
- The right to freedom of speech and association.
- The right to minimal education.
- The right to political participation.
- The right to subsistence.[23]

Some of these foundation principles are highly congruent with the labor rights identified in the preceding section of this chapter. As with the governmental foundation principles, the foundational human rights also foster democratic values (i.e., the right to political participation and the freedoms of speech and association) rather than more authoritarian values. Simultaneously, these rights allow for individual, national, and cultural differences (i.e., nondiscriminatory treatment and the freedom of speech and association), in what Donaldson and Dunfee term the "moral free space" in which individual differences of opinions about right and wrong exist.

Sustainability: Ecological Sphere Foundation Principles

If nature can be said to have a goal, it is likely to be ecologizing. The economizing that is inherent in industrialization when combined with the basic ecologizing processes of nature points in the direction of a possible foundation value for the nature environment of:

- Sustainability or ecologizing.

Nature, that is, wastes nothing. What is waste for one process becomes food for others, creating a cycle that sustains itself in creating the conditions for life on earth as we know it, or what some have called the Gaia hypothesis, the hypothesis that the earth itself is a living system.[24]

The UN Global Compact, building on the consensus fostered through the UN's Agenda 21 and the Declaration on Human Rights and Environment, reinforces the need for sus-

TABLE 9.2 Foundation Values in the Spheres of Human Civilization and Natural Environment

Source: Sandra Waddock, "Foundation Principles for Making Corporate Citizenship Real," *Journal of Business Ethics* 50 (2004), pp. 313–27.

Economic Sphere	Governmental Sphere	Civil Society Sphere	Ecological Sphere
• Just and favorable working conditions • Minimum age and working conditions for child labor • Nondiscrimination • Freedom from forced labor • Free association	• Participation • Decentralization • Diversity • Accountability • Transparency	• Freedom of physical movement • Ownership of property • Freedom from torture • Right to a fair trial • Nondiscriminatory treatment • Physical security • Freedom of speech and association • Right to at least a minimal education • Right to political participation • Right to subsistence	• Sustainability • Precautionary (preventative) approach to environmental challenges • Responsible and ethical management products and processes • Development and diffusion of environmentally sound technologies

tainability by emphasizing the following core environmental principles as its foundation principles:

- Taking a precautionary (preventative) approach to environmental challenges.
- Responsible and ethical management products and processes from the point of view of health, safety, and environmental aspects.
- Development and diffusion of environmentally sound technologies.[25]

This extended discussion of values as they apply to the spheres is summarized in Table 9.2. An example of one company's attempts to respond to a moral and strategic challenge is given in Case 9.1.Global Standards/Global Village

Emerging Trends in Standards, Principles, Codes of Conduct

During the late 1990s and early 2000s, an enormous wave of scandals brought attention to the need to provide coherent, consistent guidelines to ensure accountability, responsibility, and transparency with respect to how businesses behave in the world and the impacts that they have. In the following sections we briefly explore some of the major initiatives attempting to evolve principles, standards, and codes of conduct to which businesses can (and should) adhere.

Protecting the Ecological Surround

The United Nations has recognized the importance of environmental sustainability through development of its Agenda 21 initiative, which was adopted at the global environmental conference held in Rio de Janeiro, on June 14, 1992.[26] Agenda 21 is based in part on the principles of environment and development adopted at the Rio conference, which was the

Pfizer's Multisector Engagement: AIDS Drugs in the Developing World

The world's largest pharmaceutical maker, Pfizer Inc., faced a moral and strategic challenge: How could it respond to the HIV/AIDS epidemic, the most devastating disease of the third world, in a way that was commensurate with the company's leading position in its field? Pfizer's own portfolio of marketable therapies had little to offer in combating the disease, yet it nonetheless faced internal and external pressures to expand access to health care for the world's most needy. In response, in 2003 Pfizer began mobilizing the technical skills and expertise of its own employees in the fight. Under the personal oversight of the company's chairman and CEO, Henry A. McKinnell, the Pfizer Global Health Fellows volunteer program, dubbed "Hank's Peace Corps," sends skilled personnel to developing countries to help nongovernmental organizations (NGOs) build the health and social infrastructure of communities ravaged by HIV/AIDS. McKinnell's vision, extending beyond traditional industry responses of cash and drug donations and ordinary volunteerism, is a novel experiment in large-scale international development: Pfizer intends to eventually scale up the program to include volunteers from many companies, and in so doing has the rare opportunity to establish a new model of cross-sector engagement at the deepest level of organizations to confront AIDS and potentially other global crises.

As many sectors of society evolve to the conclusion that medical care is a human right, the Fellows program advances the moral and practical discussion about the role and means of various institutions—especially the critical pharmaceutical industry—to ensure those rights. In its intended scale, leverage, and social value, the program demonstrates Pfizer's support for the first UN Global Compact principle that seeks the protection of human rights, by attempting to safeguard the most basic one—to life itself. As HIV/AIDS increasingly leads to inequities in the society and workplaces of developing countries, the program also addresses the goal of the sixth principle, "to eliminate discrimination in employment and occupation," by reducing the stigma of the disease through education and prevention.

In its approach to these goals, Pfizer has partnered with nonprofit aid organizations ("NGO partners") already in the target regions and steeped in a common mission. In turn, the NGOs engage their own field staffs or local organizations, such as community clinics and research and training institutions ("field organization beneficiaries") in the developing world to identify solutions to their most pressing needs. Under this arrangement, the NGO partners expect to gain a number of benefits from Pfizer personnel—generally in capacity-building analysis, planning, and training that they couldn't otherwise afford. Because each volunteer's assignment is different, these benefits take many forms, among which are improved epidemiological skills to better identify health trends and plan interventions; increased efficiency in NGO program management, learning, reporting, and fund-raising; improved drug-trial competence that in turn attracts more first-world resources; AIDS education, prevention, and economic-support tools for workplaces and care centers; and training in state-of-the-art medical skills.

Pfizer fully anticipates many advantages from the Fellows program as well. As a personnel development tool, it encourages volunteers to come home with new operational and business insights, as well as better understanding of the company's many stakeholders (patients, communities, NGOs). These insights should inform future social policies, business processes and decisions—not the least of which include bringing future AIDS therapies to market. For many employees impassioned by public-health issues, the program is also expected to be a valuable recruitment and retention tool. And, significantly, it is intended to help build relations with both critical activist organizations and powerful legislative and regulatory authorities—many of whom believe the pharmaceutical industry must make more effort to address the developing world's health crises.

A number of lessons from the early phases of implementation are valuable for the light they shed on the nuances of building cross-sector partnerships around the contributions of corporate volunteers. Some of these lessons include:

- The labor-intensive planning to accommodate the needs of all stakeholders—the corporation, the NGO, its field staff, beneficiaries, and the individual volunteer—cannot be overestimated.
- Field assignments are most productive when they're driven by beneficiary needs and not simply to accommodate the desires of available volunteers.
- The personal traits of successful corporate employees are not always suited to the rigors of the third world; thorough screening and preparation are vital.
- NGO adjustment to the culture and disciplines of for-profit corporations is nearly as significant.
- Corporate executives' enthusiasm can help but also hinder the program development process.
- First-world corporate expertise does not always transfer easily to third-world conditions, and work-arounds are difficult to find.
- Midmanagers' willingness to allow volunteers time off is critical to such a program's success, and the burden felt by colleagues back home can jeopardize that approval.
- Expectations by all parties of the others must be firmly set—and then constantly adjusted.

Clearly the challenges Pfizer has addressed with the Fellows program are profoundly significant; there is perhaps none more so than the politically charged and intractable dilemma of AIDS, especially for a pharmaceutical developer today. The volunteer approach is an innovative attempt to bring the company's core medical and managerial competencies to bear on difficult infrastructure challenges, which inhibit the efficacy of drug and cash donations and hinder the successful treatment and prevention of AIDS. While the Fellows program is admittedly a modest beginning, Pfizer ambitiously seeks to scale it to meaningful impact. This approach has been appreciably more challenging than Pfizer, the NGOs, and field organizations first imagined. Sharing the knowledge of Pfizer's own specialists shows deeper organizational commitment than other avenues it could have chosen, such as donating more cash or drugs, and is far more difficult than it probably needed to pursue if its motivation were purely image building.

The Fellows response, however, stops short of tackling knotty business strategy changes called for by critics of the pharmaceutical industry in recent years. For example, a tiered and transparent global pricing system would allow health authorities in poor countries to purchase critical drugs at lower and more predictable prices and could lead the industry to even more profound benefits for the disadvantaged. Pfizer does not pose the Fellows program as a substitute or ultimate solution to such issues. However, one can imagine that its most significant contribution ultimately may be the influence of its returning volunteers on management's future thinking about such policies. In this way, the program has the potential to create change within the company's processes, of the sort the Global Compact intends.

DISCUSSION QUESTIONS

1. How would you evaluate Pfizer's efforts to deal with the AIDS crisis?
2. Do you think Pfizer's efforts go far enough? Why or why not?
3. Does Pfizer's commitment to working with NGOs adequately show the company's commitment to the Global Compact's first principle? Why or why not?
4. What advice would you give to Pfizer to sustain its initiatives over time?

Source: Jonathan Levine, for the Center for Corporate Citizenship at Boston College, 2004.

first-ever global conference on the environment.[27] Among the most important principles for leading corporate citizens to be aware of are the sovereign right of nations to use their own natural resources to meet the needs of future and present generations. The principles emphasize the need for sustainable development and its link to environmental protection, through focusing on eradicating poverty, meeting the needs of developing countries as a priority, and paying particular attention to ensuring that the voices of vulnerable groups—such as women, youth, indigenous, and oppressed peoples—are heard.

The Rio Principles also emphasize the need for global partnership in conserving and protecting the earth's ecosystem, through an open and global economic system, with fair trade policies, discouragement of transfer of environmentally harmful activities to more vulnerable or weaker nations, and internalization of costs. Nation-states are encouraged to promote countrywide initiatives to improve sustainability, scientifically and technologically, through citizen participation, and effective environmental legislation along with active citizen participation in the setting of national laws and regulations. The principles also encourage global intercountry cooperation in the interest of the environment and a spirit of collaboration and partnership.

Agenda 21 is a comprehensive document that sets forth an ambitious series of agenda items and goals linking economic and social development with ecological sustainability. Specific goals of Agenda 21 are: (1) promoting sustainable development through trade liberalization; (2) making trade and environment mutually supportive; (3) providing adequate financial resources to developing countries and dealing with international; and (4) encouraging macroeconomic policies conducive to environment and development.[28]

Agenda 21 focuses on combating poverty, changing consumption patterns, encouraging sustainability, and responding to population or demographic shifts. It also focuses on protecting and promoting human health, while simultaneously promoting the integration of environment and development in decision-making processes. Arenas of environmental concern include the atmosphere, the forests, and fragile ecosystems (including focusing on the increasing desertification of some areas of the world resulting from overpopulation and overuse of the land and creating sustainable mountain, agricultural, and rural areas). Companies and nations need to learn to manage and protect biological diversity, and to manage biotechnology safely. Pollution and waste management systems are aimed at improving the oceans and other bodies of water and the atmosphere, and reducing hazardous wastes and toxic chemicals, solid wastes and sewage, and radioactive wastes.

Responses from Businesses

Businesses today are coming under increasing pressure from environmental activists, regulatory agencies, governments, and NGOs to move toward sustainable development. Some business groups are responding to these pressures by creating self-regulatory initiatives that focus their internal practices on more sustainable practices.

One of the foremost business-oriented organizations in fostering collaborative relationships among the many parties interested in sustainable ecology has been the Coalition for Environmentally Responsible Economies (CERES). Composed of more than 50 investor, environmental, religious, labor, and social justice organizations, CERES has drafted a set of principles that nearly 50 companies and organizations had endorsed by the end of the 20th century. Another business-oriented organization acting to promote sustainable ecology is the World Business Council for Sustainable Development (WBCSD). A third is the chemical industry's Responsible Care initiative.

CERES Principles

The CERES Principles came into existence following the Exxon *Valdez* oil spill in Alaska. The spill brought renewed activist and indeed global public attention to the need for ecologically sustainable business practices. Initiated in 1989, the CERES Principles were first called the Valdez Principles and were then broadened in scope and tactics toward influencing corporate strategies with respect to the environment through using shareholder resolutions to initiate conversations with corporate directors about company practices.[29]

The CERES coalition views itself as successfully modeling cooperation and dialogue among investors, environmentalists, and companies; as a leader in standardizing corporate reporting on the environment; and as a catalyst for measurable improvements in companies' environmental practices. CERES has accomplished much of this through its 10 principles. These principles point to specific ways that companies can change their behaviors and practices to achieve the ecological sustainability demanded by the four core principles of The Natural Step process. Among the current signatories are Sun Oil, Arizona Public Service Company, Bethlehem Steel, General Motors, H. B. Fuller, and Polaroid Corporation. By signing the CERES Principles, companies agree to meet although clearly the signatories do not yet actually operate in sustainable ways.

World Business Council for Sustainable Development

The World Business Council for Sustainable Development (WBCSD) is a coalition of 170 transnational companies from 35 countries and 20 industry sectors that have the shared goal of a commitment to sustainable development through a triple-bottom-line orientation—economic, ecological, and social. The WBCSD aims to establish business leadership in the area of sustainability, innovation, and corporate social responsibility. The coalition has four main goals: business leadership in sustainability, policy development that will help businesses create a framework for sustainability, best-practice dissemination, and global outreach.[30]

WBCSD came about as a way to get businesses involved in the UN's Earth Summit in Rio in 1992, where Agenda 21 was developed. Since that time, in addition to providing information and bringing together the nearly 1,000 business leaders involved around issues of environment, the WBCSD has undertaken a number of projects, involving accountability, advocacy, capacity building, energy and climate, the role of the financial sector, sustainable livelihoods, and water.[31]

Responsible Care

Another example of an industry-led environmental effort is the Responsible Care initiative of the Chemical Manufacturers Association, which has received considerable public attention for its leadership. The chemical industry is, for obvious reasons, under significant pressure to improve its environmental performance. Like the CERES Principles, Responsible Care is a voluntary effort by chemical companies to commit to continual environmental, health, and safety improvements in a manner that is responsive to the public interest.[32] Significant aspects of Responsible Care are that companies signing on commit themselves to continually improving performance, collaboration to help improve each others' environmental performance, measuring progress, and gaining regular public input on their efforts. The effort operates through a set of guiding principles and detailed guidelines for management practice in six operating arenas important to chemical companies.

ISO 14000

Another set of emerging environmental standards to which many companies, particularly those operating in the European Union, are paying attention are the ISO 14000 standards. Modeled in part on the International Organization for Standardization (ISO) 9000 quality standards, ISO 14000 focuses companies' attention on environmental management, that is, on avoiding or minimizing the harmful effects of corporate activities on the environment. ISO 14000 and the related ISO 14001 auditing standards are largely industry driven and, unlike the CERES Principles, generally represent internally developed standards, rather than a more globally defined set of absolute standards and principles to which a company agrees to adhere.[33]

Like the CERES Principles, ISO 14000 emphasizes the operating policies and practices within the company, rather than the nature or use of products or services generated.[34] The goal of the ISO standards is to reduce harmful environmental effects of the production process itself that occur from pollution and waste or from depletion of natural resources. ISO 14000 is actually a family of related standards that attempts to align businesses, industries, governments, and consumers around common ecological interests. Generally, ISO expects that companies will develop their own standards and environmental management systems, in compliance with relevant legislation and regulations, and then audit their practices to assure conformance to internal standards. Companies operating under the ISO 14000 standards are also expected to focus on continual improvements in their environmental practices.

ISO 14000 standards emphasize several different aspects of environmental management, including life-cycle assessment, which describes the environmental performance of products, the integration of environment into design and development to improve environmental performance, and communication about environmental performance (e.g., through labels, declarations, and general corporate communications). Other aspects of this process, which is similar to the quality management process of plan, do, check, act, are ongoing monitoring of environmental performance and auditing performance.[35] Many companies now must use the ISO 9000 quality standards to compete successfully, simply because their allies demand it. A similar developmental cycle is likely for the ISO 14000 family of environmental standards and/or the CERES Principles. Hence, it makes sense for companies that wish to be leading corporate citizens to begin moving toward meeting such standards.

Global Accountability and Sustainability

Natural Capitalism

In their *Harvard Business Review* article "A Road Map for Natural Capitalism," Amory Lovins, L. Hunter Lovins, and Paul Hawken argue that simple changes in corporate practices can provide significant benefits that will not only protect the natural environment but also potentially be very profitable.[36] If the idea of natural capitalism—sustainability—truly takes hold (and earlier chapters of this book have provided a good deal of evidence that it well might), then becoming sustainable will require four dramatic shifts in business practices:

- Dramatically increase the productivity of natural resources by reducing wasteful practices, changing production design and technology, and stretching ecological resources significantly further than they are being stretched today.

- Shift to biologically inspired closed-loop production models, in which all the by-products of one process become an input for another process so that nothing is wasted.

- Move to a solutions-based business model, in which value is delivered as a flow of services rather than products and well-being is measure by satisfying expectations for quality, utility, and performance of products and services.

- Reinvest in natural capital by restoring, sustaining, and expanding the planet's ecosystem.[37]

In part, natural capitalism is based not on the law of diminishing returns, which informs much current economic thinking, but rather on a radically different perspective: the concept of expanding returns. This concept, which underpins approaches like lean manufacturing and whole system design, implies that saving a lot of resources can be less costly than saving a smaller amount.[38]

The authors of this radical approach to capitalism argue that by thinking about the whole system–the closed loop—leaders can find numerous small changes that result in big savings, a point that Peter Senge calls finding leverage in his important book *The Fifth Discipline*.[39]

Kodak Corporation, for example, eliminated 700,000 pounds of landfill waste and produced savings of $600,000 yearly by developing a new material that wraps photographic paper.[40] By changing from a foil wrapping that could not be recycled to a more environmentally friendly wrapping for its paper, the company found that it would actually save money, eliminate the landfill problem, and address ergonomic safety issues that were the original incentive for thinking about the change. Lovins and his coauthors argue that companies can go further and rethink manufacturing processes entirely, creating new products and processes that actually prevent waste in the first place. This technique, which requires shifting one's perspective away from looking just at production to looking at the whole system, is biologically based in the concept of "waste equals food."[41]

Respect for Human Dignity

Respect for human dignity and worth is at the core of all stakeholder relationships and certainly fundamental to the global principles businesses are expected to employ regarding basic human rights. In the following sections we will briefly explore some of the most important principles, and their promulgating organizations, to help provide a framework for leading corporate citizens. Basic human rights can be found within the sphere of civil society, where we begin this exploration. In addition to the UN Global Compact, there are a number of other important initiatives worthy of discussion.

Working Conditions: The Sweatshop Controversy

Companies that outsource production to suppliers in developing nations must establish pay standards. Forced in part by pressures from activist groups like United Students Against Sweatshops, Sweatshop Watch, Corporate Watch, UNITE, and the International Labor Organization (among many others), many companies now are paying much more attention to working conditions in supplier firms than they have had to do in the past.

Nike, Reebok, Liz Claiborne, Phillips–Van Heusen, and many other companies that have faced considerable controversy about their sourcing practices have banded together to form a self-regulatory association called the Fair Labor Association (FLA). The American Apparel Manufacturers Association (AAMA), which is an industry trade group, has also created a less stringent set of standards for monitoring factories.[42]

The Union of Needletrades, Industrial and Textile Employees (UNITE), the Retail, Wholesale and Department Store Union, and the Interfaith Center on Corporate Responsibility are among the activist groups that believe that corporate-based regulation of suppliers' working conditions is mainly a public relations, rather than a substantive, move. Sweatshop Watch, which combines labor and community (civil society) interests, argues that the real solutions to sweatshop conditions will come not from industry self-regulation but from implementation of enforceable labor standards and protection in international trade agreements and relatively standardized and enforced national and international laws.[43]

The companies forming the FLA hope that by regulating themselves, they will be able to avoid some of the negative publicity and associated diminishment of, their reputational capital and customer loyalty associated with activists uncovering human rights and worker abuses in supplier companies. Companies in industrialized nations sourcing from developing nations naturally argue that if they were to pay prevailing domestic wage rates to workers in developing nations, they would lose the very competitive advantage and economizing benefits they had sought to gain in outsourcing production in the first place.

Human rights and labor activists, on the other hand, argue that working conditions and pay scales need to be monitored not just by industry groups like the FLA and the AAMA, which are likely to be biased in favor of the companies, but by external and more objective monitors. In fact, activist groups have strongly criticized the formation of industry-based monitoring organizations. One activist group, Corporate Watch, converted its 1998 Greenwash Award into a "Sweatwash Award," given to the FLA because it was concerned that the creation of FLA would mean that only cosmetic, rather than real, improvements in working conditions would be made.[44] Governments of developing nations, of course, argue that transnational companies bring much-needed jobs and economic development to their nations; they are therefore sometimes willing to overlook transgressions of basic human rights and dignity in the interest of economic development.

Sweatshop Watch defines a sweatshop as "a workplace where workers are subject to extreme exploitation, including the absence of a living wage or benefits, poor working conditions and arbitrary discipline."[45] The following is an excerpt from the Sweatshop Watch's homepage, describing conditions in sweatshops both in the United States and in developing nations:

> The overwhelming majority of garment workers in the U.S. are immigrant women. They typically toil 60 hours a week in front of their machines, often without minimum wage or overtime pay. In fact, the Department of Labor estimates that more than half of the country's 22,000 sewing shops violate minimum wage and overtime laws. Many of these workers labor in dangerous conditions including blocked fire exits, unsanitary bathrooms, and poor ventilation. Government surveys reveal that 75% of U.S. garment shops violate safety and health laws. In addition, workers commonly face verbal and physical abuse and are intimidated from speaking out, fearing job loss or deportation.
>
> Overseas, garment workers routinely make less than a living wage, working under extremely oppressive conditions. Workers in Vietnam average $0.12 per hour, and workers in Honduras average $0.60 per hour. Sweatshops can be viewed as a product of the global economy. Fueled by an abundant supply of labor in the global market, capital mobility, and free trade, garment industry giants move from country to country seeking the lowest labor costs and the highest profit, exploiting workers the world over.[46]

Sweatshop conditions clearly fail to respect the basic human dignity of the workers who labor there. Companies that operate with integrity and hope to implement their vision and values through their stakeholder relationships, particularly with suppliers, need to be well aware of the conditions of work in those suppliers' operations. Integrity demands closely monitoring working conditions and assuring that employees are treated with respect and dignity, including providing a living wage even when economizing pressures push a company toward exploitive practices in the interest of a better financial bottom line. The values-driven company also pays attention to the social and ecological costs of its activities in, at minimum, a triple-bottom-line framework. (See Case 9.2 for a discussion of Nike, in particular.)

The Living Wage Debate

The criterion for wage payment that is rapidly evolving in the international community is the "living wage," which pegs the wage scale in any nation relative to the standard of living in that nation. Exactly how to calculate this living wage is yet undetermined; there are, however, various approaches, all of which attempt to ensure that basic human needs for shelter, food, and clothing are met. For example, one coalition of activists, academics, and representatives of developing countries defined living wages in the global garment and shoe industries. The living wage is defined as a take-home wage earned by working within the country's legal maximum hours per week (but not more that 48 hours) that provides nutrition, water, housing, energy, transportation, clothing, health care, child care, and education for the average family, plus some savings or discretionary income.[47]

Business Week made the initial proclamation: "After years of pressure to stop abusive practices in Nike's overseas plants, CEO Philip Knight has decided to revamp labor policies. In doing so, he becomes the one applying pressure—on other US companies to match his new standards." In a program the company calls Transparency 101, Nike is working with external auditors from PricewaterhouseCoopers and Nike's internal compliance office to ensure that the company's foreign suppliers, which employ more than half a million workers, are in compliance with the company's standards.

To cope with the plethora of criticisms directed against it, Nike instituted labor standards that included external monitoring, hiring PricewaterhouseCoopers to do its audits, providing financial assistance to factories, and improving environmental standards and working conditions in its supplier factories. Among the benefits Nike hopes to supply are increased overtime pay, new counseling programs, better safety procedures, new recognition programs, better ventilation, cleaner working environments, and enhanced training programs in its supplier factories.

Of course, it's not always that easy to ensure that standards are being met. But for years Nike experienced firsthand what it is like to be targeted by human and labor rights activists unhappy with its practices—and the bad press that followed. Activist groups still keep a close watch on the company's activities in developing nations because, even with the standards in place, compliance is not always ensured. For example, after Nike instituted the new standards, activists found that the auditors overlooked major problems and therefore continued questioning both the company's motives and its performance.

Not only does Nike have to deal with the aftermath of all the bad press it received about its labor practices, but it also has to cope with competitive realities of shifting fads and fashions that have caused its sneaker sales to drop. The decline in sales occurred almost simultaneously with CEO Phil Knight's demand that the company "just do it" by meeting significantly higher labor standards while rebuilding the company competitively from top to bottom.

Despite years of efforts to improve its factories, Nike still faces criticisms from activists. The global activist nonprofit organization Oxfam has a NikeWatch Web site that tracks activities. The following is an excerpt from that site:

> Ever wondered, as you slipped on your sneakers or pulled on a pair of jogging shorts, what life might be like for the person who made them?
>
> Nike promotes sport and healthy living, but the lives of workers who make Nike's shoes and clothes in Asia and Latin America are anything but healthy. They live in severe poverty and suffer stress and exhaustion from overwork. Oxfam Community Aid Abroad is part of an international campaign to persuade Nike and other transnational corporations to respect workers' basic rights.

DISCUSSION QUESTIONS

1. Investigate Nike's current labor standards and practices.

2. Why has the company moved so aggressively to implement factory monitoring and ensure transparency?

3. What are the implications of the problems that Nike faced in the 1990s for its reputation as a leading corporate citizen?

4. Should Nike have put all of these resources into these monitoring and accountability systems? Why or why not?

Sources: Kelley Holland and Aaron Bernstein, "Nike Finally Does It," *Business Week*, May 25, 1998, pp. 46 ff; Louise Lee, "Can Nike Still Do It?" *Business Week*, February 21, 2000, pp. 12–128; www.nikebiz.com/labor/index.shtml; "Opening Comments before the Global Compact," Philip H. Knight, New York, July 26, 2000, www.nikebiz.com/media/n_compact.shtml; and Oxfam, "NikeWatch," www.oxfam.org.au/campaigns/nike/index.html (accessed July 2, 2004).

The Sweatshop Watch has also attempted to define what is meant by a living wage in a way that accommodates the different standards for meeting basic needs in different nations. The method is presented in Note 9.1.

Economic Sphere: Respect for the Economic System

By establishing high standards and operating principles and adhering to them, and, further, by engaging in dialogue about important issues with other stakeholders, business leaders can carve out a satisfactory economic agenda. If that agenda is to succeed long-term, however, it must be aligned with the agendas of stakeholders in the civil society and political spheres, who now have access to communications technology that enables them to transmit information, ideas, and plans globally virtually instantaneously. Thus, respect for all stakeholders' points of view is gaining in importance, and corporate citizens increasingly need to carry out their responsibilities with integrity, transparency, and accountability to satisfy their many constituencies.

Emerging Business Standards

Among the most notable of the groups that are developing voluntary standards for business practices with respect to labor, human rights, environment, and ethics is the Global

In 1998, a coalition of organizations hosted a Living Wage Summit, at which the following consensus about how to calculate a living wage was reached, and ultimately published by the activist organization Sweatshop Watch:

$$\text{Take home wage}[1] = \frac{\text{Average family size}[2]}{\text{Average \# of adult wage earners}} \times (\text{Cost of nutrition} + \text{Clothing} + \text{Health care} + \text{Education} + \text{Portable water} + \text{Child care} + \text{Transportation})[3] + \frac{\text{Housing} + \text{Energy}[4]}{\text{Average \# of adult wage earners}} + \text{Savings}(10\% \text{ of income})[5]$$

1. The take home wage is based on the number of hours worked in a legal working week (not exceeding 48 hours in one week). The take home wage is the worker's weekly net wage (subtracting out union dues, taxes, etc.).

2. The average family size is divided by the average number of adult wage earners in a family. As noted below, it has not yet been determined what data would be used to quantify this analysis.

3. This list of "basic needs" was derived from a larger list that also included: entertainment, vacation, paid family leave, retirement, life insurance and personal liability insurance. This list is not definitive and may vary depending on regional factors.

4. The cost of housing and energy is divided by the average number of adult wage earners. Housing and energy needs are considered to expand in proportion to the number of wage earners in the household.

5. A random factor of 10 percent has been included for savings in order to permit workers to have some discretionary income and to allow workers to send money home to their families.

DISCUSSION QUESTIONS

1. What is the living wage for your area? (You will have to gather data to make the calculation.)

2. Does the minimum wage in your area enable families to earn a living wage?

3. If not, what policy recommendations would you make to local business leaders? To government officials?

Source: Sweatshop Watch, www.sweatshopwatch.org/swatch/wages/formula.html (accessed July 2, 2004).

Reporting Initiative (GRI). The standards include the Caux Round Table Principles, the Global Sullivan Principles, and Organization for Economic Cooperation and Development's Guidelines for Multinational Enterprises. Additionally, in 2004, the International Organization for Standardization (ISO) which promulgates quality and environmental standards, announced that it would be broadening its scope to multiple stakeholders and developing guiding standards for corporate social responsibility.[48] ISO expects that its standards, which will not, at least in the short term, be used for certification purposes, will supplement existing standards and principles. The reputation of the ISO will lend great credibility to procedures that attempt to assure that companies are being responsible.

OECD Guidelines for Multinational Enterprises

Thirty-eight nations have agreed to a nonbinding set of guidelines for the behavior of multinational corporations through the Organization for Economic Cooperation and Development (OECD), to which 30 member nations and eight affiliates belong. These guidelines, called the OECD Guidelines for Multinational Enterprises, provide guidance on all aspects of firm behavior in the global arena, including employment and industrial relations, human rights, environment, information disclosure, competition, taxation, and science and technology.[49] By following these guidelines, companies can live up to societal and government expectations. Because they are issued by the OECD, the guidelines have a considerable credibility and are rapidly becoming one of the world's best sources of guidance for companies about their corporate responsibilities.[50]

Caux Principles for Business

The Caux Round Table, working in collaboration with the Minnesota Center for Corporate Responsibility, bases its principles for business on two basic ethical ideals. One ethical ideal is the Japanese concept of *kyosei*, which means living and working together for the common good, to enable cooperation and mutual prosperity to coexist with health and fair competition. The second ethical ideal is that of human dignity, which in Caux's usage simply refers to the sacredness or intrinsic value of each person as an end, not as a means to the fulfillment of others' purposes.[51] The Caux Round Table was founded in 1986 by Frederick Philips, former president of Philips Electronics, and Olivier Giscard d'Estaing, vice chairman of INSEAD. Its purpose is to reduce trade tensions by enhancing economic and social relationships among participants' countries and focus generally on building a better world. The Caux principles build on an earlier effort by the Minnesota Center for Corporate Responsibility.[52] These principles attempt to move businesses and their leaders toward a perspective that says they should look first to their own actions and behaviors when they are determining what is the right thing to do.

Global Sullivan Principles

Similar in their intent to the UN Global Compact's 10 principles, the Global Sullivan principles were developed in 1977 by the Reverend Leon Sullivan, who was concerned about businesses participating in the then-apartheid regime in South Africa. Topics covered by the Global Sullivan Principles include universal human rights, equal opportunities, respect for freedom of association, levels of employee compensation, training, health and safety, sustainable development, fair compensation, and working partnership to improve quality of life. As of 2004, about 100 companies had become signatories.

Equator Principles

Demonstrating that the financial community increasingly recognizes the importance of principles, the Equator Principles were first adopted by 10 banks in 2003 and had accumulated 25 signatories in 14 countries within a year.[53] The principles are aimed at helping financial institutions adequately manage the social and environmental risks in financing projects around the world, particularly in emerging markets.

The Equator Principles Web site quotes Herman Mulder, a banking executive who helped bring about the principles, as saying: "It is our fundamental belief that the Equator Principles are appropriately becoming the reference standard for financial institutions to ensure that the principles of responsible environmental stewardship and socially responsible development are embedded within our project finance activities. Moreover, the Equator Principles are an excellent example how our financial sector is able to self-regulate on high value issues."[54]

Political Sphere

Companies operating in the global arena know that they need to understand how local governments operate in all of the countries where they locate facilities, market products and services, or source materials. They need to be aware of local rules and regulations, as well as the ways companies are expected to operate in different cultures and with respect to governments. Different ideologies make for very different contexts, each of which must be analyzed individually and discussed by corporate leaders to ensure that integrity is maintained.

One of the serious issues facing companies when they operate outside their homelands is the apparently differing standard of integrity in different cultures. In some countries, it seems, business leaders face corrupt officials (and businesspeople) when they attempt to operate locally. What companies have discovered, however, is that, difficult as it may be, sticking to their own internally developed values and standard of integrity is, in the long run, the best practice. In this section we will focus on dealing with corruption when operating in the global arena, particularly as it applies to the political sphere of activity.

Pervasive Corruption

"Corruption is found, to some degree, in every society. As a sign that something has gone wrong in the relationship between society and the state, corruption is becoming a pervasive phenomenon."[55] So begins Transparency International's source book on national integrity systems.

Transparency International (TI) is a Berlin-based international nongovernmental organization (INGO) that has as its mission increasing government accountability and curbing national and international corruption. Founded in 1993 by Peter Eigen, TI works by creating coalitions of people with integrity from all three spheres of activity.

Because corruption undermines the integrity of not only the business system but also the political and civil society systems, Transparency International has multiple concerns:

- humanitarian, as corruption undermines and distorts development and leads to increasing levels of human rights abuse;
- democratic, as corruption undermines democracies and in particular the achievements of many developing countries and countries in transition;
- ethical, as corruption undermines a society's integrity; and
- practical, as corruption distorts the operations of markets and deprives ordinary people of the benefits which should flow from them.[56]

Using a systems perspective on each country in which it operates, TI attempts to understand the causes, loopholes, and incentives feeding corrupt practices locally. It then attempts to determine the main types of corruption within the public domain and the leverage points for change within that system. According to TI, "Policy response to combating corruption has several elements common to every society: the reform of substantive programs; changes in the structure of government and its methods of assuring accountability; changes in moral and ethical attitudes; and, perhaps most importantly, the involvement and support of government, the private business sector, and civil society."[57] Some of these areas for change can be addressed quickly, while others require longer periods of time.

According to TI, reform efforts need to be both serious and concerted in order to be effective. TI has identified eight characteristics of successful corruption reform initiatives:

1. A clear commitment by political leaders to combat corruption wherever it occurs and to submit themselves to scrutiny.
2. Primary emphasis on prevention of future corruption and on changing systems (rather than indulging in witch hunts).
3. The adoption of comprehensive anticorruption legislation implemented by agencies of manifest integrity (including investigators, prosecutors, and adjudicators).
4. The identification of those government activities most prone to corruption and a review of both substantive law and administrative procedures.
5. A program to ensure that salaries of civil servants and political leaders adequately reflect the responsibilities of their posts and are as comparable as possible with those in the private sector.
6. A study of legal and administrative remedies to be sure that they provide adequate deterrence.
7. The creation of a partnership between government and civil society (including the private sector, professions, religious organizations).
8. Making corruption a "high-risk" and "low-profit" undertaking.

According to TI, five areas of reform are particularly helpful in reducing corrupt governmental practices: public programs, government reorganization, law enforcement, public awareness, and the creation of institutions to prevent corruption. Each country's situation must be analyzed to determine what specifically can be done, in part because action in any one of these areas will have ripple effects to the others, that is, they are part of a whole system where change needs to be leveraged to have the greatest effect.

TI also annually produces a Corruption Perceptions Index that ranks countries on a scale from 10 (highly clean) to 0 (highly corrupt). To create the index, TI consolidates the results of 16 different surveys, requiring a minimum of three surveys for each country included, so as to assure validity of the results.

Bribery Is Now Outlawed Globally

To cope with corruption globally requires enforceable and consistent laws on an international scale. There are positive signs that corruption is increasingly becoming less well accepted globally. For example, not only has TI made tremendous inroads into dealing openly with corrupt systems, but also in 1998 some 34 nations signed a new international treaty designed to outlaw bribery on a global scale.[58] Of these, 29 nations are members of the OECD; that is, they are among the largest economies in the world. Prior to this treaty, only the U.S. government had outlawed bribery, through the Foreign Corrupt Practices Act, which business leaders sometimes felt put their companies at a competitive disadvantage. With passage of this treaty, bribery became a criminal act in virtually every important economy in the world.

TI points out that company directors and leaders need to understand and accept their responsibility for staying within both the letter and the spirit of the law in countries where they operate. Voluntary codes of conduct, accompanied by internal enforcement procedures, can help companies sustain their integrity in the face of potential lost business when a bribe is not paid. And, as TI points out, "grand corruption is the enemy of high standards and efficiency,"[59] and thus goes against business's core value of economizing in the long run.

Accountability: Public Policy Mandate

Although responsibility management and assurance represent improvements in leading corporate citizenship, they are in many respects incomplete without a system of accountability. The principles described in this chapter and the initiatives are still voluntary and have been adopted by but a small fraction of the estimated 70,000 transnational corporations in the world, and probably by an even smaller proportion of the many millions of small and medium-sized enterprises. Indeed, it appears that the largest, most visible brand-name companies are the ones adopting these standards of performance, while business-to-business companies and those without a certain degree of visibility go largely under the radar screen of accountability.

In the current U.S. legal system and increasingly those in other parts of the world, corporations are accountable only to their shareholders and only for profit maximization, without regard to the impacts that they might have on other stakeholders. While numerous U.S. states now permit companies to take other stakeholders' interest into consideration, the main thrust of current law is to embed a narrow shareholder orientation into corporate goals. Indeed, one legal expert and outspoken critic argues that corporate executives cannot legitimately pursue goals other than financial wealth. Further, he suggests that companies addressing any social goals at all, or even reducing profits to implement costly responsibility measures, is effectively illegitimate behavior.[60]

There is increasing recognition among critical observers of corporations that voluntary responsibility management approaches may not be enough to curb corporate power or forestall future abuses. Corporate critics argue for some significant countervailing power to the increasingly global power commanded by corporations.[61] This power could come from political nation-states or from the types of civil society and NGO interests expressed at protests against organizations like the World Trade Organization around the world during the late 1990s and early 2000s. It could involve political action by citizens to dismantle some of the privileges that have allowed corporations to gain the power they currently have.

Emerging Regulations and Laws

Despite the seemingly entrenched power of corporations and the unwillingness of many to pursue corporate citizenship in good faith, there are signs emerging in the early 2000s that accountability will be enforced through an array of new laws and regulations (see Table 9.3). In the wake of the many scandals, accounting irregularities, and evidence of financial misdealings and executive greed in the United States, the Sarbanes-Oxley Act

TABLE 9.3   Social Disclosure Regulations in Existence as of 2004

Sources: European regulations are listed in the Reputation Institute's *In-Sights*, January–February 2004; information Japan is from Masahiko Kawamura, "Japanese Companies Launch New Era of CSR Management in 2003," Social Development Research Group, www.nli-research.co.jp/eng/resea/life/li030806.pdf (accessed April 22, 2004); and www.calpers.com/index.jsp?bc=/investments/riskman-agesystem.xml (accessed April 21, 2004).

Europe	
United Kingdom	Socially Responsible Investment Regulation (2000) requires pension fund managers to disclose their policies on socially responsible investment, including shareholder activism.
Belgium	Social Label Law (2003) requires annual reporting indicating how CSR is assessed in pension funds.
France	Annual reports require social and environmental impact assessment of company activities (2001) if listed on the French stock exchange. Retirement funds should rely on financial and social criteria in investment selection.
Germany	Companies need to indicate how social and environmental policies are being integrated (2001), and companies must declare whether codes are being followed or not.
The Netherlands	Mandatory compliance with OECD guidelines for multinationals to obtain export credits (2002).
Norway	All enterprises need to include environmental reports in yearly balances (1999).
Sweden	All enterprises need to include environmental reports in yearly balances (1999).
European Commission	In a communication to the Parliament required that corporate. social responsibility criteria be introduced in legislation of member states.
Other Nations	
Japan	As of 2003, audits of listed companies are required to disclose material information on risk related to corporate viability, including financial and business risks, but extending to reputation and "conspicuous deterioration of brand image."
Australia	As of 2003, a law passed in 2002 requires all investment firms to disclose how they take socially responsible investment into account.
United States	
Sarbanes-Oxley Act (2002)	Establishes independence of audit committees on corporate boards, corporate responsibility for financial reports (CEOs and CFOs are required to certify the appropriateness of financial statements and disclosures), makes it unlawful for officers and directors to fraudulently influence, coerce, manipulate, or mislead auditors, forces repayment or forfeiture of bonuses and profits in the case of accounting restatements, allows the SEC to bar people who have violated SEC regulations from holding officer and director positions, prohibits insider trades during pension fund blackout periods, establishes rules of professional responsibility for attorneys, and authorizes the SEC to establish funds for the relief of victims.
Voluntary Pressure Tactics	CalPERS recently stated: "CalPERS has embarked on a large-scale project to develop and deploy a comprehensive framework for measuring, monitoring, and managing risk . . . Over the next several years, risk management will become a driving force in the decision-making process used for our portfolio management." A coalition of SRI firms, including Calvert, Citizens Funds, Domini Social Investments, Green Century, Capital Management, Parnassus, Trillium, and Walden Asset Management submitted a letter to the SEC in 2002 seeking disclosure of financially significant environmental risk.

establishes at least some baseline requirements for boards of directors, chief corporate officers, and those who serve them.

Other interesting nonregulatory developments that will force corporate attention to social and environmental matters, in addition to financial ones, include the California Public Employees Retirement System's emphasis on good corporate governance and more recent attention to measuring, monitoring, and managing risk, including the types of risk that come with environmental and social problems. Further, a coalition of socially responsible investment (SRI) firms petitioned the U.S. Securities and Exchange Commission (SEC) in 2002 to require that companies disclose financially significant environmental risk. While not mandated into law at this point, such moves put new pressures on companies for transparency about their impacts and seek to hold them accountable.

Around the world, more proactive governments are beginning to establish new expectations of corporations and fund managers regarding triple-bottom-line issues. In the United Kingdom, for example, the 2000 Socially Responsible Investment Regulation requires pension fund managers to disclose policies on SRI, including shareholder activism. While pension fund managers do not actually have to *do* anything differently—or even take triple-bottom-line issues into account—the regulation creates significant peer pressure on pension fund managers to think about such matters and, by implication, companies as well. In 2001 France became the first nation in the world to require social and environmental impact assessment in corporate reports for all companies listed on the French stock exchange. In the wake of this law, French retirement funds need to rely on both financial and social criteria in making investment decisions. While implementation is not yet fully achieved, some progress is being made.

Germany, since 2001, has required companies to indicate how social and environmental policies are being integrated, and to declare whether or not codes of conduct are being followed. The Netherlands has required mandatory compliance with the OECD's Guidelines for Multinational Enterprises if companies are to obtain export credits since 2002. Sweden and Norway have required environmental reports since 1999. The European Commission has signaled its support of corporate responsibility and SRI generally through a white paper issued in 2002 and has communicated to the European Union's Parliament that corporate social responsibility criteria be introduced in legislation of member states.

As of 2003, audits of listed companies in Japan are required to disclose material information on risk related to corporate viability. Included risks go beyond financial and business risks to encompass reputational and brand-image-related risks. Finally, as of this writing at least, since 2003, Australia requires investment firms to disclose how they take SRI into account.

Such laws are only the very early steps of a framework capable of holding companies and investment managers accountable for social and ecological performance as well as financial performance. They do, however, signal a future that could conceivably be different than the present with respect to the art of corporate citizenship. In some ways, regulations like these play an important role in leveling the playing field for all companies, by establishing the same—and presumably fair—rules of the game to which all must adhere, rather than allowing some companies to forgo disclosure or operate without consideration for long-term social and ecological impacts. Accountability, responsibility, and transparency are the fundamental demands that companies are facing today to sustain their legitimacy in society—or maintain their so-called license to operate.

Leading Challenge Ahead: Responsibility Assurance

This chapter has identified a set of foundational principles for the issues of labor, human rights, system integrity, and environmental practices, based on what is contained in globally agreed-on (mostly UN-based) documents and the new regulations that are beginning to evolve around corporate accountability. These initiatives promulgate basic standards that *ought* to be followed by brands, retailers, and their suppliers around the globe. Of course, as evidenced by a continuing stream of exposés put forward by the BBC, the *New*

York Times, Sixty Minutes, and a host of other outlets, frequently such standards are not met. After years of hard-won progress in the major industrialized countries on the range of issues covered by these foundation principles, the globalization of production and the disaggregation of supply chains appears to have brought us back full circle to some of the more egregious business practices of the past, including sweatshops, abusive working standards, and growing ecological deterioration.

Given this unsatisfactory state, it is not surprising to find a wide variety of initiatives emerging to better regulate companies, ensure compliance with standards, and establish some system of accountability and comparability. To avoid external regulation, many companies are engaged in the types of voluntary initiatives to monitor their own practices through codes of conduct or by joining initiatives that attest to their adherence to foundation principles.

Combined with internal responsibility management systems, these initiatives constitute the beginnings of a responsibility assurance system. We can see the outlines of a voluntary global system that establishes standards and enforces standards beginning to emerge, in part the result of civil society and NGO anticorporate activism, but at this point the system is still voluntary and many critics of globalization and of the power of the modern transnational firm believe that voluntary standards will need to be complemented by mandate. For example, the Global Compact, Global Reporting Initiative (GRI), SA 8000, and AA 1000 contain three core elements of responsibility assurance: standards of conduct or the foundational principles discussed above (e.g., the Global Compact), monitoring, verification, and certification processes to ensure that what companies say they are doing is what they are actually doing (e.g., AA 1000 and SA 8000), and reporting guidelines for reasonably standardized external communication of what is being done that is relatively comparable across companies and nations (e.g., GRI). Elements of the emerging responsibility system are:

- *Generally accepted foundation principles, values, and guidelines* that provide minimal standards that all companies are expected to meet with respect to core stakeholders and the natural environment.

- *Globally recognized systemic approaches to responsibility management* that can be applied uniquely to each company but provide for comparable levels of responsibility and stakeholder-related outcomes.

- *Globally accepted multiple-bottom-line audit and reporting guidelines* and principles that detail the content, scope, and credibility of what is reported, comparable to generally accepted accounting principles (GAAP).

- *Credible external verification, monitoring, and certification systems* built around overall responsibility management practices or related to specific issues (e.g., child labor, sweatshop working conditions, labor rights, living wage, environment, corruption).

Such voluntary initiatives may never satisfy corporate critics, particularly in light of the reality that, for example, of the nearly 70,000 transnational corporations, only about 1,500 had signed the Global Compact by late 2004, whose reach hardly extends to the millions of small and medium-sized enterprises in the world today. Peer pressure from companies within the same industry does have the capacity to shift corporate attention to the reporting of social and ecological as well as economic/financial performance—and what gets measured is what mangers tend to pay attention to.

Here we can make an analogy to the quality movement. Quality became a business imperative during the 1980s in part because of customer demands for better quality, in part because the Japanese had already set a high standard of quality that forced others to focus on quality, and in part because European Union companies began requiring that suppliers meet ISO quality standards.[62] Perhaps it will take a similar sequence of events around corporate responsibility, underlying corporate responsibility for all companies, branded or not, to begin taking foundation principles seriously. For instance, what might be the impact of current European Union companies requiring their suppliers to meet SA 8000 labor standards, to join the Global Compact, and to uphold the principles, reporting out using GRI standards?

Alternatively, what if several major transnational corporations that have long or extensive supply chains (e.g., Wal-Mart) or employ people on a global basis (e.g., McDonald's) determined that they and all of their suppliers had to be certified as meeting foundational standards? The chain reaction of such a move would create a cascade effect, as in the quality movement, that would make the meeting of foundation principles a way of doing business. Resultant attention from the general public, the press, and competitors could conceivably create an entirely new context in which foundation principles are met as part of the company's basic license to operate—its fundamental social contract.

The world today is far from either voluntary or mandated assurance that foundation principles—basic human and labor rights, ecological principles, or the transparency that provides trust in the integrity of the system—are in fact being implemented. Yet forces are pushing companies to make corporate citizenship real, not just rhetoric. Only time, competitive conditions, political will, and underlying social movements will determine whether the ultimate outcome is in the best interests of humanity—meeting the basic needs of people for respect and dignity, of human civilization for a sustainable global ecology, of democracy for systemic integrity.

For leaders of corporate citizens, the emergence of standards, and continued demands for transparency and accountability pose significant new challenges— and new ways of doing business in the global context. Standards around labor practices, human rights, the use of environmental resources, and government regulations have gained great public awareness over the past two decades. This attention to making corporations accountable for their impacts is unlikely to diminish in an age where members of civil society who care about the ways in which people are treated and about the health of the natural environment are now globally connected. Corporations, it is likely, will be held accountable for their actions and held to very high standards indeed if they hope to continue their global march.

For leading corporate citizens, the message is clear. Being out in front of the wave of potential global regulation is one way to achieve competitive advantage. Companies that attempt to hide behind veils of secrecy will only become subject to activism, protests, and negative publicity that damage their reputations and their credibility. Leaders of corporate citizens who recognize the significant advantages to be gained in being forthcoming with and respectful of external stakeholders by adhering to high standards will truly put their companies into the lead. We all depend on a healthy ecological system for our very breath and sustenance. The economic system needs to be free, but it also needs to operate within the rules that societies establish in order to balance the interests of consumption and materialism with other values in society. The political sphere needs to operate with integrity, free of corruption and abuse if people are to live freely themselves and if democratic values are truly to spread throughout the world, as many people believe desirable. And enterprises in civil society need to be active participants in the economic and political systems, carrying a strong voice for the socializing effects of relationships, meaning, and values that bring civility to the world.

The principles and standards discussed in this chapter, and others that had to be omitted in the interests of time and space, are among the most important features of the modern economic and societal systems in which we live. We all need to learn to operate with integrity, individually and organizationally, and these standards provide a positive and proactive set of guideposts to help us along the way.

Endnotes

1. Portions of this chapter are drawn from two of my papers. The discussion on principles, and some of the conclusions, are from Sandra Waddock, "Creating Corporate Accountability: Foundational Principles to Make Corporate Citizenship Real," *Journal of Business Ethics* 50 (2004), pp. 313–27. The discussion on emerging regulations is drawn from Sandra Waddock, "Unfolding Corporate Citizenship: New Demands for a New Era," in *Corporate Social Responsibility*, ed. José Allouce (New York: Palgrave-McMillan, in press).

2. See, for example, Naomi Klein *No Logo: No Space, No Choice, No Jobs* (New York: Picador, 2000); or Eric Schlosser, *Fast Food Nation: The Dark Side of the All-American Meal* (Boston: Houghton Mifflin, 2001).

3. See, www.investorhome.com/sri.htm (accessed July 6, 2004). This screen is notably broad, including shareholder resolutions as well as direct investments in screened companies and mutual funds.

4. See, for example, Pietra Rivoli, "Labor Standards in the Global Economy: Issues for Investors," *Journal of Business Ethics* 43, no. 30 (March 2003), pp. 223–32; see also Samuel B. Graves, Kathleen Rehbein, and Sandra Waddock, "Fad and Fashion in Shareholder Activism: The Landscape of Social Policy Resolutions, 1988–1998," *Business and Society Review* 106, no. 4 (Winter 2001), pp. 293–314.

5. See Rivoli, "Labor Standards in the Global Economy."

6. See ILO, "Business and Social Initiatives," http://oracle02.ilo.org:6060/vpi/VpiSearch.First?p_lang=en.

7. See, for example, D. O'Rourke, "Monitoring the Monitors: A Critique of PricewaterhouseCooper's Labor Monitoring," white paper, released September 28, 2000; and Stephen J. Frenkel, "Globalization, Athletic Footwear Commodity Chains and Employment Relations in China," *Organization Studies* 22, no. 4 (2001), pp. 531–62.

8. Thomas Donaldson and Thomas W. Dunfee, "Toward a Unified Conception of Social Contracts Theory," *Academy of Management* 19, no. 2 (1994), pp. 252–84; and Thomas Donaldson and Thomas W. Dunfee, *Ties That Bind: A Social Contracts Approach to Business Ethics* (Boston: Harvard Business School Press, 1999), p. 265. See also, Thomas Donaldson, "Values in Tension: Ethics Away from Home," *Harvard Business Review*, September–October 1996, Reprint # 96402, pp. 1–12.

9. M. S. Schwartz, "A Code of Ethics for Corporate Codes of Ethics," *Journal of Business Ethics* 41, no. 1/2 (November–December 2002), pp. 27–42.

10. J. N. Behrman, "Adequacy of International Codes of Behavior," *Journal of Business Ethics* 31, no. 1 (May 2001), pp. 51–63.

11. Donaldson and Dunfee, *Ties That Bind*.

12. Donaldson, "Values in Tension," p. 6.

13. James McGregor Burns, *Leadership* (New York: Harper Torchbooks, 1978).

14. Donaldson, "Values in Tension," pp. 7–8.

15. UNWire, "Globalization: NGOs Assail UN Ties to Corporate-Led Trend," September 7, 2000, www.unfoundation.org/unwirebw/archives/show_article.cfm?article=1173 (accessed July 6, 2004).

16. Laura P. Hartman, Bill Shaw, and Rodney Stevenson, "Exploring the Ethics and Economics of Global Labor Standards: A Challenge to Integrated Social Contract Theory," *Business Ethics Quarterly* 13, no. 2 (April 2003), pp. 193–225.

17. Donaldson and Dunfee, *Ties That Bind*.

18. Hartman, Shaw, and Stevenson, "Exploring the Ethics and Economics of Global Labor Standards."

19. Ibid.

20. Transparency International Web site, www.transparency.org/welcome.html.

21. Ibid.

22. UN Global Compact Web site, www.unglobalcompact.org/Portal/?NavigationTarget=/roles/portal_user/dialogue/Dialogue/nf/nf/transparency (accessed July 2, 2004).

23. Donaldson and Dunfee, *Ties That Bind*, p. 68.

24. James Lovelock, *Gaia: A New Look at Life on Earth* (New York: Oxford University Press, 2000).

25. UN Global Compact Web site, www.unglobalcompact.org/Portal/?NavigationTarget=/roles/portal_user/aboutTheGC/nf/nf/theNinePrinciples (accessed July 2, 2004).

26. The full text of Agenda 21 can be found at www.unep.org/Documents/Default.asp?DocumentID=52unep/neworg.htm (accessed July 6, 2004).

27. The Rio Declaration can be found at www.unep.org/unep/rio.htm (accessed July 6, 2004).

28. From Agenda 21, gopher://unephq.unep.org:70/00/un/unced/agenda21/a21c02.txt.

29. Additional information about CERES and the CERES Principles can be found at www.ceres.org (accessed July 6, 2004).

30. World Business Council for Sustainable Development Web site, www.wbcsd.ch/templates/TemplateWBCSD1/layout.asp?type=p&Menuld=NjA&doOpen=1&ClickMenu=LeftMenu (accessed July 2, 2004).

31. Ibid.

32. Information and the complete set of principles for Responsible Care can be found at www.dowethics.com/r/environment/care_info.html (accessed July 6, 2004).

33. For an extended discussion of ISO 14000 and 14001, see Amy Pesapane Lally, "ISO 14000 and Environmental Cost Accounting: The Gateway to the Global Market," *Law & Policy in International Business* 29, no. 4 (Summer 1998), pp. 401–538.

34. Additional information on ISO and the various sets of standards can be found at www.iso.ch.

35. Information about the ISO 14000 family of standards can be found at www.iso.ch/iso/en/prods-services/otherpubs/iso14000/index.html (accessed June 15, 2004).

36. Amory B. Lovins, L. Hunter Lovins, and Paul Hawken, "A Road Map for Natural Capitalism," *Harvard Business Review*, May–June 1999, pp. 145–58.

37. Ibid., pp.146–48.

38. Ibid., p.148.

39. Peter M. Senge, *The Fifth Discipline* (New York: Free Press, 1990).

40. See www.kodak.com/US/en/corp/environment/1998/kodakPark/savingsRecycling.shtml.

41. Lovins et al., "A Road Map for Natural Capitalism," p. 152.

42. See, for example, Aaron Bernstein, "Sweatshop Reform: How to Solve the Standoff," *Business Week*, May 3, 1999, pp. 186–90.

43. See www.sweatshopwatch.org/swatch/about (accessed July 6, 2004).

44. See www.corpwatch.org/trac/greenwash/sweatwash.html (accessed July 6, 2004).

45. From www.sweatshopwatch.org/swatch/industry (accessed July 6, 2004).

46. Ibid.

47. From Sweatshop Watch Web site, www.sweatshopwatch.org/swatch/newsletter/4_2. html#living_wage (accessed July 6, 2004).

48. International Organization for Standardization (ISO) Web site, www.iso.org/iso/en/commcentre/pressreleases/2004/Ref924. html (accessed July 12, 2004).

49. For more information, see the OECD Web site, www.oecd.org (accessed July 2, 2004).

50. OECD Guidelines, "Report by the Chair, 2003." www.oecd.org/dataoecd/3/47/15941397.pdf (accessed July 2, 2004).

51. Details about the Caux Round Table and this framing of the two ethical ideals can be found at www.cauxroundtable.org/default.htm.

52. The Caux Roundtable principles can be found at http://astro.temple.edu/~dialogue/Codes/caux./htm (accessed July 2, 2004).

53. Information on the Equator Principles can be found at www.equator-principles.com (accessed July 2, 2004).

54. Quoted in ibid.

55. Jeremy Pope, *TI Source Book 2000: Confronting Corruption: The Elements of a National Integrity System*, www.transparency.org/source-book/index.html (accessed July 6, 2004).

56. Transparency International Web site, www.transparency.com

57. Pope, *TI Source Book*, Executive Summary, p. 2.

58. Information in this paragraph is from Skip Kaltenheuser, "Bribery Is Being Outlawed Virtually Worldwide," *Business Ethics*, May–June 1998, p. 11.

59. Pope, *TI Source Book*, Part B, p. 3.

60. Joel Bakan, *The Corporation: The Pathological Pursuit of Profit and Power* (New York: Free Press, 2004).

61. Ibid. See also John Cavanagh and colleagues, *Alternatives to Economic Globalization* (San Francisco: Berrett-Koehler, 2002); Charles Derber, *Regime Change Begins at Home: Freeing America From Corporate Rule* (San Francisco: Berrett-Koehler, 2004).

62. J. R. Evans and W. M. Lindsay, *The Management and Control of Quality*, 4th ed. (New York: West, 1999).

Values Added: Global Futures

Mister! He said with a sawdusty sneeze,
I am the Lorax. I speak for the trees.
I speak for the trees, for the trees have no tongues.
And I'm asking you, sir, at the top of my lungs—
He was very upset as he shouted and puffed—
What's that THING you've made out of my Truffula tuft?

. . . So I quickly invented my Super-Axe-Hacker
which whacked off four Truffula Trees at one smacker.
We were making Thneeds
four times as fast as before!
And that Lorax? . . . He didn't show up any more.

But the very next week
he knocked
on my new office door.
He snapped. I'm the Lorax who speaks for the trees
which you seem to be chopping as fast as you please . . .

I meant no harm. I most truly did not. But I had to grow bigger. So big-
    ger I got.
I biggered my factory. I biggered my roads.
I biggered my wagons. I biggered the loads
of the Thneeds I shipped out. I was shipping them forth
to the South! To the East! To the West! To the North!
I went right on biggering . . . selling more Thneeds
And I biggered my money, which everyone needs . . .

I yelled at the Lorax, Now listen here, Dad!
All you do is yap-yap and say, Bad! Bad! Bad! Bad!
Well, I have my rights, sir, and I'm telling *you*

I intend to go on doing just what I do!
And, for your information, you Lorax, I'm figgering
on biggering
and biggering
and BIGGERING
and BIGGERING,
turning MORE Truffula Trees into Thneeds
which everyone, EVERYONE, *EVERYONE* needs!

And at that very moment, we heard a loud whack!
From outside in the fields came a sickening smack
of an axe on a tree. Then we heard the tree fall.
The very last Truffula Tree of them all!
No more trees. No more Thneeds. No more work to be done.

Dr. Seuss, The Lorax[1]

Scanning the Future: Finding Pattern in Chaos

Leading corporate citizens know that they need to think through the consequences of their decisions and actions carefully, lest we end up with "No more trees . . . No more work to be done." They also need to understand very clearly the forces at play not only in the competitive/economic sphere but also in the political and civil society spheres. Corporate leaders are learning that they need to operate in sustainable ways with respect to the natural environment because of the limitations of the ecological system in supporting life as we know it on earth. To further this learning, we need to enhance awareness of what is likely to happen in the future.

We cannot predict the future, but we can understand patterns and potentials. Like many of the dynamics and relationships we have explored in this book, future trends are embedded in chaotic processes, the immediate outcomes of which cannot be known. Chaos and complexity theories tell us that *we can seek patterns that provide significant insights*. These patterns become evident when we look carefully at dynamics and think creatively about what is happening now, what might happen, and what the implications are.

Using all of our leadership insights and our expanded awareness so that we can hold multiple perspectives (remember the higher stages of development), we can explore what might initially seem to be a chaos of information, trends, and interrelationships. The future actually exhibits large-scale patterns that can help us think through appropriate actions that provide significant expertise in coping with a changing world. To do this effectively, we need to know how to study the future, what data to look at, and how to think more creatively about possibilities.

To do futures pattern seeking, leading corporate citizens carefully monitor the shifting dynamics and concerns of their multiple stakeholders, as well as the broader (and, importantly, more subtle) technological, competitive, and social shifts that take place throughout the various societies in which they operate. They do this monitoring not only because these forces and dynamics may pose problems but also because they represent interesting and potentially profitable new opportunities for business development. If one company overlooks opportunities or challenges, other companies that pay closer attention can gain competitive advantage.

Once a company uncovers current trends, data, and patterns, it can use a range of techniques to project these patterns out into the future and think about their potential implications for the enterprise. One such technique, called scenario analysis, has been used success-fully by Royal Dutch/Shell, among other prominent companies. Scenario analysis was particularly helpful to Shell in preparing for falling oil prices (which some observers had considered unrealistic) in the 1980s. Other techniques are future search conferences and open space meetings; we will explore these at the end of the chapter.

For any corporate citizen, having a futures monitoring role is a critical element of the boundary-spanning functions. The company can use information gathered within functions to develop future scenarios to help prepare for any of multiple possible out-comes. It is important that leaders of corporate citizens heed the advice of baseball great Yogi Berra, who once said, "If you don't know where you're going, you wind up somewhere else."[2]

This chapter will explore some of the current dynamics and trends that will shape the future. It will provide a basic framework for thinking about the ways in which leading cor-porate citizens can cope with the inevitable patterns of change and complexity they will face in creating and sustaining positive relationships with their stakeholders. The values are added, as the chapter title suggests, because we need to think not only about sustain-ability but also about what is meaningful to people, to stakeholders, and ultimately to our-selves as citizens of organizations, of particular societies, and of the world.

The Shape of the Future

What is it that shapes our future? Although we as human beings have little control over nature, we do in many senses control our own destiny. We make decisions that impact our future on a daily basis, whether in our leadership capacities or within the companies we manage. For example, to the extent that we take stewardship responsibility for our own impacts on the ecological environment, nature will reward us bountifully. To the extent that we provide for appropriate balance among the three spheres of activity in human civ-ilization, not only with respect to the natural environment but also with respect to each other, societies will be productive and meaningful places in which to live, work, and play. And it is developing meaningful relationships within society and respecting all stake-holders that are keys to long-term effectiveness (and efficiency, or economizing) of lead-ing corporate citizens.

The world of tomorrow will continue to change rapidly, even chaotically. But, as we have learned from thinking about life processes organically and applying that thinking to our ideas of management, even chaotic systems have patterns that are, to a large extent, comprehensible and understandable. Understanding patterns and developing new ways of thinking about the implications of even potential patterns can help raise awareness of the implications of corporate decisions on stakeholders and nature. Ultimately, it can also help us lead better lives as individuals in society and as corpo-rate citizens.

Clearly, understanding future patterns demands relatively high levels of cognitive, emotional, and moral development. As developmental psychologist Robert Kegan puts it, without this development, we will really be *In Over Our Heads*[3] amid the "mental demands of modern life." Tomorrow's leaders will need to work productively to develop a sense of what is meaningful to others and to think through the systems implications of their decisions to move themselves toward understanding the future. Such systems thinking—built as it is on understanding where the points of leverage are and what the interactions among different variables, issues, and relationships mean—also requires shifting perspectives to encompass data that might ordinarily be ignored or overlooked. Small shifts, as chaotic systems illustrate, can result in large changes down the road. As leaders of corporate citizens, we need to be intensely aware not only of the larger pat-terns of society but also of the small shifts that can provide meaningful opportunities—or challenges—in the future.

This chapter presents some current data on the state of the world, then looks at some of the predictions that futurists—people who study the future—are making that are likely to affect leaders and leading corporate citizens. Let us begin this exploration with some information about the current state of the world's social, political, economic, and ecological spheres. Then we will look at predictions of challenges and opportunities made by futurists that will inevitably (even if we don't know exactly how) shape global futures.

The State of the World

The United Nations Development Program (UNDP) established a set of Millennium Goals in 2000 that it hoped to achieve by 2015. (Table 10.1 lists the goals and summarizes progress made toward them as of 2004.) These goals deal with the world's major problems of poverty, lack of education, and inequity. Businesses have important roles to play in achieving these goals.

TABLE 10.1   The UNDP's Millennium Goals and Progress Made toward Them

Source: UNDP Web site, www.undp.org/mdg/abcs.html#Indicators (accessed July 7, 2004).

1. Eradicate Extreme Poverty and Hunger

Target for 2015: Halve the proportion of people living on less than a dollar a day and those who suffer from hunger.

More than a billion people still live on less than a dollar a day; sub-Saharan Africa, Latin America and the Caribbean, and parts of Europe and Central Asia are falling short of the poverty target.

2. Achieve Universal Primary Education

Target for 2015: Ensure that all boys and girls complete primary school.

As many as 113 million children worldwide do not attend school, but the target is within reach. India, for example, should have 95 percent of its children in school by 2005.

3. Promote Gender Equality and Empower Women

Targets for 2005 and 2015: Eliminate gender disparities in primary and secondary education preferably by 2005, and at all levels by 2015.

Two-thirds of illiterates are women, and the rate of employment among women is two-thirds that of men. The proportion of seats in parliaments held by women is increasing, reaching about one-third in Argentina, Mozambique, and South Africa.

4. Reduce Child Mortality

Target for 2015: Reduce by two-thirds the mortality rate among children under five.

Every year nearly 11 million young children die before their fifth birthday, mainly from preventable illnesses, but that number is down from 15 million in 1980.

5. Improve Maternal Health

Target for 2015: Reduce by three-quarters the ratio of women dying in childbirth.

In the developing world, the risk of dying in childbirth is 1 in 48, but virtually all countries now have safe motherhood programs.

6. Combat HIV/AIDS, Malaria and Other Diseases

Target for 2015: Halt and begin to reverse the spread of HIV/AIDS and the incidence of malaria and other major diseases.

Forty million people are living with HIV, including 5 million newly infected in 2001. Countries like Brazil, Senegal, Thailand, and Uganda have shown that the spread of HIV can be stemmed.

7. Ensure Environmental Sustainability

Targets:

- *Integrate the principles of sustainable development into country policies and programs and reverse the loss of environmental resources.*
- *By 2015, reduce by half the proportion of people without access to safe drinking water.*
- *By 2020 achieve significant improvement in the lives of at least 100 million slum dwellers.*

More than 1 billion people lack access to safe drinking water, and more than 2 billion lack sanitation. During the 1990s, however, nearly 1 billion people gained access to safe water and the same number to sanitation.

continued

concluded

8. Develop a Global Partnership for Development

Targets:

- *Develop further an open trading and financial system that includes a commitment to good governance, development and poverty reduction—nationally and internationally.*
- *Address the least developed countries' special needs, and the special needs of landlocked and small island developing states.*
- *Deal comprehensively with developing countries' debt problems.*
- *Develop decent and productive work for youth.*
- *In cooperation with pharmaceutical companies, provide access to affordable essential drugs in developing countries.*
- *In cooperation with the private sector, make available the benefits of new technologies—especially information and communications technologies.*

Indicators

Many developing countries spend more on debt service than on social services. New aid commitments made in the first half of 2002 could mean an additional $12 billion per year by 2006.

UNDP, in collaboration with national governments, is coordinating reporting by countries on progress toward the UN Millennium Development Goals. The framework for reporting includes eight goals—based on the UN Millennium Declaration. For each goal there is one or more specific target, along with specific social, economic, and environmental indicators used to track progress toward the goals.

The eight goals represent a partnership between the developed countries and the developing countries determined, as the Millennium Declaration states, "to create an environment—at the national and global levels alike—which is conducive to development and the elimination of poverty."

Support for reporting at the country level includes close consultation by UNDP with partners in the UN Development Group, other UN partners, the World Bank, IMF and OECD and regional groupings and experts, The UN Department of Economic and Social Affairs is coordinating reporting on progress toward the goals at the global level.

Monitoring progress is easier for some targets than for others and good quality data for some indicators are not yet available for many countries. This underscores the need to assist countries in building national capacity in compiling vital data.

Huge social problems exist in the world beyond the ecological problems. For example, although there are reports that the AIDS epidemic may be slowing down, the U.S. National Institute of Allergy and Infectious Diseases reported in January 2004 that some 40 million people globally—37 million adults and 2.5 million children—were living with HIV/AIDS. Nearly two-thirds of these people live in sub-Saharan Africa, and another 18 percent are in Asia and the Pacific. These numbers translate to a global epidemic affecting about 11 of every 1,000 adults, with as much as 8 percent of the population in sub-Saharan Africa affected.[4] Further, the UNDP reports that 28 million people had already died of HIV/AIDS by 2001 and that without a massive intervention as many as 100 million people were expected to be affected; seven countries already have more than 20 percent of their populations affected, and two countries, Botswana and Zimbabwe, have rates as high as 39 percent and 34 percent, respectively.[5]

Other problems are highlighted by the following statistics. For example, although the percentage of people in the world living on less than a dollar a day dropped from 40 percent to 21 percent between 1981 and 2001, progress is unevenly distributed, with countries in Asia and Southeast Asia benefiting the most from economic development, and countries in Africa, Latin America, Eastern Europe, and Central America the least.[6] A group called World Centric has gathered some startling statistics that are included in Table 10.2. The challenge for leading corporate citizens is to find ways of doing business in a world that increasingly demands attention to issues of not only ecology but

TABLE 10.2   Some Facts about Our World

Source: World Centric, www.worldcentric.org/state/#rich (accessed July 7, 2004).

Rich and Poor World

- The amount of money that the richest 1 percent of the world's people make each year equals what the poorest 57 percent make.
- The world's 358 billionaires have assets exceeding the combined annual incomes of countries with 45 percent of the world's people.
- The richest 5 percent of the world's people have incomes 114 times that of the poorest 5 percent.
- The combined wealth of the world's 200 richest people hit $1 trillion in 1999; the combined incomes of the 582 million people living in the 43 least developed countries is $146 billion.
- The GDP (Gross Domestic Product) of the poorest 48 nations (i.e., a quarter of the world's countries) is less than the wealth of the world's three richest people combined.
- A few hundred millionaires now own as much wealth as the world's poorest 2.5 billion people.
- An analysis of long-term trends shows the distance between the richest and poorest countries was about: 5 to 1 in 1820; 11 to 1 in 1913; 35 to 1 in 195-; 44 to 1 in 1973; 72 to 1 in 1992.

Consumption/Waste

- 20% of the population in the developed nations consume 86% of the world's goods.
- A mere 12% of the world's population uses 85% of its water, and these 12% do not live in the Third World.
- Globally, the 20% of the world's people in the highest-income countries account for 86% of total private consumption expenditures—the poorest 20% a minuscule 1.3%. More specifically, the richest fifth:
  1. Consume 45% of all meat and fish, the poorest fifth 5%.
  2. Consume 58% of total energy, the poorest fifth less than 4%.
  3. Have 74% of all telephone lines, the poorest fifth 1.5%.
  4. Consume 84% of all paper, the poorest fifth 1.1%.
  5. Own 87% of the world's vehicle fleet, the poorest fifth less than 1%.
- U.S. per capita consumption of paper is 681 pounds per year—7 trees a year.
- 91% of paper comes at the expense of 4 billion trees per year.
- The human race as a whole generates over 350 million metric tons of hazardous waste each year; the United States generates 180 million tons, or 4 pounds a day per person.
- 5 percent of the world's population lives in the U.S., but Americans produce 50 percent of the world's waste.
- Mobile phones will be discarded at a rate of 130 million per year by 2005, resulting in 65,000 tons of waste.
- 75% of all carbon dioxide emissions are caused by the industrialized world.
- The cost of providing basic health care and nutrition for all would be less than is spent in Europe and the U.S. on pet food.

also social sustainability—and to do so in a way that fosters social justice rather than injustice.

The statistics in Table 10.2 are startling enough, but evidence of the gap between the haves and the have-nots in the world continues to mount. This shift in the distribution of wealth brings significant implications for the potential growth and prosperity of nations as well as of companies. Thinking about the differences between wealthy and less wealthy nations and people suggests that there may be new business opportunities in serving less developed nations with ecologically sustainable products that still meet their needs, while attempting to close the growing gap between rich and poor.

We have already recognized that economic development cannot continue apace without consideration of what is ecologically and socially sustainable. Sustainability in this case also includes the sustainability of democratic institutions, free-market economies, and healthy local communities in the face of enormous inequities in the distribution and use of resources. The wide availability of information will create significant disturbances among peoples with less if some moves are not made to close the growing gap, sometimes called the digital divide. The gap exists between rich and poor in most if not all nations, as well as, generally speaking, between northern and southern countries or, alternatively, developed and developing nations.

New, more ecologically sensitive and responsible practices are needed to serve the needs of the billions of people in the world who now live in poverty. Businesses, obviously, have an essential role to play in developing the goods and services needed to close these gaps. What is true, however, is that facing up to these global realities means that some significant shifts in lifestyle and production processes may be needed, particularly for wealthier and more powerful citizens. For aware and innovative leading corporate citizens, significant opportunities may exist.

Global Trends, Issues and Opportunities

Certain significant trends, issues, and opportunities—some technological, some economic, others social and political—make understanding the complexities of global dynamics an imperative for those leading corporate citizens today. Some trends may also provide significant business opportunities for creative entrepreneurs. Futurists can help provide understanding by identifying significant shifts in the world around us. The next two sections of this chapter will briefly explore some of the major shifts likely to affect corporate citizens in the 21st century.

Trends

The Center for Strategic and International Studies (CSIS) in Washington, D.C., has developed a project called the Millennium Project, which has attempted to identify the major trends in the world today.[7] Michael J. Mazarr, author of a report titled *Global Trends 2005*, says of the current era:

> The basic transition . . . is from the industrial era of human society, around since the late 18th century, to a new age that goes by a variety of names—the information age, the postmodern era, and others. We call it the "knowledge era," because one way (though only one) of understanding it is as a time when the acquisition, diffusion, use, storage, and transmission of knowledge becomes the basic activity of human societies. This one fundamental shift will refashion all the institutions of our lives.

If Mazarr and the panel of experts that CSIS has put together are correct, leaders of corporate citizens have a lot to think about in figuring out how to responsibly manage their relationships in all spheres of human society and the environment. *Global Trends 2005* focuses on six major trends, which can be presented here only in simplified terms, hardly in all of their complexity. Citizens in all spheres of society, and particularly corporate citizens, clearly need to be aware of and know how to cope with these trends effectively if they hope to sustain competitive advantage—and, simultaneously, build collaborative relationships with stakeholders essential to productive engagement in their worlds.

Mazzar and the other futurists identify several foundations as part of the first trend: demography, natural resources, and the environment and culture.

Demography, Ecology, Culture

Although the world's population *growth rate* is slowing (see Case 10.1), population itself continues to grow and will do so until it levels off somewhere between 8 and 12 billion people globally. Trends of modernization, education, and expansion of women's rights reduce fertility and have tended to slow the rate of population growth. But because 95 percent of that growth will occur in less developed countries, the gap between rich and poor can be expected to widen and processes of urbanization, already under way, will likely continue.

Although sustainable development is gaining momentum, population growth and many current organizational practices will place significant strains on the natural environment. Although knowledge businesses are less dependent on the ecology than industrial busi-

If asked to make a list of the top 5 or 10 problems facing the world, most people educated in developed countries would include over-population. We have grown up with the threat of the population bomb, and with great hoopla and concern the global population crossed the 6 billion mark in the year 2000.

What if population growth were no longer a problem? Sometime within the next 10 years a global conference will convene on the question, "What are we to do about the declining population in the world?"

This still surprises most people, though we are beginning to wake up in the past year or so. What is actually happening? The rate of global population growth is slowing steadily. In the year 2000 it is expected that 78 million persons will be added to the global population, compared to 86 million at the peak of population growth a few years ago. More than 60 nations in the world, including Russia, Canada, Australia, Japan, all of Europe, and elsewhere have fertility rates which have fallen below the rate needed to maintain a steady state population. This rate is 2.1 children per woman. Only four nations in the world have seen their fertility rate increase since 1980—Denmark, Norway, Sweden, and Ethiopia—and among these only Ethiopia has a fertility rate greater than 2.1.

The United Nations has been revising its population forecasts downward, and while it still assumes nearly a century of growth and a peak near 9.5 billion, it seems more likely that further downward revisions are likely. In fact, the best bet is that the world population will peak by 2025, at something around 7.8 billion, and decline after that.

Don't believe this? Russia, Germany, and Japan have all officially raised alarms this year about declining population in their countries, and more countries will soon follow. Among the implications:

- The need to open immigration laws to allow for greater movement of the global work force.
- The likelihood of intense values-based political debate about whether to encourage larger families in developed nations, eventually in all nations.
- Whether advances in longevity will offset the decline in birth rates such that population growth will be sustained longer into the 21st century.
- A declining number of young people compared to a growing number of old people.
- How we will maintain a growing global economy if there are fewer customers each year (and debate whether we should grow).

DISCUSSION QUESTIONS

1. What are the business implications of global population decline?
2. Is holding the world's population steady a good or bad thing? Why?
3. How should leading corporate citizens begin to think about issues related to population?
4. Are there inherent business opportunities in this situation? What are some of them?

Source: © 2000 Glen Hiemstra, Futurist.com, www.futurist.com/portal/science/science_population_explosion.htm (accessed July 7, 2004).

nesses are, significant ecological problems can be expected with respect to agricultural yields, demand for crop lands, the intensity of modern farming methods, with resulting soil erosion, desertification, and overfarming, and a crisis in fisheries. Some 80 countries already face significant water shortages, and this problem is only likely to be exacerbated by continued population growth.

Culture and ideology are essential aspects of human life and one of the foundational elements of the Millennium Project's projections. As Mazarr points out, culture plays an essential role in determining a nation's economic prospects, as well as its international relationships.[8]

Science, Technology, Modernization

An important factor in the dynamics facing corporate citizens, according to the Millennium Project, has to do with the push supplied by science and technology, which in turn contribute to the process of modernization. Among the technological and scientific shifts that can be expected are processes of miniaturization, biogenetic engineering, and continued revolution in information and communications technology (including the information thereby made available). The gap between rich and poor will intensify the gap between the information/technology rich and poor as well, as access to technological advances becomes essential to taking a role in the modern world.

Mazarr observes, "Richer countries tend to look the same—freer, more individualistic and less hierarchical, more concerned with the environment."[9] Not only does this "looking alike" tend toward greater homogeneity, but it also places considerable pressures for constructive—toward democratic—reform on repressive regimes. And, Mazarr notes, this process may well result in more peace and less war!

Human Resources and Complexity

The third trend identified by the Millennium Project involves the move toward a knowledge-based economic system and the resulting expected increased attention to and value on human resources—employee stakeholders. Mazarr identifies four features of the "new economy" to which leading corporate citizens will need to pay attention:[10]

- Human capital—because knowledge resides in human beings.
- Freedom and empowerment—because empowered people create and innovate.
- Disorganization—because companies using complexity and chaos theories as a base for organizing will outpace companies organized more hierarchically and traditionally.
- Networks and alliances—because partnerships will become critical to organizational effectiveness and efficiency.

Mazarr identifies the principles of the knowledge era as being speed, flexibility, decentralization, and empowerment. Using these principles implies that organizations trust their stakeholders, in particular their employees, and give them responsibilities that go far beyond traditional responsibilities. Ultimately, what these principles mean is that companies will have to design themselves in the ways we have been discussing throughout this book so that integrity and responsibility are values embedded within all of their operations.

Global Tribalism

Although processes of globalism proceed apace on a global basis, much trading occurs *within*, not among, the three major trading blocs of Europe, the Americas, and East Asia.[11] Mazarr points out that this globalization process will demand increased global awareness, resulting from enhanced communications and the rise of the multinational corporation as a powerful social institution. But, when threatened, such ideological forces tend to erupt in the forms of tribalism that political scientist Benjamin Barber calls Jihads. Thus, we can expect continued attempts by various ethnic, religious, political, and cultural groups to sustain their identities in the face of global pluralism.[12]

Transforming Authority

According to the Millennium Project, traditional institutions will face increased challenges to their authority in the knowledge era, in which communications are instantaneous and information is widely shared. This trend is most related to the political sphere of activity, because it foresees a trend toward greater levels of democratization throughout the world, as information becomes more readily available and widely shared.

Among the factors that will influence authorities are tendencies to decentralize their organizations, creating virtual structures (as many companies already are doing), influencing through knowledge and allegiance rather than coercion, and acquisition of power from competence and effectiveness rather than tradition.[13]

Cognitive, Emotional, Moral Demands on Humans

As Robert Kegan notes, the many demands on human beings today place considerable strain on our capacity to understand and step into the perspectives of others, as well as to hold multiple perspectives in our heads simultaneously.[14] Mazarr, writing for the Millennium Project, also believes that the knowledge era will stretch the limits of human understanding. These demands will push the need for many more people to develop higher level skills of cognitive, moral, and emotional development. The pace of change, the multiplicity of stakeholders and their numerous demands, and the complexity of coping simultaneously with technology all create the potential, Mazarr says, for anxiety and alienation.

Chapter 10   *Values Added: Global Futures*   **229**

Lessons from the Global Trends

Mazarr concludes *Global Trends 2005* with three major lessons that strike to the core of what this book is all about:

> The three most important lessons suggested by this transition are these: the decisive role of education, as the activity that equips people for success in the knowledge era; the primacy of moral values and social responsibility at a time when both are urgently needed; and the need for a "New Capitalism," a reform of some elements of capitalist theory to ensure that markets capture the true costs and implications of economic activities.[15]

Issues and Opportunities

The coming of the new millennium has challenged many thinkers and leaders to work together to try to predict the major issues and opportunities the planet will face. Another initiative, also called the Millennium Project, has brought together more than 200 futurists and scholars from over 50 countries to analyze what issues, opportunities, and strategies are arising globally. This project is organized by the American Council for the United Nations University, in cooperation with the Smithsonian Institution, the Futures Group, and the United Nations University. Funded by the U.S. Environmental Protection Agency, the United Nations Development Program (UNDP), and UNESCO, the project's goal is to develop capacity to think about the future globally.[16]

The Millennium Project's "2004 State of the Future" report identified 15 global issues, 15 challenges, and 15 opportunities to which leading corporate citizens—as well as members of society generally and political leaders generally—need to pay attention in the next century. These issues and opportunities, which remain current, create potential new economic opportunities, as well as significant problems to be solved. The issues are reproduced in Table 10.3.

The Millennium Project's report discusses each issue in greater detail. Coping with these issues demands collaboration among organizations from all sectors of society, including corporations that will have to meet the economic demands of the future and do so responsibly, with vision and values guiding the way. Significant creativity and capacity to understand the fundamental problems, while simultaneously maintaining respect for others' needs and dif-

TABLE 10.3   The Millennium Project's 15 Global Issues

Source: www.acunu.org/millennium/isandop.html.

1. World population is growing; food, water, education, housing, medical care must grow apace.
2. Fresh water is becoming scarce in localized areas of the world.
3. The gap in living standards between rich and poor promises to become more extreme and divisive.
4. The threat of new and re-emerging diseases and immune microorganisms is growing.
5. Diminishing capacity to decide (as issues become more global and complex under conditions of increasing uncertainty and risk).
6. Terrorism is increasingly destructive, proliferating, and difficult to prevent.
7. Adverse interactions between the growth of population and economic growth with environmental quality and natural resources.
8. The status of women is changing.
9. Increasing severity of religious, ethnic, and racial conflicts.
10. Information technology's promise and perils.
11. Organized crime groups becoming sophisticated global enterprises.
12. Economic growth brings both promising and threatening consequences.
13. Nuclear power plants around the world are aging.
14. The HIV epidemic will continue to spread.
15. Work, unemployment, leisure, and underemployment are changing.

TABLE 10.4   **The Millennium Project's 15 Opportunities**

Source: www.acunu.org/millennium/isandop.html.

1. Achieving sustainable development.
2. Increasing acceptance of long-term perspectives in policy making.
3. Expanding potential for scientific and technological breakthroughs.
4. Transforming authoritarian regimes to democracies.
5. Encouraging diversity and shared ethical values.
6. Reducing the rate of population growth.
7. Emerging strategies for world peace and security.
8. Developing alternative sources of energy.
9. Globalizing the convergence of information and communications technology.
10. Increasing advances in biotechnology.
11. Encouraging economic development through ethical market economy.
12. Increasing economic autonomy of women and other groups.
13. Promoting the inquiry into new and sometimes counterintuitive ideas.
14. Pursuing promising space projects.
15. Improving institutions.

ferences, especially when they are in deprived economic circumstances or from very different cultures, will be necessary to find effective and efficient—or economizing—solutions to some of these issues.

Where there are issues, there are also opportunities, some for economic development and others for collaboration among the three spheres of human society, as the Millennium Project's list of 15 global opportunities indicates (see Table 10.4).

There are significant business opportunities embedded in the opportunities noted in Table 10.4 for leaders who can understand how to tap into them. Of course, the future is much more chaotic and emergent than these neat lists of possibilities suggest. What techniques such as scenario analysis can do is help those who must cope with the future figure out both the messy aspects and ways to cope, as well as creative approaches for handling the inherent uncertainty of the future.

Because messy problems frequently cross sector and sphere boundaries, however, individual companies acting alone may be less successful in tapping into them than companies that know how to collaborate with enterprises from the other spheres. What this blurring of boundaries means is that advantage will go to those companies, countries, and alliances that can generate new ideas for dealing with the emerging issues and opportunities. The next section will briefly explore new research on such trisector collaborations.

Intersector Partnership and Collaboration

The interactions among enterprises in the civil society sphere,[17] the political sphere, and the business/economic sphere have typically been given scant attention in management thought. To their credit, many global business leaders have recognized the need to create strategic alliances and more cooperative strategies not only with each other but also with governmental and nongovernmental organizations, as the burgeoning in social and trisector partnerships around the world attests.[18] Clearly this aspect of the pluralistic global economic and societal situation demands new skills of collaboration and mutual understanding of differences in perspective, culture, and ideology, among other factors, some of which shape the economic and political worlds as well as the relational world of civil society.

The kinds of problems identified above suggest that old-fashioned single-sector solutions will no longer work. These problems by their nature cross boundaries and are what scholar Russell Ackoff has termed "messes," that is, intractable and difficult problems that various organizations, groups, and individuals must work together to resolve. Such unstructured problems require innovation and creativity, placing significant demands on any one organization's knowledge, skills, and resource base, and thus elicit multisector approaches for their solutions.

When problems cross organizational and sector (sphere) boundaries, when stakeholders are interdependent in dealing with problems, and when there is a rich network of ties—or social capital—among the stakeholders, then multisector collaboration becomes a useful vehicle for effecting social change. Businesses have found this out in the United States, where for years they have been working with schools to help schools reform themselves. Increasingly it has become clear that not only do businesses and schools need to be involved in these improvement efforts, but because education is at its root a social problem, all the relevant stakeholders, from all three spheres of activity, need to be involved in such efforts.[19]

Although establishing multisector collaborations is not easy, there is increasing information on some of factors that make such collaboration successful. First, there has to be some overriding reason why the actors should work together—a compelling shared vision, a common problem, a crisis to overcome, or a leader everyone wants to work with. Then there need to be ways in which the relevant actors and organizations can be brought together, through networks and alliances, through a "brokering" or mediating enterprise of some sort (e.g., a grant or an organization that plays a mediating role). Finally, there needs to be sufficient mutual education about other stakeholders and their interests, and sufficient benefits to be gained by all to keep these parties, which typically may never interact, working together over time.[20]

In recent research on trisector collaborations, involving organizations from the civil society, economic, and political/governmental spheres, Steve Waddell shows how these factors interact to make partnership feasible. For example, he studied a road maintenance project in Madagascar, a country that has a weak governmental infrastructure but that needed improved roads. So poorly maintained were the roads that anarchy and banditry were serious problems. To solve the problem, villagers formed nongovernmental "road users associations," and the government delegated its authority to those associations. By financing much of the improvement work with tolls, working with road contractors to improve their road-building techniques, and working on a peer basis with government officials, the associations brought villagers, government, and private contractors into a collaboration that has been largely successful in improving the roads.[21]

Such collaborative efforts will become more and more necessary in dealing with global futures issues. As perhaps the most powerful among institutions in societies today, corporate citizens will be increasingly looked on as resources for helping to resolve societies' significant problems, challenges, and opportunities.

Only if they operate with integrity, transparency, sustainability, and respect for stakeholders in all spheres of society will corporate citizens be in a position to be effective (and efficient) in their emerging leadership roles. Further, leading corporate citizens anticipate rather than react to future trends, issues, and problems and work interactively with the appropriate stakeholders in different spheres of activity to find solutions. They can do so best if they are engaged in continuing activities with their stakeholders to scan the future. Just how future scanning by leading corporate citizens in conjunction with stakeholders from other spheres can be done will be briefly explored in the next sections.

Scenarios and Future Searches

Having scanned the current situation and sought out important trends, as well as the weak signals that might become levers of dramatic change, how do companies cope with all of this information? A technique called open space technology, developed by Harrison Owen, can be helpful in determining what is going on and what needs to be changed in highly complex, emergent, and generally messy situations.

Two other techniques specifically aim at helping decision makers plan for the future: scenario analysis, which has been extensively used by Shell Oil, and future search conferences, which have been used by communities and others to assess what issues are likely to arise. To conclude our look at the future, we will briefly explore some key aspects of each of these important techniques.

Open Space Technology

Open space technology is a technique, developed and written about by Harrison Owen (with, as he admits, input from many others).[22] Open space technology enables multiple stakeholders with widely divergent perspectives to come together around a problem of mutual interest to develop workable solutions.[23] Typically, an open space meeting brings together many interested parties to work together in a circle on the problem at hand. Open spaces can be used to devise corporate citizenship and competitive strategies, or to bring multiple resources to bear on a strategic, community-based, or technological problem. Or they can be used effectively to deal with large-scale social problems.

An open space can be created anywhere a circle large enough to contain as many participants—stakeholders—as are relevant to the problem can be formed. Owen believes that setting stakeholders into a circular format enables the type of interaction that will be necessary to create the type of third-way thinking or boundary-less thinking that is needed to deal with complex problems. One of the first rules of open space, then, is to invite to the meeting "Whoever cares," and a second important rule is that once the relevant stakeholders have been invited, "Whoever comes is the right group." Open space has been used successfully with groups as small as 5 and as large as 1,000.

The time frame for an open space meeting also needs consideration. While they can be held for periods of less than a day, most successful open space meetings last between two and three days (at the outside) to give participants sufficient time to deal with the complexity of the issues at hand. While space prohibits a complete description of the open space technology, Owen emphasizes that there are four principles and one law to any open space meeting (see Table 10.5).

Basically, the open space technique involves everyone present placing his or her ideas onto a board (typically using stickies or other ways to attach notes of some kind). Those present then organize the stickies into activities on which those present will work, assuming that someone is willing to lead a session and ultimately (within the time frame of the meeting) produce a report on that topic, and then allowing those present to self-organize into a working group.

The basic idea is that if the key stakeholders have been invited to the open space, then the important issues related to the topic at hand will be raised and organized by those present. Anyone interested in a particular aspect of the issue will then either post a meeting on that issue and run it or attend a meeting that someone else has organized. Interested parties will contribute to the way in which that issue is framed and possible resolutions

TABLE 10.5 Open Space Technology

Source: Harrison Owen, *Open Space Technology: A User's Guide*, 2nd ed. (San Francisco: Berrett-Koehler, 1997).

The Four Principles of Open Space

- Whoever comes is the right people.
- Whatever happens is the only thing that could have.
- Whenever it starts is the right time.
- When it's over, it's over.

The One Law of Open Space

- The law of two feet: if during the course of the gathering, any person finds him- or herself in a situation where they are neither learning nor contributing, they must use their two feet and go to some more productive place.

and action steps developed. Small groups meet on particular aspects of the issue to consolidate their ideas and develop strategies and creative new approaches for dealing with that aspect. After each group meeting, those in attendance are expected to produce a report that can be combined, at the end of the entire meeting, into a book of action plans and projects that have come out of the open space meeting.

Although open space technology is not explicitly designed to deal with the future, it can provide a platform for understanding the complexities of the present and lead interested parties into designing a way forward into the future. In that sense, open space technology can be considered a useful futures planning tool.[24]

Future Search

A related technique, but more explicitly futures-focused, is the future search conference. Developed by Marvin Weisbord and others, the future search conference involves bringing a diverse group of stakeholders interested in an issue, industry, community, or problem together to share their views and wisdom about it.[25] The outcome of a future search conference is an action plan that stakeholders, who participate actively in identifying and analyzing the issues as well as developing the action steps, are expected to implement. The general idea is to get the relevant stakeholders together so that they can devise workable solutions together. As with open space meetings, future search conferences use emerging knowledge of how groups work to design the meeting so that everyone's input is taken seriously in the process of devising solutions and action steps.

The future search conference focuses on five tasks: reviewing the past, exploring the present, creating ideal future scenarios, identifying common ground among participants, and making action plans. A future search conference brings together groups of stakeholders that may not interact or join in conversations under normal circumstances (i.e., groups from different spheres of activity). A future search conference—or similar open space technology event—can thus get people working together in new and exciting ways. Examples of the use of future search conferences include gaining citywide consensus on future city plans, bringing a union and management together for joint planning, and doing regional economic development.[26]

Future search conferences, like open space meetings, need to bring together all of the relevant stakeholders into a common location to do the planning together. Future searches, like open space meetings, also use techniques to get the group to self-manage and tend to be organized in three-day blocs. The general idea is to get the gathered participants to think about the current reality and explore—together—possible common futures.[27]

Several ground rules apply to future search conferences. First, as with brainstorming techniques, all ideas are valid. Second, participants should record everything on flip charts (this creates a record that can be used later on). Third, listen to each other (remember the techniques of dialogue discussed earlier in the book?). Fourth, observe established time frames, which respects everyone's time. Finally and importantly, seek common ground and action rather than problems and conflicts.

The approach for a future search conference is to get the whole system into the room. Then the group explores, also using flip charts and stickies, what each participant's view of the situation, problem, or issue is, by getting everything onto large spaces, where lines can be drawn and the system can basically be described according to everyone present's input. Using techniques of dialogue in which active listening, respect, and sharing are important, conversations can be held even about highly conflictual situations or issues.

The focus of a future search is on finding *common ground*, rather than on differences, and is *future-oriented*, rather than oriented to the past or present. In other words, the idea is that participants will not dwell on current conflicts and problems, but will focus rather on ways of thinking creatively about what values and goals they share, so as to be able to come up with creative new ways of dealing with the problems at hand.

The design for a future search conference involves getting stakeholders to sit together in mixed groups. For example, in an economic development conference, the stakeholders from the economic sphere should be mixed with those from civil society and government. The first step is to review the past by creating a timeline to the present about the relevant topic, a step Weisborg terms "recalling the past." The next step is to focus on the present: external trends affecting the relevant topic, a step termed "appreciating the present." It is in this step that a complex diagram of the situation, called a "mind map," is generally created on large boards or walls using the inputs of everyone present. The mind map serves as an essential vehicle for creating a picture of the future: what is needed, what links exist between what is already present and what is needed, and where new ideas can be generated.

Four rules are essential to creating the mind map: (1) all ideas are valid, (2) the person who names the issue says where it goes, (3) opposing trends are OK, and (4) examples must be concrete.

The critically important next step is to be "living the future," that is, creating a desirable future based on input from all and creative ideas about what might emerge—in terms of common goals and ideas—from what is already present now. Then the groups, if there are multiple groups at work, consolidate their ideas into the common themes and ideas, and move into an action planning stage.

Scenario Analysis

One other technique that has been widely used specifically to help companies plan strategically to cope with otherwise unforeseen events is scenario analysis. It also has broad applicability for coping with multiple stakeholder interests. Groups interested in using scenarios undertake significant research on the topic of interest, seeking out all the available information, and also being sure that relevant stakeholders are participating in the process since all points of view need to be represented. The group gets together to construct alternative scenarios, that is, different descriptions of the future. Typically, several scenarios are constructed: a best case, worst case, and at least one radically different alternative where the unexpected happens.[28]

By developing the scenarios as stories, planners can make them compelling and begin to think through the implications for a specific company and its vision, or for a group of stakeholders to a key issue or concern. One company that has had a great deal of success using scenarios is Shell Oil, which was able to prepare itself for the October 1973 oil shock and subsequent energy crisis using scenarios.[29]

Scenario analysis is helpful because it provides for multiple different alternative futures and helps break leaders out of the notion that simply extrapolating from the present is the only likely outcome of present trends. By asking for best and worst case scenarios as well as radically different alternatives, scenario analysis allows for possible discontinuities that make current projections meaningless—and helps prepare organizations for those potentialities.[30]

Scenario Analysis Process

Scenario planning is simple in its concept, although doing it well requires considerable research into current trends, gathering of extensive data, and synthesizing it into meaningful stories. First, a team of scenario analysts (anyone interested in a particular problem, issue, or strategy) is gathered and discusses its perceptions of the key uncertainties around whatever the focal issue or topic is. The topic might be future strategy of a company, new competitive threats, or how to proceed with economic development for a region, just as examples. The group should outline and define the relevant environment or issue, then determine key uncertainties, whether they are inside or outside of that group's control. The group should also consider the major constraints facing the planning group or company, because these define available strategic responses to the issue and determine what the major decisions or decision points might be with respect to the issue. The key issue is to determine how the future environment will be defined and constrained.

Next the group establishes a priority ranking with respect to the uncertainties identified, focusing on those with the greatest potential impact and those that are most poorly understood. The group then selects two or three critical uncertainties as the "driving uncertainties" and combines them for developing future scenarios.

Scenario development involves exploring the selected driving uncertainties and their implications in great detail. Typically, groups will create stories, or narratives based on

TABLE 10.6   **Guidelines for Future Responses by Scenario Analysts**

Source: Eric K. Clemons, "Using Scenario Analysis to Manage the Strategic Risks of Reengineering," *Sloan Management Review*, Summer 1995, pp. 61–71.

Determine the applicability of potential decisions and action steps by asking:

- What are the "no brainers," the actions common to all scenarios, that will be required in all foreseeable futures? These actions should be undertaken.
- What are the "no regrets," the actions that may be valuable in some scenarios, less valuable in others, but not damaging in any way? These actions might be undertaken, but might be stopped if they become damaging in any way.
- What are the "contingent possibilities," the actions that may be valuable in only selected scenarios?
- What are the "no ways!" the scenarios that are deemed unacceptable? How should such actions be avoided?

the driving uncertainties with an internal logic. Stories are compelling ways for leaders to begin to understand the implications of the uncertainties on the relevant organizations and stakeholders, especially if widely differing points of view have been incorporated into the different scenarios. As each story is written, different possible advantages and disadvantages, or implications, for the relevant organizations and stakeholders emerge, and possible strategic, development, or stakeholder-relationship responses begin to emerge.

The scenarios then are used to explore possible futures and to test out how different strategies for coping with the scenario will work. A critical test of a strategy, for example, is to see how it would work under vastly different scenarios. Doing such testing can help determine the robustness of a particular response. If a response to one scenario seems as though it will dramatically falter under another scenario, planners may wish to evolve a different strategy that would have a better chance of working under both scenarios. Key questions that should be asked—and answered—by scenario analysts are summarized in Table 10.6, as a way of guiding decision making and future strategies by the group of stakeholders that has been gathered to address an issue of relevance to all.

Common Ground on Planning the Future

Obviously, there are many more details that go into planning a successful future search conference, open space meeting, or scenario analysis. It is clear, however, that all of these techniques use inputs from *all* relevant stakeholders, provide for sharing of concerns and ideas, use dialogical and brainstorming techniques, and demand that participants let go of preconceived ideas and agendas. Only in these ways can stakeholders to an issue work toward common ground—*and* analyze possibilities without being biased by any one point of view. The general idea is to bring participants onto common ground, where fruitful generative new ways of working collaboratively can be developed, where there is open sharing of multiple points of view, and where reaching common ground—and shared solutions—is the goal.

Such techniques can be an important basis for generating not only innovative ideas (as Fetzer Vineyards does, see Case 10.2) but also actual commitments to carrying them out, especially when the issues and opportunities to be addressed are open-ended and ambiguous, and when decision makers are present.[31] At some level these types of techniques also can help companies that want to be leading corporate citizens do far more than respond to the future: They can help companies work together with groups from the political and economic spheres, as well as those representing the interests of the natural environment, to create a common world that we can all live in. Futures assessments can also be helpful to companies and other organizations in avoiding significant problems that might otherwise arise because they are completely unexpected.

Fetzer Vineyards' CEO, Paul Dolan, long ago saw the future—and made the move to becoming totally organic for his vineyard. Not only are all 2000 acres of Fetzer-owned vineyards certified organic, but Dolan has plans to convert all 200 of the growers who supply Fetzer to organic growing by 2010. Dolan knows what he is talking about, since he converted Fetzer to organic ways as long ago as 1986, when he was still head winemaker at the company. An organic gardener hired to grow delicious foods to be served with the Fetzer wines challenged Dolan and his boss, Jim Fetzer, about why they were using poisons in growing the grapes. When they tried an experimental patch using organic methods, the improved taste led the team toward the eventual outcome—full organic production on Fetzer-owned land and a commitment to convert suppliers by 2010.

An article in *Fast Company* magazine in 2003 highlighted the dramatic shift that has taken place within the company since those early trials and some of the thinking that lies behind the progressive, profitable, and highly productive methods in use at Fetzer, which have resulted in the company's being the best-selling brand in the $7–$10 category in 2002 and awards for the quality of its wines too numerous to mention. According to *Fast Company*:

> The results of the experiment convinced Dolan that years of applying chemical pesticides and fertilizers had stripped the soil of its richness and that the resulting dull grapes were affecting the quality of Fetzer's wine. In 1991, Fetzer launched a label called Bonterra (meaning "good earth"), made of 100% organically grown grapes. It was the first mass-marketed organic wine in the United States. The philosophy extends even to the packaging: To spare trees, Bonterra labels are made from a plant fiber known as kenaf and are printed with soy-based inks; the corks aren't sanitized with chlorine; and the cases are made from recycled cardboard.

> A year later, Louisville, Kentucky-based Brown-Forman purchased Fetzer (adding the winery to its existing brands including Jack Daniel's, Southern Comfort, and Finlandia Vodka), and named Dolan president of Fetzer. One of his first decisions was to commit to going 100% organic by 2010. All the grapes on Fetzer-owned land—about 20% of the total—are already organic. Without chemicals to fertilize the grape crop and keep insects and fungi away, growers had to learn different ways to address these same problems. They undertook what was then a fairly unusual practice of growing "cover crops," which have since become standard at wineries around the world. In the aisles between the vines as well as in fallow fields, growers plant different crops to crowd out weeds, repel bugs, and provide soil nutrients. If diseases persist, growers have other remedies, such as sprinkling sulphur dust and copper sulfates (which are approved for organic use) on the roots of vines and spraying assorted oils on the grapes to keep away pests and fungi.

> Dolan is a fourth-generation wine maker who grew up steeped in the wine country's culture. His organic conversion led him to believe that protecting the environment meant more than simply growing grapes without chemicals. It meant improving the environment for workers and investing in their skills and futures. It meant reducing emissions from farm vehicles and figuring out how to eliminate solid waste at the winery. And it meant making enough money so that Fetzer could serve as an industry example of how to

do things differently. Fetzer employees named this vision E3, which stands for economics, environment, and equity, or the triple bottom line. Every decision at the company is put to the E3 test: Does it support fair and safe standards for employees? Does it protect or improve the environment? Does it make economic sense?

The commitment to organic production, employee development, and the triple bottom line extends to all aspects of the business at Fetzer, including seeking input from employees—and improving pay scales as a result, running farming equipment on a fuel composed of soy and used cooking oils from local fast food restaurants, teaching English to laborers (and thereby avoiding translation problems), to name just a few.

In his 2003 book *True to Your Roots*, Dolan argues that all businesses should commit to the triple bottom line of economic, social, and ecological impacts and performance, and provides some insights into the visionary and farsighted business principles his company lives by:

- Your company's culture is determined by the context you create for it.
- Your business is part of a much larger system.
- True power is living what you know.
- The soul of your company is found in the hearts of its people.
- You can't predict the future, but you can create it.
- There is a way to make an idea's time come.

Clearly Dolan and Fetzer have seen the future—and are, in fact, leading the wine industry in California toward more sustainable growing practices. In 2003, inspired by Fetzer's successes not just with organic growing but also in producing better wines, California's wine industry introduced a Code of Sustainable Winegrowing Practices, a harbinger of a drive toward more ecological sustainability in a state with a fast-growing population and an industry that has frequently been criticized for lack of attention to environmental matters. Developed partially as a survival plan for the $33 billion industry, the code aimed to have at least 10 percent of the state's 600,000 acres of vineyards environmentally assessed during the first year. The voluntary initiative exceeded all expectations when during the first year 29 percent of the vineyards and 53 percent of the production facilities completed the assessment. In a model of responsibility management, the goal of the effort is to measure the current status then by adhering to the code's standards, emphasizing constant improvement in their practices.

DISCUSSION QUESTIONS

1. Do you believe that Fetzer might have a competitive edge because of its approaches to the environment and successes in producing high-quality wine using organic methods?

2. How do you think customers are likely to respond to organic wines? Why?

3. Assume you are a winemaker using traditional methods. What kinds of future-scanning methods would help you figure out how to successfully compete with Fetzer?

Sources: Paul Dolan, *True to Our Roots: Fermenting a Business Revolution* (Bloomberg Press, 2003); Alison Overholt, "The Good Earth," *Fast Company* 77 (December 2003), p. 85, www.fastcompany.com/magazine/77/goodearth.html (accessed July 8, 2004); and Tim Tesconi, "California Wine Growers Moving Toward Sustainability," *Organic Consumers Association*, October 15, 2003, www.organicconsumers.org/organic/wine102303.cfm (accessed July 8, 2004).

Leading Challenges: We Cannot Predict the Future, but We *Can* Create Relationships

Leading corporate citizens cannot predict the future, as it is an inherently chaotic process in which small changes can make large and fundamental differences. They *can*, however, prepare themselves and their organizations to cope with whatever happens by being aware of the changes that impact both internal and external stakeholders. They *can* implement dialogue and conversation with primary and critical secondary stakeholders who are capable of providing important input into the company's future plans, and they *can* continually scan the horizon for significant developments, whether technological, ecological, social, or political. By establishing these *relationships* with key stakeholders, companies can prepare themselves—in an ongoing way—for what the future is likely to bring.

Leading corporate citizens need not be surprised by technological advances, activism, or social changes that put their businesses at risk. As the sections on future search conferences, open space meetings, and scenario analysis indicate, there are numerous techniques available that companies can use on a continual basis to establish communication links with potential critics, key stakeholders, and social activists. Getting the kind of information that can only be gained when people with *different* points of view are brought together can not only enhance a company's capacity to be a respected corporate citizens but also provide the basis for revealing new trends, competitive threats, and possible new opportunities. Many of these possibilities could never be discovered through traditional channels of market research and new product/service development.

By putting in place the types of dialogic processes with stakeholders that have been described above, by focusing on continually learning and incorporating that learning into constructive new stakeholder practices, leading corporate citizens can, in fact, operate with integrity and be successful. They can also provide the means to achieve a better balance among the spheres in society and with the natural environment because the different points of view represented in these spheres will be better understood.

Is using these dialogic techniques easy? Of course not. They require a commitment to internal learning and change—and a commitment to real and recognized input from outsiders. They imply a willingness to listen to those who may be less powerful or have fewer resources than the company itself. But using such dialogue-based techniques to raise up the emerging issues, concerns, technologies, and problems, may be, in fact, a better way of operating with integrity than to assume that economizing is all important. Business, after all, was created to serve society's interests, not vice versa. All of this, of course, suggests the need for a shift of paradigm in organizing and leading corporate citizens.

Endnotes

1. From The Lorax by Dr. Seuss, copyright® and copyright © by Dr. Seuss Enterprises, L.P. 1971, renewed 1999. Used by permission of Random House Children's Books, a division of Random House Inc.

2. Robert Spiegel, "Yogi Berra's Business Wisdom, Growth and Leadership," *Business Know-How,* www.business knowhow.com/growth/yogi.htm (accessed July 6, 2004).

3. Robert Kegan, *In Over Our Heads: The Mental Demands of Modern Life* (Cambridge, MA: Harvard University Press, 1994).

4. National Institute of Allergy and Infectious Diseases, "HIV/AIDS Statistics," January 2004, www.niaid.nih.gov/factsheets/aidsstat.htm (accessed July 7, 2004).

5. Hákan Björkman, "HIV/AIDS and Poverty Reduction Strategies," UNDP Policy Note, 2002, www.undp.org/hiv/docs/hivprsEng25oct02.pdf (accessed July 7, 2004).

6. World Bank, www.worldbank.org/WBSITE/EXTERNAL/NEWS/0..contentMDK:20194973~menuPK:34463~pagePK:64003015~piPK:64003012~theSitePK:4607.00.html (accessed July 7, 2004).

7. See, for instance, the Center for Strategic and International Studies website, www.csis.org. Trends identified in this section are from Michael J. Mazarr, *Global Trends 2005: The Challenge of a New Millennium* (Washington, DC: Center for Strategic and International Studies, 1997) See www.csis.org/gt2005.

8. See Mazarr, *Global Trends 2005*.

9. Ibid., p. 13.

10. Ibid., pp. 16–24.

11. Ibid., p. 25.

12. Benjamin Barber, *Jihad vs. McWorld* (New York: Times Books; Random House, 1995).

13. Mazarr, *Global Trends 2005*, p. 31.

14. Kegan, *In Over Our Heads*.

15. Mazarr, *Global Trends 2005*, p. 37.

16. See www.geocities.com/CapitolHill/Senate/4787/millennium/new.html.

17. This topic is discussed at length by Robert D. Putnam in *Making Democracy Work: Civic Traditions in Modern Italy* (Princeton, NJ: Princeton University Press, 1993); also see his articles "Bowling Alone: America's Declining Social Capital," *Journal of Democracy* 6, no. 1 (January 1995), pp. 65–78, and "The Strange Disappearance of Civic America," *American Prospect* 24 (Winter 1996), http://epn.org/prospect/24/24putn.html.

18. See Sandra Waddock, "Public-Private Partnership as Product and Process" in *Research in Corporate Social Performance and Policy*, Vol. VII, James E. Rest, ed. (Greenwich, CT: JAI Press, 1986) and "Building Successful Social Partnerships," *Sloan* Management Review 29, no. 4 (Summer 1988), pp. 17–23; also Steve Waddell, "Market–Civil Society Partnership Formation: A Status Report on Activity, Strategies, and Tools," *IDR Reports* 13, no. 5 (1998).

19. See, for example, Sandra Waddock, *Not by Schools Alone: Sharing Responsibility for America's Education Reform* (Greenwich, CT: Praeger, 1995).

20. See, for example, Sandra Waddock, "Understanding Social Partnerships: An Evolutionary Model of Partnership Organizations," *Administration and Society* 21, no. 1 (May 1989), pp. 78–100.

21. Steve Waddell, "Business-Government-Nonprofit Collaborations as Agents for Social Innovation and Learning," paper presented at the 1999 Academy of Management Annual Meeting, Chicago, IL, 1999.

22. Information about Harrison Owen's development of open space technology can be found at www.openspaceworld.com/index.htm (accessed July 4, 2004).

23. See Harrison Owen, *Open Space Technology: A User's Guide*, 2nd ed. (San Francisco: Berrett-Koehler, 1997); and *Expanding Our Now: The Story of Open Space Technology* (San Francisco: Berrett-Koehler, 1997).

24. More details about open space technology can be found at www.change-management-toolbook.com/OpenSpace.htm (accessed July 7, 2004). By clicking on Home, you can link to other change management tools and techniques as well.

25. Marvin R. Weisbord and Sandra Janoff, *Future Search: An Action Guide to Finding Common Ground in Organizations & Communities* (San Francisco: Berrett-Koehler, 1995).

26. Information on future searches can be found at www.future-search.net (accessed July 7, 2004).

27. More information about future searches can be found at www.change-management-toolbook.com/FS.html (accessed July 7, 2004).

28. The steps are outlined online at www.du.edu/~bhughes/WebHelpIFs/ifshelp/scenario_ analysis.htm (accessed July 7, 2004).

29. For a good overview of how to do scenario analysis see Peter Schwartz, *The Art of the Long View: Planning for the Future in an Uncertain World* (New York: Doubleday Currency, 1996).

30. Ibid. See also Eric K. Clemons, "Using Scenario Analysis to Manage the Strategic Risks of Reengineering," *Sloan Management Review*, Summer 1995, pp. 61–71.

31. To learn about future search conferences, see Marvin R. Weisbord and Sandra Janoff, *Future Search: An Action Guide to Finding Common Ground in Organizations & Communities* (San Francisco: Berrett-Koehler, 1995). For information on open space technology, see Harrison Owen's two books *Open Space Technology: A User's Guide*, 2nd ed. (San Francisco: Berrett-Koehler, 1997), and *Expanding Our Now: The Story of Open Space Technology* (San Francisco: Berrett-Koehler, 1997).

CHAPTER ELEVEN

Leading Global Futures: The Emerging Paradigm of Leading Corporate Citizenship

Imagine a global economy that is healthy and self-governing. Imagine markets that are organized to empower people. Imagine an economy that is free, humane, competitive, profitable, decentralized, nonbureaucratic, and socially accountable. Imagine a global economy that operates for the common good, a market that develops local-to-global structures to build sustainable community.

This sort of economy is what we are talking about in civil development. It requires a new order of thinking about global markets characterized by freedom and accountability.

Severyn Bruyn, *A Civil Economy: Transforming the Market in the Twenty-First Century.* Published by the University of Michigan Press, 2000.

Severyn Bruyn's remarkable statement synthesizes much of what this book is about: creating corporate citizens that have respect for human dignity, and the natural ecology that supports it, through a balanced approach to the three spheres of human activity that constitute civilization—economic, political, and civil society. All along we have been talking about developing managers into leaders who take their responsibilities seriously and proceed with their decisions and their impacts wisely by consistently implementing a value- and values-added approach.

Economic success is the result when companies treat stakeholders with dignity and respect, and when their practices match their rhetoric about vision and values. We have seen the need for balance among economic, political, and civilizing interests, all three of which are necessary to create successful and ecologically sustainable societies. We have seen the need for higher levels of awareness and development, both individually and organizationally, to cope with today's, and particularly tomorrow's, complexities and challenges. We have seen, in short, the need for and the beginnings of a shift of perspective on what it means to be a leading corporate citizen, both individually and organizationally.

Shifting Perspectives

This book has presented what I hope is a realistic but fairly radical perspective on how companies as citizens in the global village can be successful not alongside or separate from but rather with, in, and of societies. The systems perspective presented through the three-spheres framework, combined with the links among vision, values, and value added integrates responsibility, meaningfulness, and the energy and capacity of whole persons directly into organizational life.

By understanding that responsibility is integrated into all of the organizational practices that impact stakeholders and the ecological environment, organizations are discovering the power of vision to create meaning and purpose for the orga-nization and its stakeholders, as well as the power of treating others with respect and dignity. Such a stance not only balances power among the three spheres of human activity but also tends to bring more equity and power balance into relationships within organizations as well. When companies tap the full resources of individuals and treat them as human beings, the tendency to treat people as mere cogs in the great machine of business diminishes. Respect and dignity are enhanced.

Transformation Based on Nature

Fully incorporating the emerging paradigm of corporate citizenship into the dominant management paradigm will require radical shifts in the current business model, in power dynamics, and in balance among the three spheres of human activity, which themselves must be put into sustainable *relationships* with stakeholders and the natural environment. Part of the needed wisdom can derive from principles embedded in nature itself, using what author David Korten terms a "life-centered approach" that taps the wisdom of nature and ecological systems. Certainly, if we hope to sustain productivity and use ecological resources wisely, a shift of balance in the powers among the spheres is needed.

Balancing power means that corporate activities can be undertaken on a scale accessible to human beings and with the best interests of all stakeholders kept firmly in mind and well balanced. Duly elected democratic governments can resume their rightful powers to determine the public interest and the common good. And the relationships fostered and sustained in civil society can nourish the spirit and the bodies of productive members of societies and productive corporate stakeholders.

Korten offers six lessens drawn from what is now known about self-organizing ecological systems that potentially help in rethinking the way that corporate life is currently scaled and operates (see Table 11.1).[1] We can relate these, to some extent, to some of the design elements that Korten develops for his visionary postcorporate world. And many of them are similar to ideas that we have been discussing throughout this book. Perhaps it is time to begin imagining different types of futures that provide inspiration for human life in the midst of nature, where resources are equitably distributed among all of the peoples of the world.

First, Korten says, life favors self-organization, and companies would be wise to do so as well. Self-organization is the process of organizing that tends to emerge when (in this case)

TABLE 11.1 **Korten's Lessons of Life's Wisdom and Progressive Design Elements**

Source: Adapted from David Korten, *The Post-Corporate World* (San Francisco: Berett-Koechler, 1999).

Lessons of Life's Wisdom	Progressive Corporate Design Elements
1. Life favors self-organization.	Human-scale self-organization.
2. Life is frugal and sharing.	Renewable energy self-reliance. Closed-cycle materials use. Regional environmental balance.
3. Life depends on inclusive, place-based communities.	Village and neighborhood clusters. Towns and regional centers.
4. Life rewards cooperation.	Mindful livelihoods.
5. Life depends on boundaries.	Interregional electronic communication.
6. Life banks on diversity, creative individuality, and shared learning.	Wild spaces in nature and within organizations.

people are together for a purpose. But self-organization is best suited to reasonably small-scale endeavors that are rooted locally, thus favoring human-scale enterprises that not just rhetorically but truly empower people to self-organize. Human-scaled enterprises allow people to engage in a positive vision that enables them to achieve *meaningful* personal *and* company purposes. Second, Korten notes, life is frugal and sharing, values that are certainly found in the economizing that underpins corporate efficiency. But from an ecological perspective, this also means thinking about operating in a sustainable manner for the long term, hence ecologizing, which effectively means wasting nothing.

Third, life depends on inclusive, place-based communities, what we earlier termed rootedness. Corporations that are accountable to the communities that depend on them and their numerous stakeholders within those communities will respect the boundaries that communities attempt to erect. Communities develop on a human scale, not globally, though clearly technology permits some global communities to exist electronically. It is not protectionism, in the negative sense, that exists when a community attempts to sustain its uniqueness and sense of place, but rather an attempt to free the human spirit with the sustenance of relationships, personal knowledge, and a shared sense of the common good found in community.

Fourth, as noted early on in this book, life rewards cooperation. Symbiosis (i.e., interdependency) strengthens the bonded organism, whether individual or community, in its attempts to compete for necessary life resources. Rather than fostering a dog-eat-dog hypercompetitive environment based on the accumulation of material goods, the whole human being is rewarded by helping others, and doing his or her bit to make the world a better place for self and others. This is not altruism but rather a belief in the goodness of the human spirit. Such a spirit is fostered by what Korten calls "mindful livelihoods," which entails finding meaning in work no matter where one works or what one does.

Finally, life banks on diversity, creative individuality, and shared learning, as do successful companies in the global environment. Only by tapping what Korten calls "wild spaces" can this diversity of enterprise be maintained. But these wild spaces need to be more than based in the natural environment (though these are certainly important). Wild spaces are those that allow for innovation and personal meaning-making to develop within leaders throughout an enterprise. Organizational wild spaces turn everyone into leaders because they tap the richness of potentialities that are inherent in every human being and allow for that richness in the context of shared vision and values.

Wild spaces can be created through the types of dialogic practices discussed as part of the exploration of the future and also can be created by engaging regularly with stakeholders who have different perspectives than leaders of a company. Creating wild spaces in leading corporate citizens ultimately means hiring many different types of people with many different backgrounds, and tapping their insights and knowledge extensively. It means having the self-confidence—as a leader and as a company—to bring in diverse points of view, and incorporate them into corporate values and operating practices. Doing so successfully may necessitate a significant shift of perspective.

Metanoia: A Shift of Perspective

Leading corporate citizens create meaningful visions and underpin those visions with operating practices that result in integrity in all senses of the word. Powerful and meaningful visions create a sense of higher purpose for the enterprise that brings everyone involved into a common vision and helps create a strong internal community and sense of belonging, where all know what they individually have to contribute and how that contribution helps move the vision along. Such visions are underscored by constructive values that help stakeholders, employees in particular, know their place in the organization's efforts to make significant contributions to building a better world and a sustainable future. The combination of vision and stakeholder-meaningful values results in the development of responsible day-to-day practices that allow the organization to add value in the by-product of profits and wealth generation. Combined, all of this means operating with integrity.

We have argued that it is leading corporate citizens with these characteristics that will succeed in the complexities, dynamism, and connectedness likely to continue to evolve in the future. They will do so in conversation with their stakeholders. Such corporate citizens also incorporate not only objective data and information—that which can be observed— but also the subjective and intersubjective or more interpretive elements of life, such as aesthetics, emotions, and meaningfulness, into their everyday activities. They understand the need for ecological and community sustainability and are prepared to operate with issues of sustainability fully in mind. Developing corporate citizens that have these attributes calls for nothing less than a shift of mind. Peter Senge calls this shift *metanoia*, which literally means a shift of mind, even transcendence toward a higher purpose.[2]

This *metanoia* takes leading corporate citizens away from thinking that their actions— as individuals or as organizations—can be taken in isolation. It moves them toward more ecological or systems understanding of embeddedness, interconnectedness, and interdependence. It also asks them to think about the decisions they make as managers/leaders in an integrated way, that is, not only with their heads but also with their hearts and spirits. It asks leaders to think about the meaning their decisions and actions have and the meaning embedded in the work that they and others jointly do—and then to create and tell stories that help them to share the meanings with others.

The new perspective thus asks leaders of and within corporate citizens to think deeply about the meaning and implications of *all* of the decisions they are making and what their impact on the world around us is likely to be. Leading citizens can do this because they explicitly recognize that there will be impacts and consequences of decisions. They know that *all* decisions are embedded with a set of values that either honors the relationships and stakeholders they impact or not. They are *engaged* in ongoing *relationships* with stakeholders and understand their perspectives, even when they are radically different from the company's internal perspective. This *metanoia* asks leading citizens to seek meaning and meaningfulness in decisions so that everyone can bring his or her whole self—mind, heart, body, spirit—to work (as opposed to checking their brains or heart at the door). It demands mindful rather than mindless action, thought, and decisions from managers who are connected to their hearts as well as their pocketbooks.

The changes in organizations and societies today also demand that leadership be distributed throughout the enterprise rather than held closely in a few top managers' hands. Distributed leadership means taking responsibility for the consequences of one's actions (and thinking through what those consequences are likely to be). It also asks many— most—individuals to assume qualities more like entrepreneurs, self-initiators, and leaders than ever before, to be responsible for their own productive engagement with others and for the results that the decisions they make achieve. Leadership, in this sense, falls to everyone who takes part in bringing to reality the vision embodied in the higher purposes shared by individuals within the enterprise.

Ultimately, this *metanoia* asks leaders in corporate citizens to seek *wisdom* and *mindfulness* in their work as leaders of and within corporate citizens.[3] Mindful and wise leaders think through the consequences of their decisions to all of the stakeholders those decisions impact. Mindful leaders are aware that they do not and cannot know all that they need to know, but take seriously the responsibilities—all of them—attendant on their leadership. They continue to grow, learn, develop, and embed learning practices within their enterprises as part of the culture. They seek wisdom, knowing that, in the words of leading management thinker Russell Ackoff:

> *Wisdom is the ability to perceive and evaluate the long-run consequences of behavior*. It is normally associated with a willingness to make short-run sacrifices for the sake of long-run gains.[4]

Imaginization and the Leading Corporate Citizen

As difficult as the developmental task for achieving the emergent *metanoia* in real-world corporate citizens might be for some individuals and organizations, it is possible to begin to imagine what an individual working in a new-paradigm organization might experience. This task of what management thinker Gareth Morgan terms "imaginization" will be the subject of the next several sections.[5] Imaginization asks us to think in terms of metaphors and images of what might be, not necessarily what is. Imaginization is a technique for enhancing leadership and management creativity that helps leaders understand situations in new ways, find new images about organizing, create shared understandings, and link those capacities to both personal and organizational learning and continued development. Adapting the technique of imaginization for our purposes here, we will explore in this chapter the vision, values, leadership attributes, individual and organizational work shifts, and structures that might be able to provide leading corporate citizens with patterns for coping in the turbulent world of the future. We will explore emerging new values and logics, or ways of thinking, as well as societal implications of these logics in an imaginary trip into a true leading corporate citizen.

Vision Shifts

The first stop in our imaginary trip into the emerging-paradigm organization will be at some of the implications of the new *metanoia* for vision. (See Table 11.2 for the shifts that are likely to take place.)

Imagine living and working with passion for your work and the purposes of your employing organization, a leading corporate citizen! Imagine a company with a vision embedded with bigger meanings and purposes that draw people in so that they can bring mind, heart, body, and spirit to work, where leaders and managers learn and practice mindfulness in all their decisions and actions. Imagine that the vision is clearly enough articulated that all of the relevant stakeholders understand it, acknowledge it, share it, and value it. Understanding the vision, primary stakeholders can live it because it is not just articulated but also is fully implemented, a lived, live, living, and lively vision. Imagine that this enterprise treats all of its stakeholders, internal and external, primary and secondary, with dignity and respect and is rewarded with long-term success and profitability. This is what vision in the emerging paradigm for leading corporate citizens is.

TABLE 11.2 **Vision Shifts Needed in Emerging Leading Corporate Citizens**

Vision Shifts From . . .	To . . .
Maximizing shareholder wealth without regard for other stakeholders	Doing something important and useful for customers using the full resources of employees in a way that treats all stakeholders with dignity and respect resulting in success and profitability
General, nonspecific core purpose	Building a better world in some way, creating meaning and higher purpose generating passion and commitment to that purpose and vision among stakeholders, especially employees
Corporate vision and strategy available only to top managers	Corporate vision and strategy shared by all primary stakeholders, clearly articulated, and related to higher purposes
Business separate from society	Business integral to society
Discretionary responsibility	Responsibility integral to and implicit in all practices that impact human and natural ecologies
Stakeholder management	Stakeholder relationships
Authority from the top	Meaningful leadership that guides core purposes and enables others to act in their own and the enterprise's best interest

Further, imagine that the organization is a business, a business that sees itself and its impacts as an integral part of the broader set of societies in which it operates so that it carefully acknowledges the inherent and unavoidable responsibility in all of its practices, decisions, and impacts. Imagine that top leadership is acknowledged as developing the core vision, a vision that demonstrates the enterprise's higher purpose and benefits stakeholders and societies, and guiding practices by enabling, truly empowering, others to act in their own and the enterprise's best interest. Imagine that everyone involved knows exactly what that vision is and what his or her contribution is to achieving it.

Imagine a company that understands—and acts on—the need for balancing its own power, resources, and strategies with those of other stakeholders. Imagine that all relationships with stakeholders are engaging, dialogue based, and mutually respectful. Imagine that rather than managing the stakeholders, which implies an unbalanced power relationship, this company develops and manages its relationships carefully by respecting the interests, needs, and dignity of other stakeholders. Now imagine that responsibility is integral to and implicit in all of the multifaceted day-to-day operating practices the company develops. No longer is responsibility considered discretionary or something that is done after business is taken care of. Instead, business is undertaken responsibly, in a "both/and" logic that accepts the inherent tension and paradoxes of such a stance. Such is the nature of vision in the emerging paradigm organization.

Values in the Emerging Paradigm

The second part of our imaginization takes us to the realm of values. What are the values that underpin the leading corporate citizens as compared to more traditional organizations? (See Table 11.3 for a summary of the shifts in values accompanying the shift to the emerging paradigm.)

Economizing and power-aggrandizing values underpin all business activity as we know it today. Even as the new paradigm emerges, we can imagine that these values are likely to sustain business enterprise, but that they will be supplemented and complemented by the values that help balance the other spheres of activity. Thus, imagine economizing and power-aggrandizing values complemented by values of civilizing, which helps to build community internally and externally, and ecologizing, which provides for community and ecological sustainability. Imagine that leaders of future corporate citizens are far more likely to operate with an understanding of the importance of community, relationships, civilizing than do most present-day companies, to think relationally and systemically. In operationalizing this understanding, leaders create numerous means of engaging in mutually respectful conversations with stakeholders, some of which appropriately influence corporate

TABLE 11.3 **Value Shifts in the Emerging Paradigm**

Values Shift From . . .	To . . .
Economizing and power aggrandizing	Inclusion of civilizing and ecologizing
Imbalance	Balance
No respect or dignity for stakeholders	Respect and dignity for all stakeholders
Hierarchy	Shared power, empowerment with *appropriate* hierarchy
Dominance	Partnership, equality
Authority	Democracy
Competition	Collaboration *and* competition
Control through systems	Control through goals and values
Exclusive	Inclusive
Value the objective, scientific, observable	Value the objective and subjective, interobjective and intersubjective
Disconnected, fragmented, autonomous	Connected, holistic, networked (linked)

practices. Simultaneously, imagine that current and future pressures from the resource constraints imposed by the natural environment may well heighten sensitivity to values of ecologizing, increasing attention to natural ecology and sustainable development.

Further, imagine that, pushed by communications technology and the ready availability of information, the trend toward democracy in societies continues unabated and even enters the workplace. Imagine that the workplace itself has structurally transformed so that many individuals, wherever they are in the company, are expected (as they largely are today) to exert more entrepreneurial qualities than they did in the past. The combination of entrepreneurial attitudes and the independence among stakeholders it is likely to foster may well move companies away from valuing hierarchy and dominance. Companies may move toward truly sharing power and empowering employees, but will likely sustain appropriate levels of hierarchy in the firm (some of which is likely to continue to be necessary as a structural element).

Along with this shift, imagine that companies move away from stakeholder management toward developing stakeholder relationships because they value the mutuality inherent in the relationship itself. Even more radically, perhaps, imagine that leading corporate citizens come to value the synthesis and generativity that is inherent in fostering collaborative as well as competitive relationships with stakeholders in all spheres of society. Values of collaboration and competition, rather than simple competition, might, in this world, meld in a tension of opposite and paradox that yet provides a basis for continual creativity and innovation.

In organizations with clearly articulated vision and core values, where leadership involves creating meaning rather than directing through authority and hierarchy, we can imagine that controls through organizational systems will be supplemented by controls provided by the glue of common goals and shared values. Organizations thereby respect and value employees (in particular) and the contributions they wish to and will make toward accomplishing the organization's vision. And such enterprises are, we might think, also likely to value the diversity of inclusive stakeholder relations in their primary relationships, whether with customers, suppliers, owners, or employees, rather than explicitly or implicitly generating exclusive tactics and policies.

Finally, we can imagine that there will be value for the holons (whole/parts) that corporate citizens recognize are always present in the connected, holistic, and networked system they call an organization. Individual stakeholders are holons that may form into groups that are themselves holons, which are part of larger organizations. All of these levels are respected as the wholes that they are, while recognizing that each is yet incomplete without the rest. Leaders in the emerging-paradigm organization recognize the interrelatedness of the parts of the whole system and are careful about developing operating practices so that the integrity of each holon is maintained and negative ripple effects are minimized.

Individuals Leading Corporate Citizens

Individuals operating within leading corporate citizens will need skills tomorrow that they probably can get away without today. Table 11.4 lists a few of the more obvious attitudinal (or mind-set) attributes and developmental characteristics, as well as some implications for the nature of work in leading corporate citizens where, remember, we have argued that leadership needs to come from everyone at every level. Let us continue our imaginary trip into the leading corporate citizen of the future at the individual level. What would this organization be like for people and for working?

Imagine coming to work every day knowing that your best contribution is expected. That best contribution taps all of you. Of course your mind in this knowledge-based economy is a crucial part of doing your work. And for some employees, physical labor is still demanded. But your contribution also involves thinking about the ways in which what you do and how you do it affects others in an emotional and aesthetic sense. You are also called upon to consider the ways your activities, especially in working with others, develop a meaningful and important contribution to making the world around you a better place, contribute to the organization's achievement of its vision, and enhance your feeling of being in a worthwhile community.

TABLE 11.4   Individuals and Work Shifts in the Emerging Paradigm

Individual Mind-set Shifts From . . .	To . . .
Self-interest	Self- and other interests
Contributions using body or mind	Contributions using mind, body, heart, spirit
Conventional reasoning, awareness	Postconventional reasoning, awareness
Single perspective held	Multiple perspectives held simultaneously
Mindlessness, lack of awareness	Mindful, aware, fully conscious
Do the job as structured	Learn constantly; improve the job and its results
Instrument of the corporation, a tool	Purposeful, self-directed
Moral reasoning from society's demands	Principled, care-based moral reasoning
Emotionally immature	Emotional maturity
Developmental Perspectives Move From . . .	**To . . .**
Individualistic ideology	Individualistic *and* communitarian ideologies
Single-perspective stages of development	Multiple-perspective stages of development
Reactive, proactive stakeholder relations	Interactive stakeholder relations
One-way (top-down) communication	Dialogue and mutual conversation
Just do my job	Constant scanning the environment for trends, opportunities, challenges
Work Shifts From . . .	**To . . .**
Meaningless	Meaningful
Powerless	Empowered
Individual gain	Individual and community gain
Not visibly connected to larger purpose	Visibly connected to larger purpose

In coming to your job every day, you know that the organization (and life itself) has high expectations of that type of learning that you will do. You are expected to always be pushing the edges of your own learning to enhance the organizational vision and community, and to push yourself toward the higher stages of individual development demanded by an increasingly complex and dynamic world. You work at mindfulness—awareness of the implications of each decision and presence here and now—so that you are aware of what you and others do and fully conscious of how others (other stakeholders) are affected by the decisions you make and the practices you develop.

Thus, developmentally you have moved toward the capacity to hold multiple perspectives simultaneously and are very skilled at taking the other's (whichever "other" is relevant in a given situation) perspective when necessary. This skill helps you develop good relationships with important stakeholders whom your daily activities and work affect (or whose activities affect your work!).

You personally and the company have moved away from simply reacting to external pressures, and have even moved beyond proactive strategies to forestall others' actions, toward more consistently interactive strategies of conversing, or being in dialogue with important stakeholders. This interactive posture helps you and the organization avoid nasty surprises from the external environment. In part you can do this because you are constantly alert to any concerns from the stakeholders you interact with. In part it happens almost naturally because your constant learning means that you pay attention to signals coming in from outside (or arising inside) the organization. And because your opinion is as respected as others, you know that when you voice an idea it will be listened to.

Your work has become meaningful and you have, in this transition to the emerging-paradigm organization, become truly empowered, not just in rhetoric, but in actuality.

Power is shared and the need for power aggrandizement, whether by individuals or the company, has diminished (while still present) in favor of focusing on a combination of individual person and company gain combined with gains for the larger communities that are relevant. You handle this somewhat paradoxical "both/and" well because you see how what you do is connected to the larger purpose of the organization. You are connected to communities both within and outside your organization and know exactly how your contribution fits in to making these enterprises better.

Structure and Practice in the Emerging Leading Corporate Citizen

Accompanying the shifts in vision, values, and work in the new paradigm organization, leading corporate citizens will find themselves shifting both their structure and practices to accommodate improved relationships with stakeholders and more awareness of responsibilities. Table 11.5 lists some of the significant shifts in structure and practice that can be expected as we continue our imaginization.

Imagine an organization where there is consistent and regular interaction and dialogue between internal stakeholders and those who used to be outside, such as suppliers, customers, and community members. Because new-paradigm organizations will likely tend to structure themselves through collaborative alliances and partnerships of various kinds, the formerly clear and rather rigid boundaries separating different stakeholder groups have tended to blur. Overlapping and merging boundaries can be expected in areas such as customer relations where practices that tie one company's purchasing system directly to others can be expected to increase, or in community relations where social partnerships to solve community-based problems of mutual concern evolve.

TABLE 11.5 Structure and Practice in the Emerging Leading Corporate Citizen

Structures Shift From . . .	To . . .
Rigid boundaries	Overlapping, merging boundaries (boundary-less-ening)
Leadership through authority	Leadership through vision and values
High, relatively rigid structure	Emergent, flexible and adaptive structure
Single, simple financial bottom line, financial capital	Multiple bottom lines
One dominant stakeholder (shareholder)	Multiple primary/secondary stakeholders
Leadership at the top (top down)	Leadership is everywhere (top down and bottom up)

Practices Move From . . .	To . . .
Economizing, power aggrandizing	Inclusion of civilizing and ecologizing
Exploitative practices, disrespectful	Integrity in practices, respectful
Reactive, proactive strategies	Interactive strategies
Objective, unemotional, meaningless	Objective/subjective, emotional/meaningful
Discretionary corporate responsibility	Responsibility integral to operating practices
Managing stakeholders	Developing stakeholder relationships
Fragmented functions	Integral systems
Operating instrumentally	Operating with integrity
Valuing contributions from and to owners	Valuing contributions of all stakeholders
Lack of accountability and transparency	Necessary accountability and transparency
Externalizing costs	Internalizing costs
Wasteful, exploitive operations	Ecologizing, nature-based operations

Leadership through vision and values continues apace, creating the organizational glue and direction that provides structure, substituting emergent, flexible, and adaptive teams, ad hoc groupings, task forces, and project/process units for formerly readily identifiable (and permanent) structures and units. This adaptive structure, while complex and somewhat difficult to understand, allows the company to meet different stakeholders' needs as they arise in what might be called emergent structure or webs of connected groups that develop sustaining relationships over time.

The respectful and interactive stakeholder relationships point the company in the direction of being accountable for and to multiple rather than a single stakeholder. Indeed, the company has moved from managing stakeholders to a more respectful stance of managing stakeholder relationships and assuring their mutuality of interests. Thus, measurement systems and the relevant reward systems are geared to performance in the essential primary and secondary stakeholder domains of not only owners (financial performance and wealth generation), but also employee relations, customer relations, supplier relations, community relations, public and governmental affairs, and others as relevant. Multiple bottom lines are followed and reported on externally so that the company's responsibility and practices are transparent to and accountable for impacts on key external stakeholders.

Imagine that internal corporate practices have also shifted so that the dominant behaviors associated with economizing and power-aggrandizing values have expanded to also include values of civilizing (relationship building) and ecologizing, assuring ecological, community, and company sustainability over the long term. Because of the transparency of corporate actions to stakeholders, the company is clear that it operates in all respects with integrity in both of its definitions, honesty/straightforwardness and wholeness. Responsibility is considered integral to all operating practices; little is done without considering the stakeholder and ecological implications: thus, accountability is built into the operating practices.

The close link of the company's vision and articulated higher purposes helps generate meaning for stakeholders who interact with the firm. Clear attention is paid to the corporate environment aesthetically, as well as to assuring that stakeholders are satisfied, in the traditional sense of customer satisfaction and quality management. To cope with the complexity of knowing that stakeholders are whole individuals, care is taking in developing all relationships so that abuses and exploitation of stakeholders, wherever they are, are practically nonexistent. Stakeholder contributions are valued, wherever they come from.

Costs are fully internalized, with accounting systems incorporating the full product or service life cycle and all associated environmental costs. The company is an industry leader in advancing full-costing processes globally. Operations are based on ecologizing and natural principles that indicate no-waste practices.

New Logics across the Globe

Gaining the needed new perspective or *metanoia* involves incorporating into our thinking a new set of logics, or ways of thinking and new values that accompany those logics.[6] Some years ago scholars Douglas Austrom and Lawrence Lad neatly synthesized these new logics and values that appear to be emerging globally. (See Table 11.6, which has been supplemented with ideas from Ken Wilber and the present author.) As has been discussed throughout this book, even Western thinking is rapidly moving from the fragmentation and atomization of the mechanistic Western view of science, nature, and the world at large, in part because of the influence of the new chaos and complexity theories.

In many respects, progressive thinking about business in society is already generally moving toward a more integrated and holistic view that includes an ecological and systems perspective. It also is beginning to incorporate the nonobservable elements of emotions, aesthetic appreciation, and individual and collective meaning, sometimes characterized as creating meaningful work, other times as spirituality in work. These new logics and values are manifesting themselves in many of the companies, research, and ways of thinking cited earlier in this book, as well as many others omitted in the interests of space and time. The general movement is thus away from passive and toward engaged (interactive) behaviors,

TABLE 11.6   New Logics and New Values

Sources: This chart is adapted from Douglas R. Austrom and Lawrence J. Lad, "Issues Management Alliances: New Responses, New Values, and New Logics," in *Research in Corporate Social Performance and Policy*, vol. 2, ed. James E. Post (Greenwich, CT: JAI Press, 1989), pp. 233–355; Ken Wilber, *The Image of Sense and Soul: Integrating Science and Reason* (Boston: Shambala, 1998); plus author's additions.

Prevailing Paradigm	Emergent Paradigm
Basic World View	
Mechanistic, simple, linear	Organic, complexity, chaotic
Cartesian, Newtonian	Ecological, systemic
Atomistic, fragmented	Holistic (holons)
Objective	Objective, subjective, interobjective, intersubjective
Disengaged, passive	Engaged, active
"It" orientation	"I," "we," and "it" orientations
Implicit Logics: Perspectives	
Focus on distinctions and separations	Focus on interdependence and interrelatedness
Either/or oppositions	Both/and relations
Dualities as opposites and contradictions	Dualities as paradoxes
Top down	Top down/bottom up
Leading Values	
Self-contained individualism and agency	Communitarianism and community
Zero-sum-game mentality	Positive-sum-gain mentality
Win–lose orientation	Win–win orientation

away from fragmentation and toward interdependence and interrelatedness, encompassing the logic of both/and rather than either/or. Paradoxes emerge in this both/and logic, necessitating a need for individuals and organizations to be able to cope with tensions of the opposites, such as in the top-down/ bottom-up authority implied in the new logics.

Table 11.6 thus illuminates a decided shift away from mechanistic and inorganic perspectives on organizing and society, which foster dominance and rigidity along with a win–lose orientation. Movement is generally toward a more organic and holistic framing that incorporates a both/and rather than either/or logic, representing in some respects an integration of Western and Eastern philosophies. Although this emerging paradigm for leading corporate citizenship is fundamentally more complex than the older more linear and mechanistic approach, it can also be energizing and exciting because it asks leaders to think deeply about what they are doing and why they are doing it. The excitement comes in part because it based on a realistic assessment of the complexity of human life itself and becomes the emerging perspective as embedded in an understanding of the meaning of relationship, a fundamental aspect, as we have seen, of corporate citizenship.

Because the emerging paradigm is organic and holistic, it incorporates not only objective and scientifically observable phenomenon, but also the aesthetic, emotional, and appreciative, more subjective and intersubjective elements of living life within communities of various sorts, shapes, and sizes. Transformation in thinking—the *metanoia* we have been discussing—is thus needed in societies, too, a transformation that has implications for us all as human beings living in what we hope will be civil and democratic societies, with economies that are growing successfully, profitability, and sustainably.

Leading Corporate Citizens in Societies

The final stage of our imaginization is to assess what this metanoia might mean for the societies in which leading corporate citizens operate. Table 11.7 identifies just a few of

TABLE 11.7   Global Governance in the Emerging Paradigm

Social and Political Shifts From . . .	To . . .
Dominant economic sphere	Balance among economic, political, and civil society spheres of activity
Nonsustainable development	Sustainable development
Exploitive and abusive development	Respectful development
Uninformed, passive, voiceless stakeholders	Informed, active stakeholders with voice
Nation-state legal-regulatory framework	International legal-regulatory framework
Diminishing social capital	Enhancing constructive social capital
Few global standards, expectations	Global standards and expectations
Little enforcement capacity globally	Global enforcement mechanisms
Little stakeholder involvement in governance	Stakeholder engagement in governance

the dominant social and political shifts that can be expected in our imaginary trip into the future.

Imagine that businesses act collaboratively with nongovernmental organizations, international nongovernmental organizations, and governmental organizations (NGOs, INGOs, and GOs), to ensure that the activities of each sphere are appropriately balanced with each other. Governments, tending toward democracy because of the power of information and its ready availability, rely on businesses to provide employment, economic development, and growth in the well-being and lifestyles of their citizens. All of this economic and social development is sensitively handled, keeping in mind the core cultural identity of each society and its distinctiveness so that citizens can develop a sustained sense of local community, bolstered by appropriate local, regional, and national infrastructure.

Development in the new paradigm is handled with ecological sustainability clearly in mind. INGOs have evolved that demand accountability and transparency from the corporation, assuring responsible practice, and providing clear global standards to which all companies voluntarily adhere. Many stakeholders are now involved in assuring that companies are governed properly—and that they meet global standards, ethically, operationally, and strategically. When abuses in human rights, labor rights, or human and child welfare do occur, companies as well as organizations from the political and civil society spheres are quick to act and compel the abuser to either change its practices or drive it out of business. Independent observers regularly audit corporate practices with audits then released publicly because international standards have created high expectations that such reporting will be standard.

The wide availability of information about these practices online makes keeping abusive practices difficult, especially as governments are clear about educating all citizens to a high enough level that democracy and free markets based on the biological principles articulated by David Korten, The Natural Step, and others are followed rigorously. All market-based activities tend to support communities, rather than debilitate them, and citizens are encouraged to voice concerns so that they can be attended to by the appropriate corporate relations people, who are spread, in their leadership capacities, throughout companies.

An international legal and regulatory framework has been devised by all the nations of the world to foster sustainability, to provide opportunities for stakeholders to voice concerns, and to assure accountability in all corporate activities. Enforcement mechanisms are strong and sanctions, when necessary, are quickly imposed. Perhaps the most critical sanction is that of releasing negative reputational information about corporate abusers publicly, a type of sanction that tends to damage the company's reputation among its stakeholders sufficiently that it actually prevents abuses.

Leading Challenges: Leading Corporate Citizens in the New Paradigm

Throughout this book, we have been discussing the shift to an emerging paradigm for leading corporate citizens. Admittedly, the book takes an optimistic rather than pessimistic point of view in suggesting that such a shift is taking place and will continue to evolve in a constructive and positive direction. Clearly, power and resource inequities exist and not all corporations behave responsibly, pushed by intense competition and demands for shareholder value to economize in sometimes destructive ways.

Part of the agenda has been to look explicitly at what a new paradigm for leading corporate citizens would look like when it is more fully evolved. We have done this by using information, examples, and research that are already available as guides to what might be in a world where balance, collaboration, and respect guide operating practices and, in this chapter, by imagining the possibilities.

Why do I believe that this optimistic scenario makes sense? After all, problems abound in the economic, political, and civil society spheres of activity that constitute human civilization—as well as in the natural environment. Despite these problems and the inherent difficulties, dilemmas, and paradoxes in overcoming them, we have attempted to paint a picture of the way that companies can act if they hope to become leading corporate citizens. And there are signs that many leading corporate citizens are beginning to move in the directions articulated in this chapter.

Over the course of the book, we have looked at significant evidence that acting as a leading citizen not only results in effective behaviors—doing the right thing with respect to stakeholders and the natural environment—but also economizes, resulting in practices that are efficient and profitable. Leaders of leading corporate citizens today have begun to understand this truly bigger picture and to act accordingly. Slowly but surely, they are moving their companies along this path toward this emergent and progressive corporate paradigm.

It requires leadership and significant wisdom to take steps that others might view as against the mainstream in a time of turbulence and great performance pressures. It requires courage to take responsibility for one's (and one's company's) impacts. It demands mindfulness and true wisdom to operate with respect for stakeholders and to engage with them rather than making assumptions about them and their needs.

Is taking this path always easy? No. Is it always more profitable in the short run? No. Will competitors still act in aggressive and competitive dog-eat-dog ways trying to outstrip companies acting in the paradigm of leading corporate citizens, which is far more collaborative in its orientation? Yes. But are companies that act with respect for stakeholders, with consideration for the full impacts of their decisions, with integrity and wisdom, successful? The evidence strongly suggests that the answer is yes.

Endnotes

1. See David Korten, *The Post-Corporate World* (San Francisco: Berrett-Koehler, 1999). See also Fritjof Capra, *The Web of Life* (New York: Anchor Doubleday, 1995); and Stuart Kauffman, *At Home in the Universe: The Search for the Laws of Self-Organization and Complexity* (New York: Oxford University Press, 1995).

2. Peter M. Senge, *The Fifth Discipline* (New York: Currency Doubleday, 1990).

3. See Russell L. Ackoff, "On Learning and the Systems That Facilitate It," *Reflection* 1, no. 1 (1999), pp. 14–24, reprinted from the Center for Quality of Management, Cambridge, MA, 1996. See also Karl E. Weick, "Educating for the Unknowable: The Infamous Real World," presentation at the Academy of Management, Chicago, IL, 1999.

4. Ackoff, "On Learning," p. 16. Italics added.

5. The term *imaginization* was developed by Gareth Morgan in *Imaginization: The Art of Creative Management* (Newbury Park, CA: Sage, 1993).

6. See Douglas R. Austrom and Lawrence J. Lad, "Issues Management Alliances: New Responses, New Values, and New Logics," in *Research in Corporate Social Performance and Policy*, vol. 2, ed. James E. Post (Greenwich, CT: JAI Press, 1989), pp. 233–355.